POSUKA DEMIZU

When you overcome a hurdle, another bigger hurdle appears.

This year I learned to do a lot of things. Which means I have a lot of goals now. Will I be able to accomplish them? It's something to look forward to!

In volume 6, the secrets of this world will begin to be revealed. Please look forward to it!

KAIU SHIRAI

Writer Shirai's personal highlights for *The Promised Neverland* fanatics, part 4:

1. This might be sudden, but I'm revealing their birthdays.
   Ray ⟶ January 15
   Norman ⟶ March 21
   Emma ⟶ August 22

2. But Ray's real birthday is actually another date.

Okay, please enjoy the volume!

Posuka Demizu debuted as a manga artist with the 2013 *CoroCoro* series *Oreca Monster Bouken Retsuden*. A collection of illustrations, *The Art of Posuka Demizu*, was released in 2016 by PIE International.

Kaiu Shirai debuted in 2015 with *Ashley Gate no Yukue* on the *Shonen Jump+* website. Shirai first worked with Posuka Demizu on the two-shot *Poppy no Negai*, which was released in February 2016.

THE PROMISED NEVERLAND

VOLUME 5
SHONEN JUMP Manga Edition

STORY BY KAIU SHIRAI
ART BY POSUKA DEMIZU

Translation/Satsuki Yamashita
Touch-Up Art & Lettering/Mark McMurray
Design/Julian [JR] Robinson
Editor/Alexis Kirsch

YAKUSOKU NO NEVERLAND © 2016 by Kaiu Shirai, Posuka Demizu
All rights reserved.
First published in Japan in 2016 by SHUEISHA Inc., Tokyo.
English translation rights arranged by SHUEISHA Inc.

Printed in Italy

Published by VIZ Media, LLC
P.O. Box 77010
San Francisco, CA 94107

10 9 8 7 6
First printing, August 2018
Sixth printing, December 2021

PARENTAL ADVISORY
THE PROMISED NEVERLAND is rated T+
and is recommended for ages 16 and up.
This volume contains fantasy violence and
adult themes.

THE PROMISED NEVERLAND

5

Escape

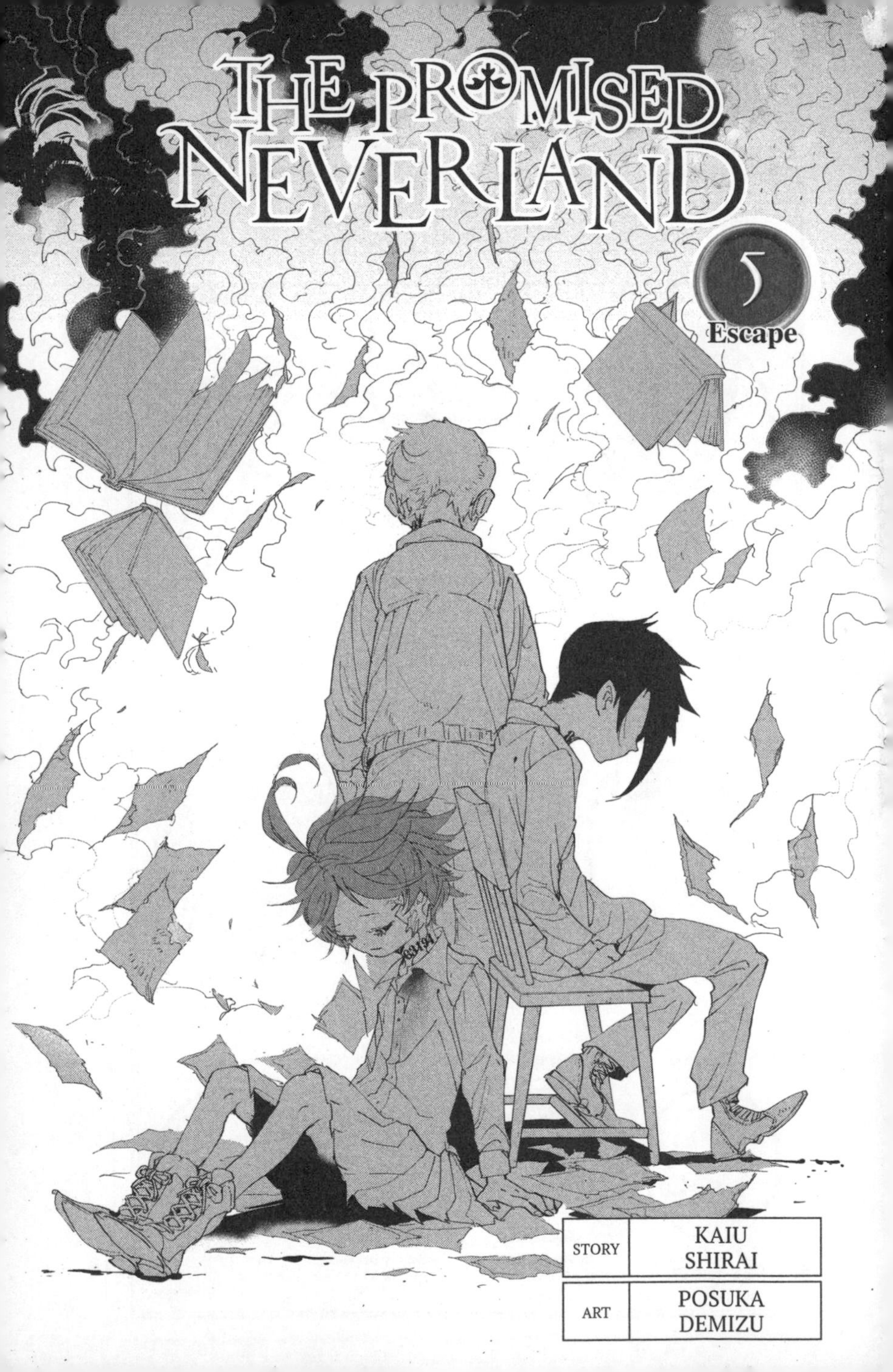

STORY	KAIU SHIRAI
ART	POSUKA DEMIZU

The Children of Grace Field House

As Norman would have wanted, they plan their escape from Grace Field House.

CHARACTERS

EMMA

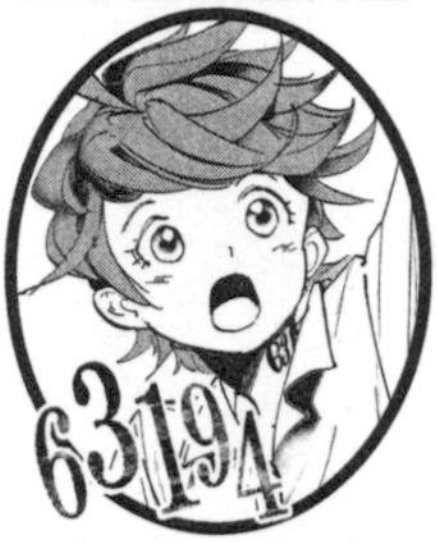
63194

An enthusiastic and optimistic girl with superb athletic and learning abilities.

RAY

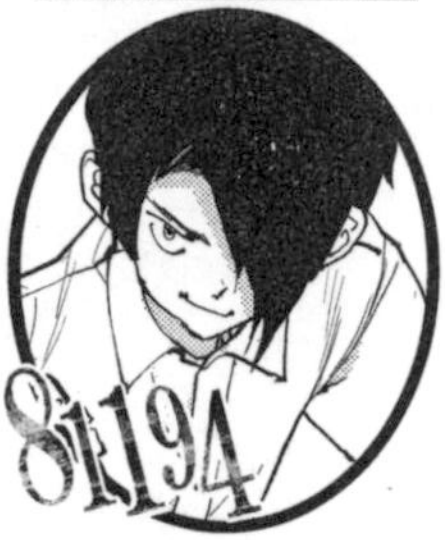
81194

The only one among the Grace Field House children who can match wits with Norman.

NORMAN

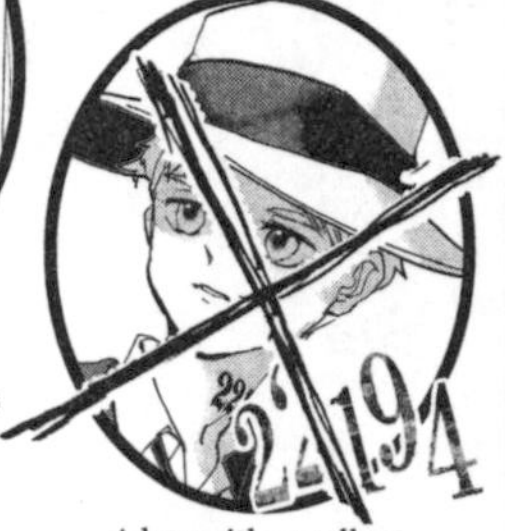
22194

A boy with excellent analytical and decision-making capabilities. He's the smartest child at Grace Field House.

PHIL

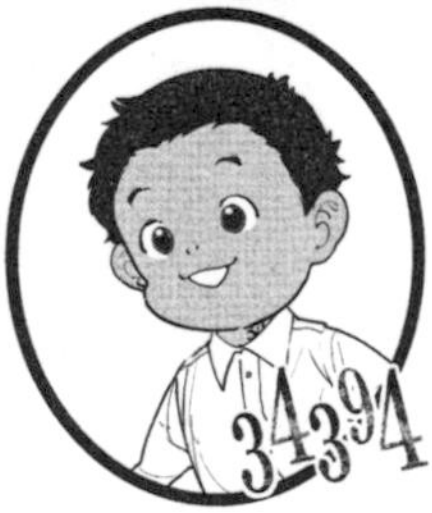

A bighearted boy who loves Emma. He is always full of energy.

GILDA

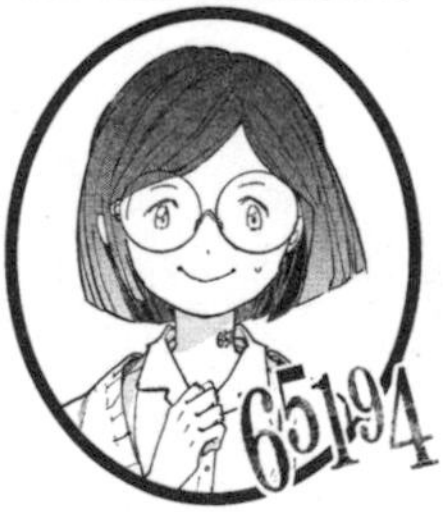
65194

A clever girl who has great insight and acts accordingly.

DON

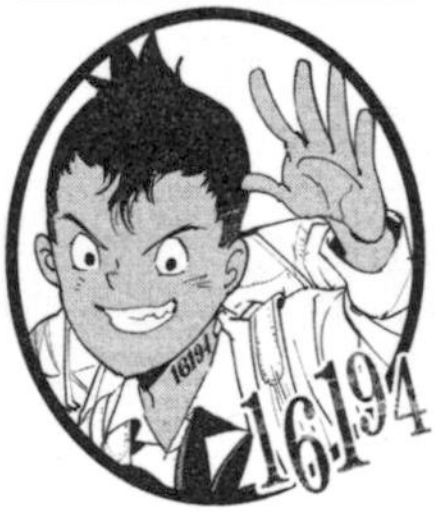
16194

A carefree boy who is cheerful but competitive.

LANNION

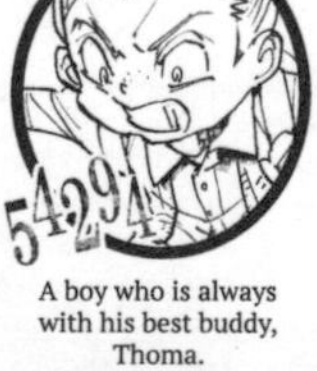
54294

A boy who is always with his best buddy, Thoma.

THOMA

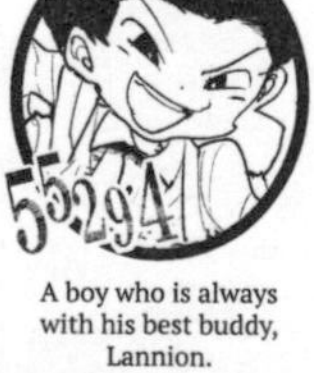
55294

A boy who is always with his best buddy, Lannion.

NAT

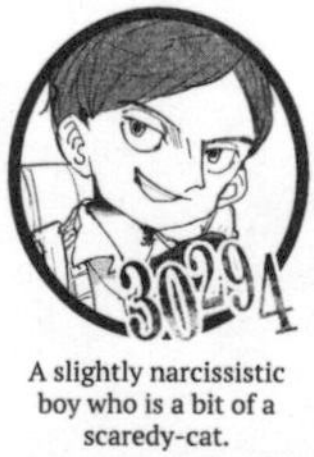
30294

A slightly narcissistic boy who is a bit of a scaredy-cat.

ANNA

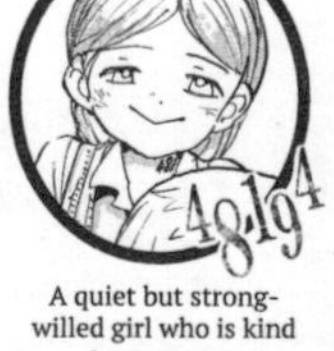
48194

A quiet but strong-willed girl who is kind to everyone.

The Adults of Grace Field House

They are kept alive to raise the children who will be presented to the demons.

KRONE

Isabella's assistant and a subordinate of the demons.

GRANDMA

The supervisor of all the adults at Grace Field House.

ISABELLA

A competent handler who raised Emma and the other children.

 ? ? ?

WILLIAM MINERVA

A mysterious figure who leaves various items that seem to help the children.

Demons of Grace Field House

They raise human children to eat their developed brains.

The Story So Far

The 38 children of Grace Field House orphanage are all living happily with their "Mom," Isabella, treating her as if she were their real mother. One day, two of the oldest children, Emma and Norman, discover the existence of demons. They find out that Isabella is raising them to be food for the demons. The two reject their fate and decide to escape with the help of their closest friend, Ray. Eventually they bring Don and Gilda in on the plan. But before they can escape, Norman is shipped off. Even in the midst of sadness and frustration, Emma and the children decide to execute his plan. They catch Isabella off guard and make their move.

THE PROMISED NEVERLAND 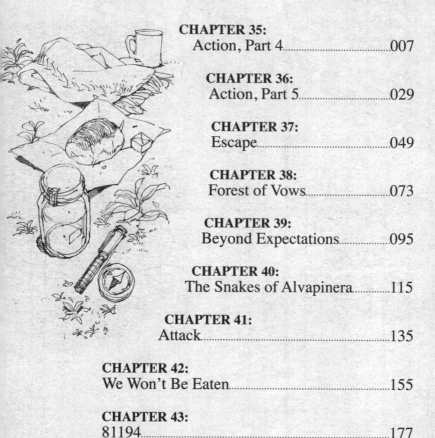 5

Escape

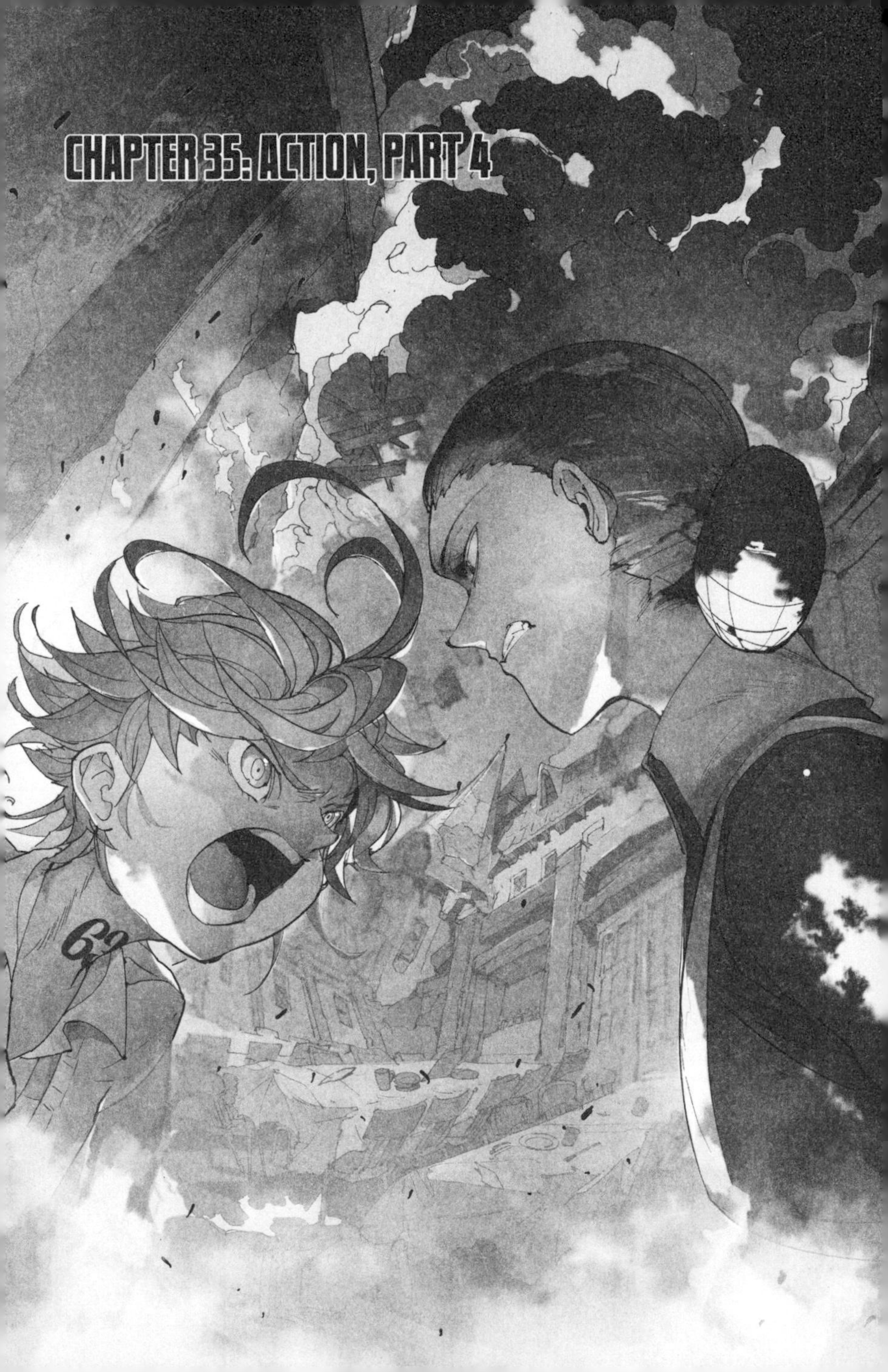
CHAPTER 35: ACTION, PART 4
63

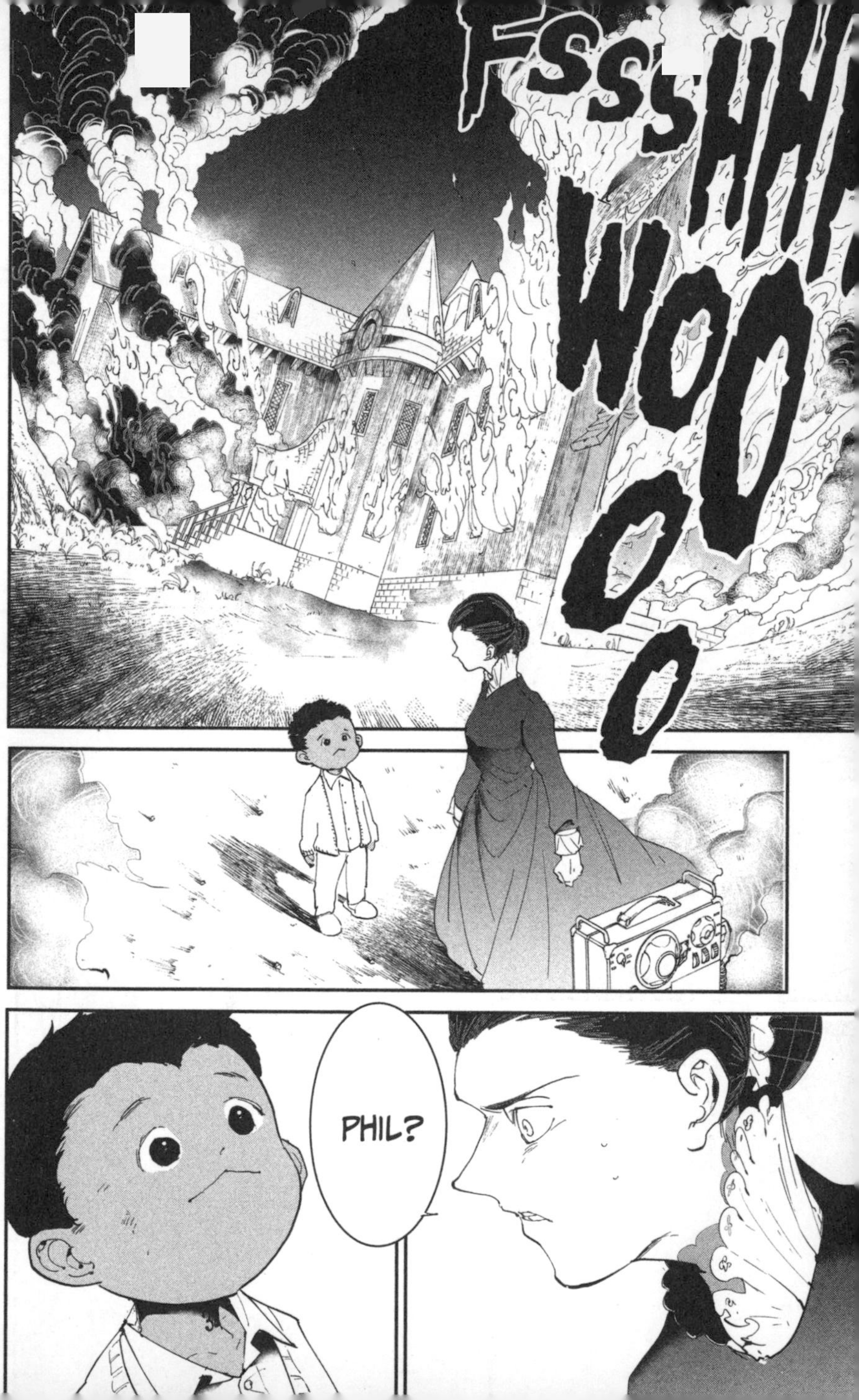
FSSHHH
WOOOOO
PHIL?

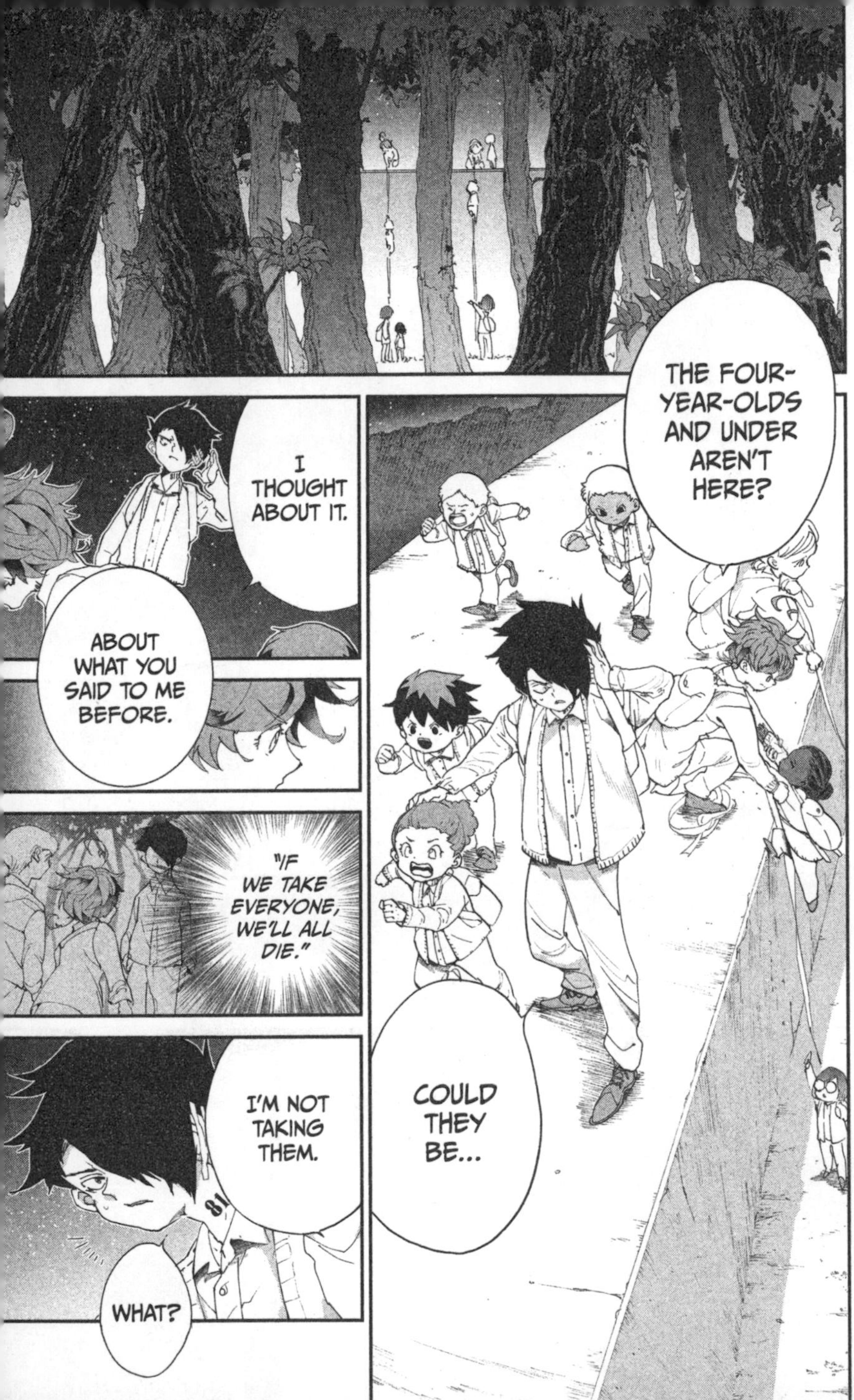
THE FOUR-YEAR-OLDS AND UNDER AREN'T HERE?
COULD THEY BE...
I THOUGHT ABOUT IT.
ABOUT WHAT YOU SAID TO ME BEFORE.
"IF WE TAKE EVERYONE, WE'LL ALL DIE."
I'M NOT TAKING THEM.
WHAT?

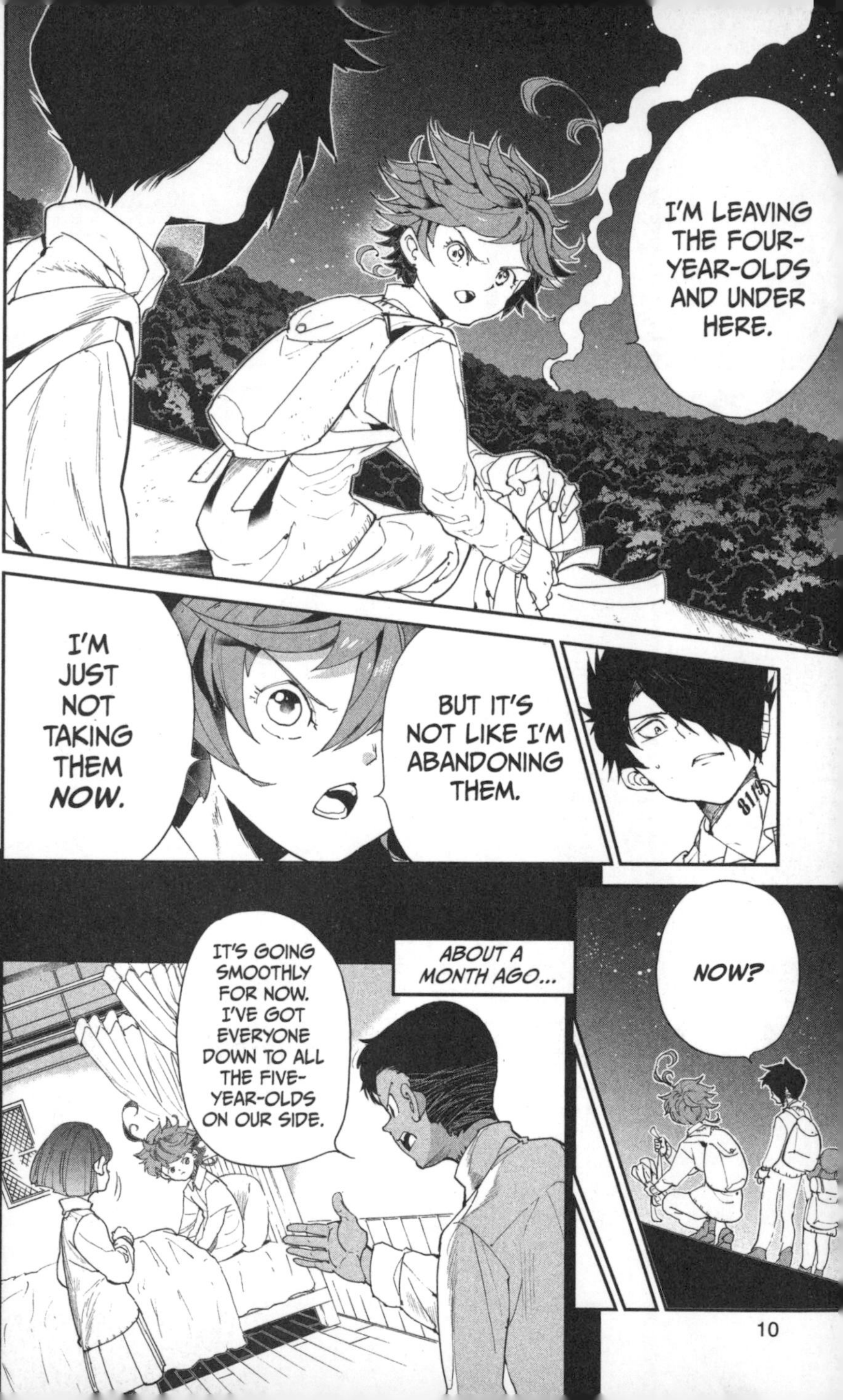
I'M LEAVING THE FOUR-YEAR-OLDS AND UNDER HERE.
BUT IT'S NOT LIKE I'M ABANDONING THEM.
I'M JUST NOT TAKING THEM *NOW.*
NOW?
ABOUT A MONTH AGO...
IT'S GOING SMOOTHLY FOR NOW. I'VE GOT EVERYONE DOWN TO ALL THE FIVE-YEAR-OLDS ON OUR SIDE.

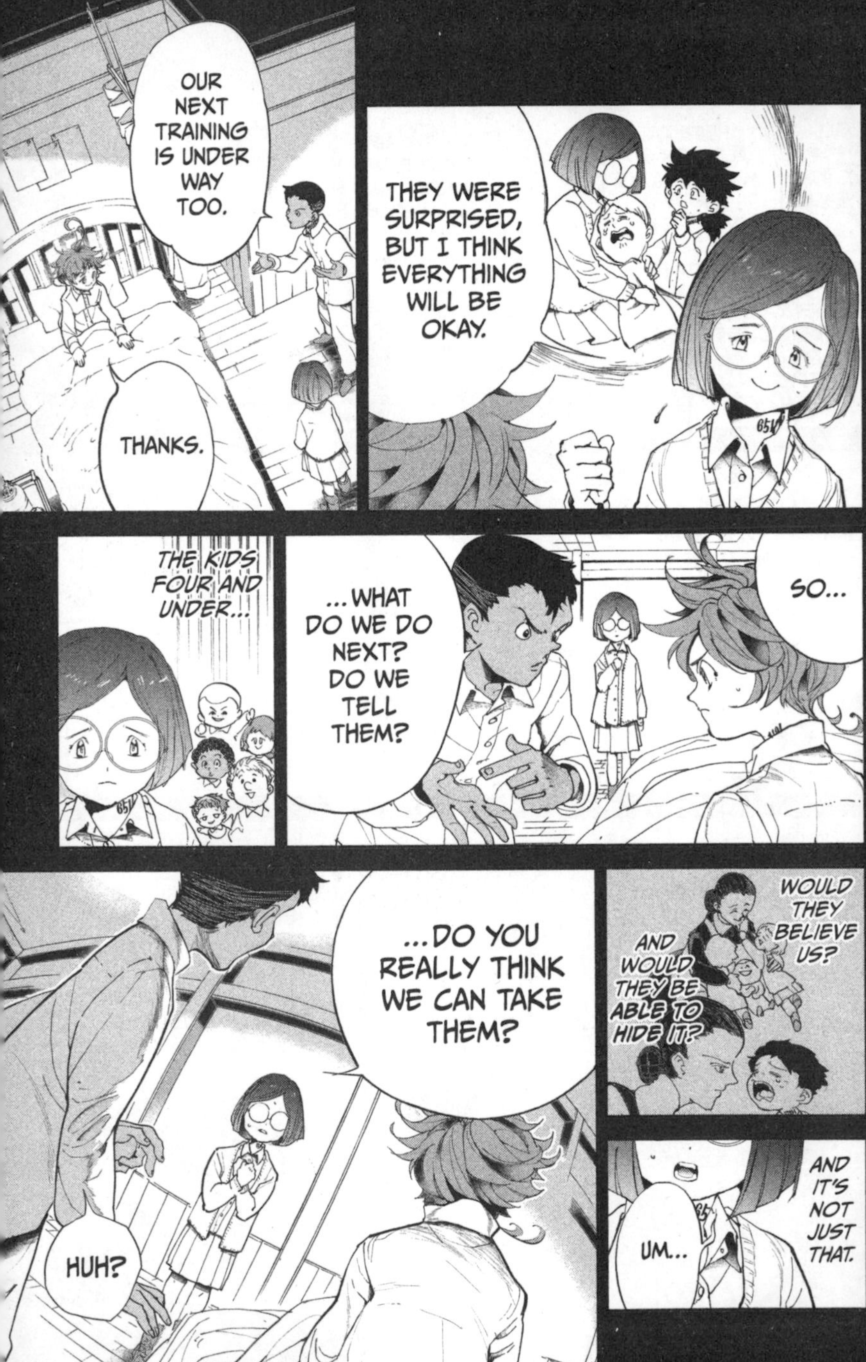
THEY WERE SURPRISED, BUT I THINK EVERYTHING WILL BE OKAY.
OUR NEXT TRAINING IS UNDER WAY TOO.
THANKS.
SO...
...WHAT DO WE DO NEXT? DO WE TELL THEM?
THE KIDS FOUR AND UNDER...
WOULD THEY BELIEVE US?
AND WOULD THEY BE ABLE TO HIDE IT?
AND IT'S NOT JUST THAT.
UM...
...DO YOU REALLY THINK WE CAN TAKE THEM?
HUH?

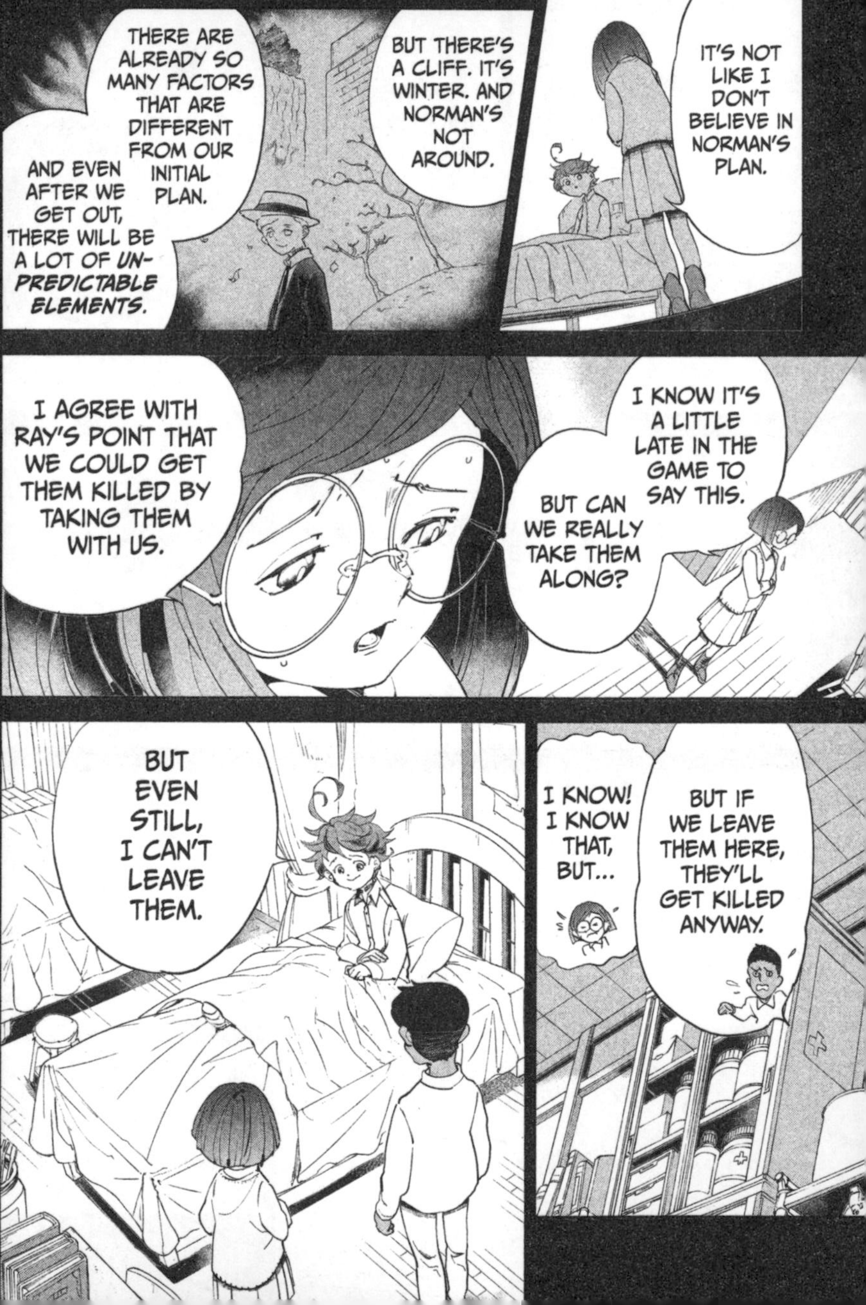
IT'S NOT LIKE I DON'T BELIEVE IN NORMAN'S PLAN.
BUT THERE'S A CLIFF. IT'S WINTER. AND NORMAN'S NOT AROUND.
THERE ARE ALREADY SO MANY FACTORS THAT ARE DIFFERENT FROM OUR INITIAL PLAN.
AND EVEN AFTER WE GET OUT, THERE WILL BE A LOT OF *UN-PREDICTABLE ELEMENTS*.
I KNOW IT'S A LITTLE LATE IN THE GAME TO SAY THIS.
BUT CAN WE REALLY TAKE THEM ALONG?
I AGREE WITH RAY'S POINT THAT WE COULD GET THEM KILLED BY TAKING THEM WITH US.
BUT IF WE LEAVE THEM HERE, THEY'LL GET KILLED ANYWAY.
I KNOW! I KNOW THAT, BUT...
BUT EVEN STILL, I CAN'T LEAVE THEM.

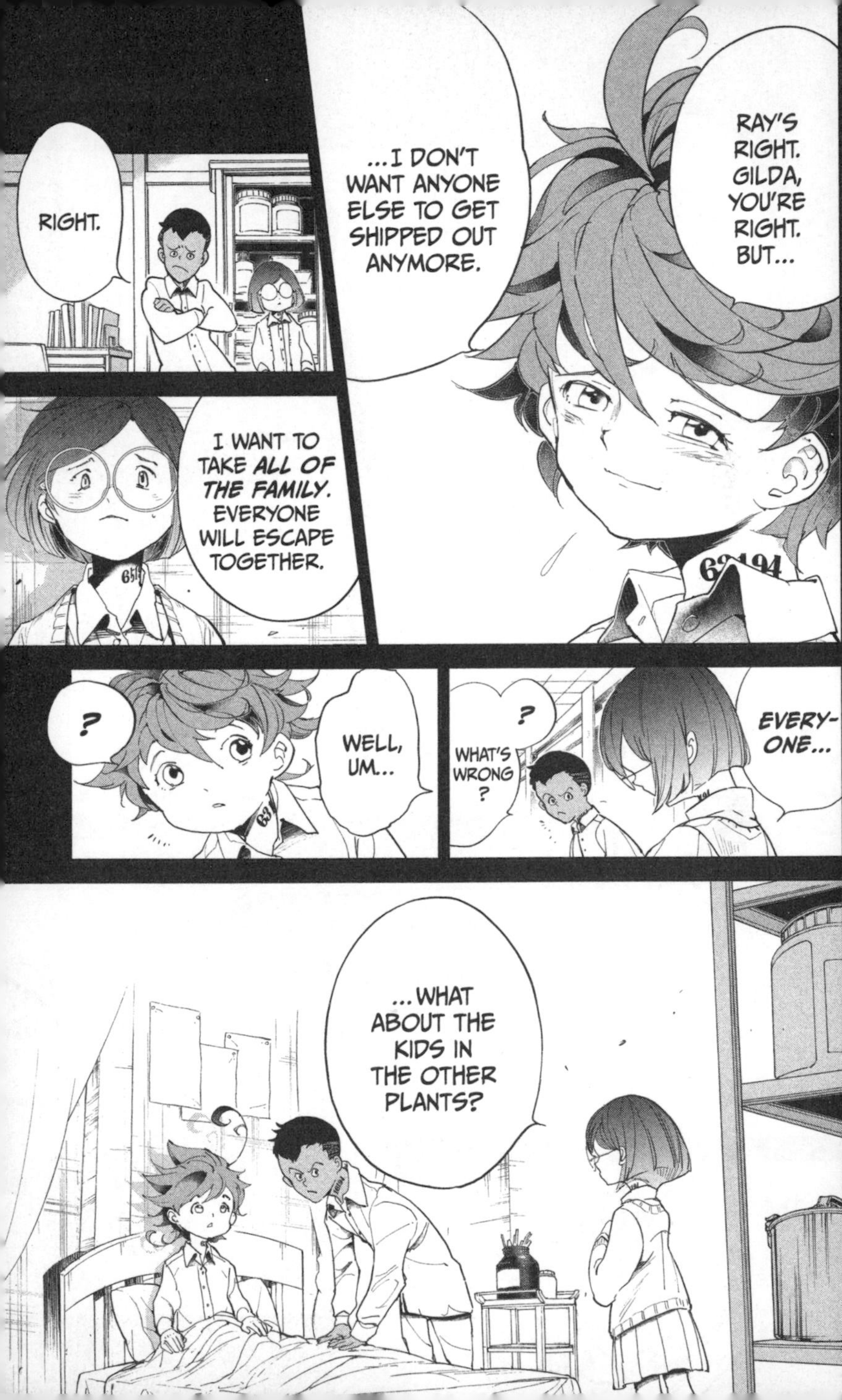
RAY'S RIGHT. GILDA, YOU'RE RIGHT. BUT...
...I DON'T WANT ANYONE ELSE TO GET SHIPPED OUT ANYMORE.
RIGHT.
I WANT TO TAKE *ALL OF THE FAMILY*. EVERYONE WILL ESCAPE TOGETHER.
EVERY-ONE...
?
WHAT'S WRONG?
?
WELL, UM...
...WHAT ABOUT THE KIDS IN THE OTHER PLANTS?

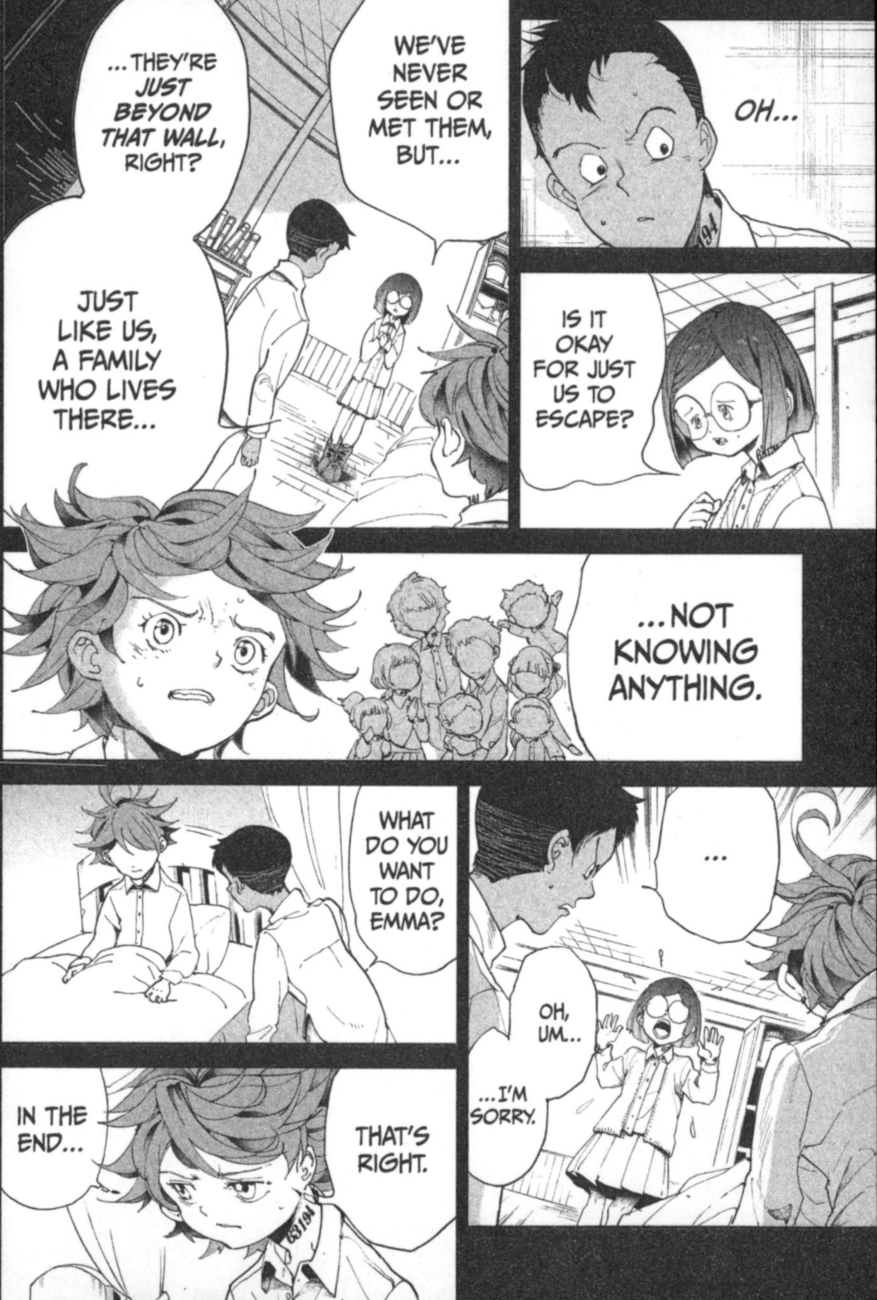
OH...
IS IT OKAY FOR JUST US TO ESCAPE?
WE'VE NEVER SEEN OR MET THEM, BUT...
...THEY'RE *JUST BEYOND THAT WALL,* RIGHT?
JUST LIKE US, A FAMILY WHO LIVES THERE...
...NOT KNOWING ANYTHING.
...
OH, UM...
...I'M SORRY.
WHAT DO YOU WANT TO DO, EMMA?
THAT'S RIGHT.
IN THE END...

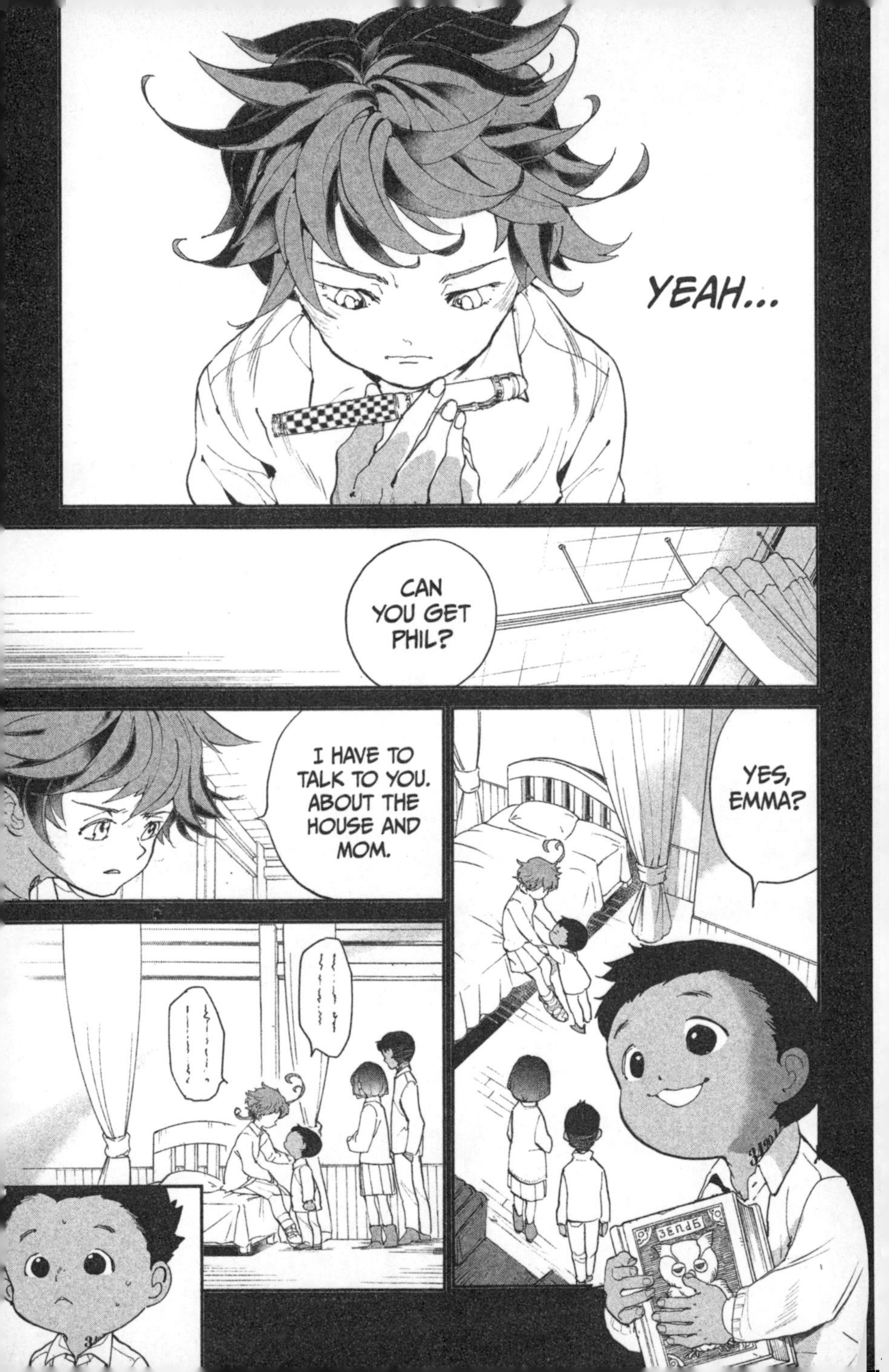
YEAH...
CAN YOU GET PHIL?
YES, EMMA?
I HAVE TO TALK TO YOU. ABOUT THE HOUSE AND MOM.

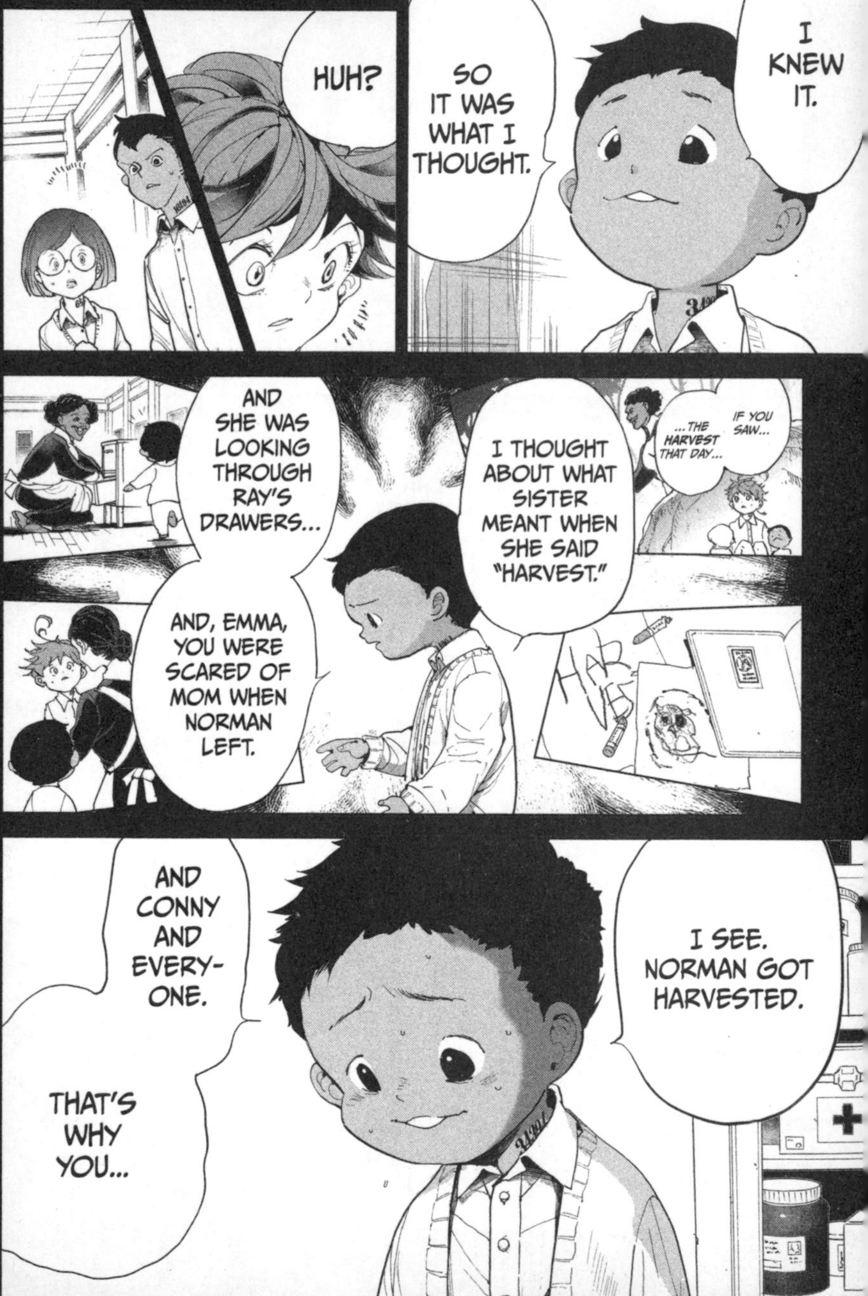
I KNEW IT.
SO IT WAS WHAT I THOUGHT.
HUH?
IF YOU SAW...
...THE HARVEST THAT DAY...
I THOUGHT ABOUT WHAT SISTER MEANT WHEN SHE SAID "HARVEST."
AND SHE WAS LOOKING THROUGH RAY'S DRAWERS...
AND, EMMA, YOU WERE SCARED OF MOM WHEN NORMAN LEFT.
I SEE. NORMAN GOT HARVESTED.
AND CONNY AND EVERY-ONE.
THAT'S WHY YOU...

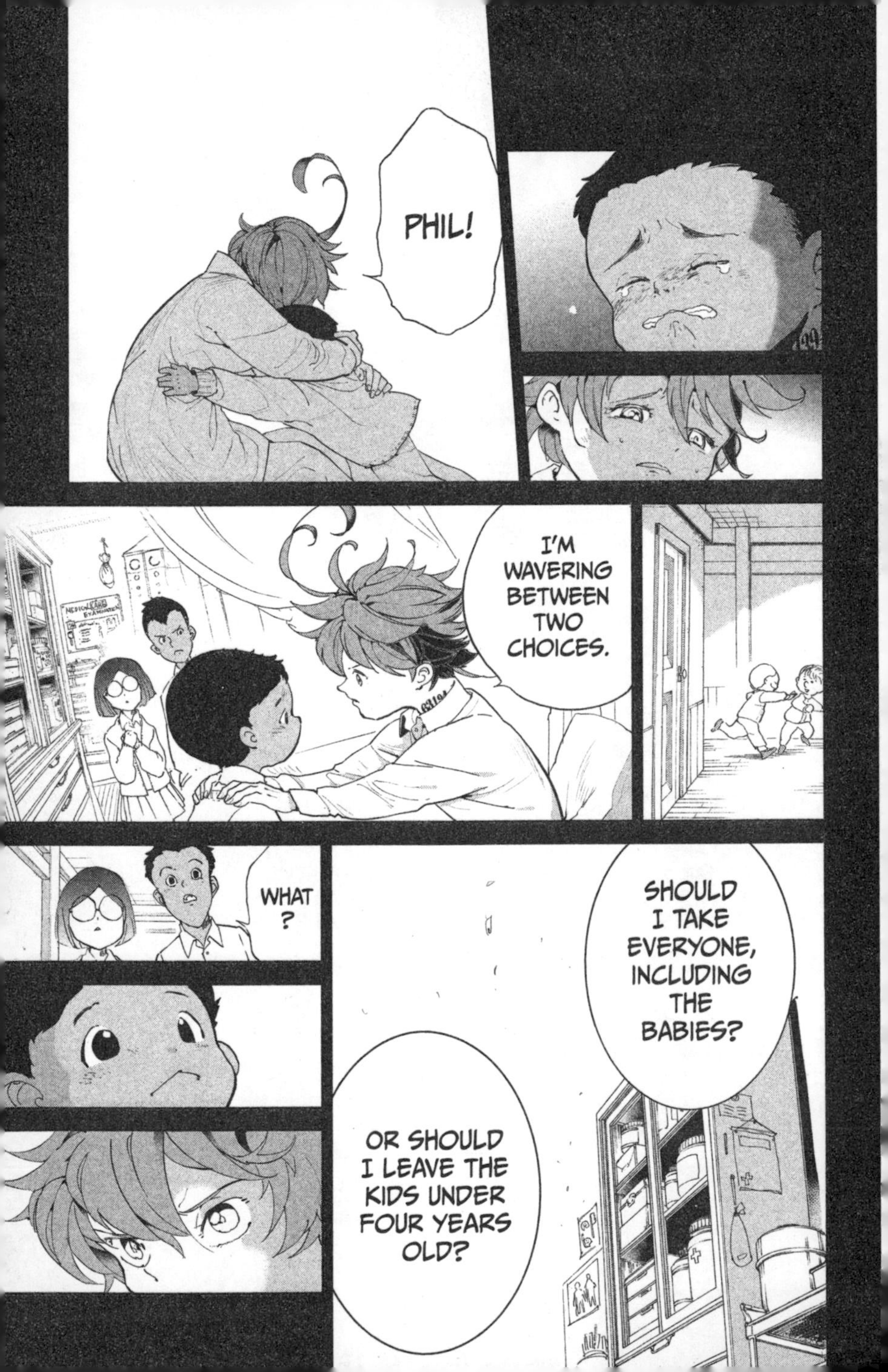
PHIL!
I'M WAVERING BETWEEN TWO CHOICES.
SHOULD I TAKE EVERYONE, INCLUDING THE BABIES?
OR SHOULD I LEAVE THE KIDS UNDER FOUR YEARS OLD?
WHAT?

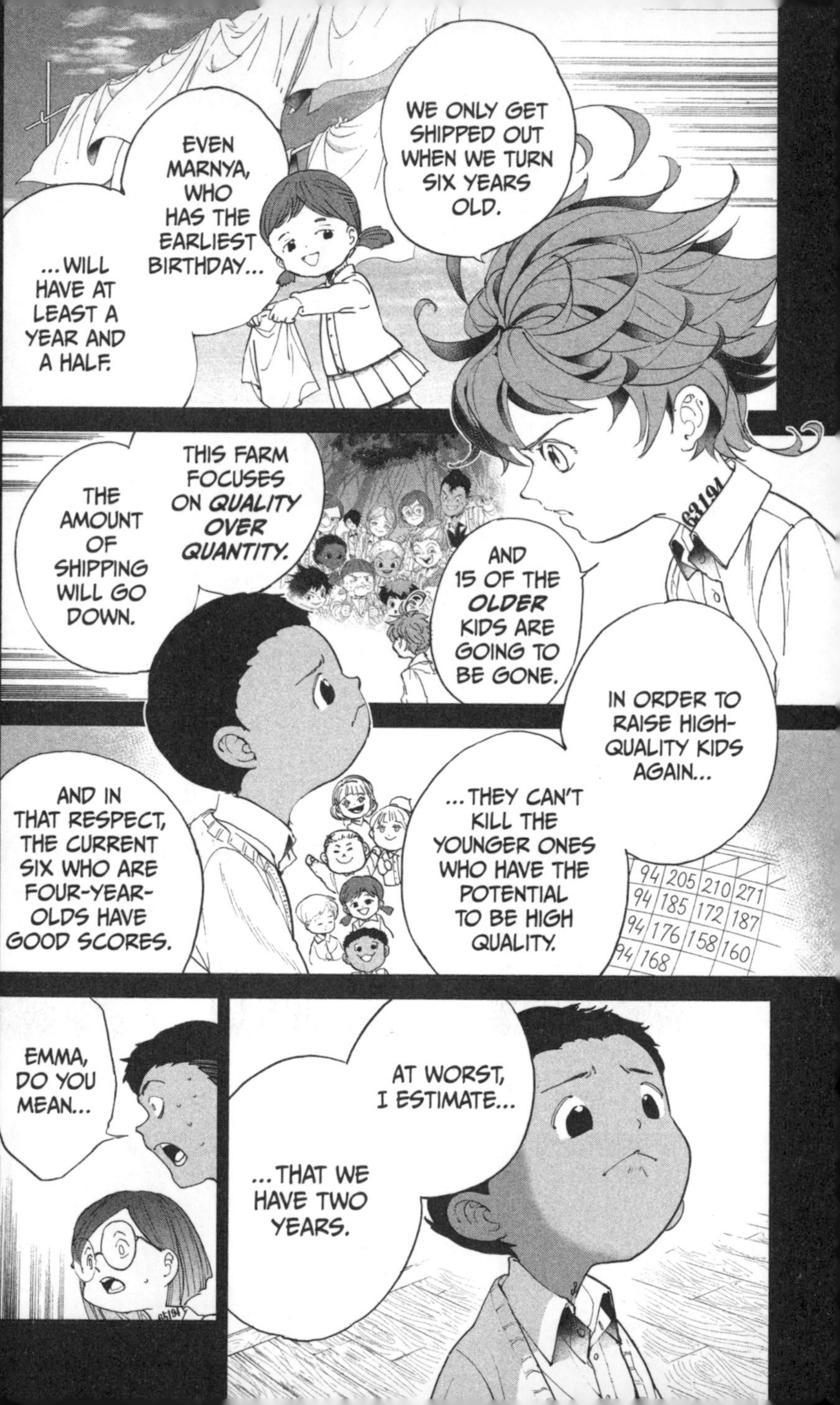
WE ONLY GET SHIPPED OUT WHEN WE TURN SIX YEARS OLD.
EVEN MARNYA, WHO HAS THE EARLIEST BIRTHDAY...
...WILL HAVE AT LEAST A YEAR AND A HALF.
AND 15 OF THE *OLDER* KIDS ARE GOING TO BE GONE.
THE AMOUNT OF SHIPPING WILL GO DOWN.
THIS FARM FOCUSES ON *QUALITY OVER QUANTITY.*
IN ORDER TO RAISE HIGH-QUALITY KIDS AGAIN...
...THEY CAN'T KILL THE YOUNGER ONES WHO HAVE THE POTENTIAL TO BE HIGH QUALITY.
AND IN THAT RESPECT, THE CURRENT SIX WHO ARE FOUR-YEAR-OLDS HAVE GOOD SCORES.
AT WORST, I ESTIMATE...
...THAT WE HAVE TWO YEARS.
EMMA, DO YOU MEAN...

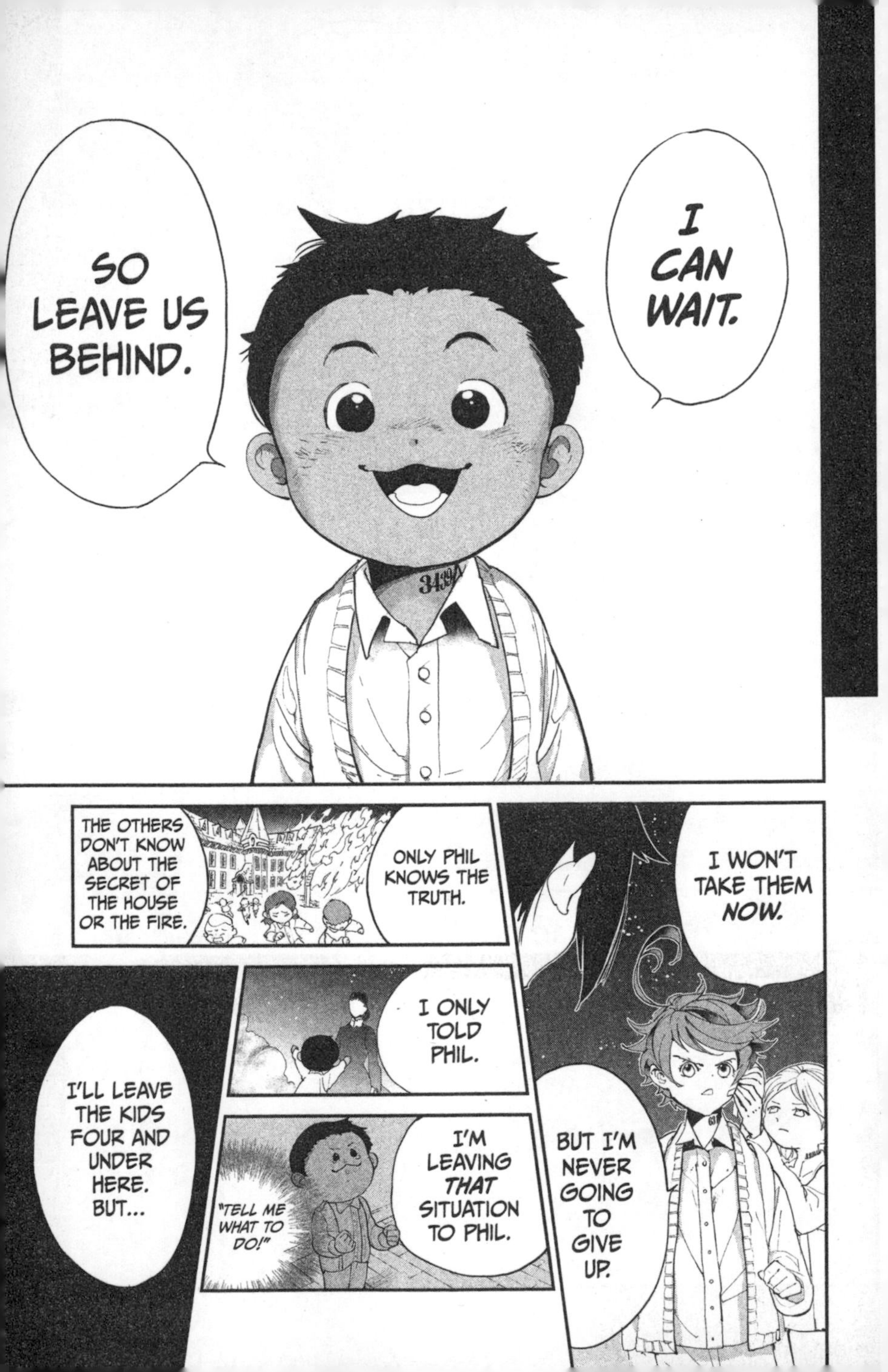
I CAN WAIT.
SO LEAVE US BEHIND.
3499
I WON'T TAKE THEM *NOW.*
BUT I'M NEVER GOING TO GIVE UP.
ONLY PHIL KNOWS THE TRUTH.
THE OTHERS DON'T KNOW ABOUT THE SECRET OF THE HOUSE OR THE FIRE.
I ONLY TOLD PHIL.
I'M LEAVING *THAT* SITUATION TO PHIL.
"TELL ME WHAT TO DO!"
I'LL LEAVE THE KIDS FOUR AND UNDER HERE. BUT...

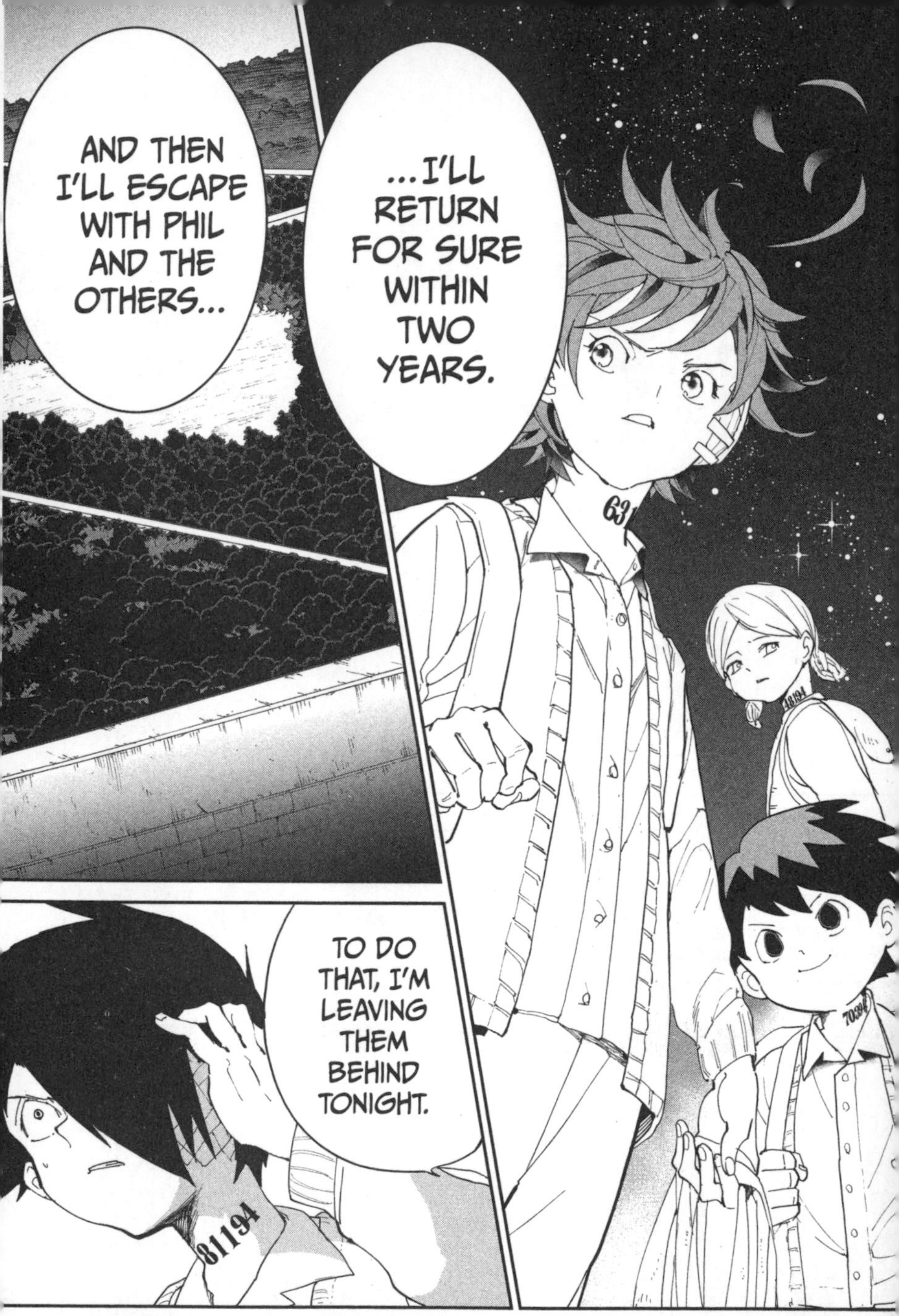
...I'LL RETURN FOR SURE WITHIN TWO YEARS.
AND THEN I'LL ESCAPE WITH PHIL AND THE OTHERS...
TO DO THAT, I'M LEAVING THEM BEHIND TONIGHT.

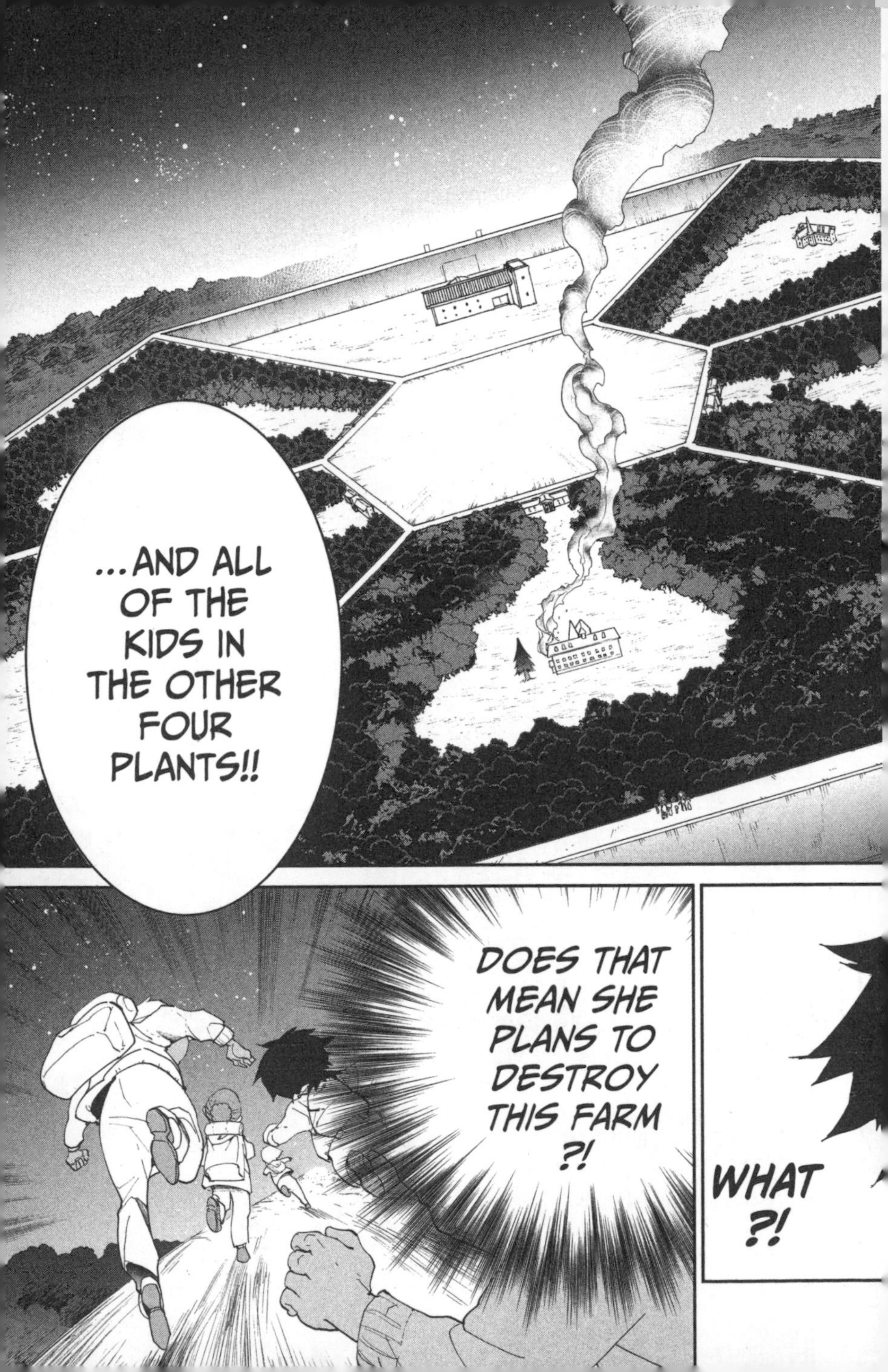
...AND ALL OF THE KIDS IN THE OTHER FOUR PLANTS!!
WHAT?!
DOES THAT MEAN SHE PLANS TO DESTROY THIS FARM?!

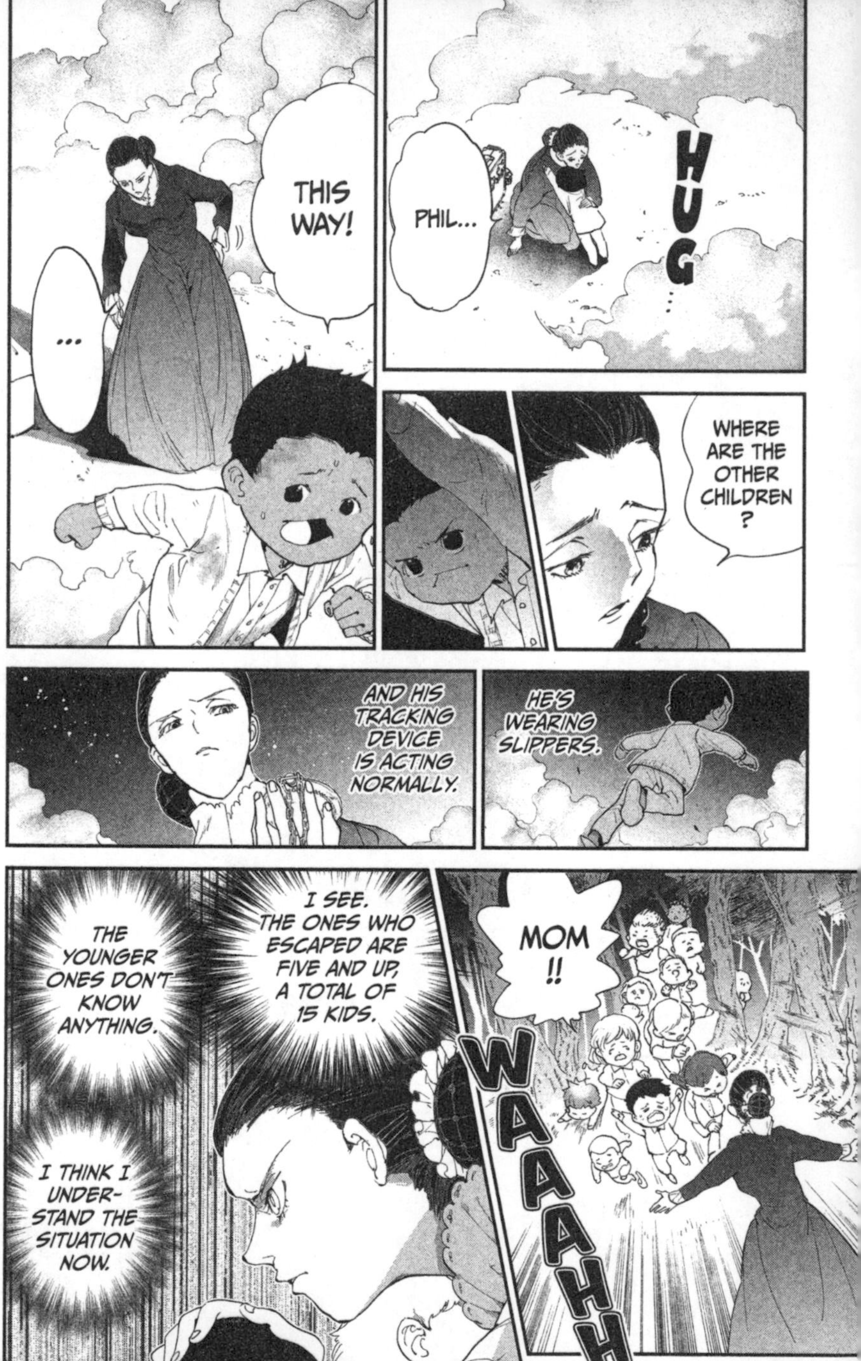
PHIL...
HUG...
WHERE ARE THE OTHER CHILDREN?
THIS WAY!
...
HE'S WEARING SLIPPERS.
AND HIS TRACKING DEVICE IS ACTING NORMALLY.
MOM!!
WAAAHH
I SEE. THE ONES WHO ESCAPED ARE FIVE AND UP, A TOTAL OF 15 KIDS.
THE YOUNGER ONES DON'T KNOW ANYTHING.
I THINK I UNDER-STAND THE SITUATION NOW.

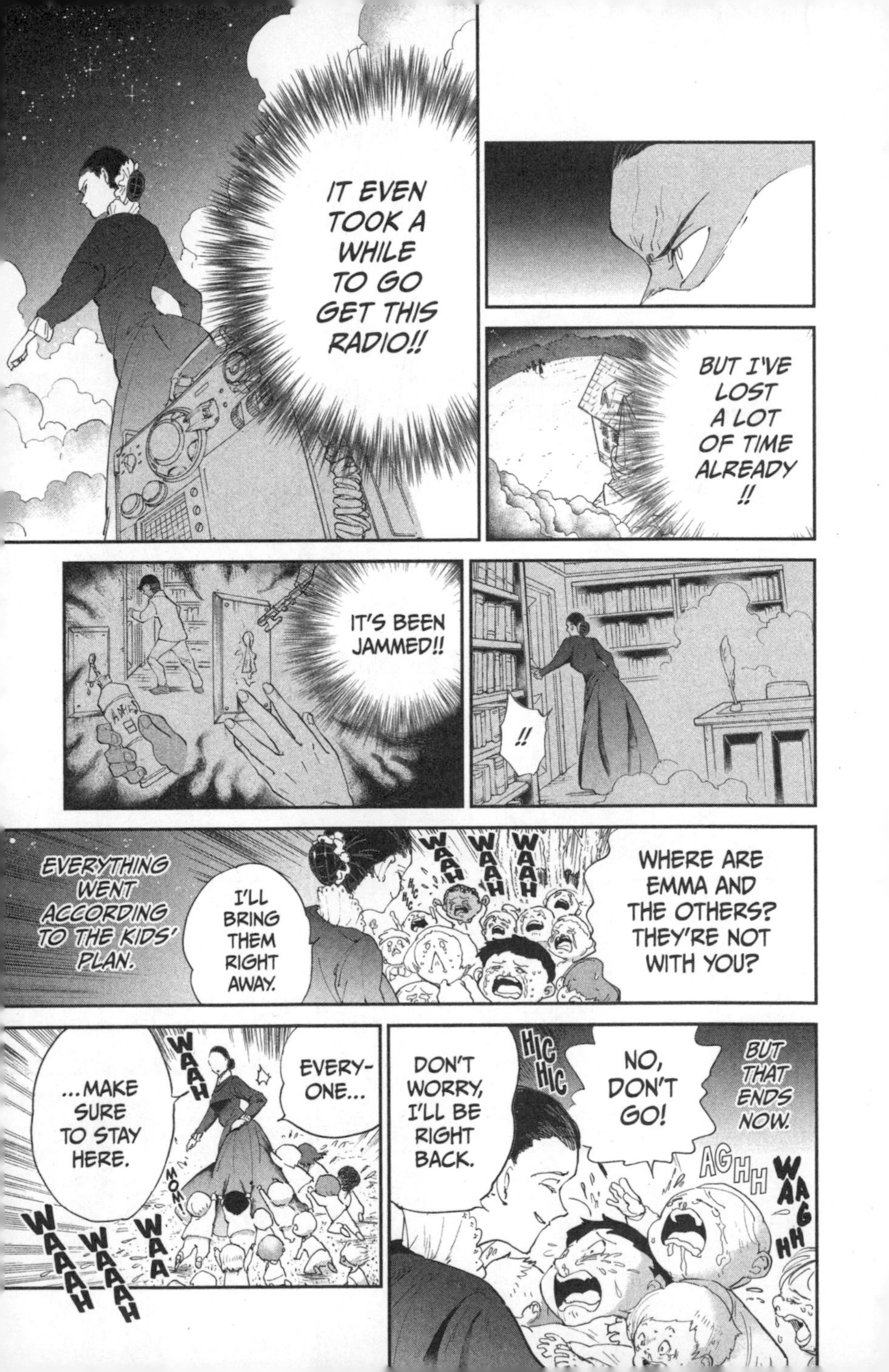
BUT I'VE LOST A LOT OF TIME ALREADY!!
IT EVEN TOOK A WHILE TO GO GET THIS RADIO!!
!!
IT'S BEEN JAMMED!!
WHERE ARE EMMA AND THE OTHERS? THEY'RE NOT WITH YOU?
WAAH
WAAH
WAAH
HIC HIC
I'LL BRING THEM RIGHT AWAY.
EVERYTHING WENT ACCORDING TO THE KIDS' PLAN.
BUT THAT ENDS NOW.
NO, DON'T GO!
HIC HIC
DON'T WORRY, I'LL BE RIGHT BACK.
AGHH
WAAGHH
EVERY-ONE...
...MAKE SURE TO STAY HERE.
WAAH
MOM!
WAAAH
WAAAAH
WAA

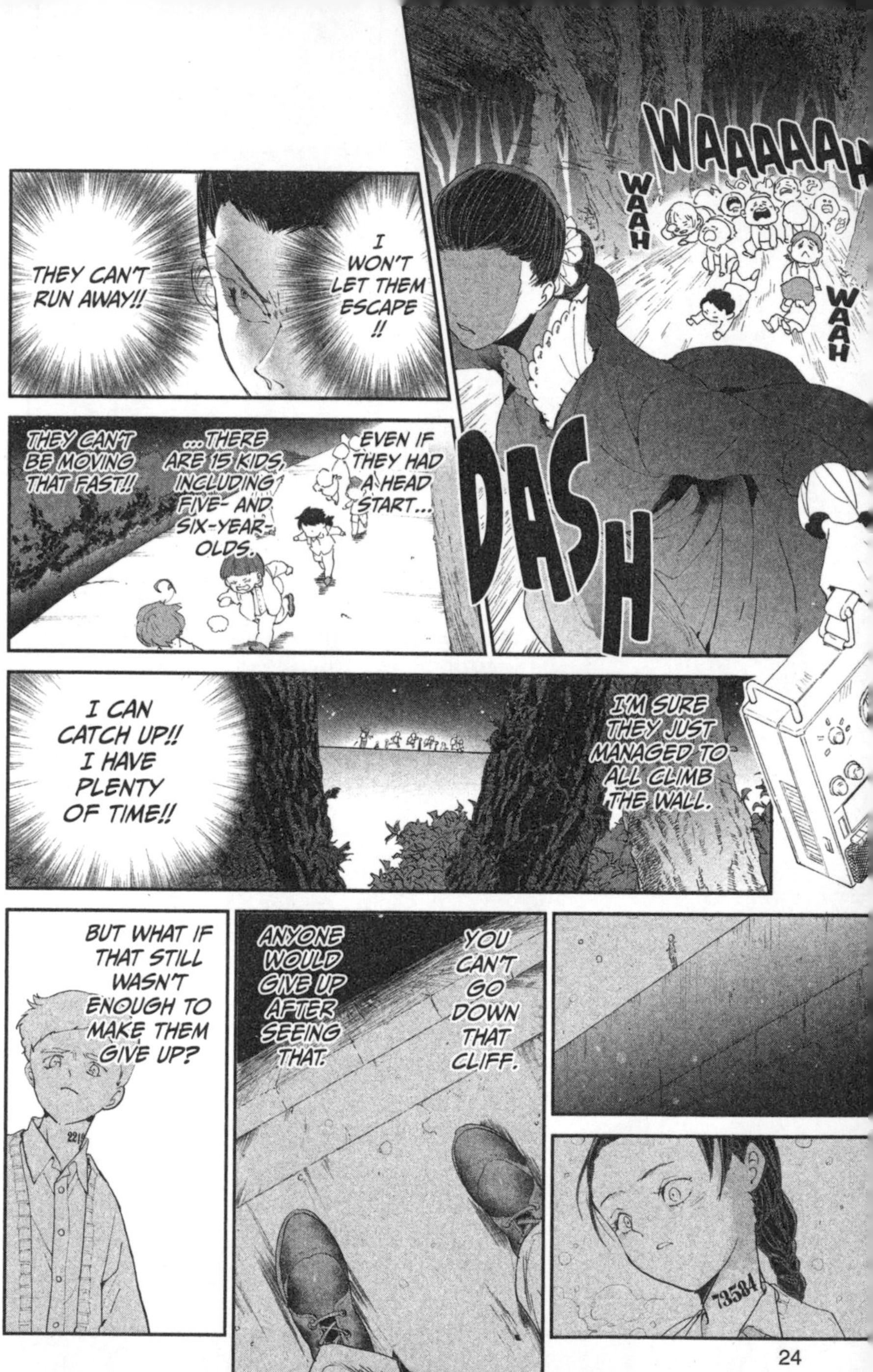
WAAAAAH
WAAH
WAAH
DASH
I WON'T LET THEM ESCAPE!!
THEY CAN'T RUN AWAY!!
EVEN IF THEY HAD A HEAD START...
...THERE ARE 15 KIDS, INCLUDING FIVE- AND SIX-YEAR-OLDS.
THEY CAN'T BE MOVING THAT FAST!!
I'M SURE THEY JUST MANAGED TO ALL CLIMB THE WALL.
I CAN CATCH UP!! I HAVE PLENTY OF TIME!!
73584
YOU CAN'T GO DOWN THAT CLIFF.
ANYONE WOULD GIVE UP AFTER SEEING THAT.
BUT WHAT IF THAT STILL WASN'T ENOUGH TO MAKE THEM GIVE UP?

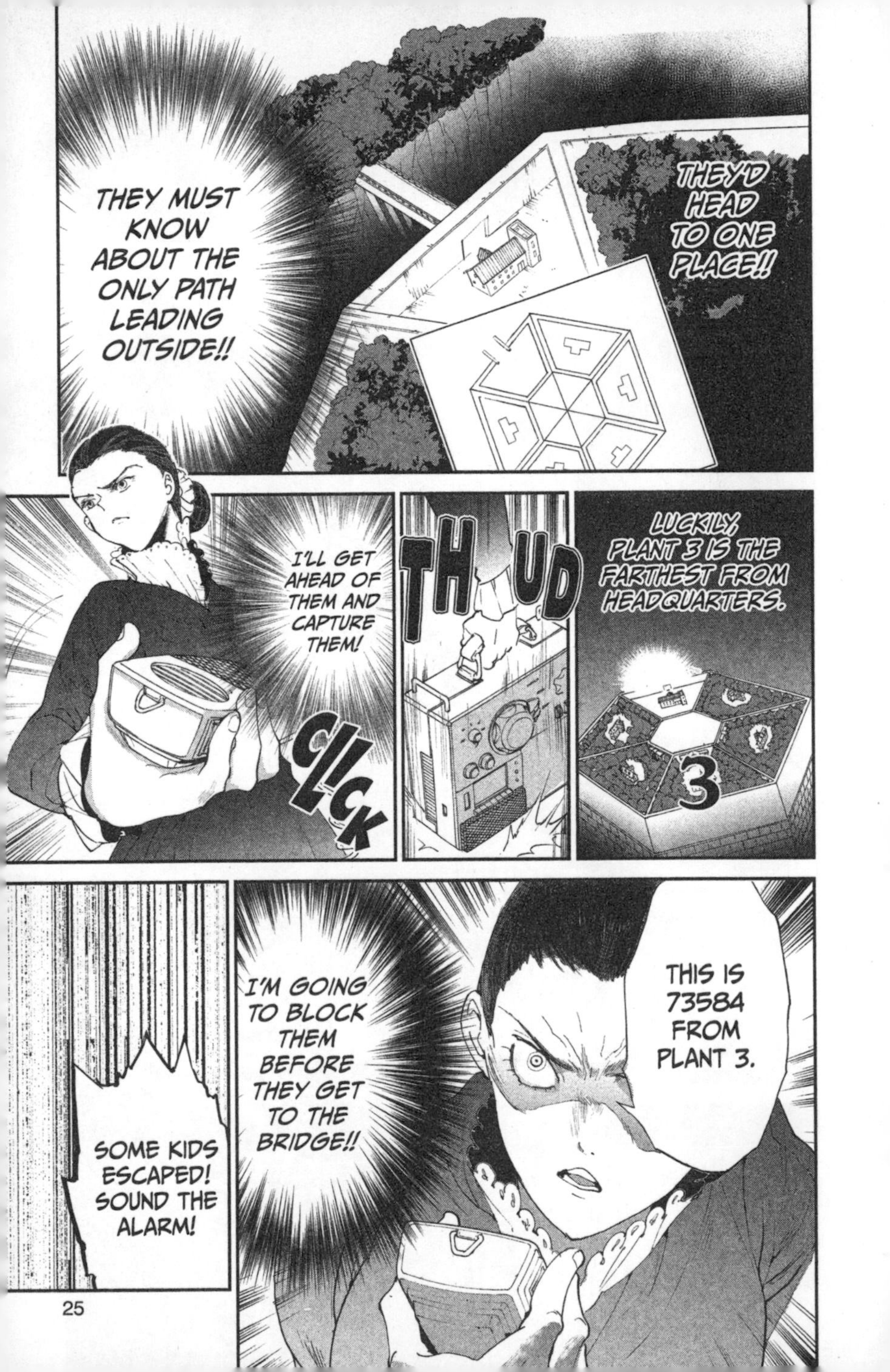
THEY'D HEAD TO ONE PLACE!!
THEY MUST KNOW ABOUT THE ONLY PATH LEADING OUTSIDE!!
LUCKILY, PLANT 3 IS THE FARTHEST FROM HEADQUARTERS.
3
THUD
I'LL GET AHEAD OF THEM AND CAPTURE THEM!
CLICK
THIS IS 73584 FROM PLANT 3.
I'M GOING TO BLOCK THEM BEFORE THEY GET TO THE BRIDGE!!
SOME KIDS ESCAPED! SOUND THE ALARM!

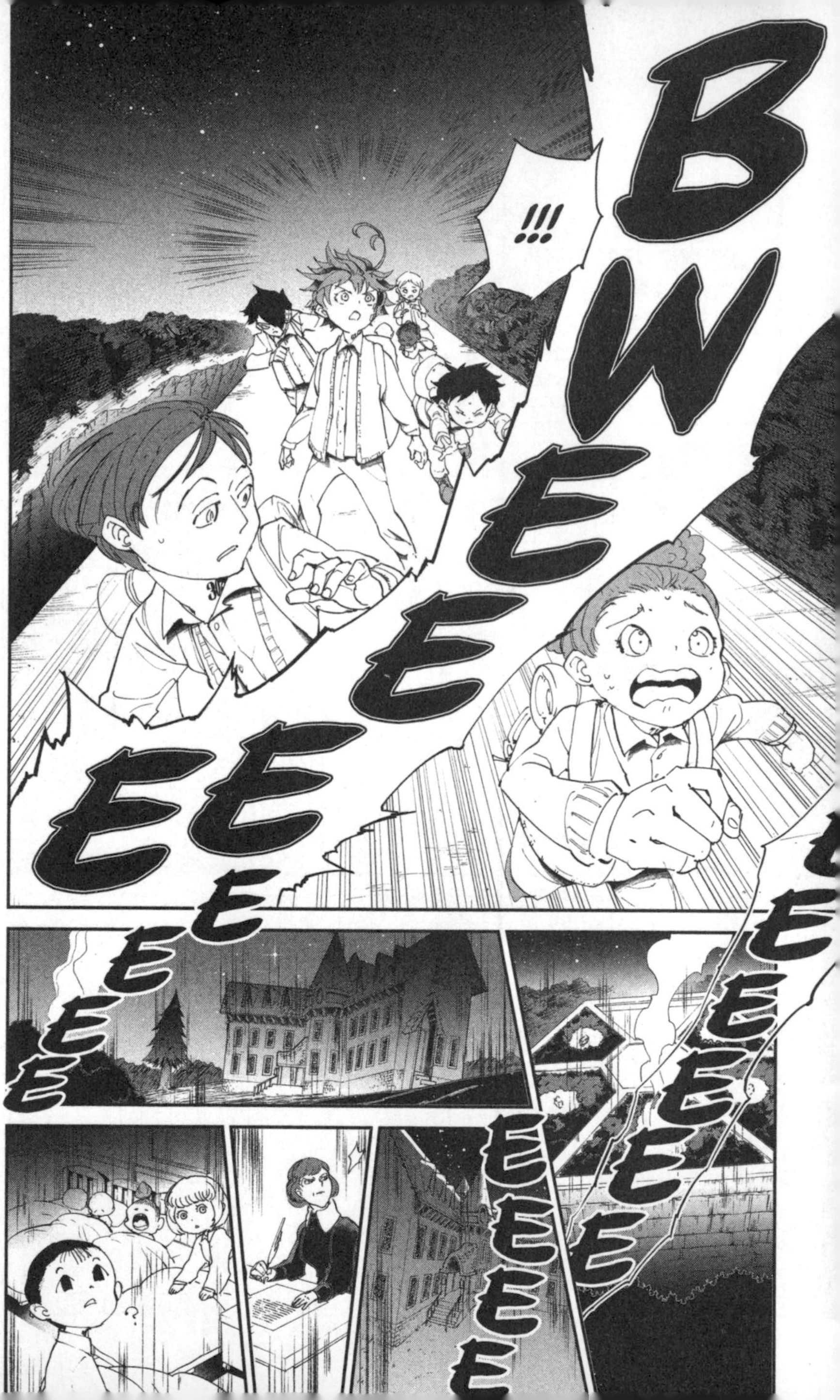

BWEEEEEE
!!!
EEEEE
EEEEEEE
EEEEEEE

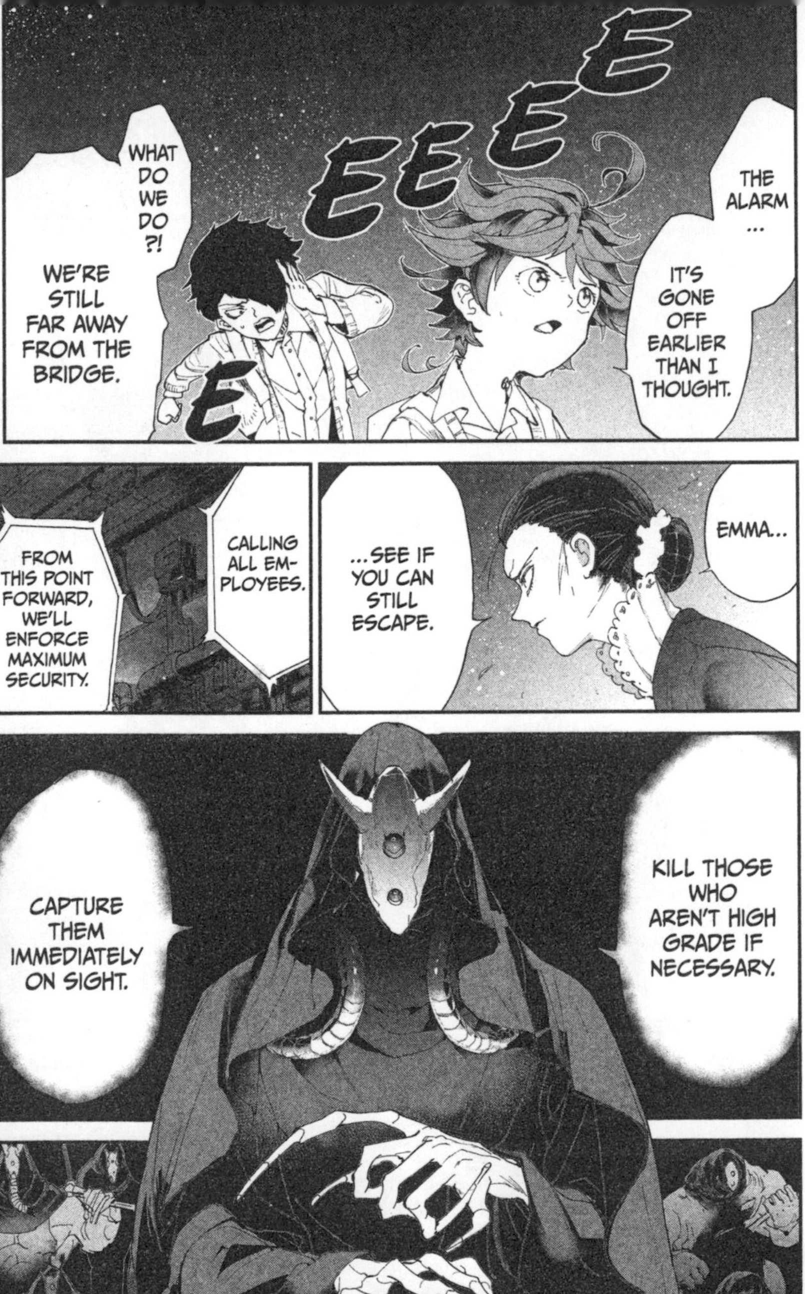
THE ALARM ...
IT'S GONE OFF EARLIER THAN I THOUGHT.
EEEEE
WHAT DO WE DO?!
WE'RE STILL FAR AWAY FROM THE BRIDGE.
E
EMMA...
...SEE IF YOU CAN STILL ESCAPE.
CALLING ALL EMPLOYEES.
FROM THIS POINT FORWARD, WE'LL ENFORCE MAXIMUM SECURITY.
KILL THOSE WHO AREN'T HIGH GRADE IF NECESSARY.
CAPTURE THEM IMMEDIATELY ON SIGHT.

THE PROMISED NEVERLAND SIDE SCENE 009

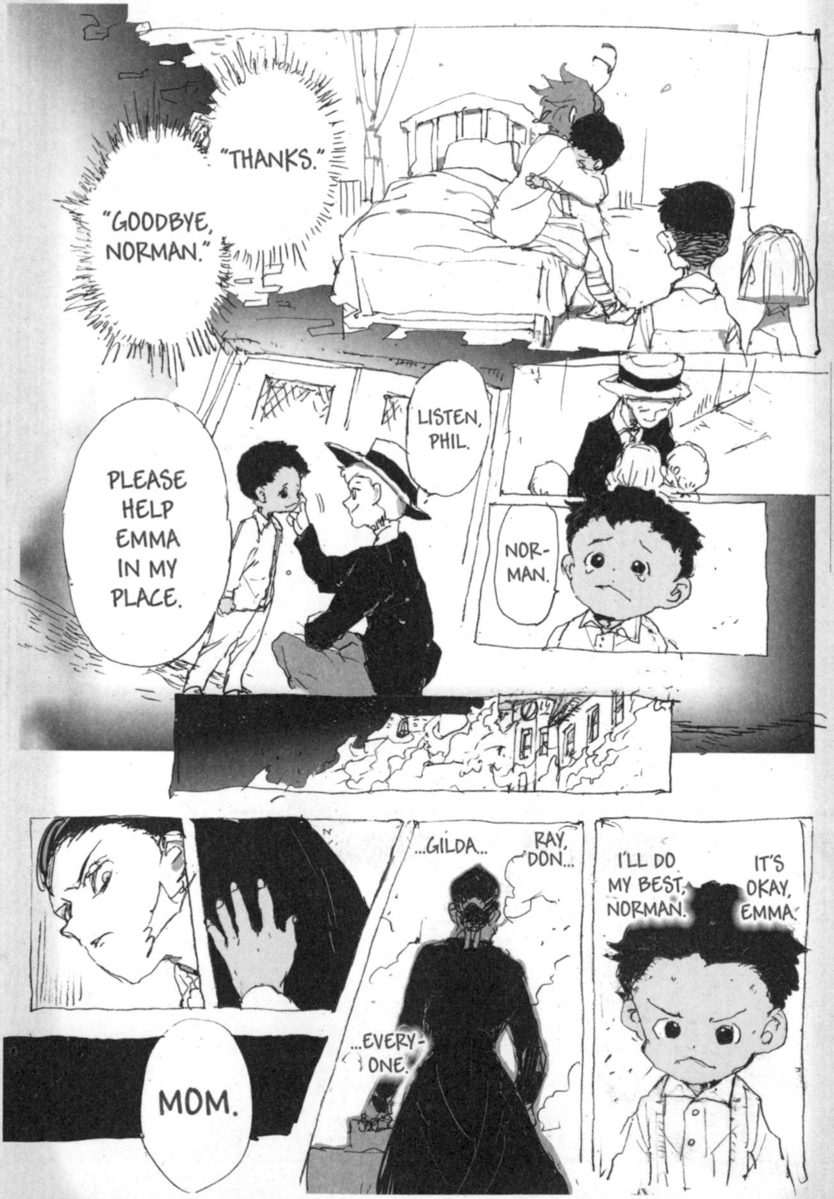
"THANKS."
"GOODBYE, NORMAN."
NOR-MAN.
LISTEN, PHIL.
PLEASE HELP EMMA IN MY PLACE.
IT'S OKAY, EMMA.
I'LL DO MY BEST, NORMAN.
RAY, DON...
...GILDA...
...EVERY-ONE.
MOM.

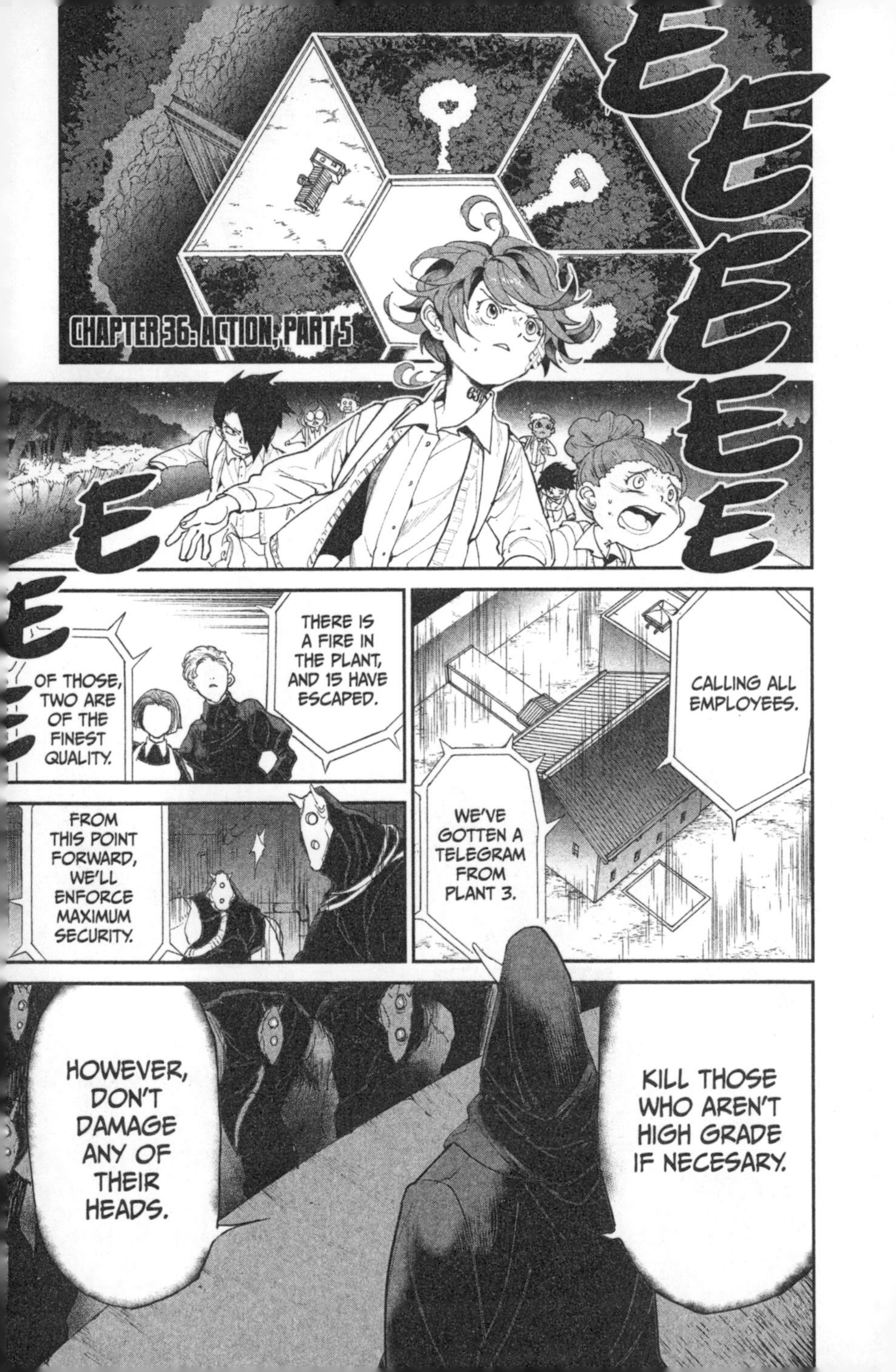
EEEEEEEEEE
CHAPTER 36: ACTION, PART 5
CALLING ALL EMPLOYEES.
WE'VE GOTTEN A TELEGRAM FROM PLANT 3.
THERE IS A FIRE IN THE PLANT, AND 15 HAVE ESCAPED.
OF THOSE, TWO ARE OF THE FINEST QUALITY.
FROM THIS POINT FORWARD, WE'LL ENFORCE MAXIMUM SECURITY.
KILL THOSE WHO AREN'T HIGH GRADE IF NECESARY.
HOWEVER, DON'T DAMAGE ANY OF THEIR HEADS.

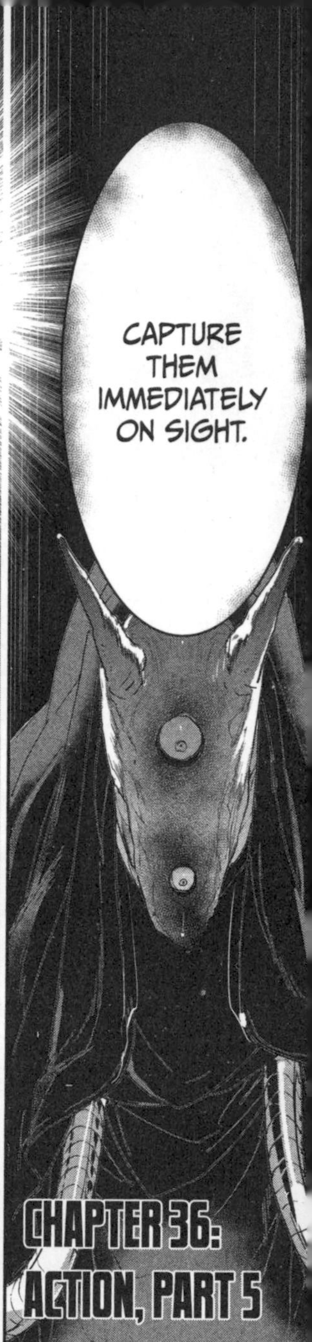
CAPTURE THEM IMMEDIATELY ON SIGHT.
CHAPTER 36: ACTION, PART 5
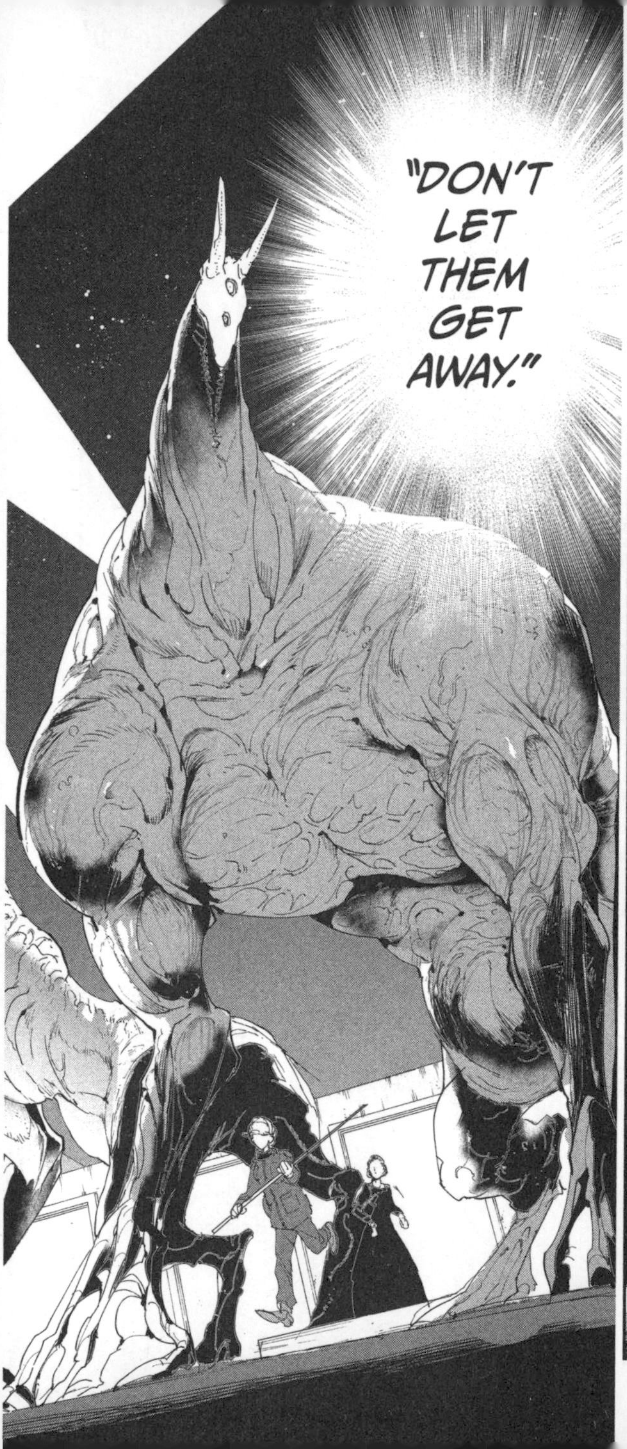
"DON'T LET THEM GET AWAY."

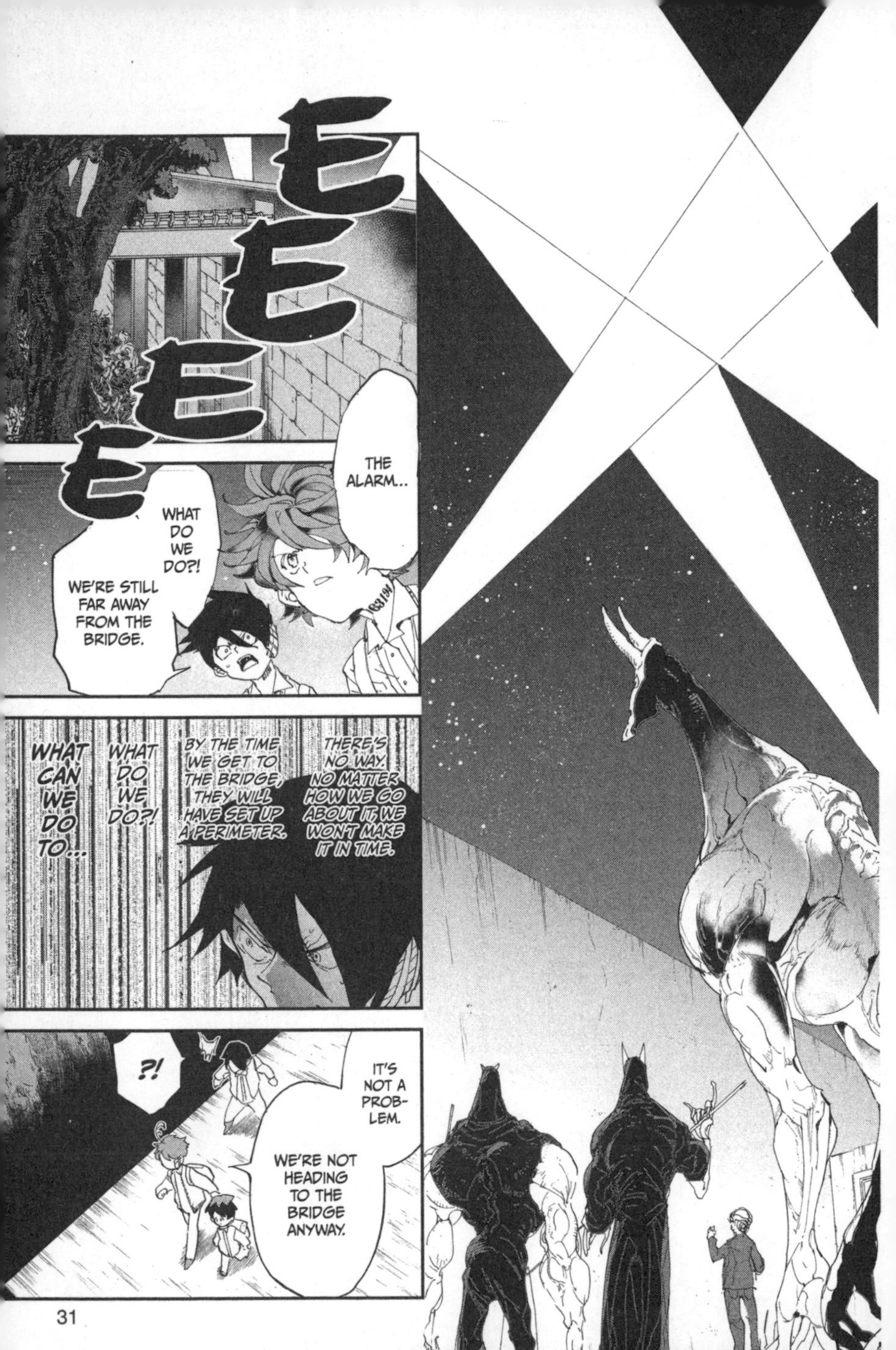

EEEE
THE ALARM..
WHAT DO WE DO?!
WE'RE STILL FAR AWAY FROM THE BRIDGE.
THERE'S NO WAY. NO MATTER HOW WE GO ABOUT IT, WE WON'T MAKE IT IN TIME.
BY THE TIME WE GET TO THE BRIDGE, THEY WILL HAVE SET UP A PERIMETER.
WHAT DO WE DO?!
WHAT CAN WE DO TO...
IT'S NOT A PROB-LEM.
?!
WE'RE NOT HEADING TO THE BRIDGE ANYWAY.

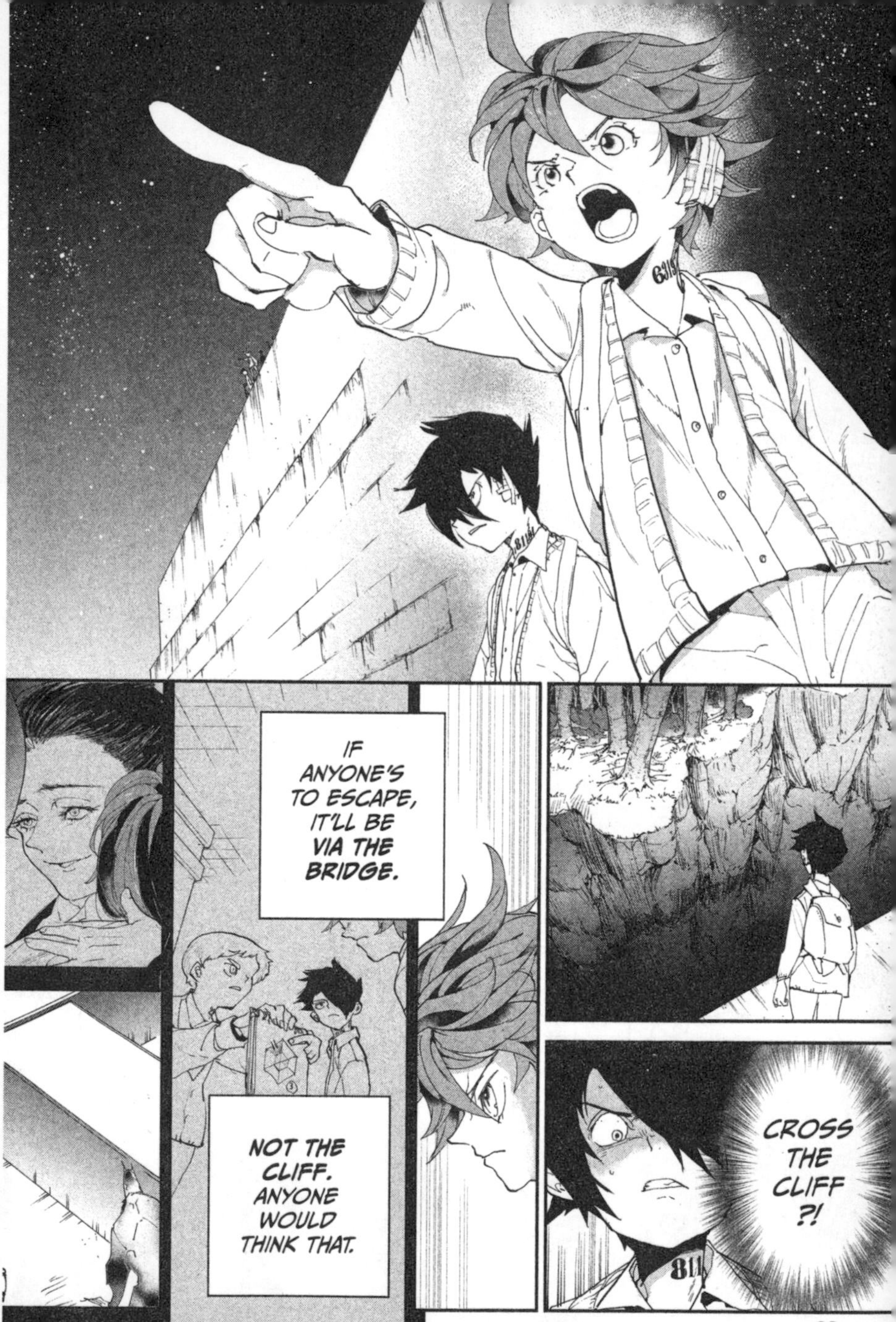
CROSS THE CLIFF ?!
IF ANYONE'S TO ESCAPE, IT'LL BE VIA THE BRIDGE.
NOT THE CLIFF. ANYONE WOULD THINK THAT.

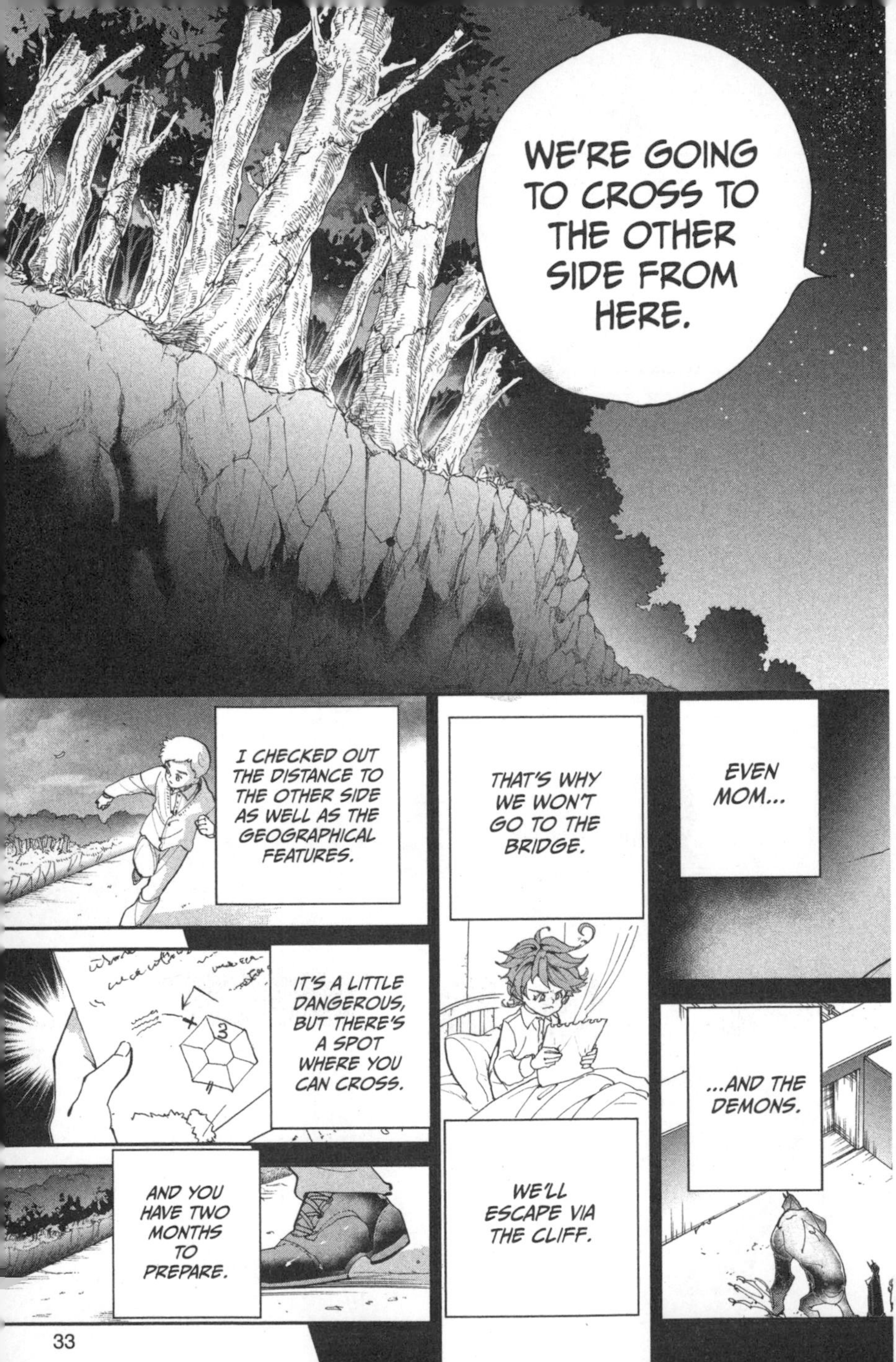

WE'RE GOING TO CROSS TO THE OTHER SIDE FROM HERE.
EVEN MOM...
...AND THE DEMONS.
THAT'S WHY WE WON'T GO TO THE BRIDGE.
WE'LL ESCAPE VIA THE CLIFF.
I CHECKED OUT THE DISTANCE TO THE OTHER SIDE AS WELL AS THE GEOGRAPHICAL FEATURES.
IT'S A LITTLE DANGEROUS, BUT THERE'S A SPOT WHERE YOU CAN CROSS.
AND YOU HAVE TWO MONTHS TO PREPARE.

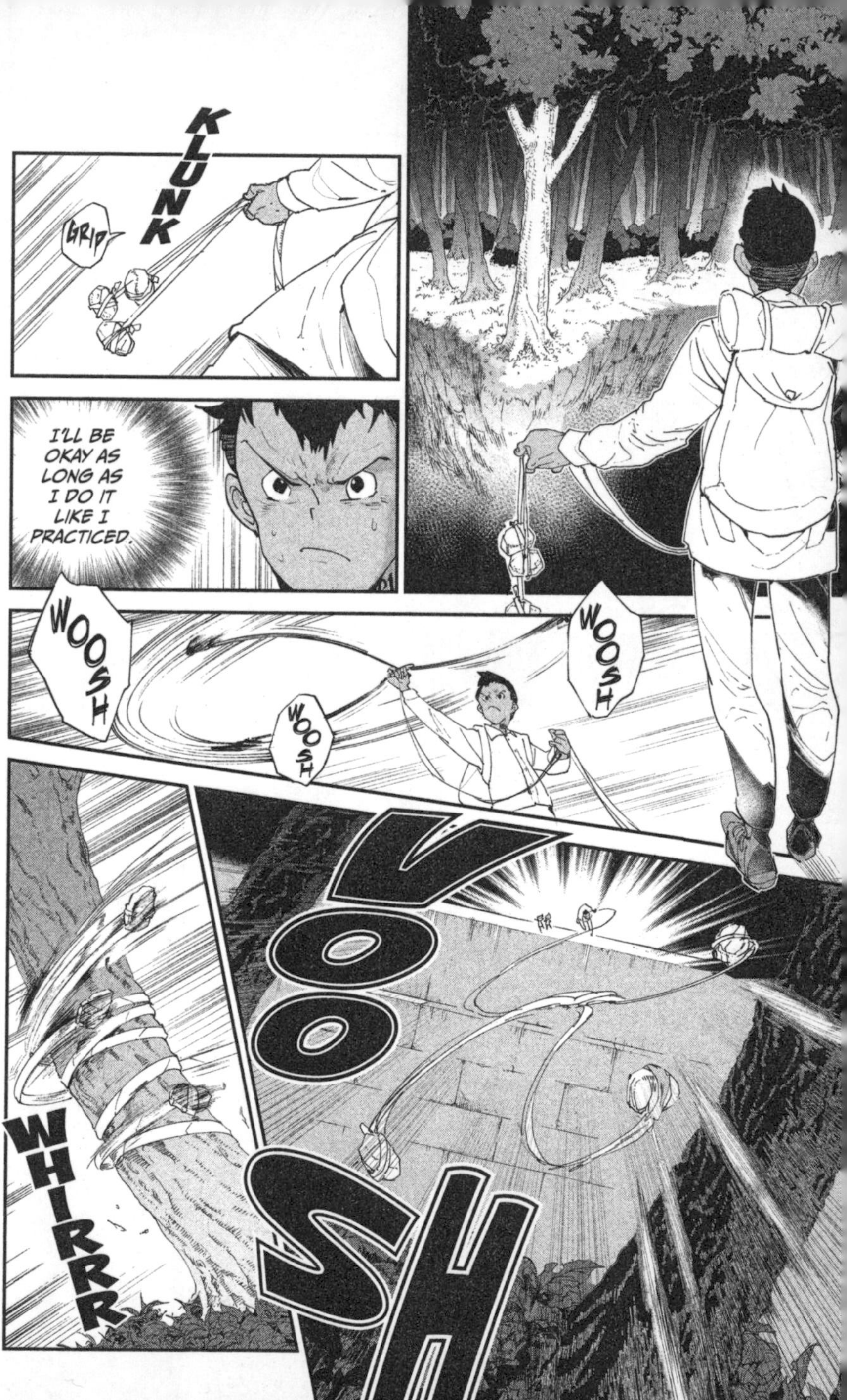
KLUNK
GRIP
I'LL BE OKAY AS LONG AS I DO IT LIKE I PRACTICED.
WOOSH
WOOSH
WOOSH
VOOSH
WHIRRR

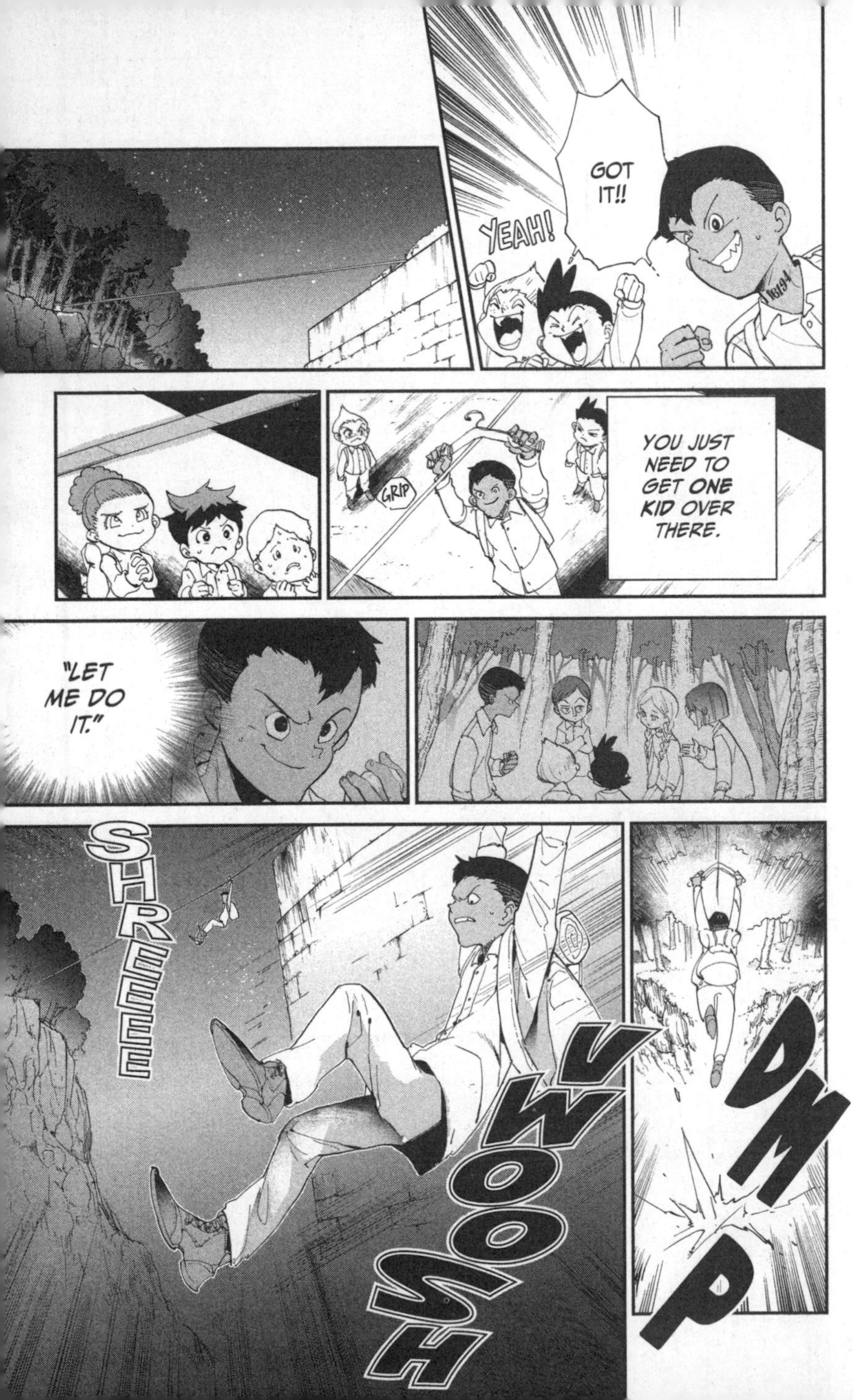
GOT IT!!
YEAH!
YOU JUST NEED TO GET ONE KID OVER THERE.
GRIP
"LET ME DO IT."
DMP
WOOSH
SHREEEE

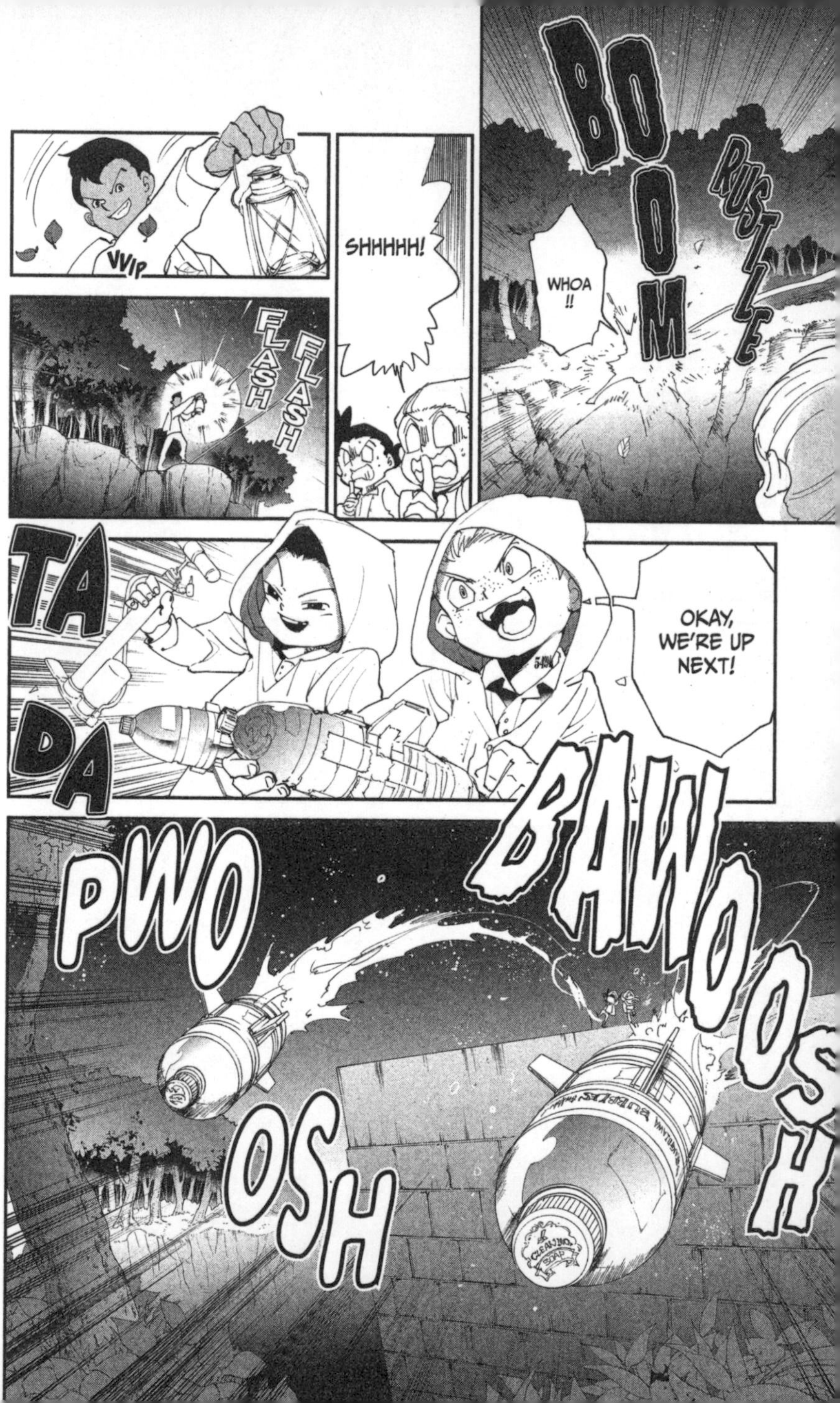
BOOOM
RUSTLE
WHOA!!
SHHHHH!
VVIP
FLASH
FLASH
OKAY, WE'RE UP NEXT!
TA DA
BAWOOOSH
PWOOSH

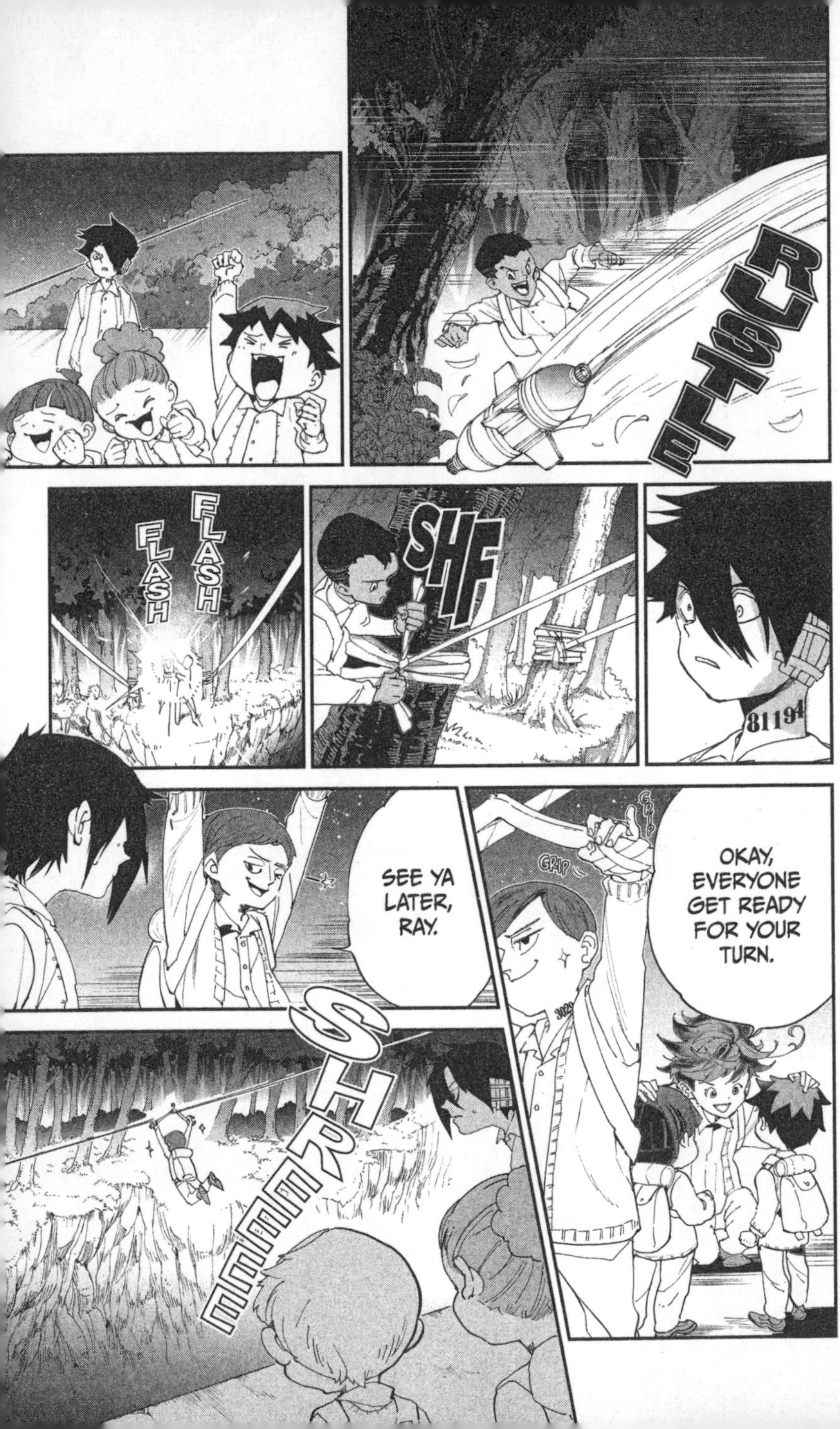
RUSTLE
81194
SHF
FLASH
FLASH
GRIP
GRIP
OKAY, EVERYONE GET READY FOR YOUR TURN.
SEE YA LATER, RAY.
SHREEEEE

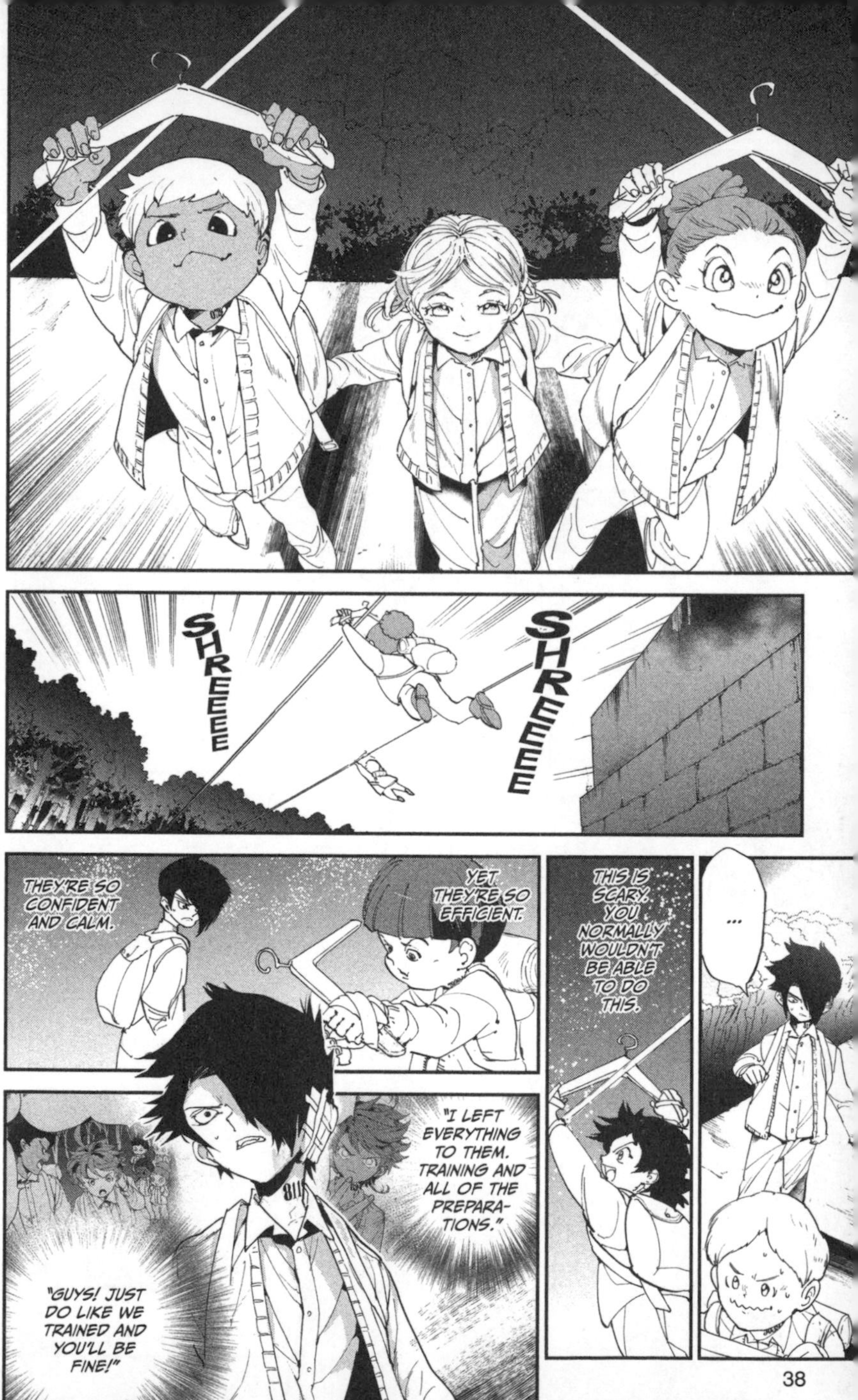
SHREEEE
SHREEEE
...
THIS IS SCARY. YOU NORMALLY WOULDN'T BE ABLE TO DO THIS.
YET THEY'RE SO EFFICIENT.
THEY'RE SO CONFIDENT AND CALM.
"I LEFT EVERYTHING TO THEM. TRAINING AND ALL OF THE PREPARATIONS."
"GUYS! JUST DO LIKE WE TRAINED AND YOU'LL BE FINE!"

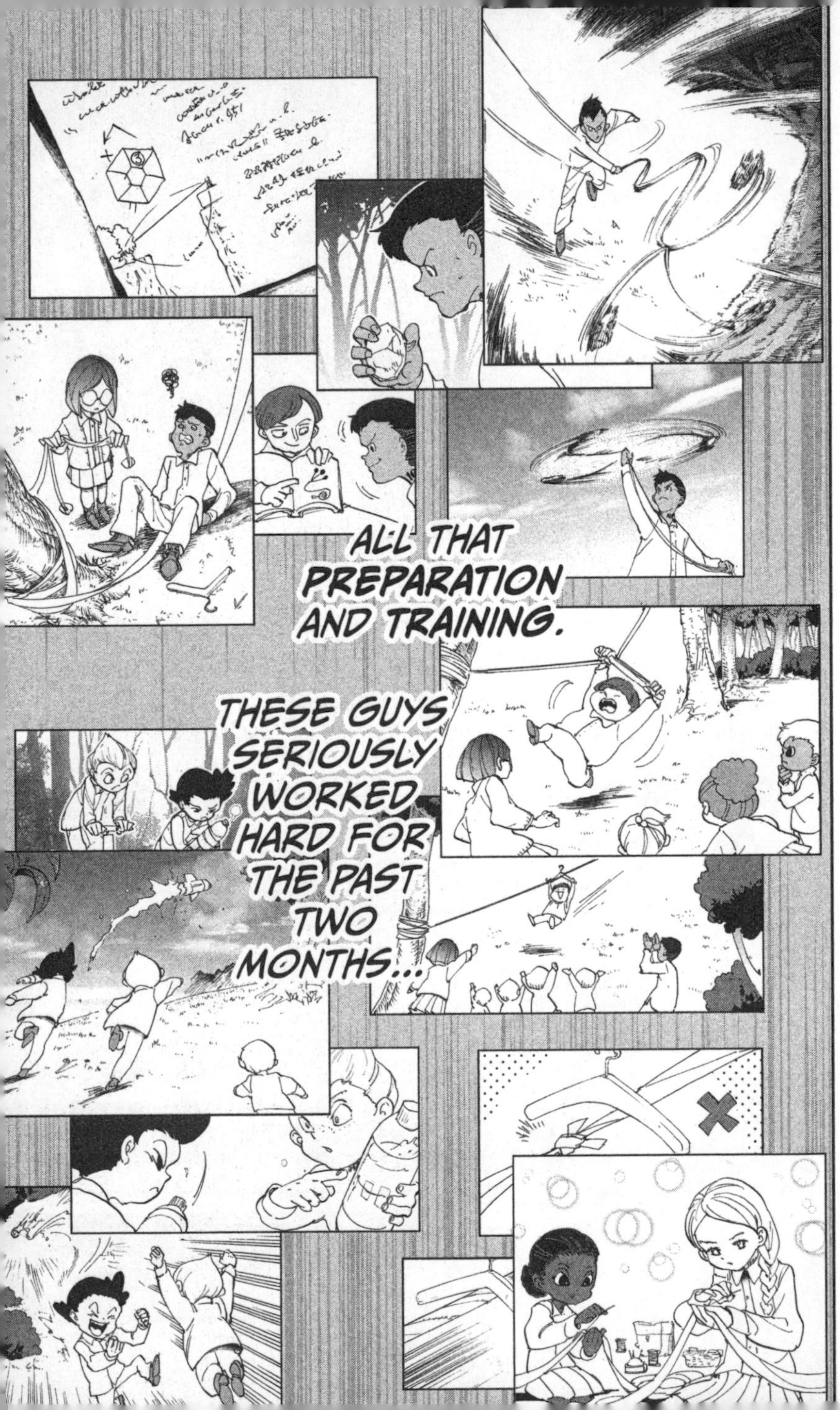
ALL THAT PREPARATION AND TRAINING.
THESE GUYS SERIOUSLY WORKED HARD FOR THE PAST TWO MONTHS...

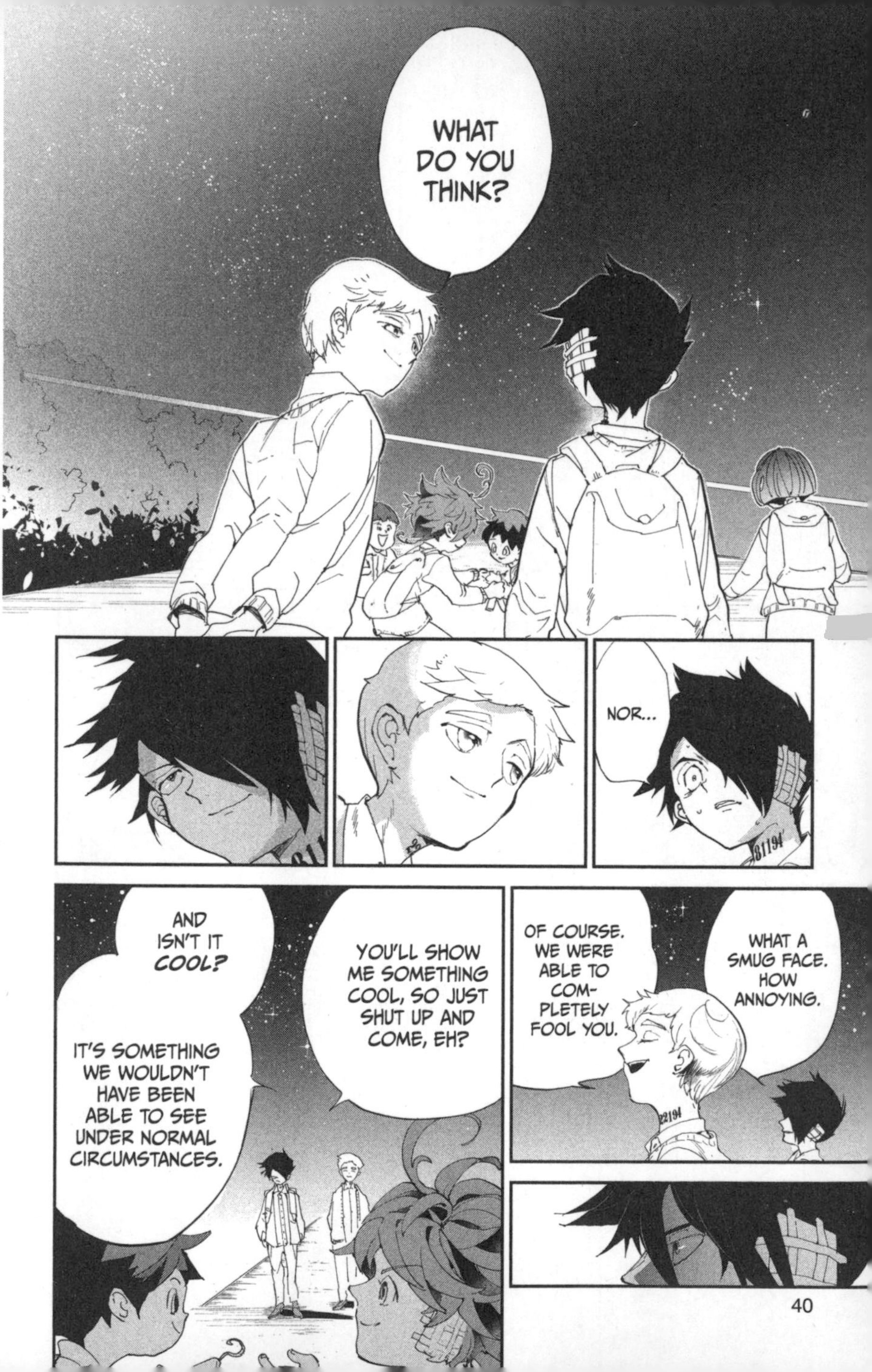
WHAT DO YOU THINK?
NOR...
WHAT A SMUG FACE. HOW ANNOYING.
OF COURSE. WE WERE ABLE TO COM-PLETELY FOOL YOU.
YOU'LL SHOW ME SOMETHING COOL, SO JUST SHUT UP AND COME, EH?
AND ISN'T IT *COOL?*
IT'S SOMETHING WE WOULDN'T HAVE BEEN ABLE TO SEE UNDER NORMAL CIRCUMSTANCES.

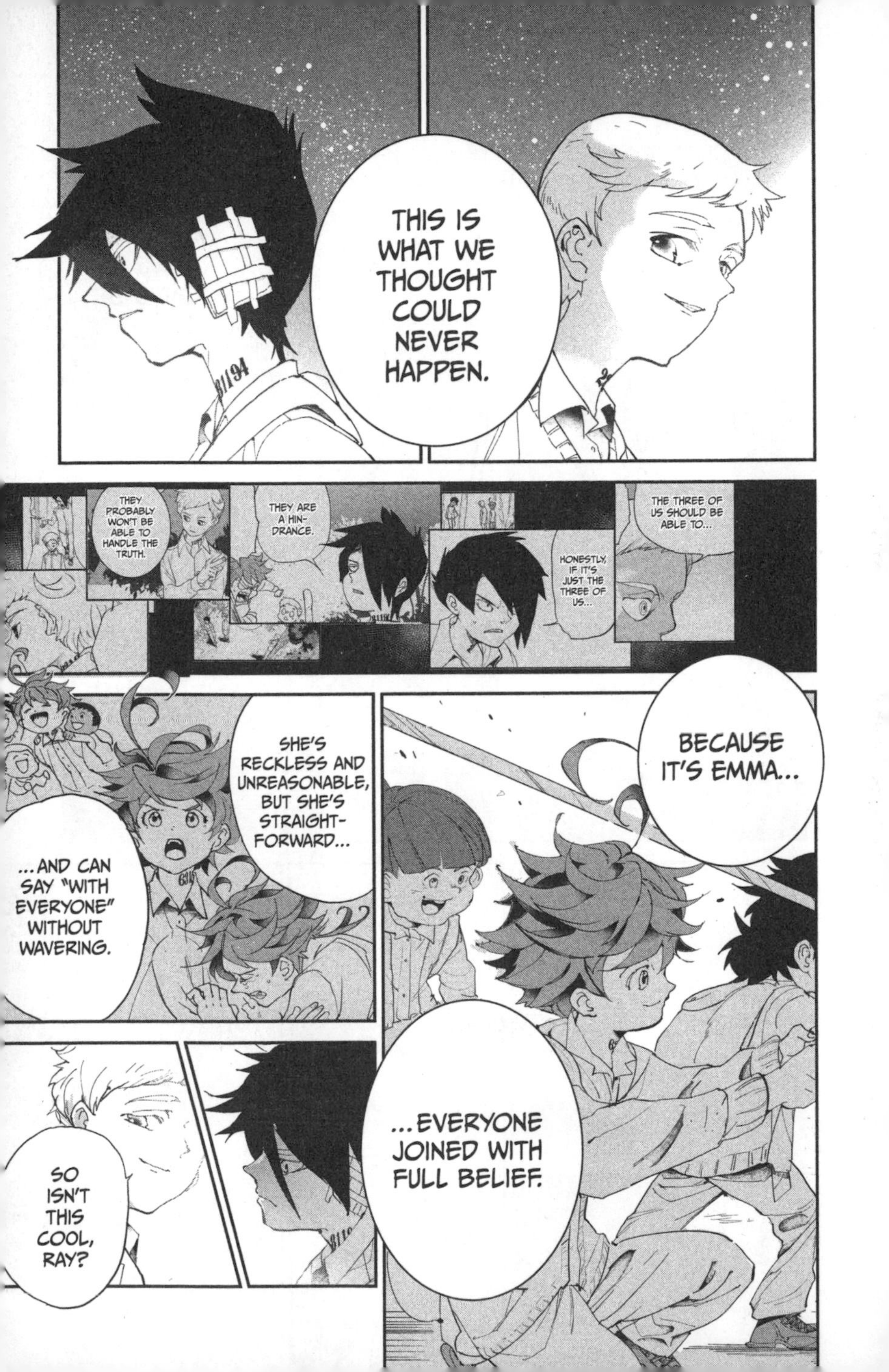
THIS IS WHAT WE THOUGHT COULD NEVER HAPPEN.
THE THREE OF US SHOULD BE ABLE TO...
HONESTLY, IF IT'S JUST THE THREE OF US...
THEY ARE A HIN-DRANCE.
THEY PROBABLY WON'T BE ABLE TO HANDLE THE TRUTH.
BECAUSE IT'S EMMA...
SHE'S RECKLESS AND UNREASONABLE, BUT SHE'S STRAIGHT-FORWARD...
...AND CAN SAY "WITH EVERYONE" WITHOUT WAVERING.
...EVERYONE JOINED WITH FULL BELIEF.
SO ISN'T THIS COOL, RAY?

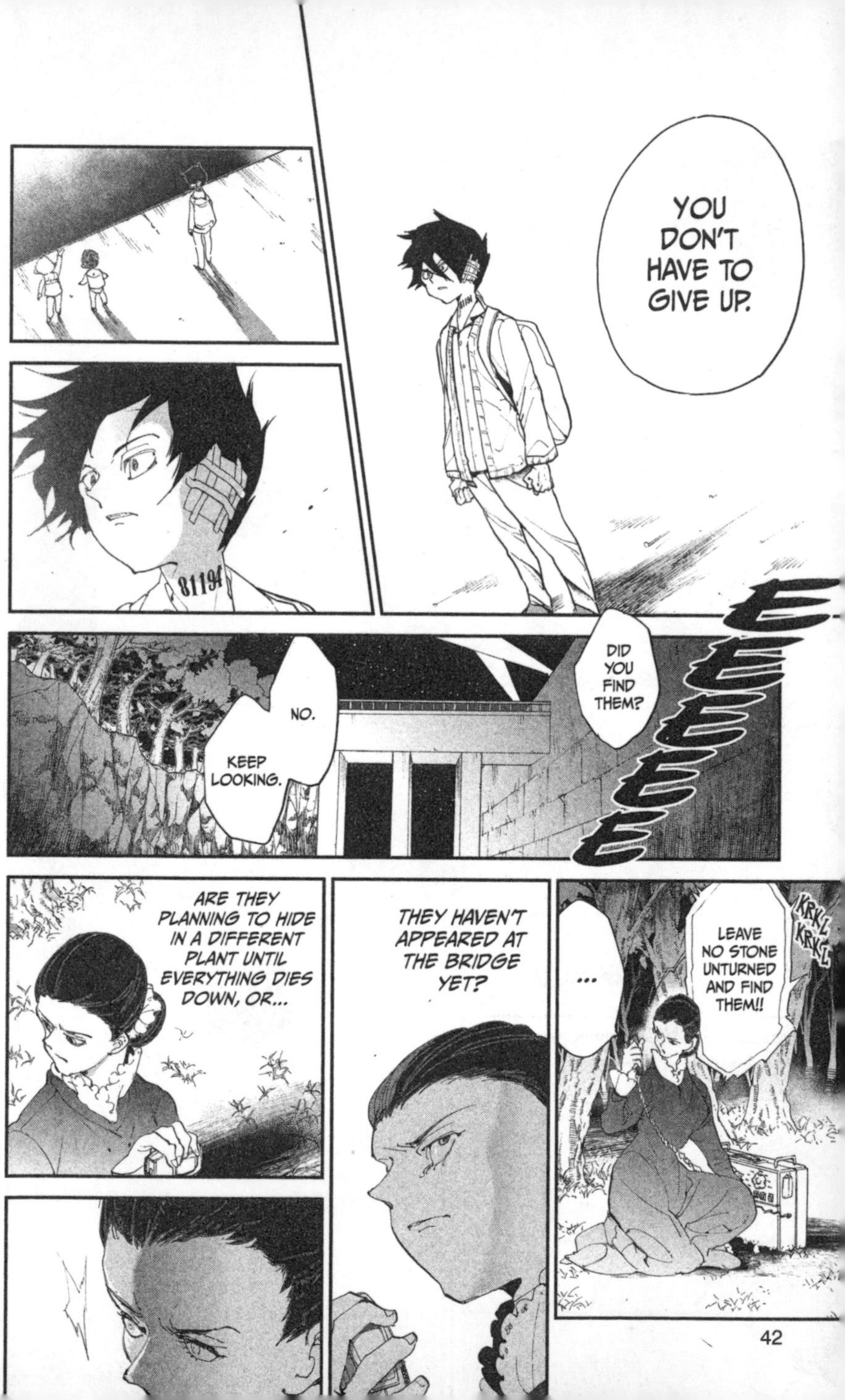
YOU DON'T HAVE TO GIVE UP.
DID YOU FIND THEM?
NO.
KEEP LOOKING.
EEEEEEE
KRK'L KRK'L
LEAVE NO STONE UNTURNED AND FIND THEM!!
...
THEY HAVEN'T APPEARED AT THE BRIDGE YET?
ARE THEY PLANNING TO HIDE IN A DIFFERENT PLANT UNTIL EVERYTHING DIES DOWN, OR...

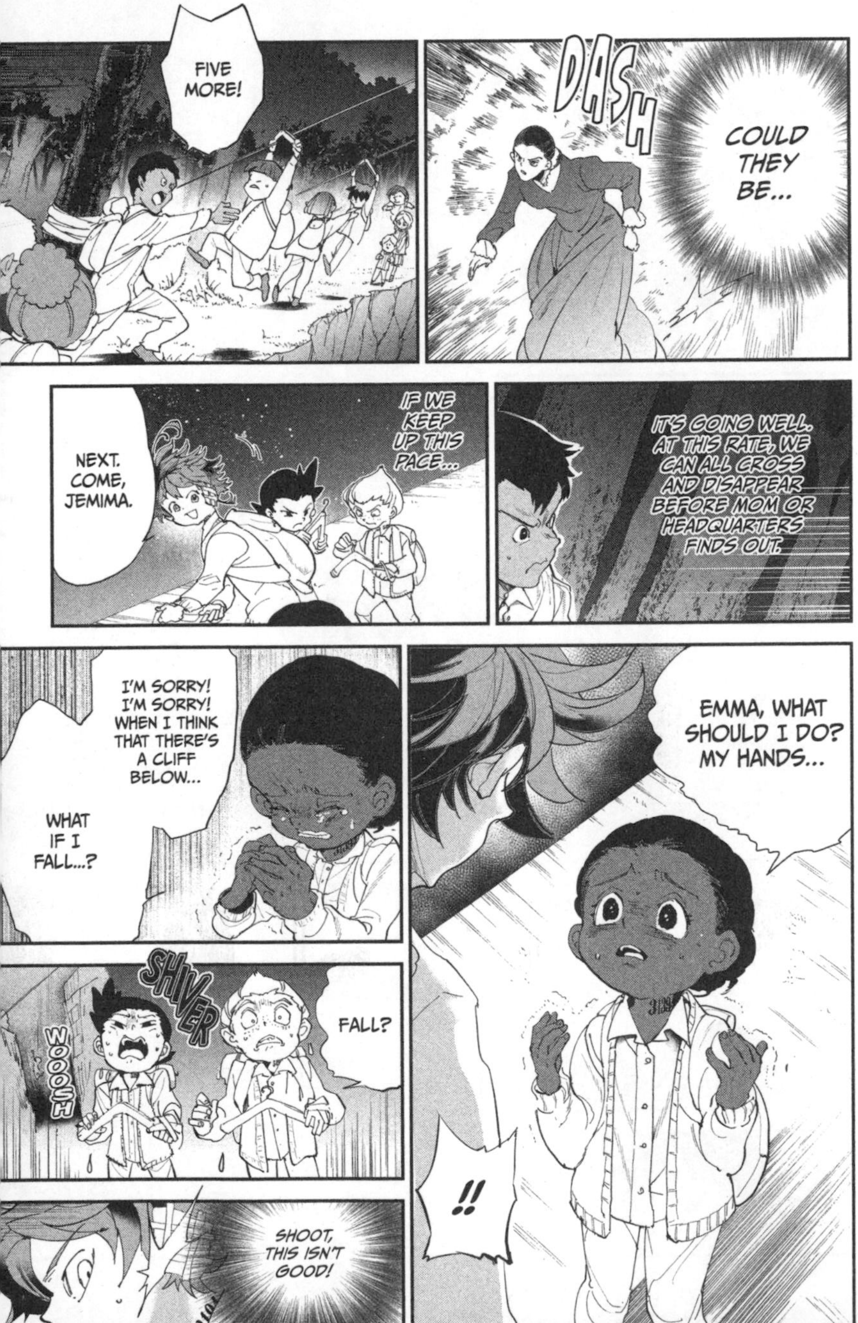
DASH
COULD THEY BE...
FIVE MORE!
IT'S GOING WELL. AT THIS RATE, WE CAN ALL CROSS AND DISAPPEAR BEFORE MOM OR HEADQUARTERS FINDS OUT.
IF WE KEEP UP THIS PACE...
NEXT. COME, JEMIMA.
EMMA, WHAT SHOULD I DO? MY HANDS...
!!
I'M SORRY! I'M SORRY! WHEN I THINK THAT THERE'S A CLIFF BELOW...
WHAT IF I FALL...?
FALL?
SHIVER
WOOOSH
SHOOT, THIS ISN'T GOOD!

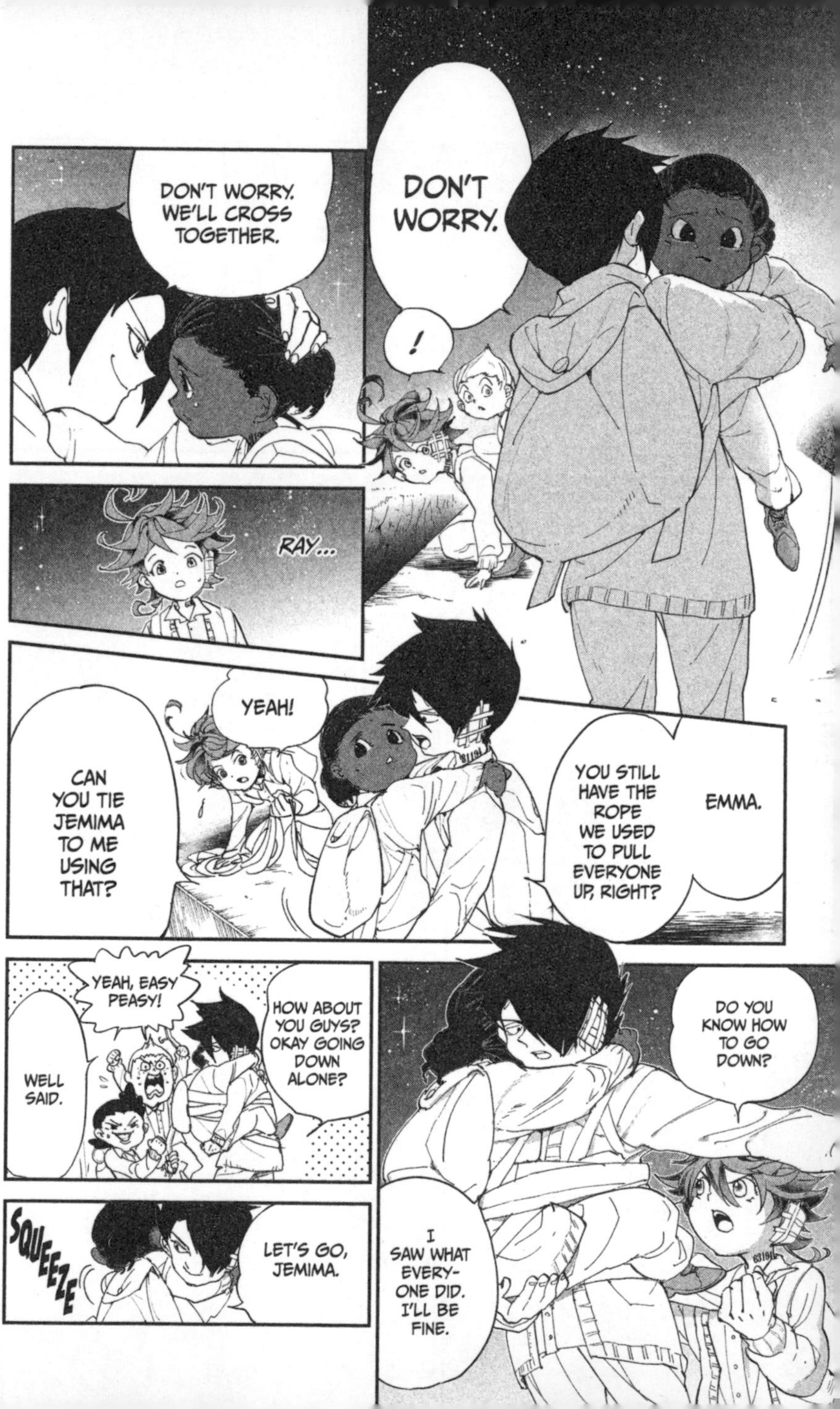
DON'T WORRY.
!
DON'T WORRY. WE'LL CROSS TOGETHER.
RAY...
EMMA.
YOU STILL HAVE THE ROPE WE USED TO PULL EVERYONE UP, RIGHT?
YEAH!
CAN YOU TIE JEMIMA TO ME USING THAT?
DO YOU KNOW HOW TO GO DOWN?
I SAW WHAT EVERY-ONE DID. I'LL BE FINE.
HOW ABOUT YOU GUYS? OKAY GOING DOWN ALONE?
YEAH, EASY PEASY!
WELL SAID.
SQUEEZE
LET'S GO, JEMIMA.

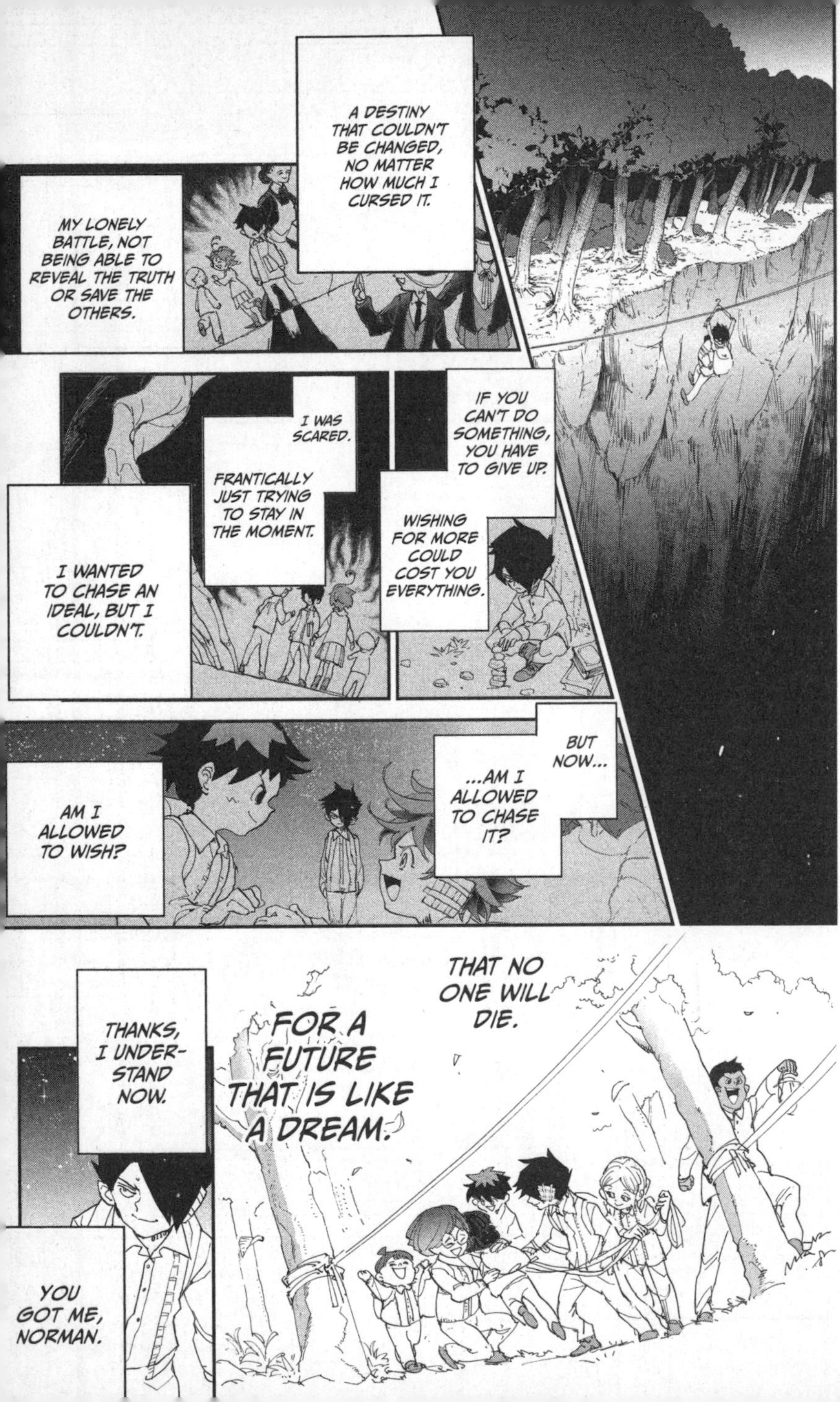
A DESTINY THAT COULDN'T BE CHANGED, NO MATTER HOW MUCH I CURSED IT.
MY LONELY BATTLE, NOT BEING ABLE TO REVEAL THE TRUTH OR SAVE THE OTHERS.
IF YOU CAN'T DO SOMETHING, YOU HAVE TO GIVE UP.
WISHING FOR MORE COULD COST YOU EVERYTHING.
I WAS SCARED.
FRANTICALLY JUST TRYING TO STAY IN THE MOMENT.
I WANTED TO CHASE AN IDEAL, BUT I COULDN'T.
BUT NOW...
...AM I ALLOWED TO CHASE IT?
AM I ALLOWED TO WISH?
THAT NO ONE WILL DIE.
FOR A FUTURE THAT IS LIKE A DREAM.
THANKS, I UNDER-STAND NOW.
YOU GOT ME, NORMAN.

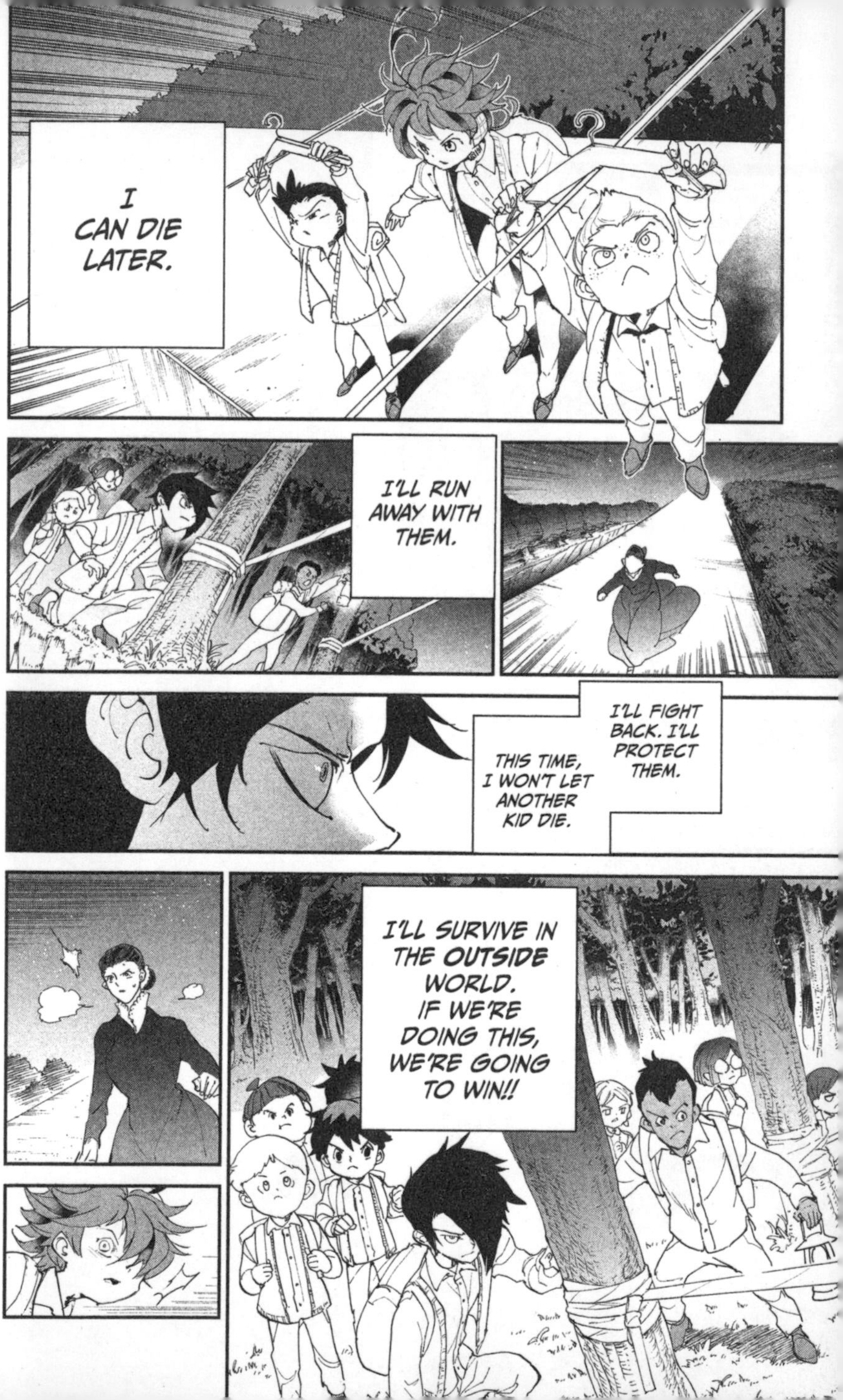
I CAN DIE LATER.
I'LL RUN AWAY WITH THEM.
I'LL FIGHT BACK. I'LL PROTECT THEM.
THIS TIME, I WON'T LET ANOTHER KID DIE.
I'LL SURVIVE IN THE OUTSIDE WORLD. IF WE'RE DOING THIS, WE'RE GOING TO WIN!!

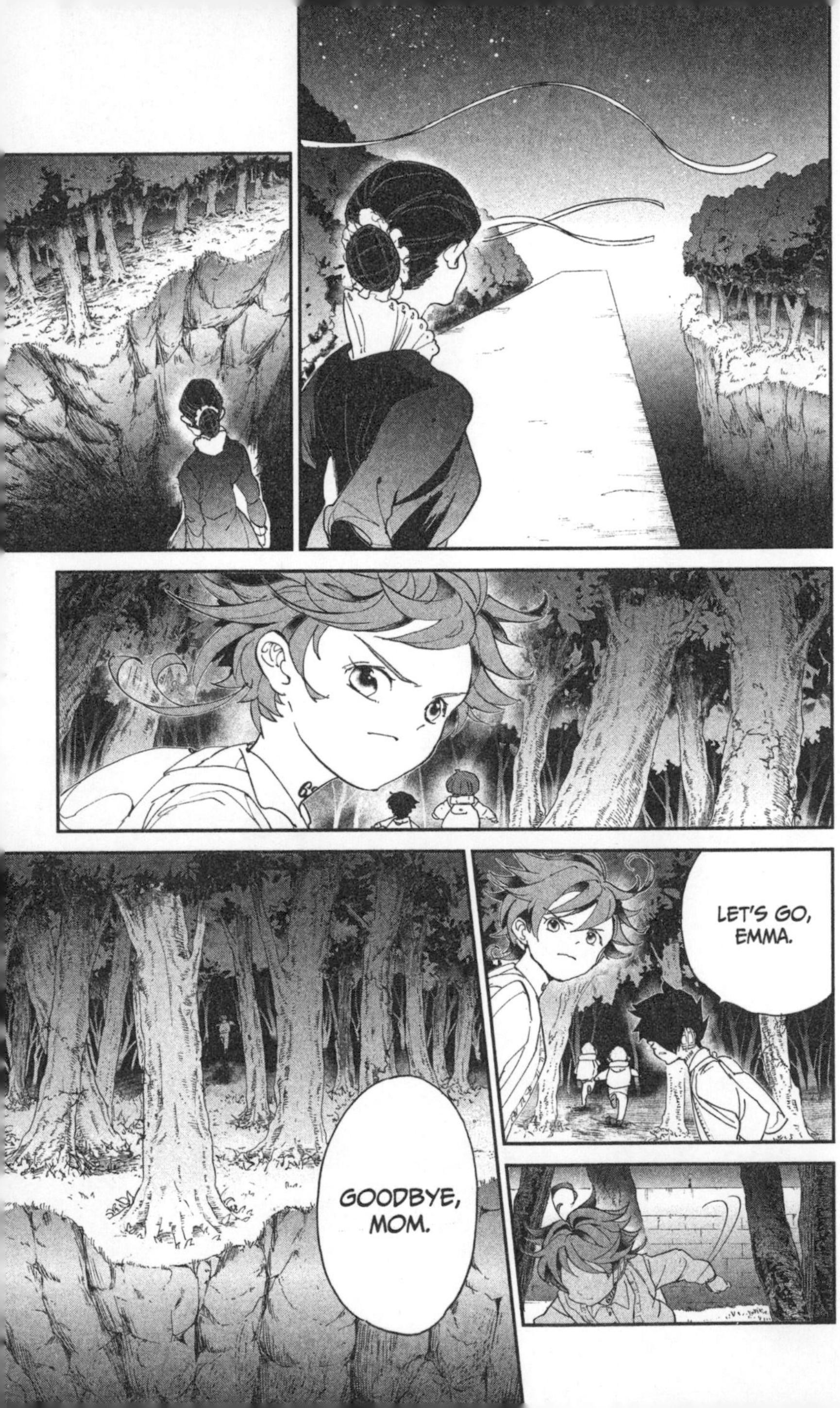
LET'S GO, EMMA.
GOODBYE, MOM.

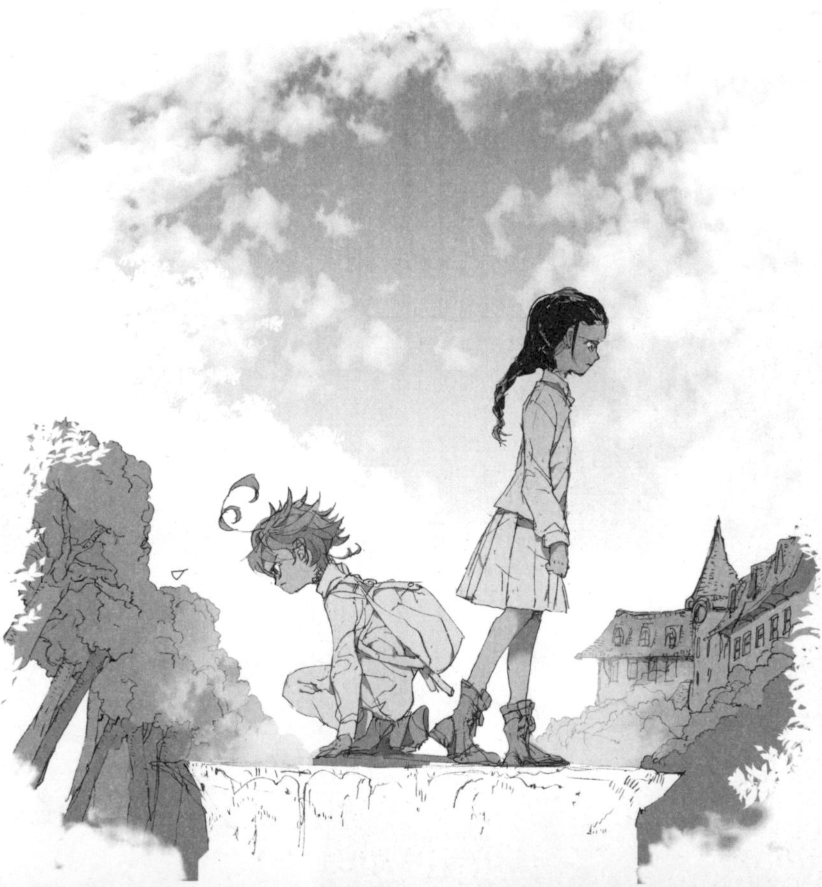

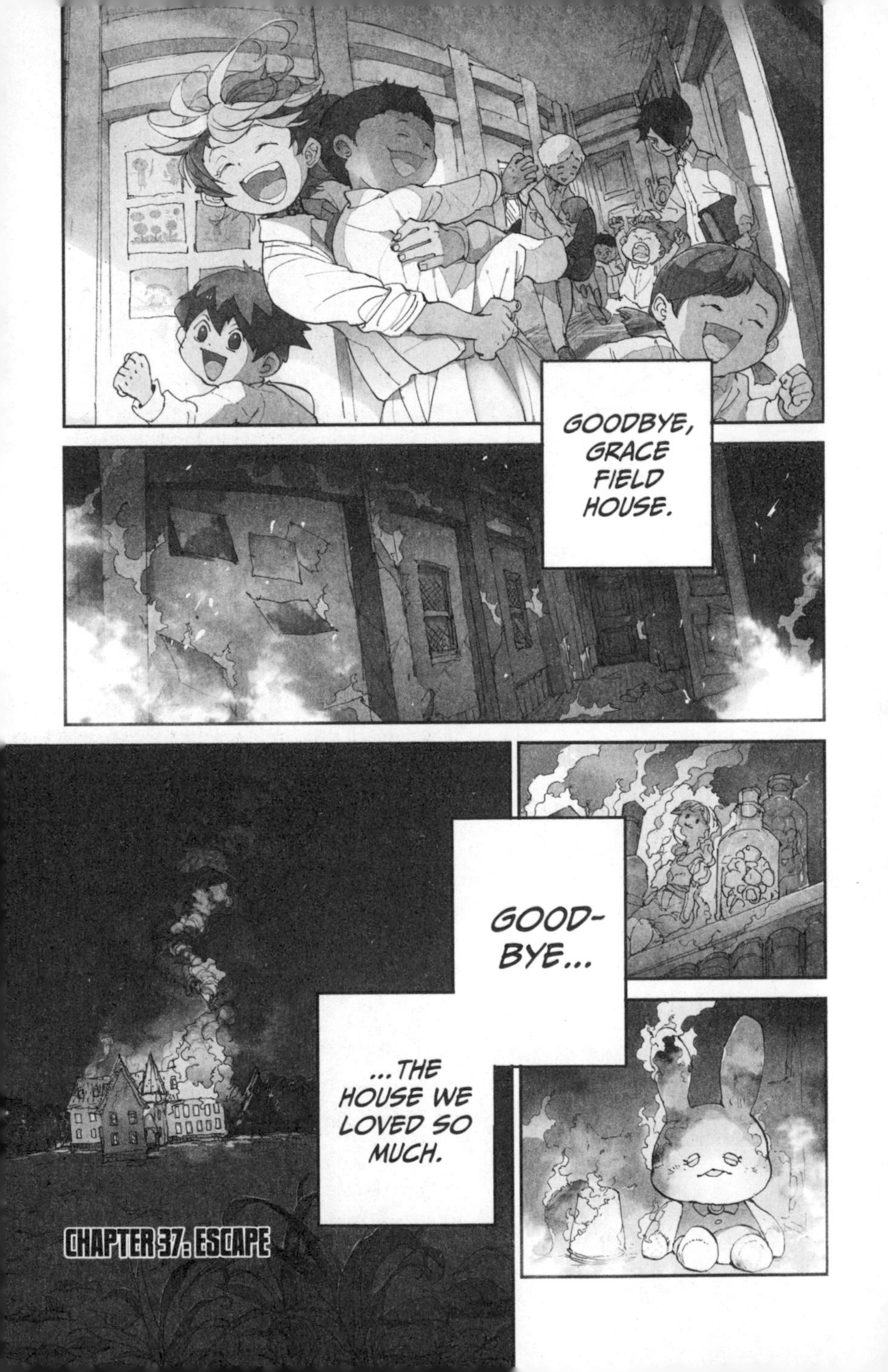
GOODBYE, GRACE FIELD HOUSE.
GOOD-BYE...
...THE HOUSE WE LOVED SO MUCH.
CHAPTER 37: ESCAPE

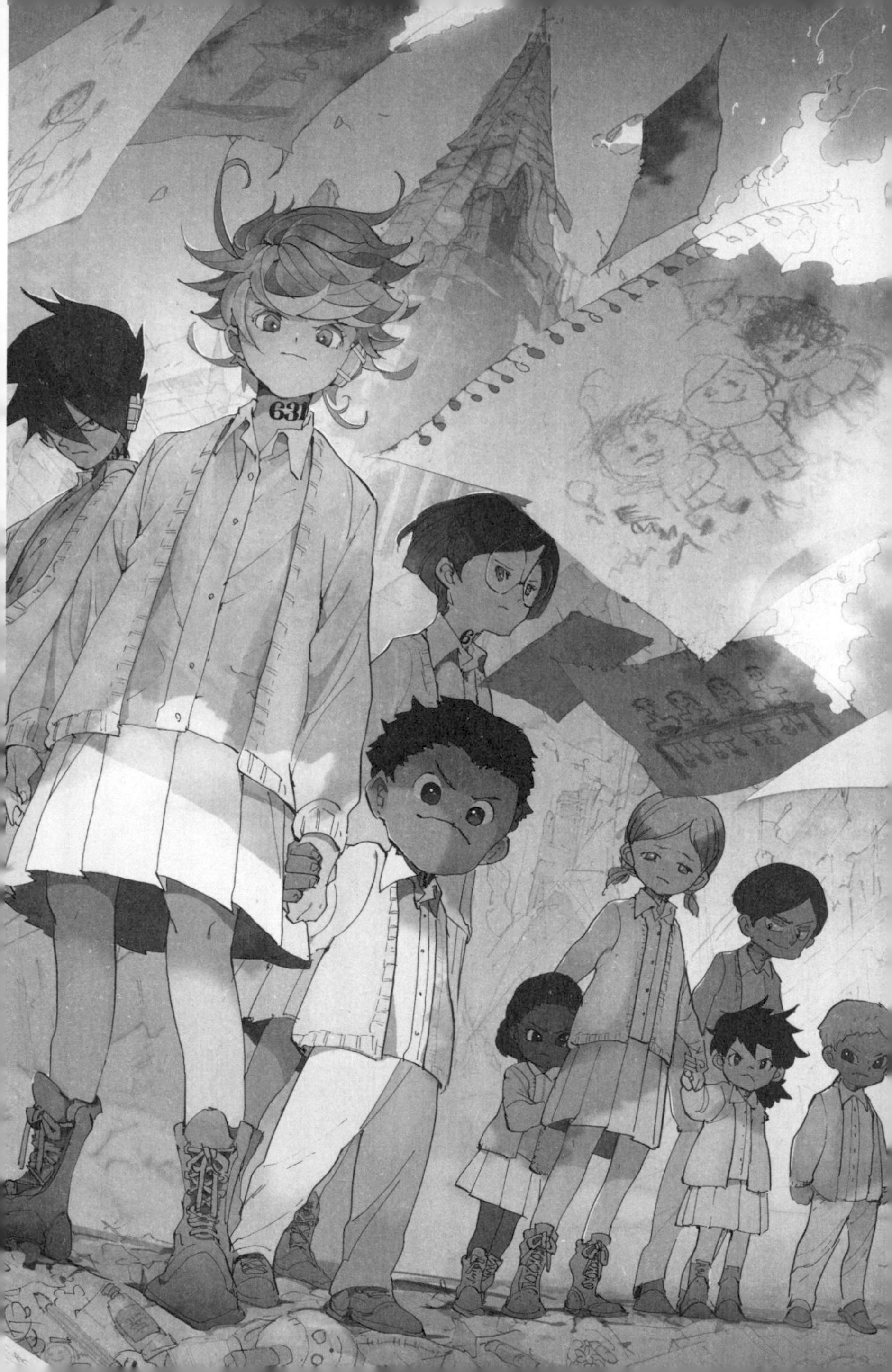

CHAPTER 37: ESCAPE

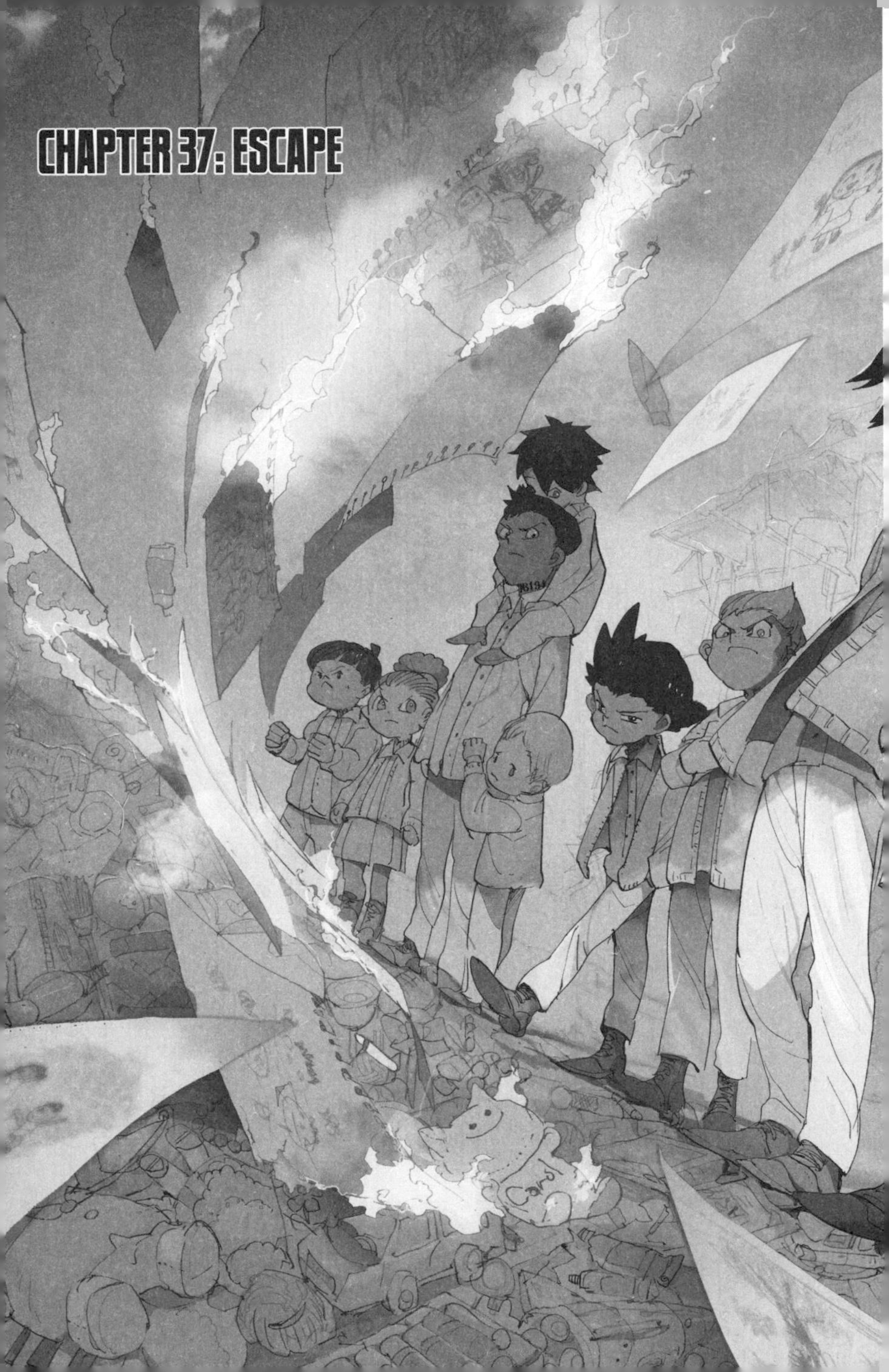

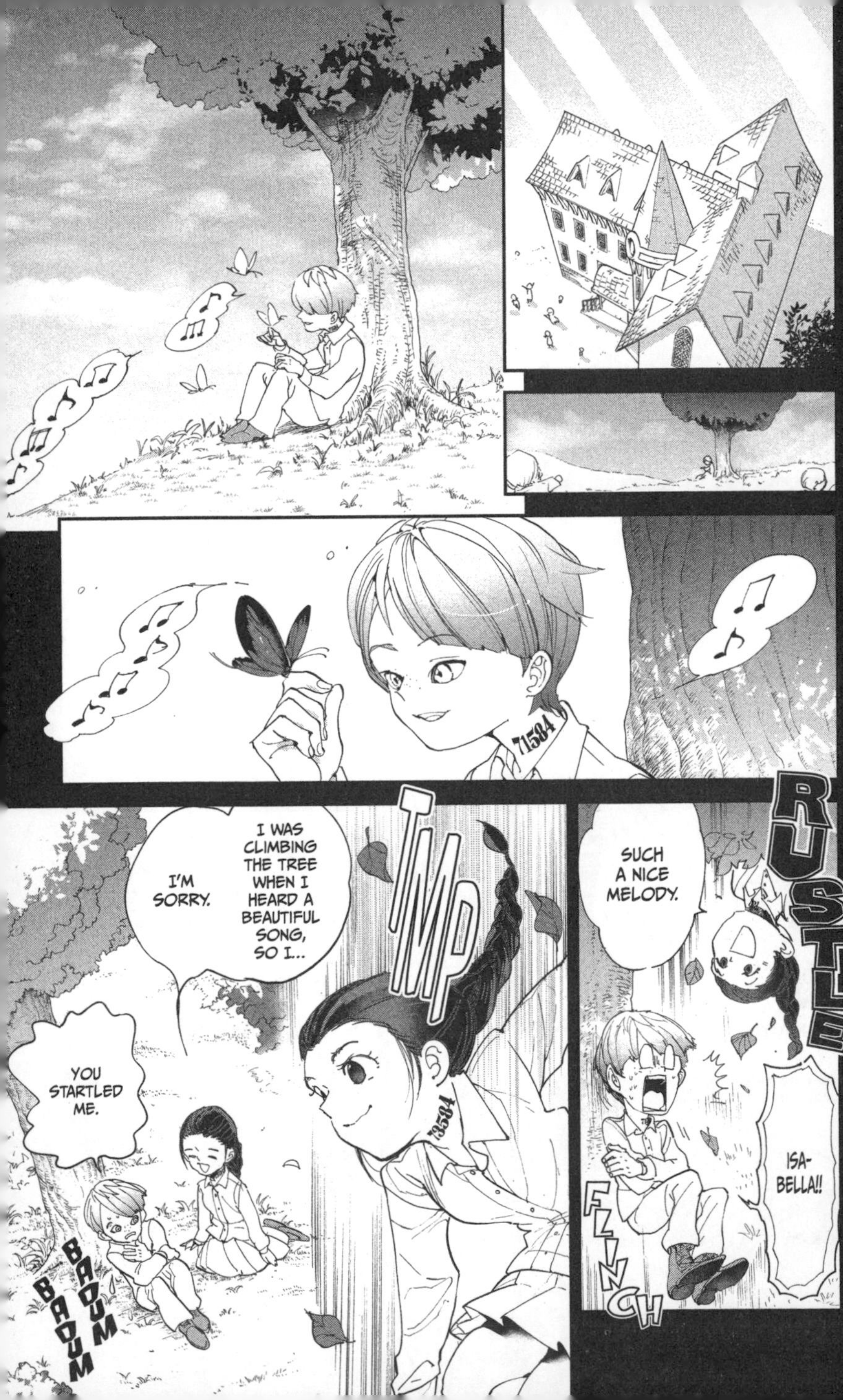
71584
RUSTLE
SUCH A NICE MELODY.
ISA-BELLA!!
FLINCH
TMP
I WAS CLIMBING THE TREE WHEN I HEARD A BEAUTIFUL SONG, SO I...
I'M SORRY.
73584
YOU STARTLED ME.
BADUM BADUM

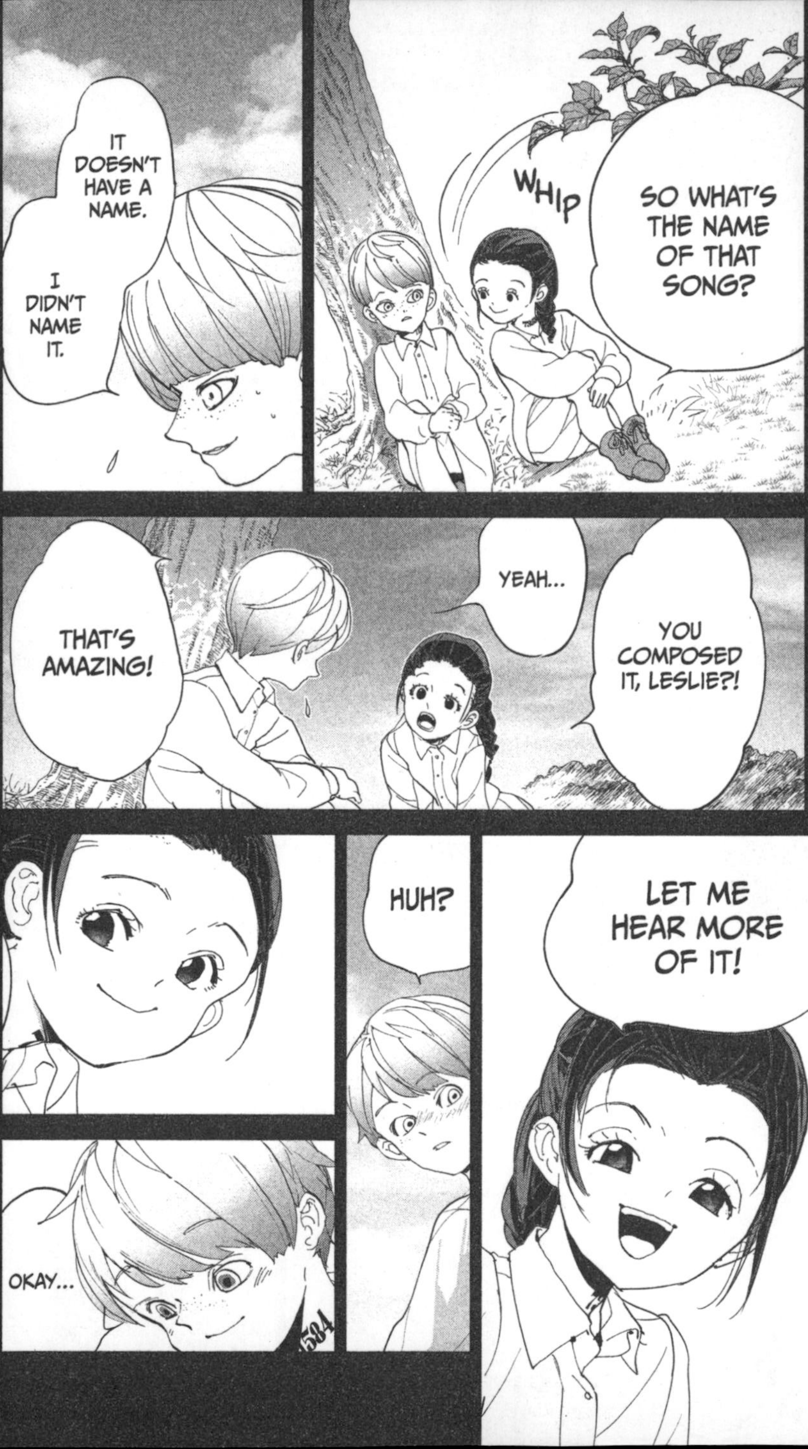
WHIP
SO WHAT'S THE NAME OF THAT SONG?
IT DOESN'T HAVE A NAME.
I DIDN'T NAME IT.
YOU COMPOSED IT, LESLIE?!
YEAH...
THAT'S AMAZING!
LET ME HEAR MORE OF IT!
HUH?
OKAY...
584

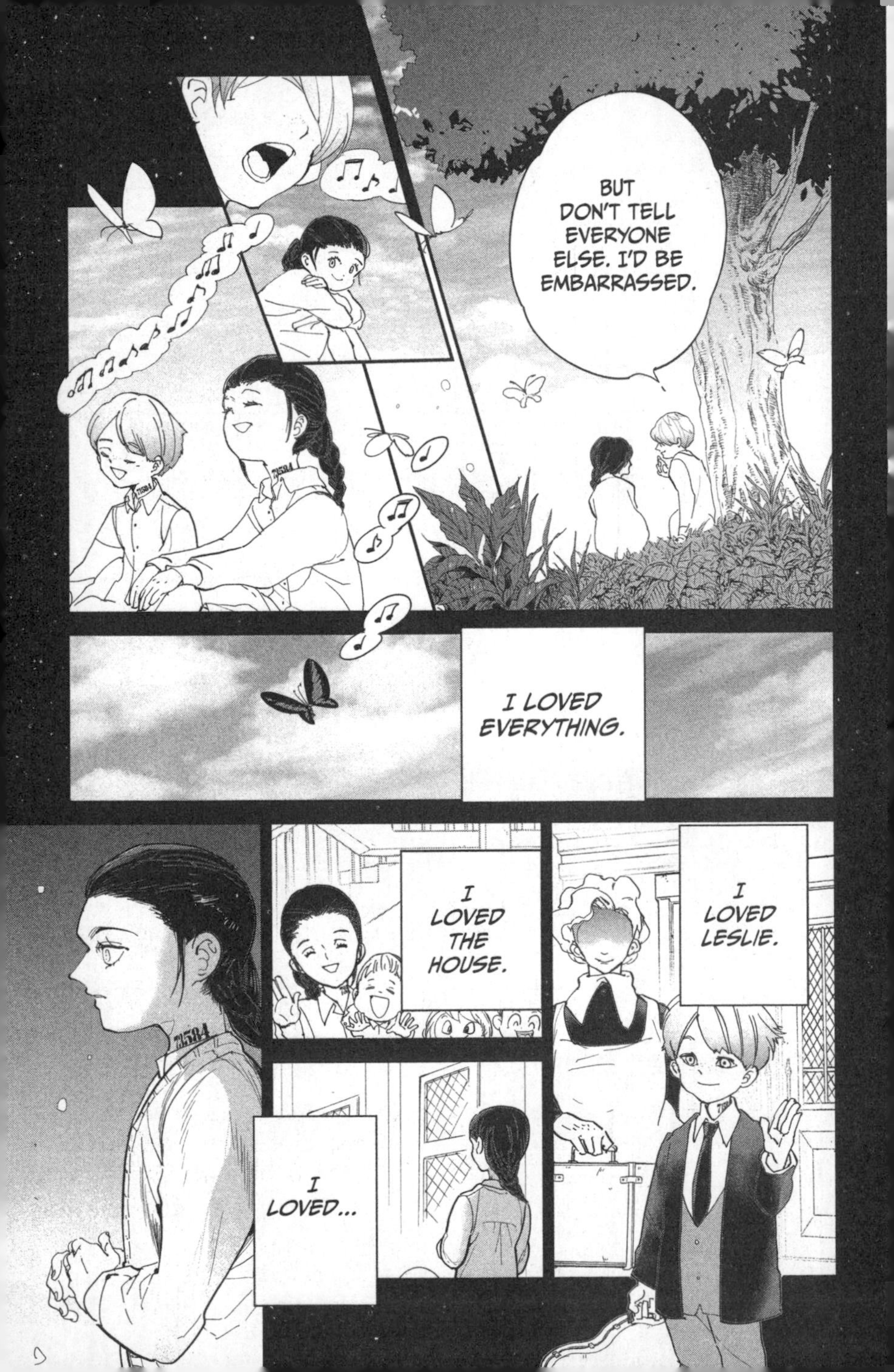
BUT DON'T TELL EVERYONE ELSE. I'D BE EMBARRASSED.
I LOVED EVERYTHING.
I LOVED LESLIE.
I LOVED THE HOUSE.
I LOVED...

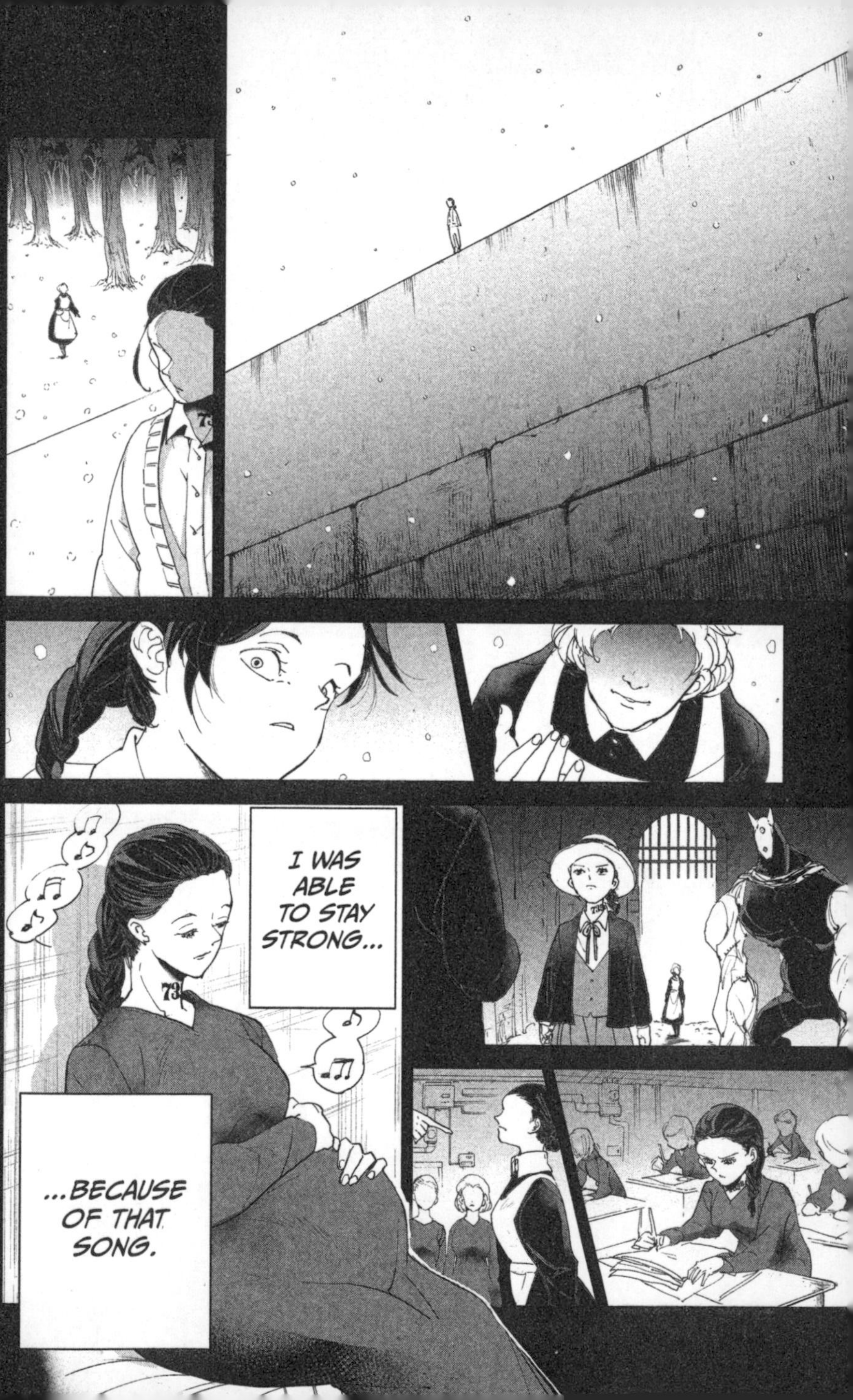
I WAS ABLE TO STAY STRONG...
...BECAUSE OF THAT SONG.

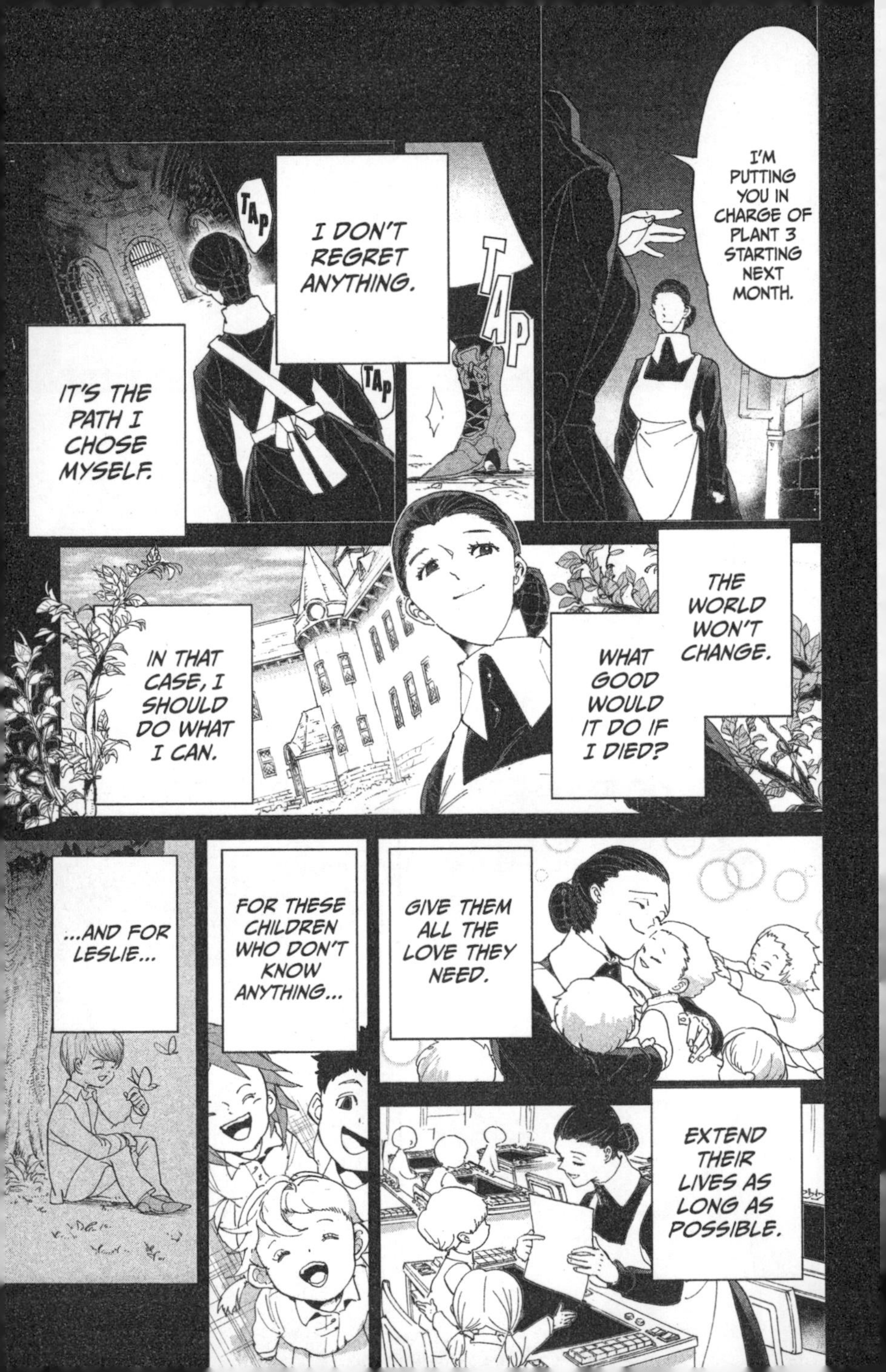
I'M PUTTING YOU IN CHARGE OF PLANT 3 STARTING NEXT MONTH.
TAP
TAP
I DON'T REGRET ANYTHING.
TAP
IT'S THE PATH I CHOSE MYSELF.
THE WORLD WON'T CHANGE.
WHAT GOOD WOULD IT DO IF I DIED?
IN THAT CASE, I SHOULD DO WHAT I CAN.
GIVE THEM ALL THE LOVE THEY NEED.
EXTEND THEIR LIVES AS LONG AS POSSIBLE.
FOR THESE CHILDREN WHO DON'T KNOW ANYTHING...
...AND FOR LESLIE...

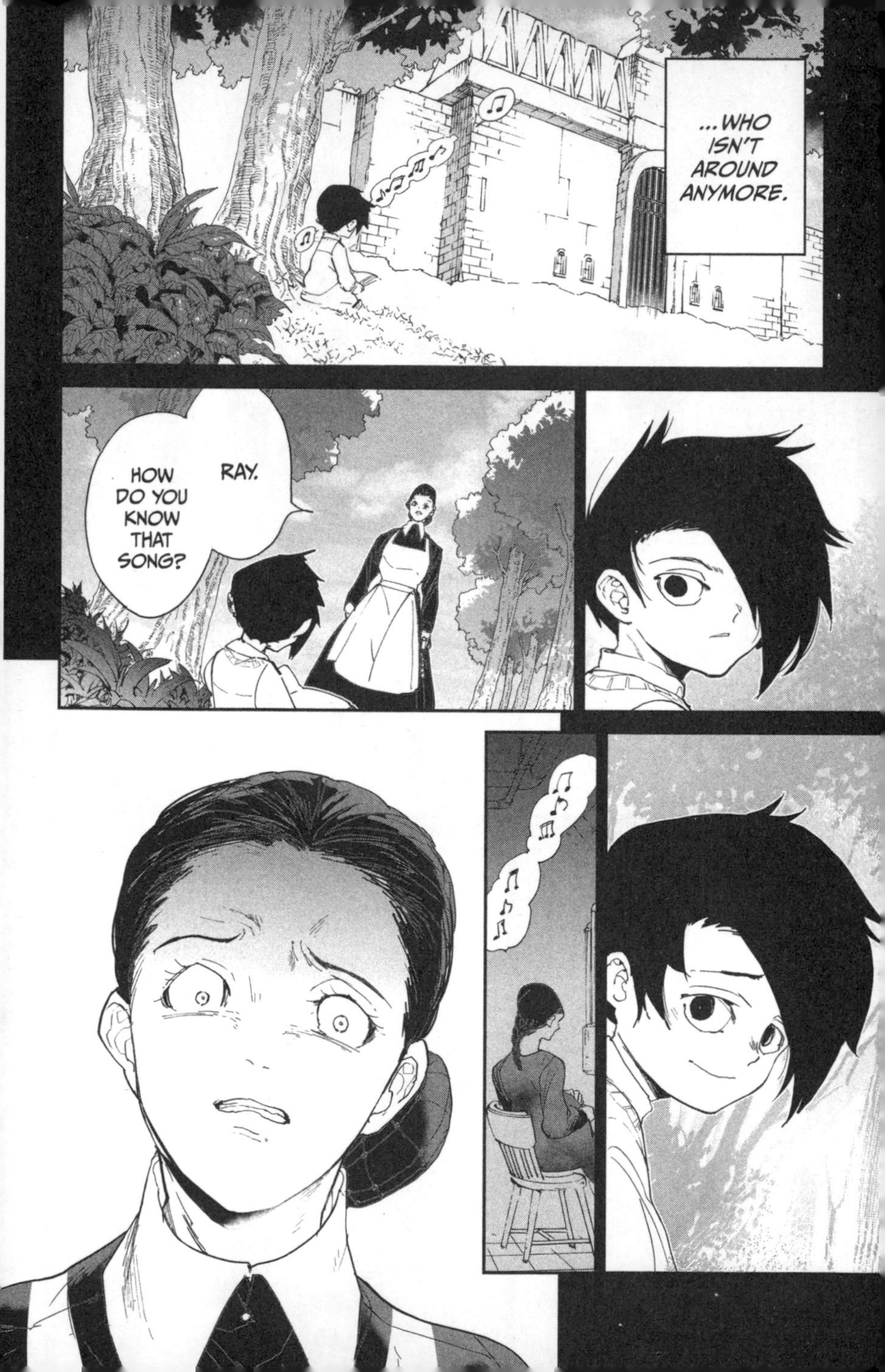
...WHO ISN'T AROUND ANYMORE.
RAY. HOW DO YOU KNOW THAT SONG?

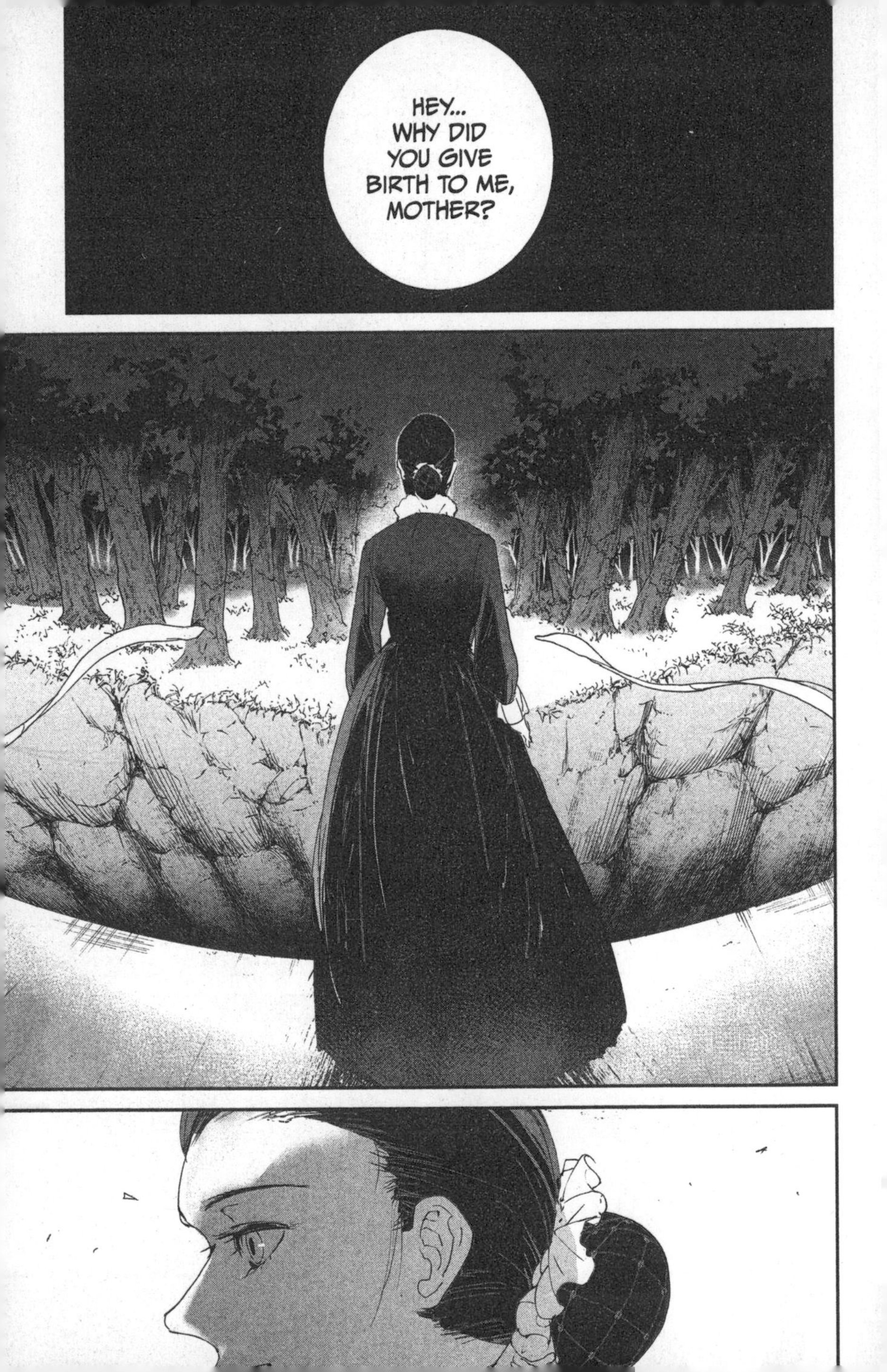
HEY... WHY DID YOU GIVE BIRTH TO ME, MOTHER?

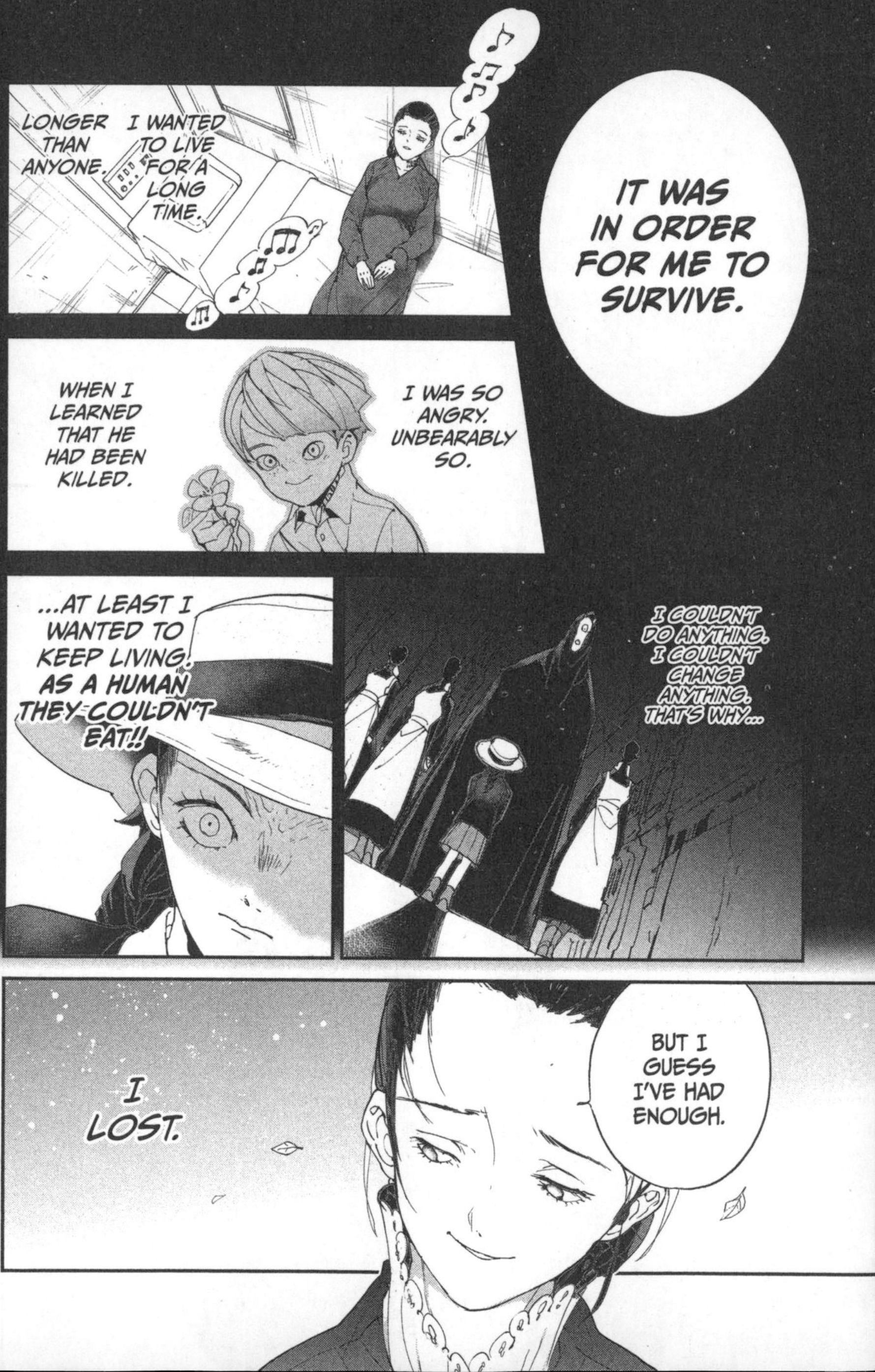
IT WAS IN ORDER FOR ME TO SURVIVE.
I WANTED TO LIVE FOR A LONG TIME.
LONGER THAN ANYONE.
I WAS SO ANGRY. UNBEARABLY SO.
WHEN I LEARNED THAT HE HAD BEEN KILLED.
I COULDN'T DO ANYTHING. I COULDN'T CHANGE ANYTHING. THAT'S WHY...
...AT LEAST I WANTED TO KEEP LIVING! AS A HUMAN THEY COULDN'T EAT!!
BUT I GUESS I'VE HAD ENOUGH.
I LOST.

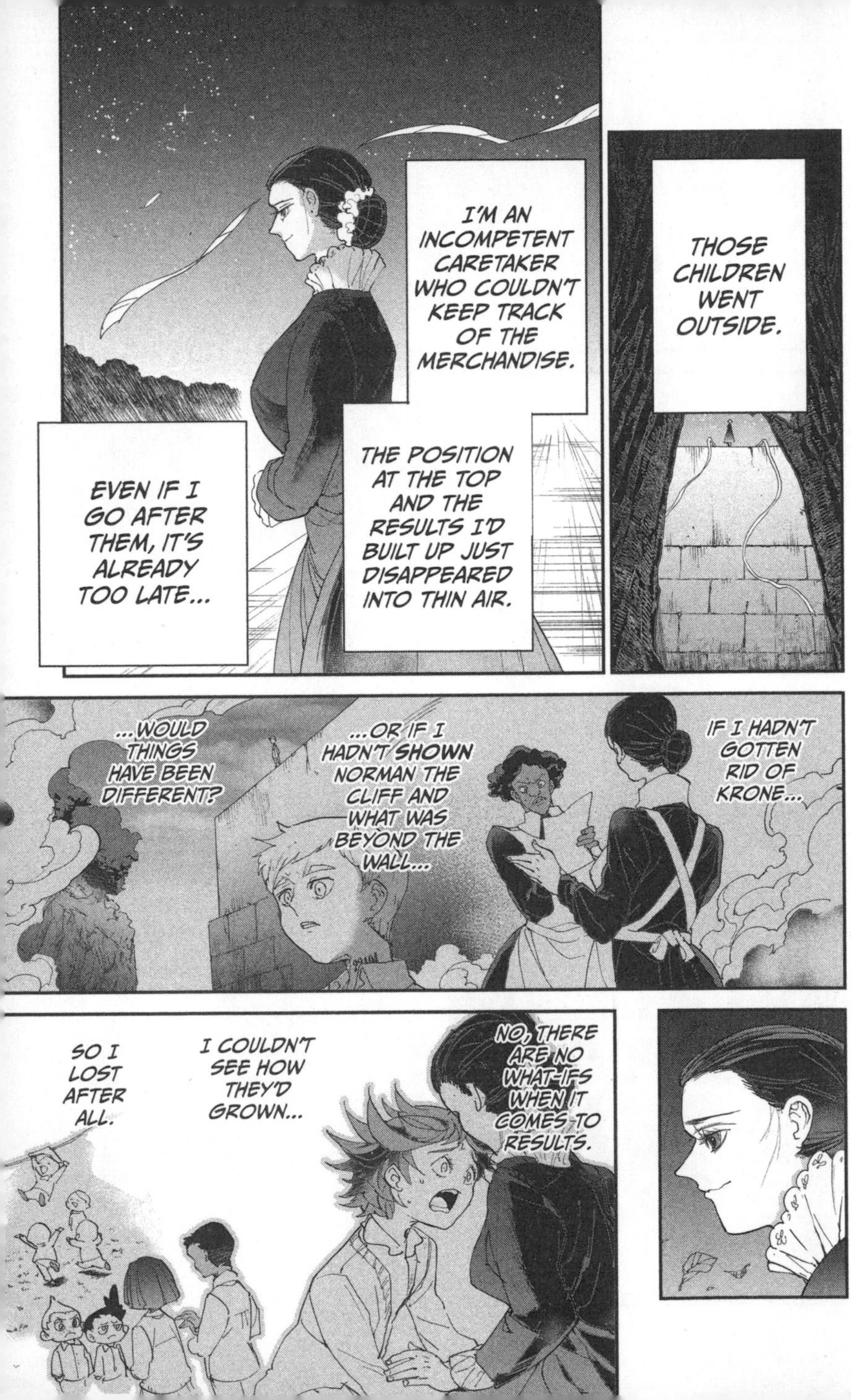
THOSE CHILDREN WENT OUTSIDE.
I'M AN INCOMPETENT CARETAKER WHO COULDN'T KEEP TRACK OF THE MERCHANDISE.
THE POSITION AT THE TOP AND THE RESULTS I'D BUILT UP JUST DISAPPEARED INTO THIN AIR.
EVEN IF I GO AFTER THEM, IT'S ALREADY TOO LATE...
IF I HADN'T GOTTEN RID OF KRONE...
...OR IF I HADN'T SHOWN NORMAN THE CLIFF AND WHAT WAS BEYOND THE WALL...
...WOULD THINGS HAVE BEEN DIFFERENT?
NO, THERE ARE NO WHAT-IFS WHEN IT COMES TO RESULTS.
I COULDN'T SEE HOW THEY'D GROWN...
SO I LOST AFTER ALL.

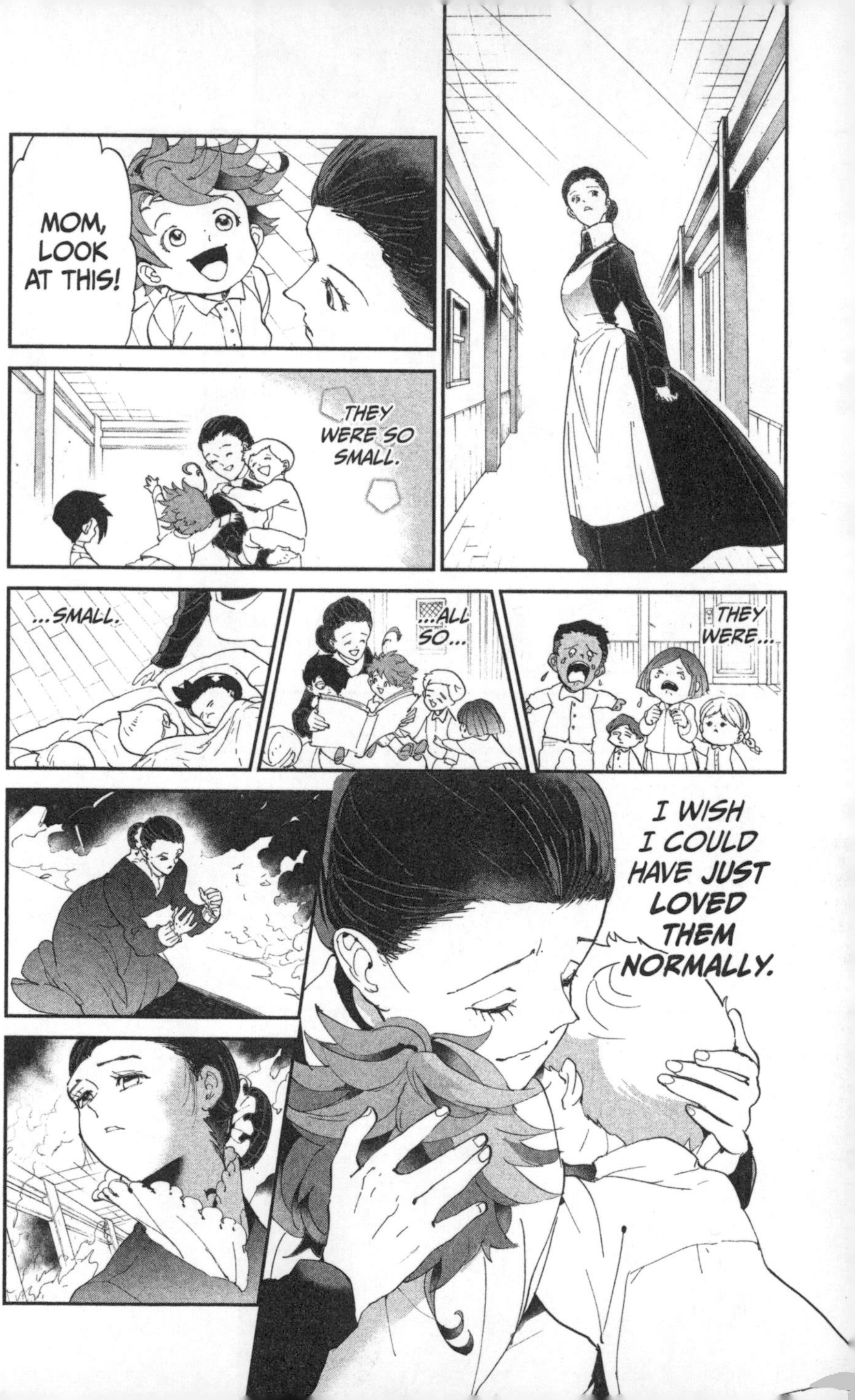
MOM, LOOK AT THIS!
THEY WERE SO SMALL.
THEY WERE...
...ALL SO...
...SMALL.
I WISH I COULD HAVE JUST LOVED THEM NORMALLY.

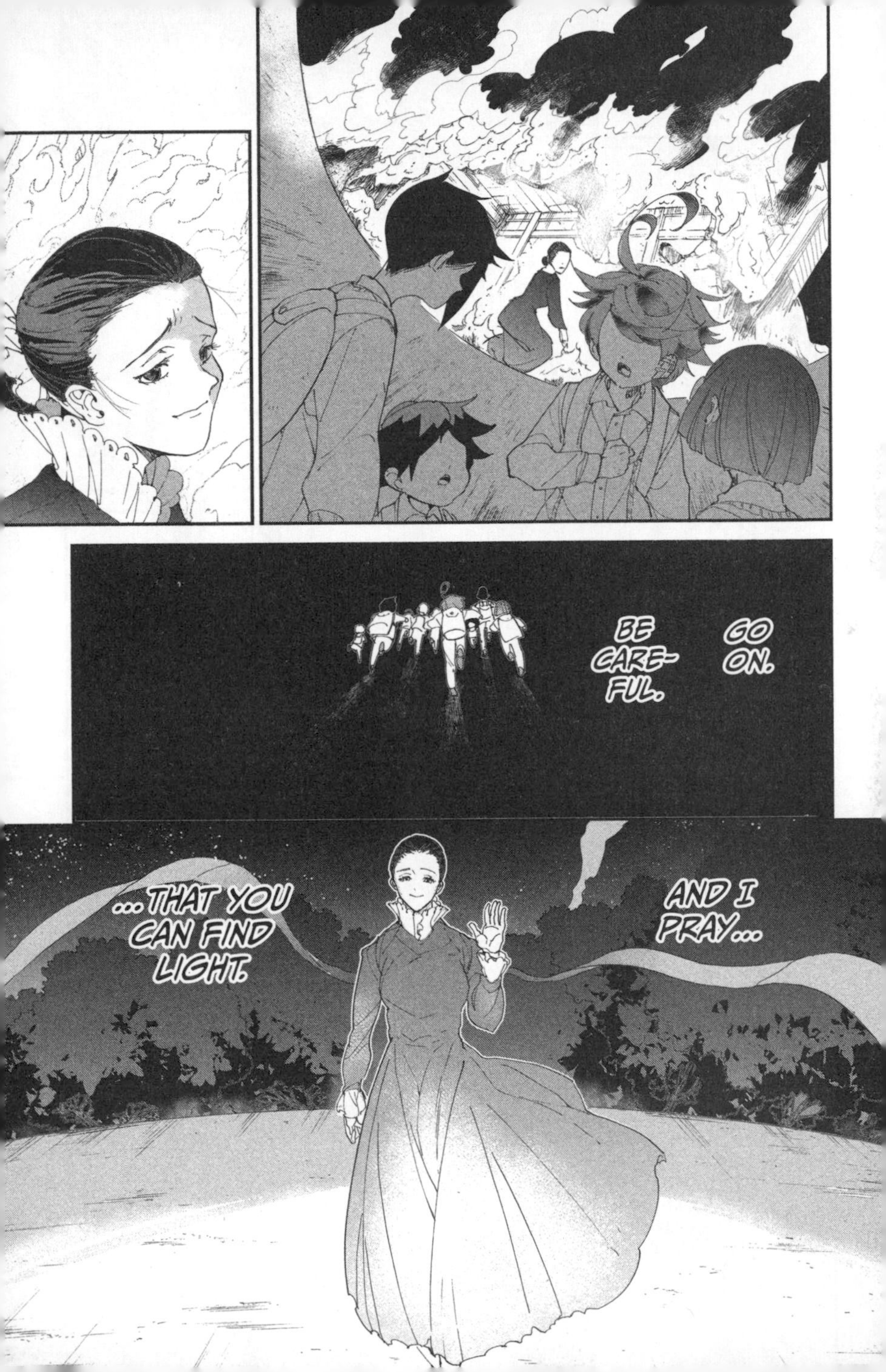
GO ON.
BE CARE-FUL.
AND I PRAY...
...THAT YOU CAN FIND LIGHT.

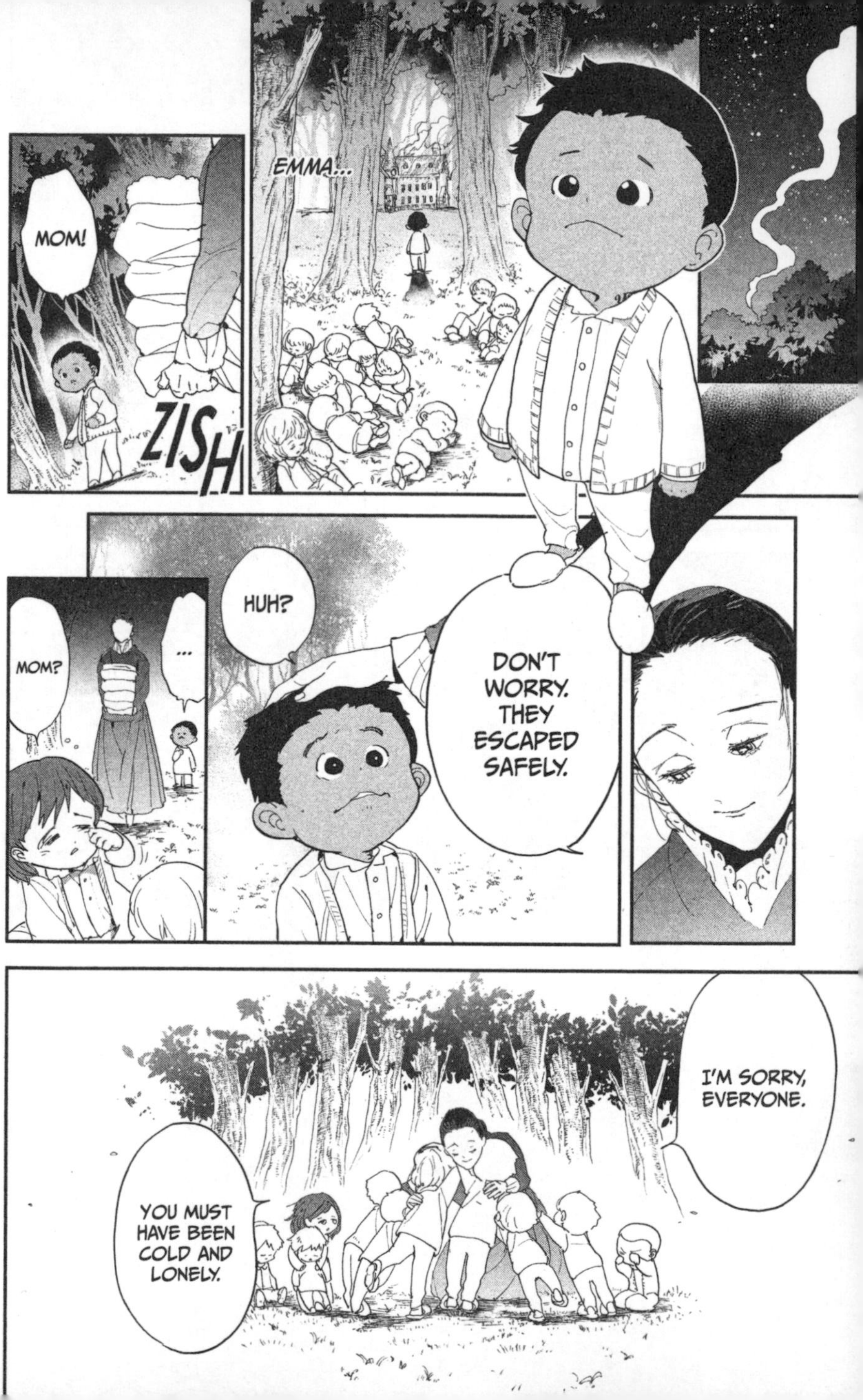
EMMA...
MOM!
ZISH
HUH?
DON'T WORRY. THEY ESCAPED SAFELY.
...
MOM?
I'M SORRY, EVERYONE.
YOU MUST HAVE BEEN COLD AND LONELY.

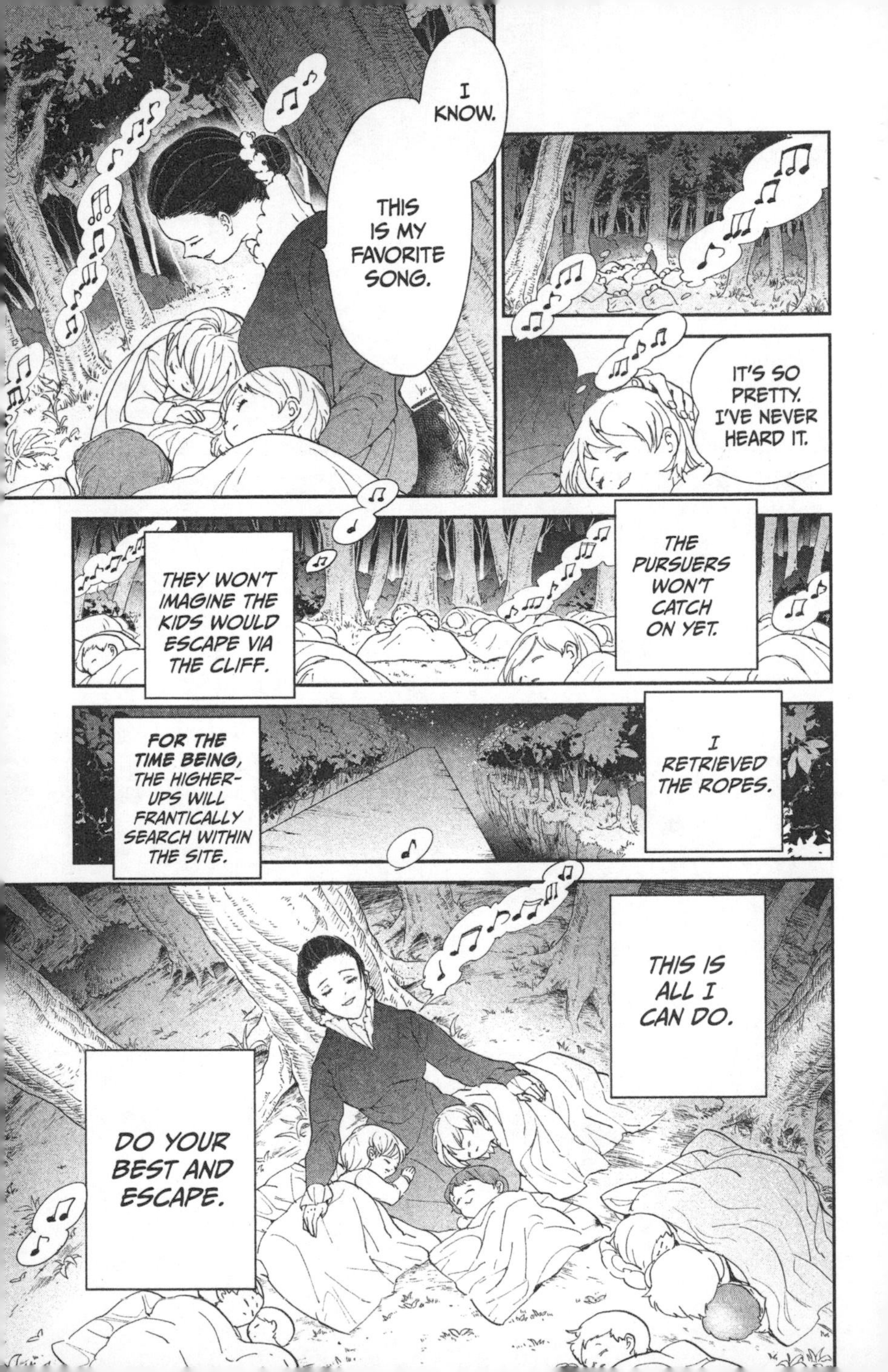
IT'S SO PRETTY. I'VE NEVER HEARD IT.
I KNOW.
THIS IS MY FAVORITE SONG.
THE PURSUERS WON'T CATCH ON YET.
THEY WON'T IMAGINE THE KIDS WOULD ESCAPE VIA THE CLIFF.
I RETRIEVED THE ROPES.
FOR THE TIME BEING, THE HIGHER-UPS WILL FRANTICALLY SEARCH WITHIN THE SITE.
THIS IS ALL I CAN DO.
DO YOUR BEST AND ESCAPE.

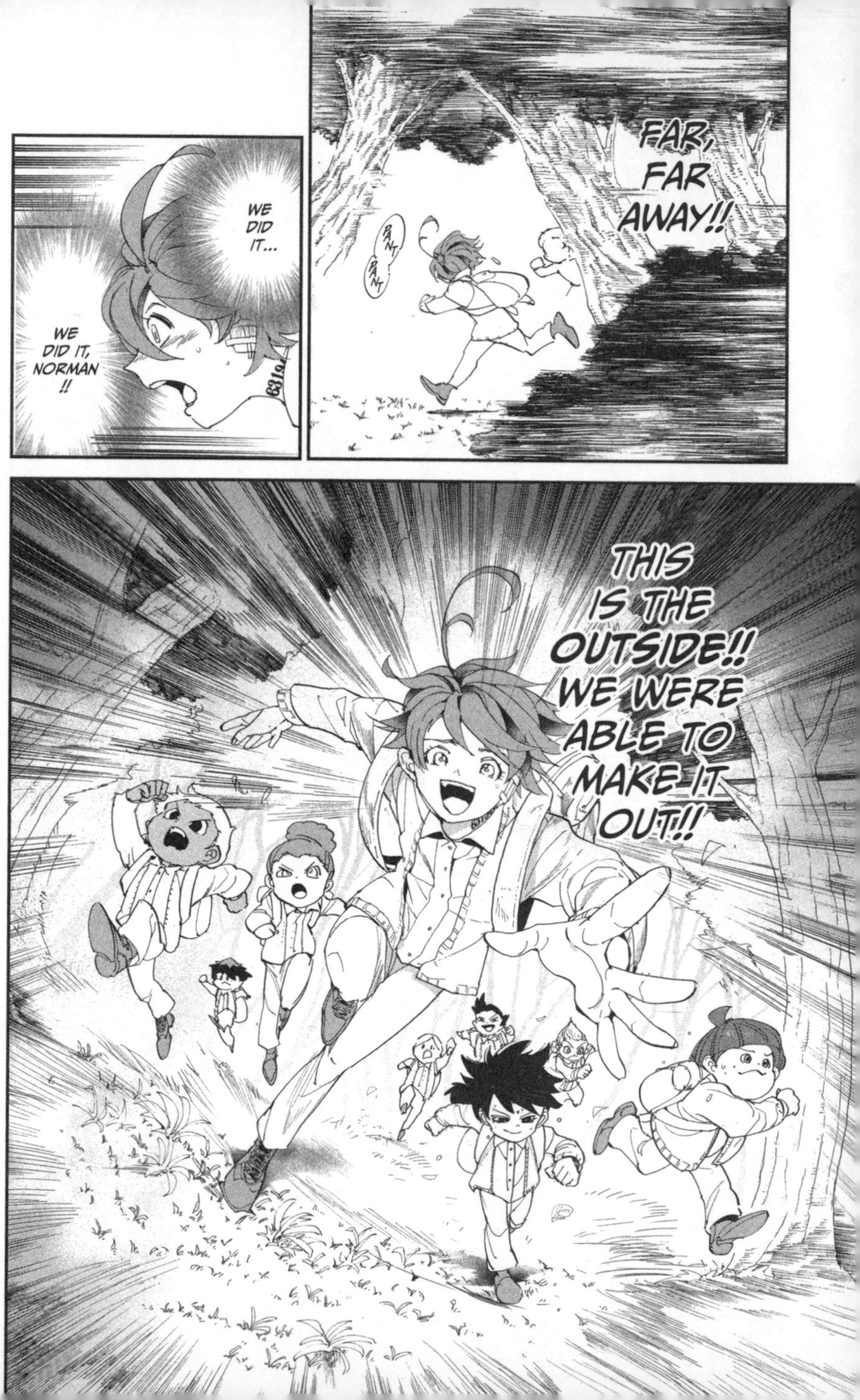
FAR, FAR AWAY!!
PANT PANT
WE DID IT...
WE DID IT, NORMAN!!
THIS IS THE OUTSIDE!! WE WERE ABLE TO MAKE IT OUT!!

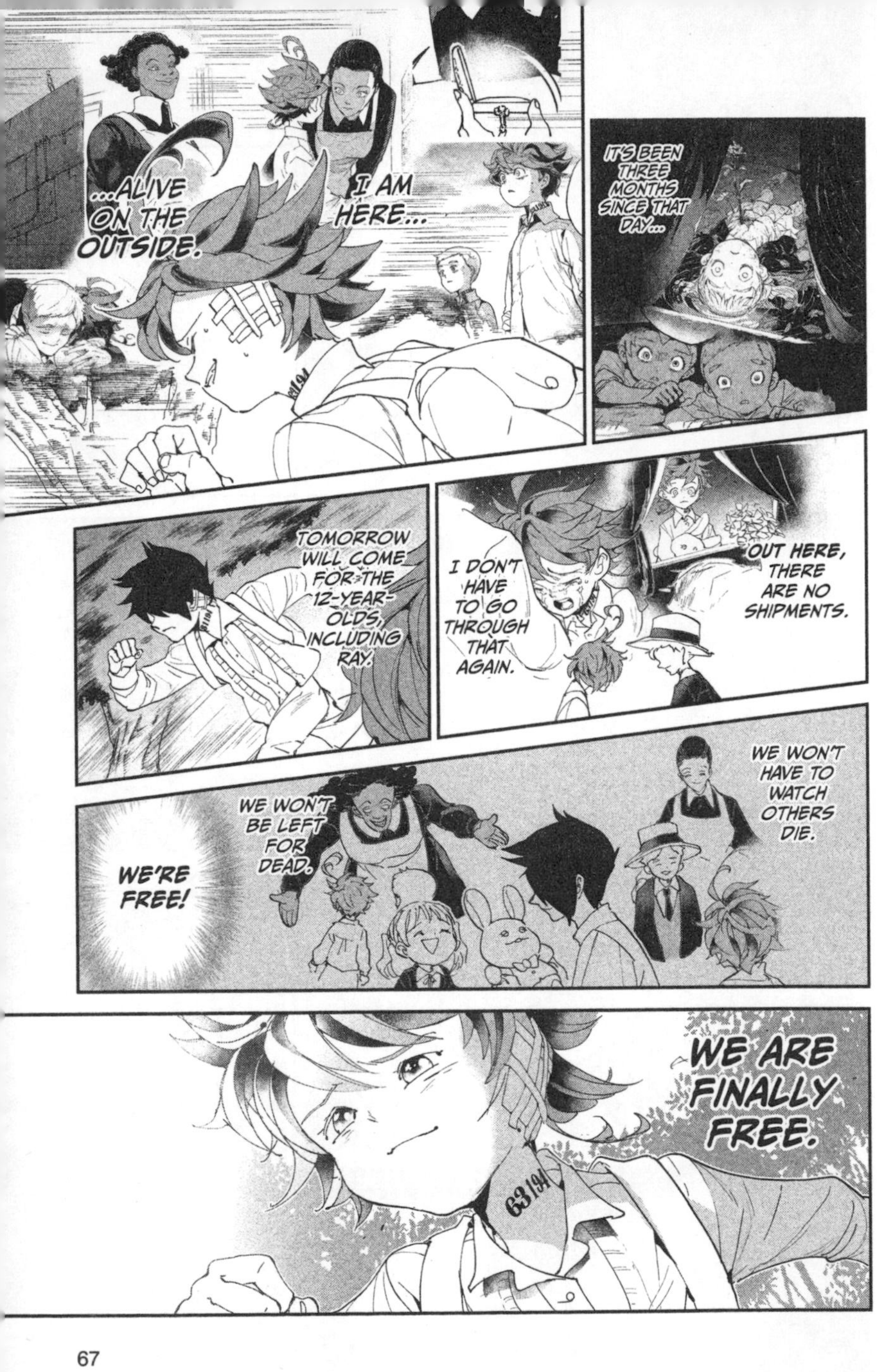
IT'S BEEN THREE MONTHS SINCE THAT DAY...
I AM HERE...
...ALIVE ON THE OUTSIDE.
OUT HERE, THERE ARE NO SHIPMENTS.
I DON'T HAVE TO GO THROUGH THAT AGAIN.
TOMORROW WILL COME FOR THE 12-YEAR-OLDS, INCLUDING RAY.
WE WON'T HAVE TO WATCH OTHERS DIE.
WE WON'T BE LEFT FOR DEAD.
WE'RE FREE!
WE ARE FINALLY FREE.
63194

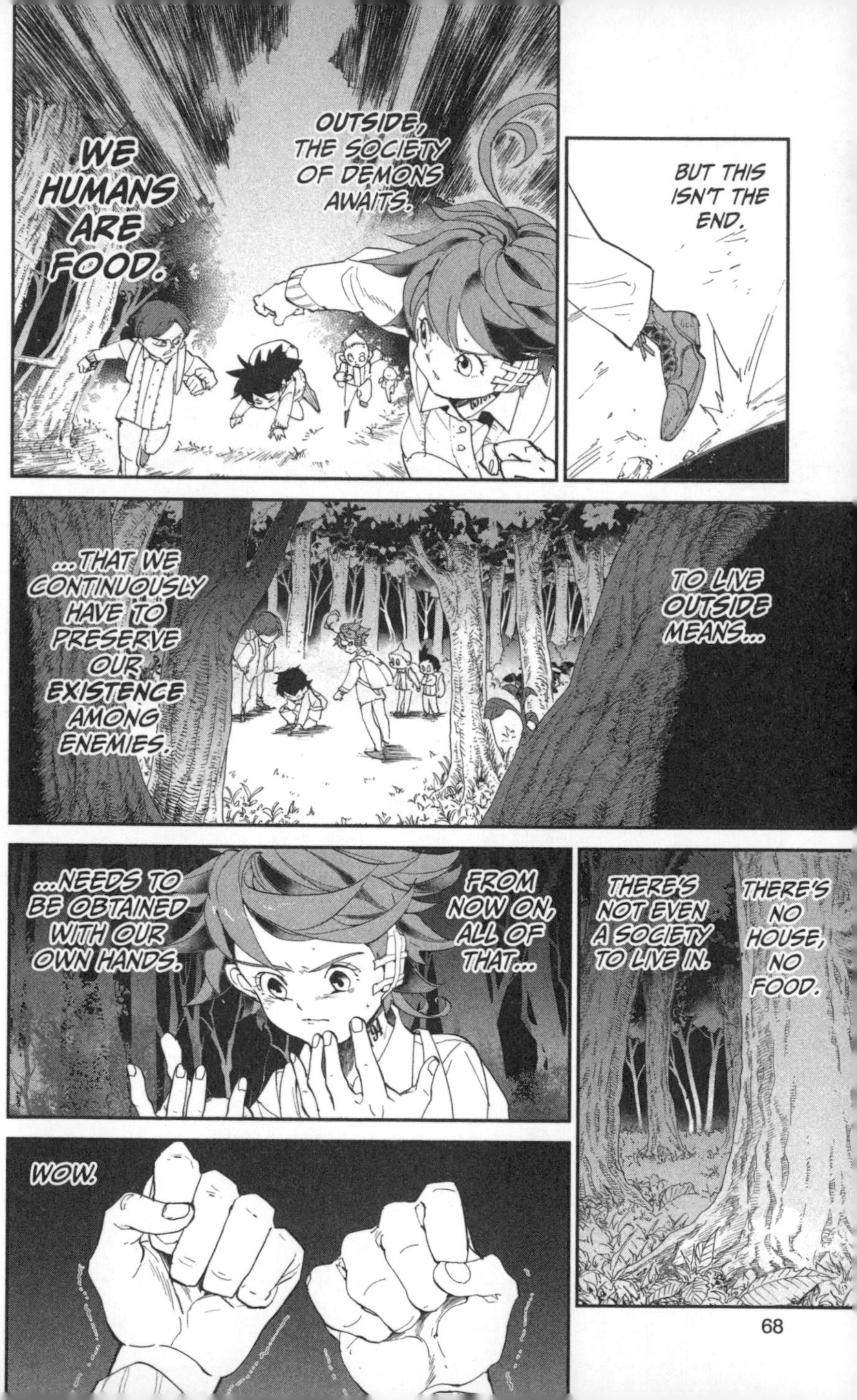
BUT THIS ISN'T THE END.
OUTSIDE, THE SOCIETY OF DEMONS AWAITS.
WE HUMANS ARE FOOD.
TO LIVE OUTSIDE MEANS...
...THAT WE CONTINUOUSLY HAVE TO PRESERVE OUR EXISTENCE AMONG ENEMIES.
THERE'S NO HOUSE, NO FOOD.
THERE'S NOT EVEN A SOCIETY TO LIVE IN.
FROM NOW ON, ALL OF THAT...
...NEEDS TO BE OBTAINED WITH OUR OWN HANDS.
WOW.

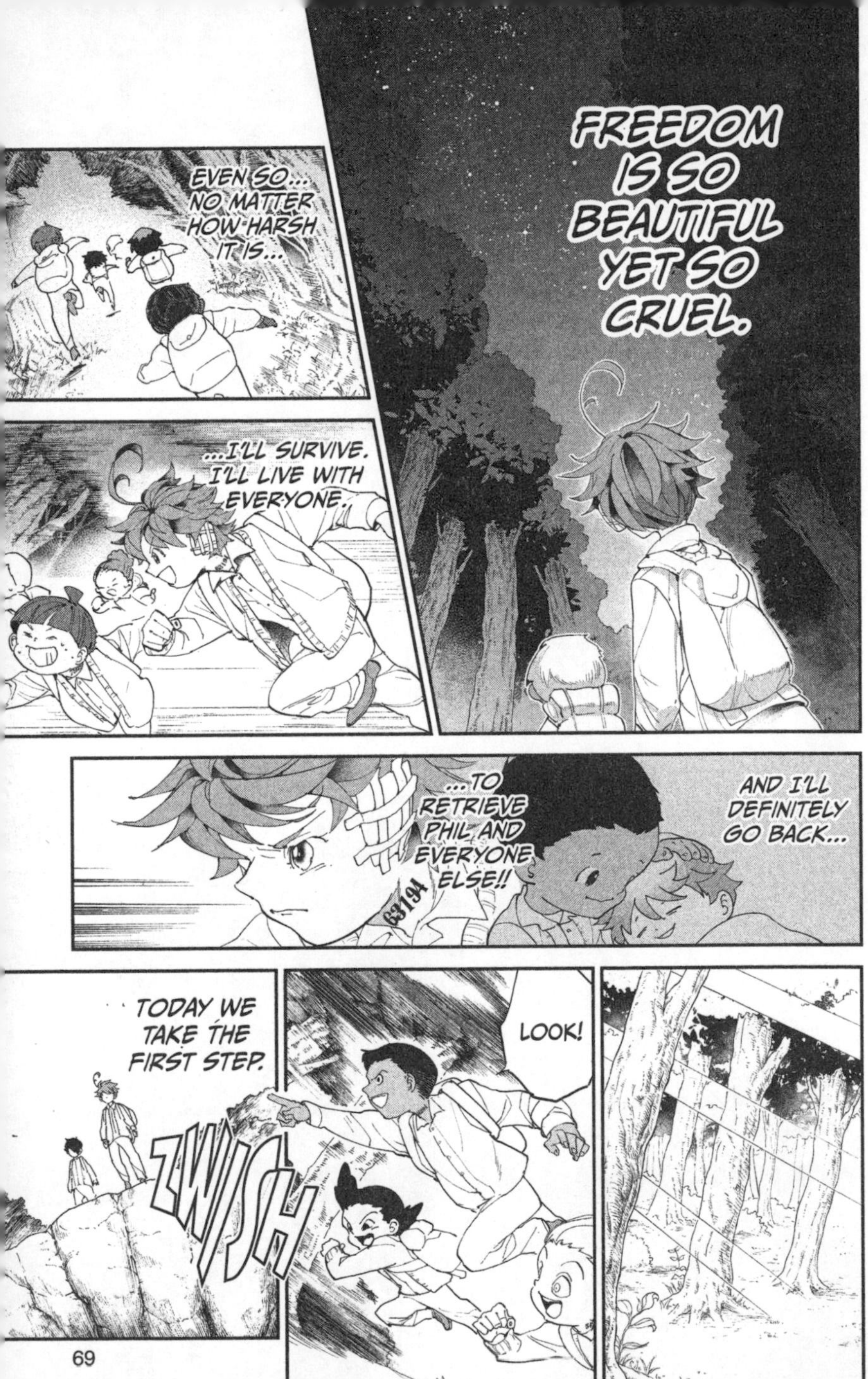
FREEDOM IS SO BEAUTIFUL YET SO CRUEL.
EVEN SO... NO MATTER HOW HARSH IT IS...
...I'LL SURVIVE. I'LL LIVE WITH EVERYONE.
AND I'LL DEFINITELY GO BACK...
...TO RETRIEVE PHIL AND EVERYONE ELSE!!
63194
LOOK!
ZWISH
TODAY WE TAKE THE FIRST STEP.

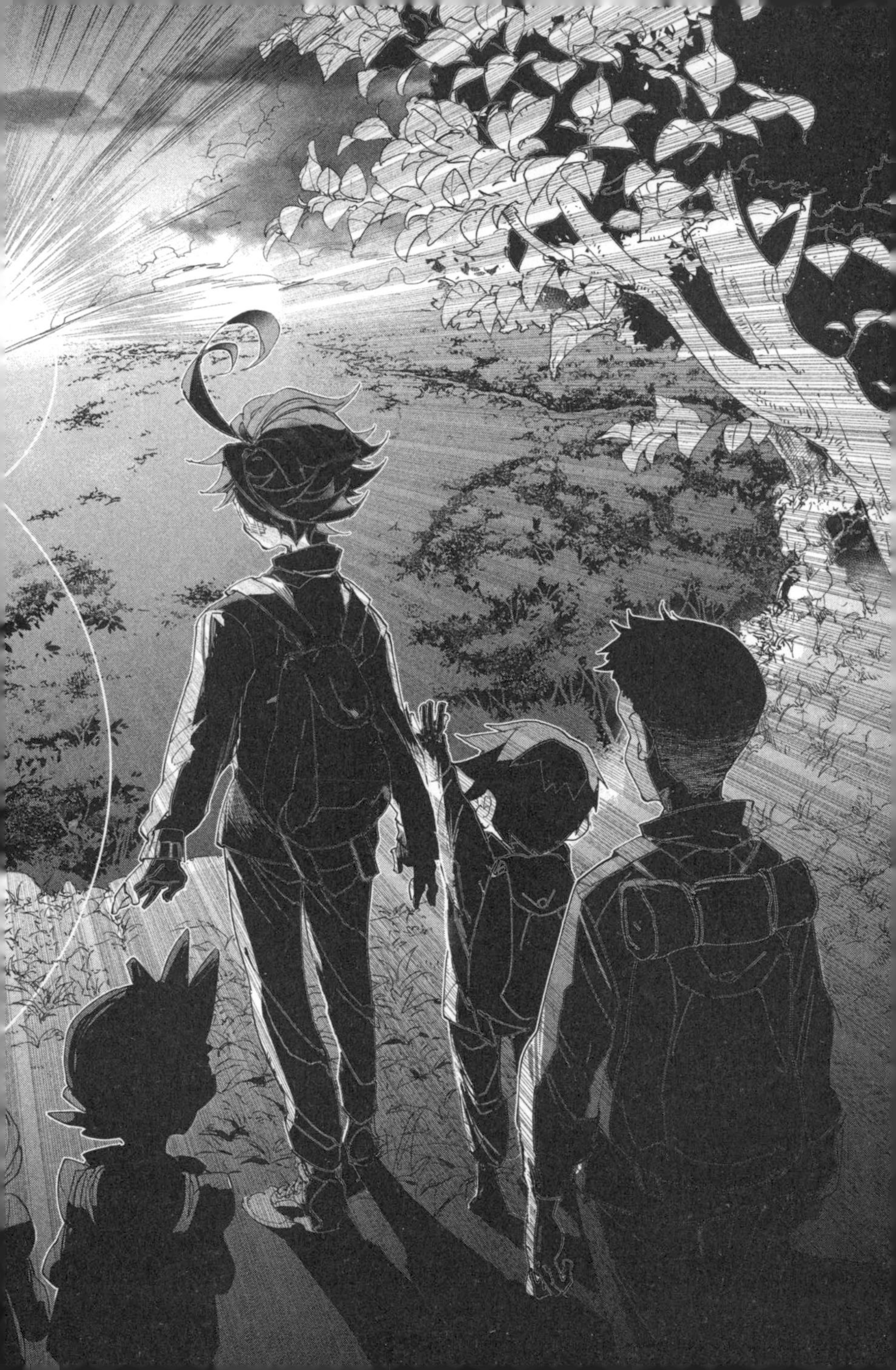

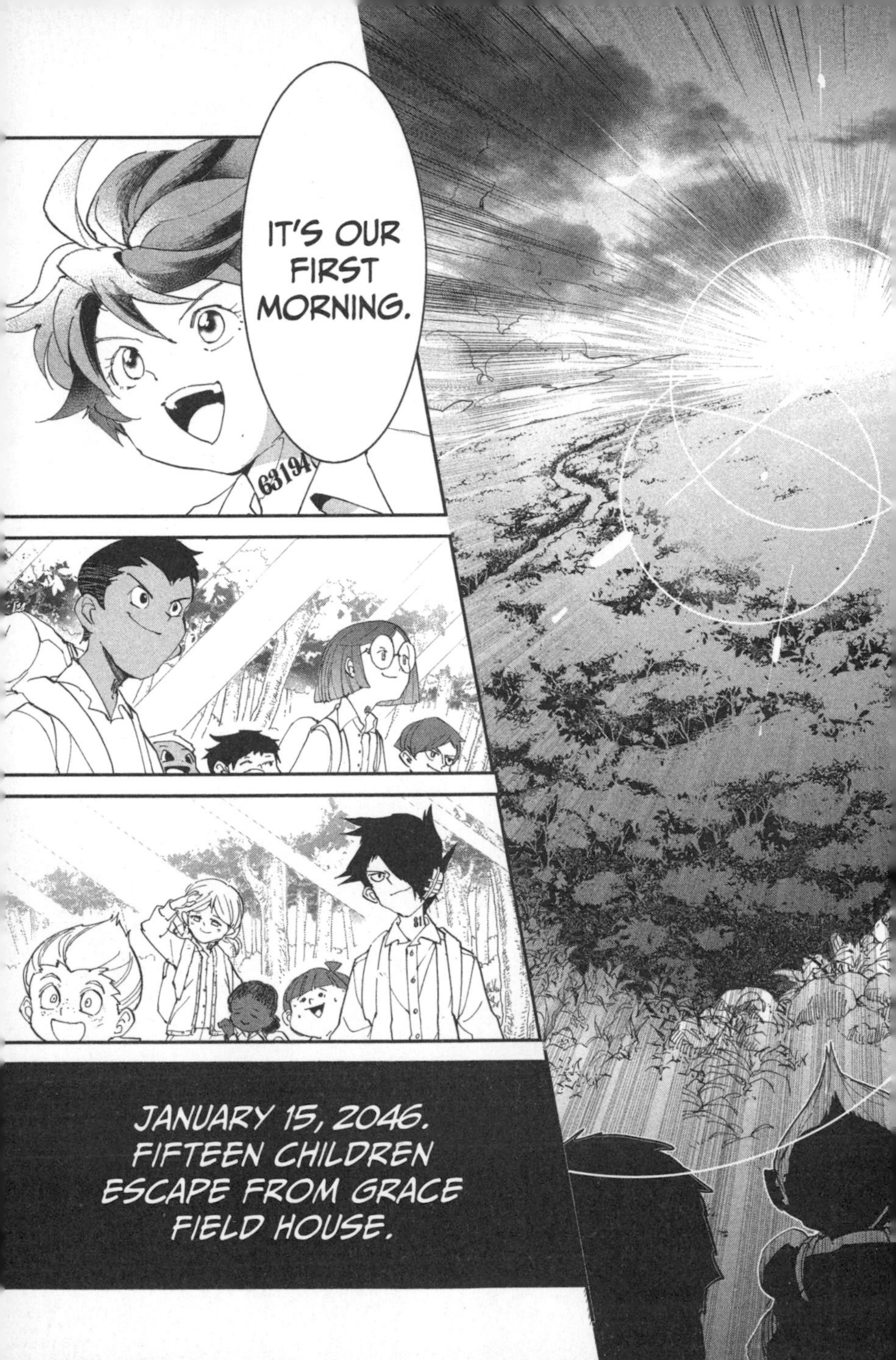
IT'S OUR FIRST MORNING.
63194
JANUARY 15, 2046. FIFTEEN CHILDREN ESCAPE FROM GRACE FIELD HOUSE.

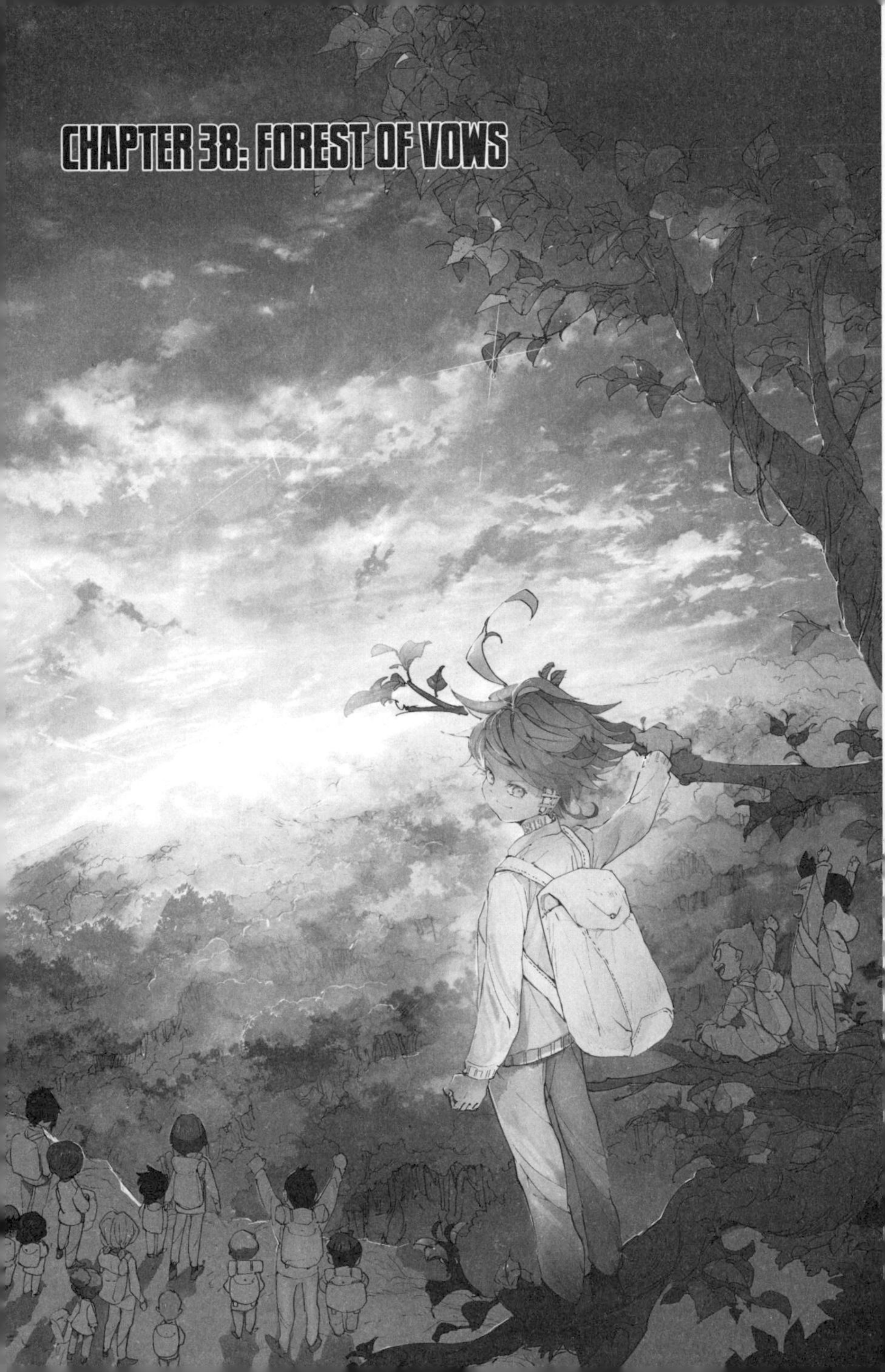
CHAPTER 38: FOREST OF VOWS

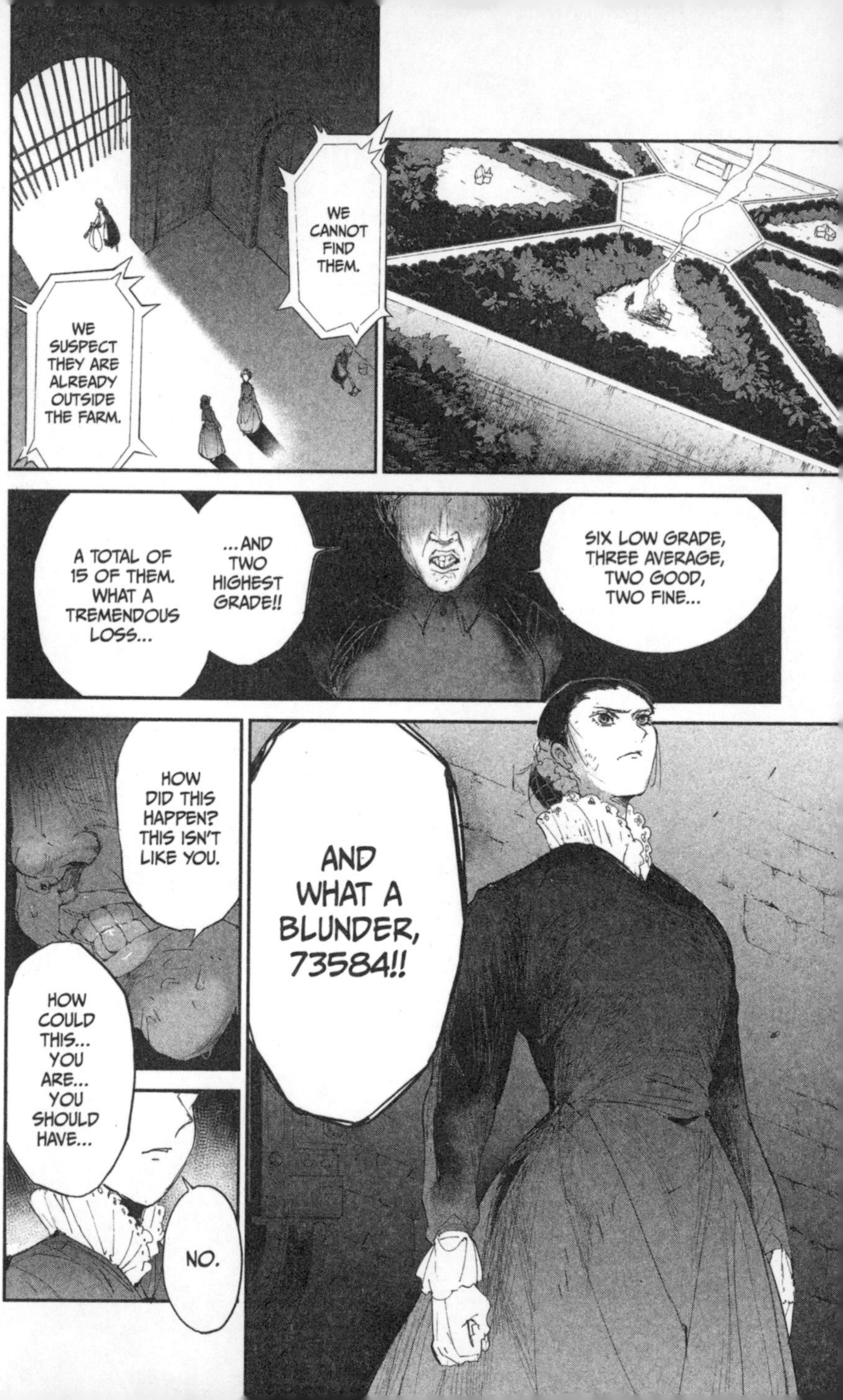
WE CANNOT FIND THEM.
WE SUSPECT THEY ARE ALREADY OUTSIDE THE FARM.
SIX LOW GRADE, THREE AVERAGE, TWO GOOD, TWO FINE...
...AND TWO HIGHEST GRADE!!
A TOTAL OF 15 OF THEM. WHAT A TREMENDOUS LOSS...
AND WHAT A BLUNDER, 73584!!
HOW DID THIS HAPPEN? THIS ISN'T LIKE YOU.
HOW COULD THIS... YOU ARE... YOU SHOULD HAVE...
NO.

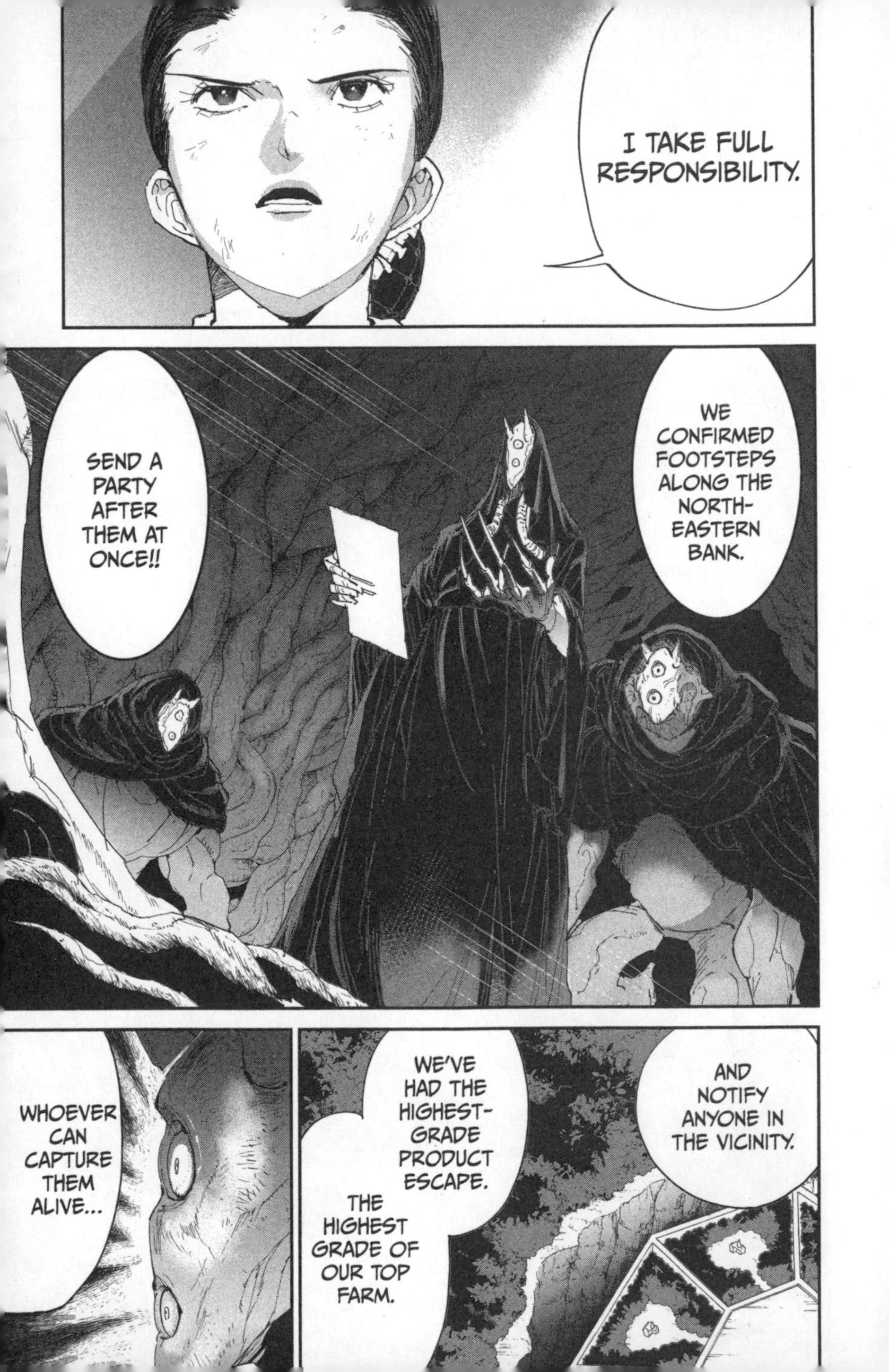
I TAKE FULL RESPONSIBILITY.
WE CONFIRMED FOOTSTEPS ALONG THE NORTH-EASTERN BANK.
SEND A PARTY AFTER THEM AT ONCE!!
AND NOTIFY ANYONE IN THE VICINITY.
WE'VE HAD THE HIGHEST-GRADE PRODUCT ESCAPE.
THE HIGHEST GRADE OF OUR TOP FARM.
WHOEVER CAN CAPTURE THEM ALIVE...

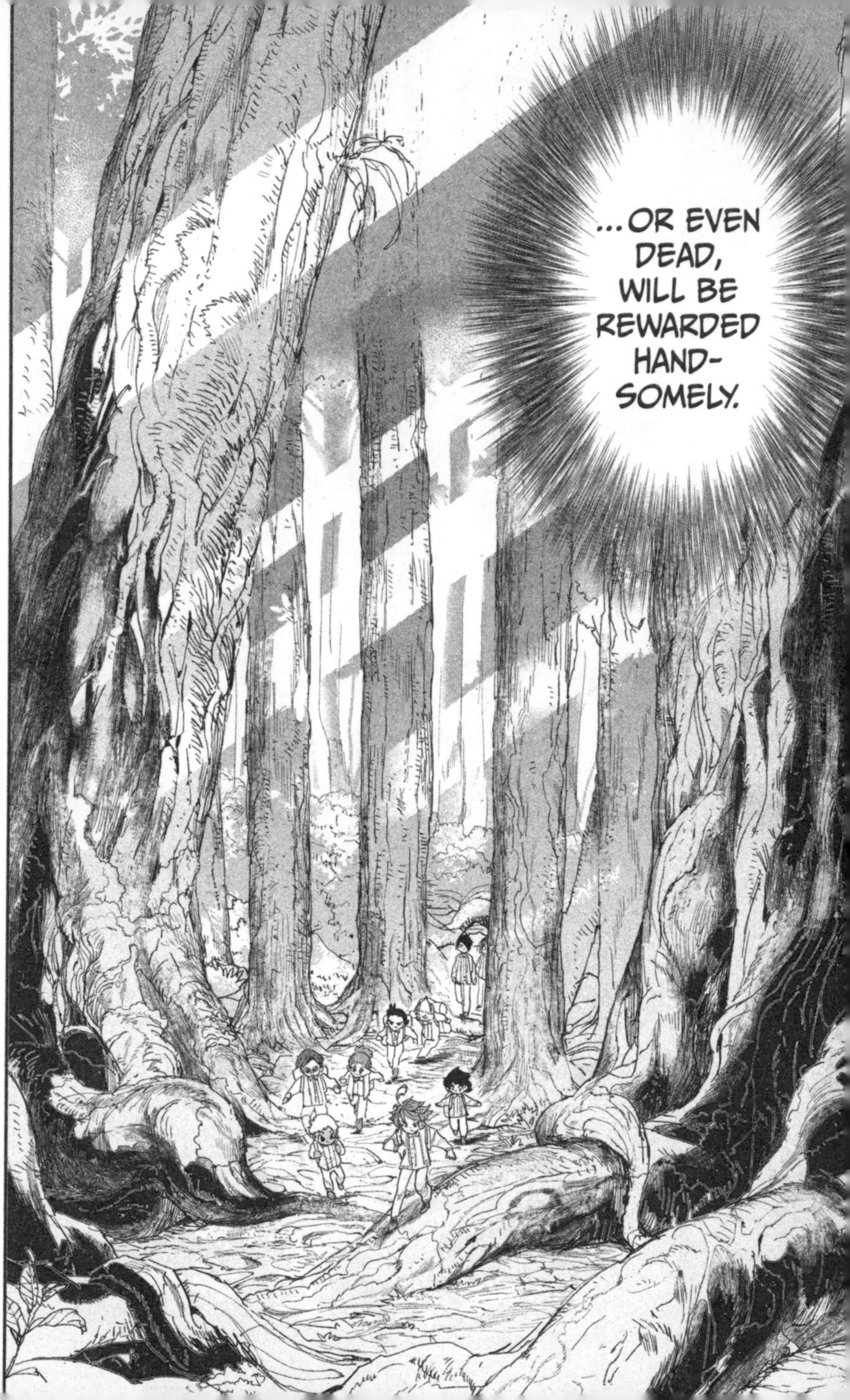
...OR EVEN DEAD, WILL BE REWARDED HAND-SOMELY.

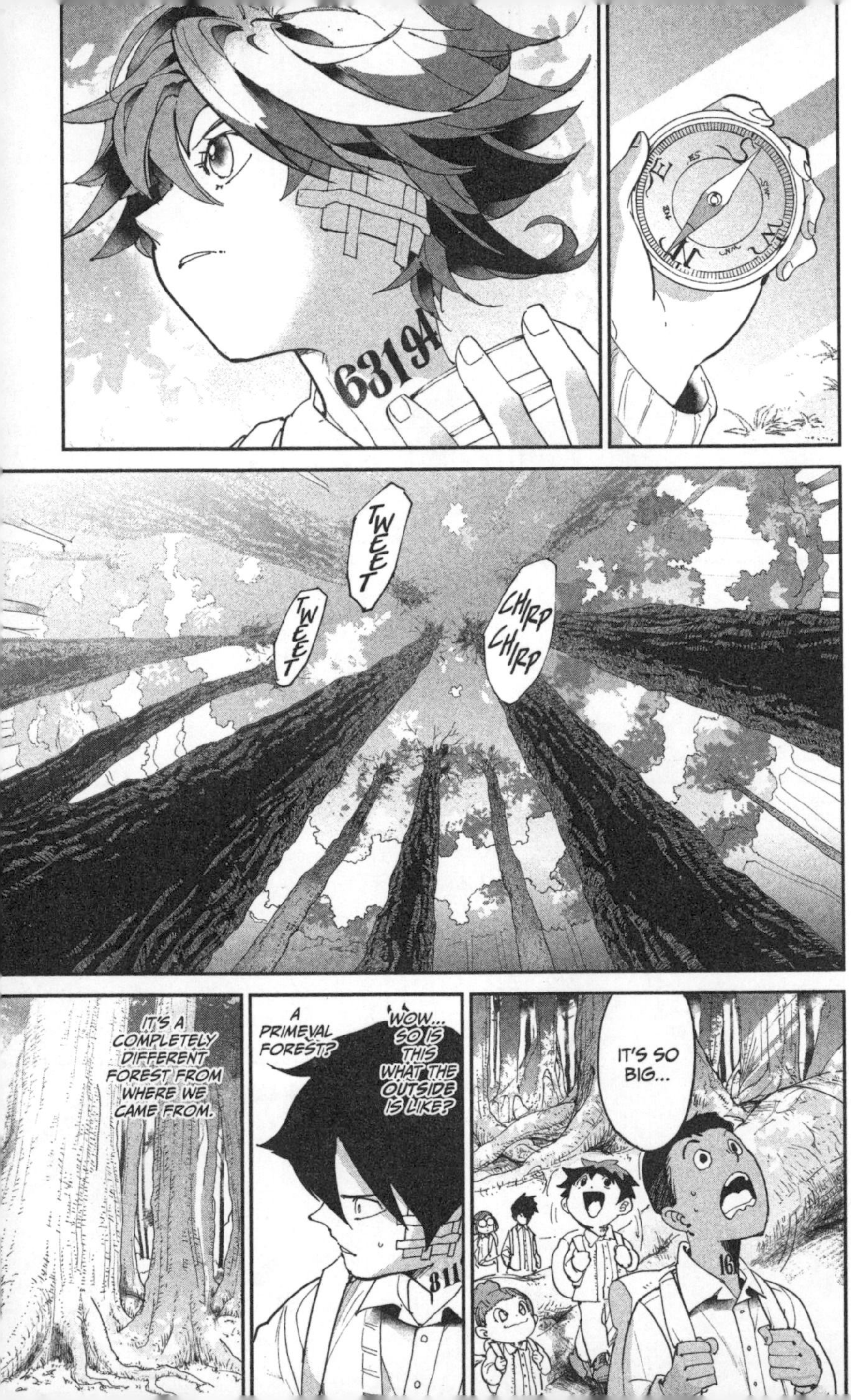
63194
CHIRP CHIRP
TWEET TWEET
TWEET TWEET
IT'S SO BIG...
WOW... SO IS THIS WHAT THE OUTSIDE IS LIKE?
A PRIMEVAL FOREST?
IT'S A COMPLETELY DIFFERENT FOREST FROM WHERE WE CAME FROM.

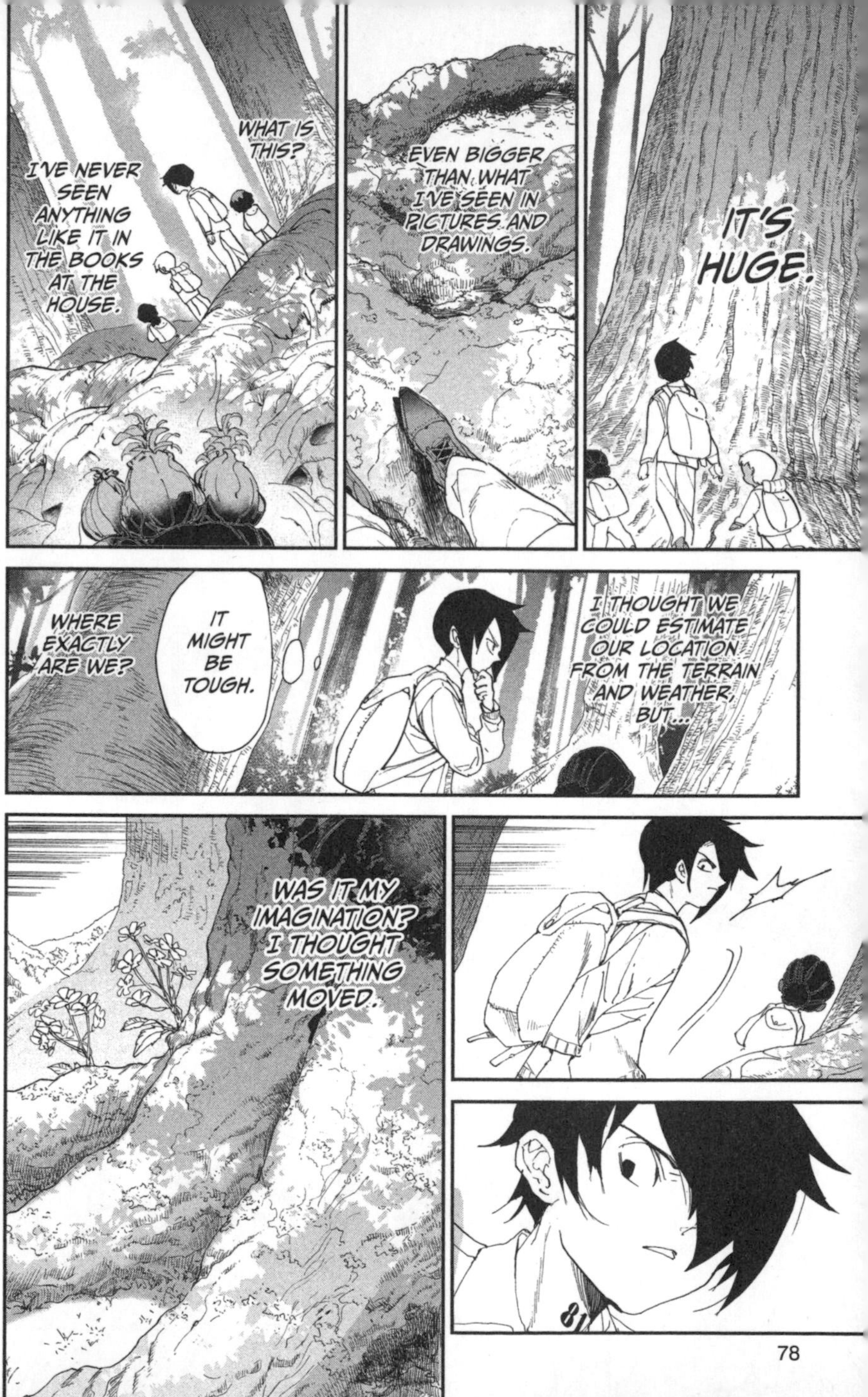
IT'S HUGE.
EVEN BIGGER THAN WHAT I'VE SEEN IN PICTURES AND DRAWINGS.
WHAT IS THIS?
I'VE NEVER SEEN ANYTHING LIKE IT IN THE BOOKS AT THE HOUSE.
I THOUGHT WE COULD ESTIMATE OUR LOCATION FROM THE TERRAIN AND WEATHER, BUT...
IT MIGHT BE TOUGH.
WHERE EXACTLY ARE WE?
81
WAS IT MY IMAGINATION? I THOUGHT SOMETHING MOVED.

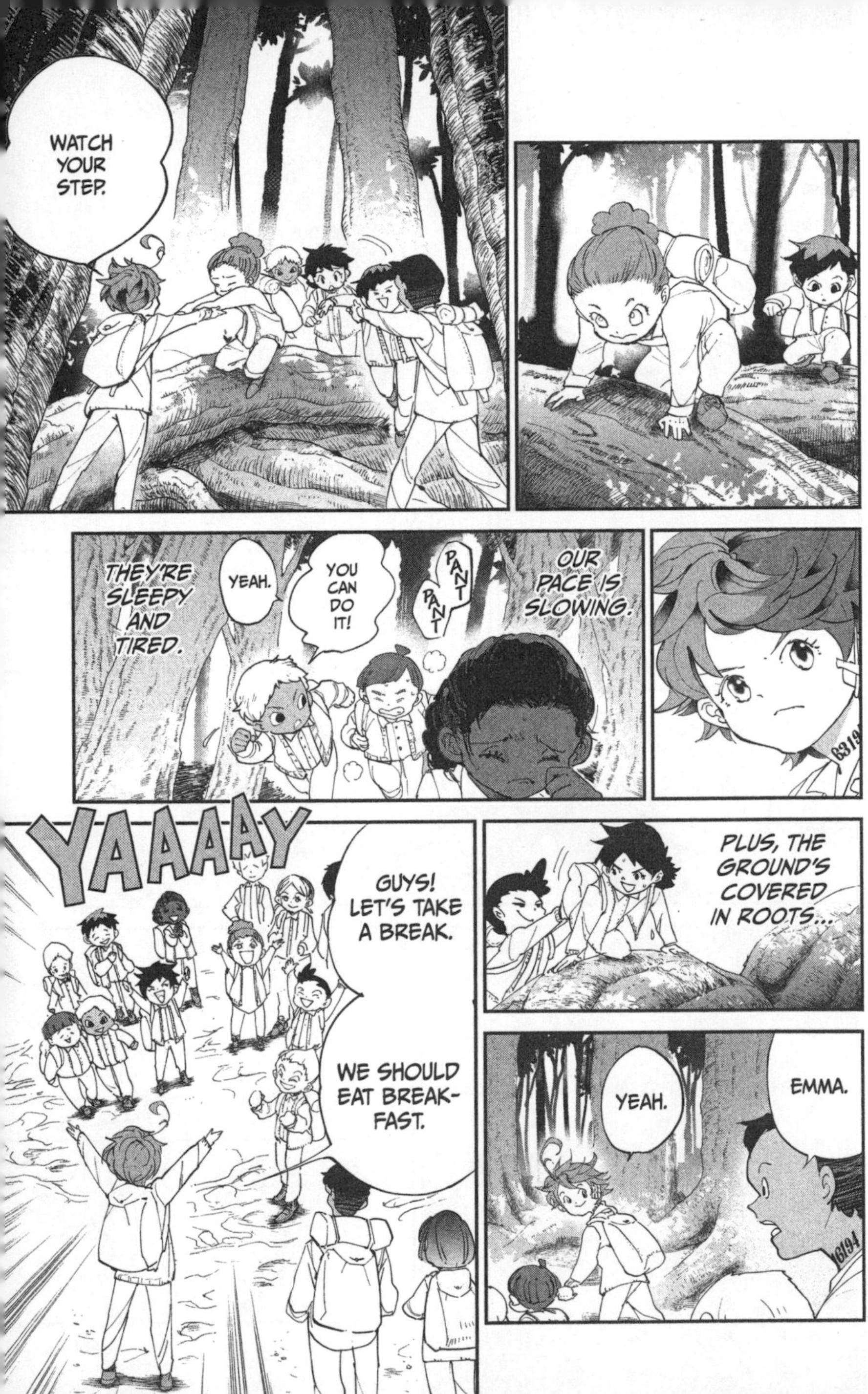
WATCH YOUR STEP.
OUR PACE IS SLOWING.
PANT PANT
YOU CAN DO IT!
YEAH.
THEY'RE SLEEPY AND TIRED.
PLUS, THE GROUND'S COVERED IN ROOTS...
EMMA.
YEAH.
GUYS! LET'S TAKE A BREAK.
WE SHOULD EAT BREAK-FAST.
YAAAAY

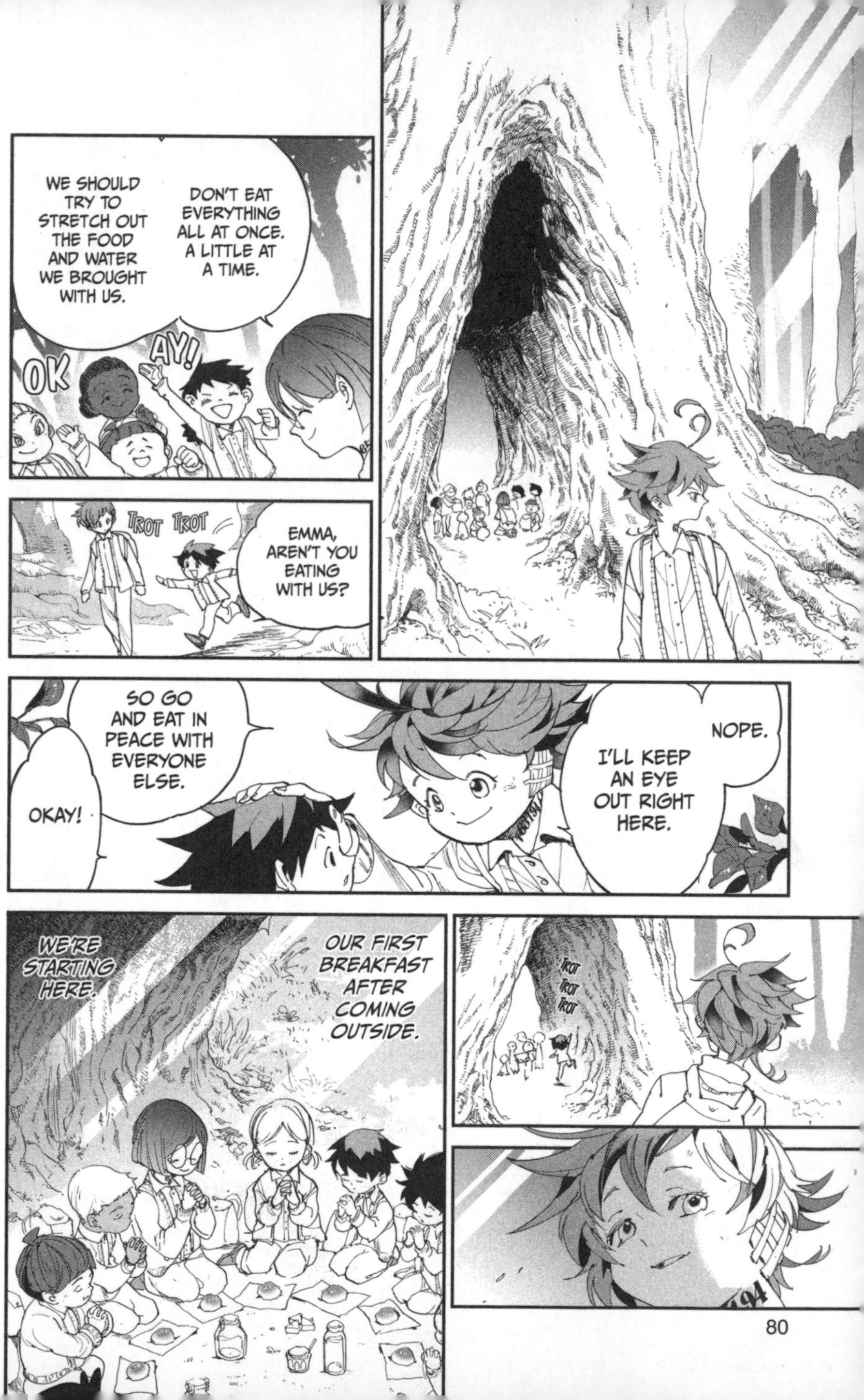
DON'T EAT EVERYTHING ALL AT ONCE. A LITTLE AT A TIME.
WE SHOULD TRY TO STRETCH OUT THE FOOD AND WATER WE BROUGHT WITH US.
AY!
OK
TROT TROT
EMMA, AREN'T YOU EATING WITH US?
NOPE.
I'LL KEEP AN EYE OUT RIGHT HERE.
SO GO AND EAT IN PEACE WITH EVERYONE ELSE.
OKAY!
TROT TROT TROT
OUR FIRST BREAKFAST AFTER COMING OUTSIDE.
WE'RE STARTING HERE.

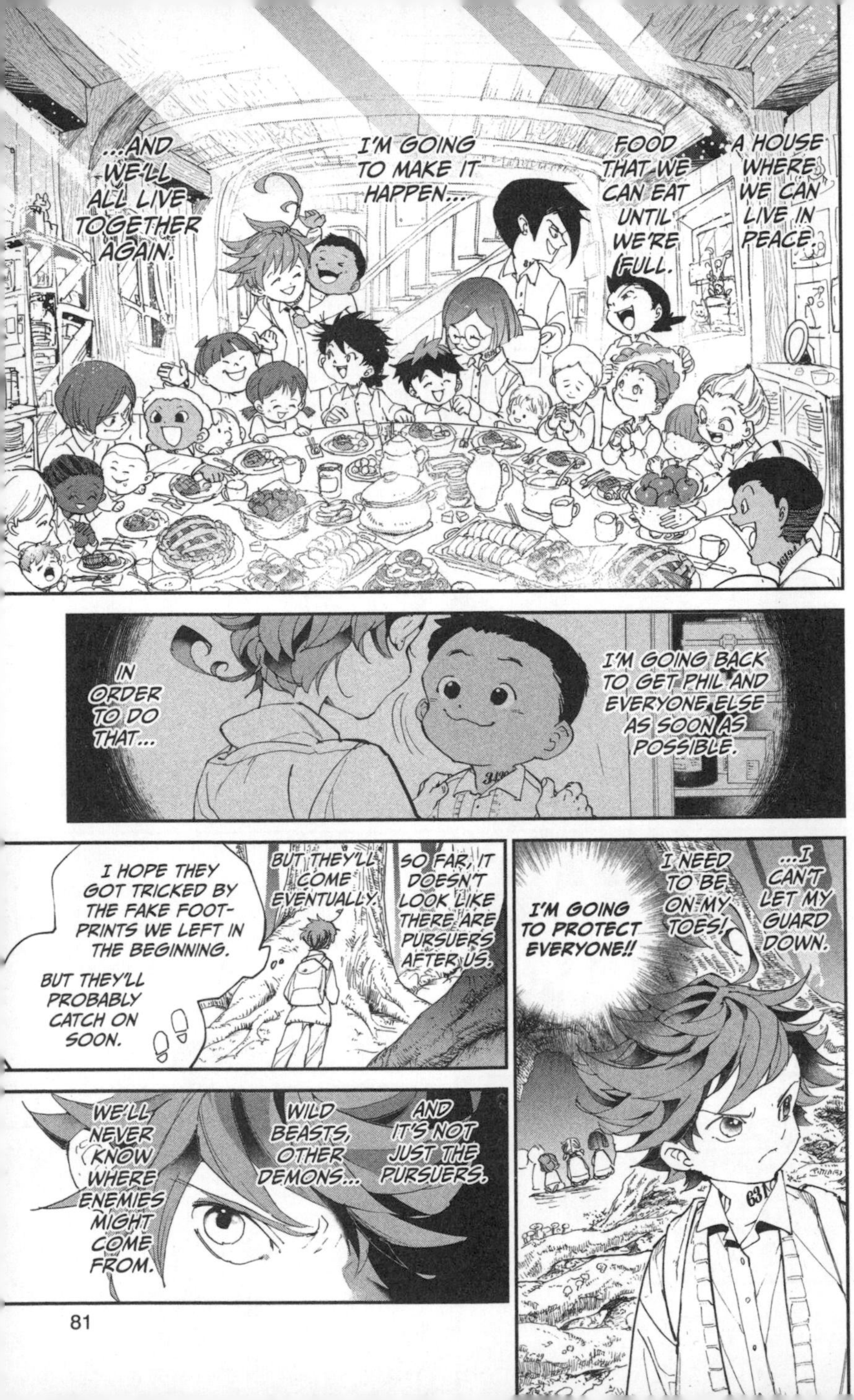
A HOUSE WHERE WE CAN LIVE IN PEACE.
FOOD THAT WE CAN EAT UNTIL WE'RE FULL.
I'M GOING TO MAKE IT HAPPEN...
...AND WE'LL ALL LIVE TOGETHER AGAIN.
I'M GOING BACK TO GET PHIL AND EVERYONE ELSE AS SOON AS POSSIBLE.
IN ORDER TO DO THAT...
...I CAN'T LET MY GUARD DOWN.
I NEED TO BE ON MY TOES!
I'M GOING TO PROTECT EVERYONE!!
SO FAR, IT DOESN'T LOOK LIKE THERE ARE PURSUERS AFTER US.
BUT THEY'LL COME EVENTUALLY.
I HOPE THEY GOT TRICKED BY THE FAKE FOOT-PRINTS WE LEFT IN THE BEGINNING.
BUT THEY'LL PROBABLY CATCH ON SOON.
AND IT'S NOT JUST THE PURSUERS.
WILD BEASTS, OTHER DEMONS...
WE'LL NEVER KNOW WHERE ENEMIES MIGHT COME FROM.

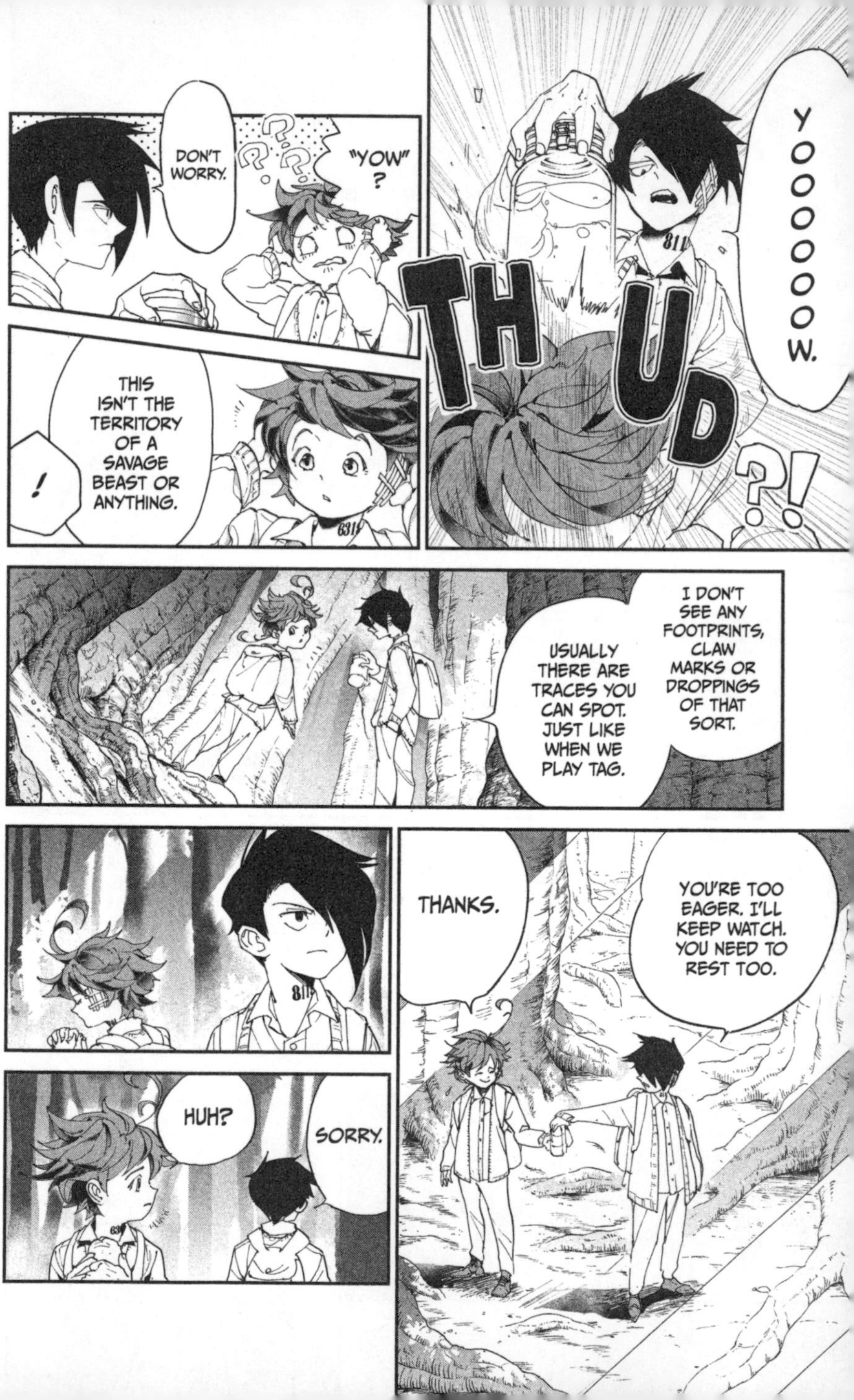
YOOOOOOW.
THUD ?!
"YOW" ?
DON'T WORRY.
THIS ISN'T THE TERRITORY OF A SAVAGE BEAST OR ANYTHING.
!
I DON'T SEE ANY FOOTPRINTS, CLAW MARKS OR DROPPINGS OF THAT SORT.
USUALLY THERE ARE TRACES YOU CAN SPOT. JUST LIKE WHEN WE PLAY TAG.
YOU'RE TOO EAGER. I'LL KEEP WATCH. YOU NEED TO REST TOO.
THANKS.
SORRY.
HUH?

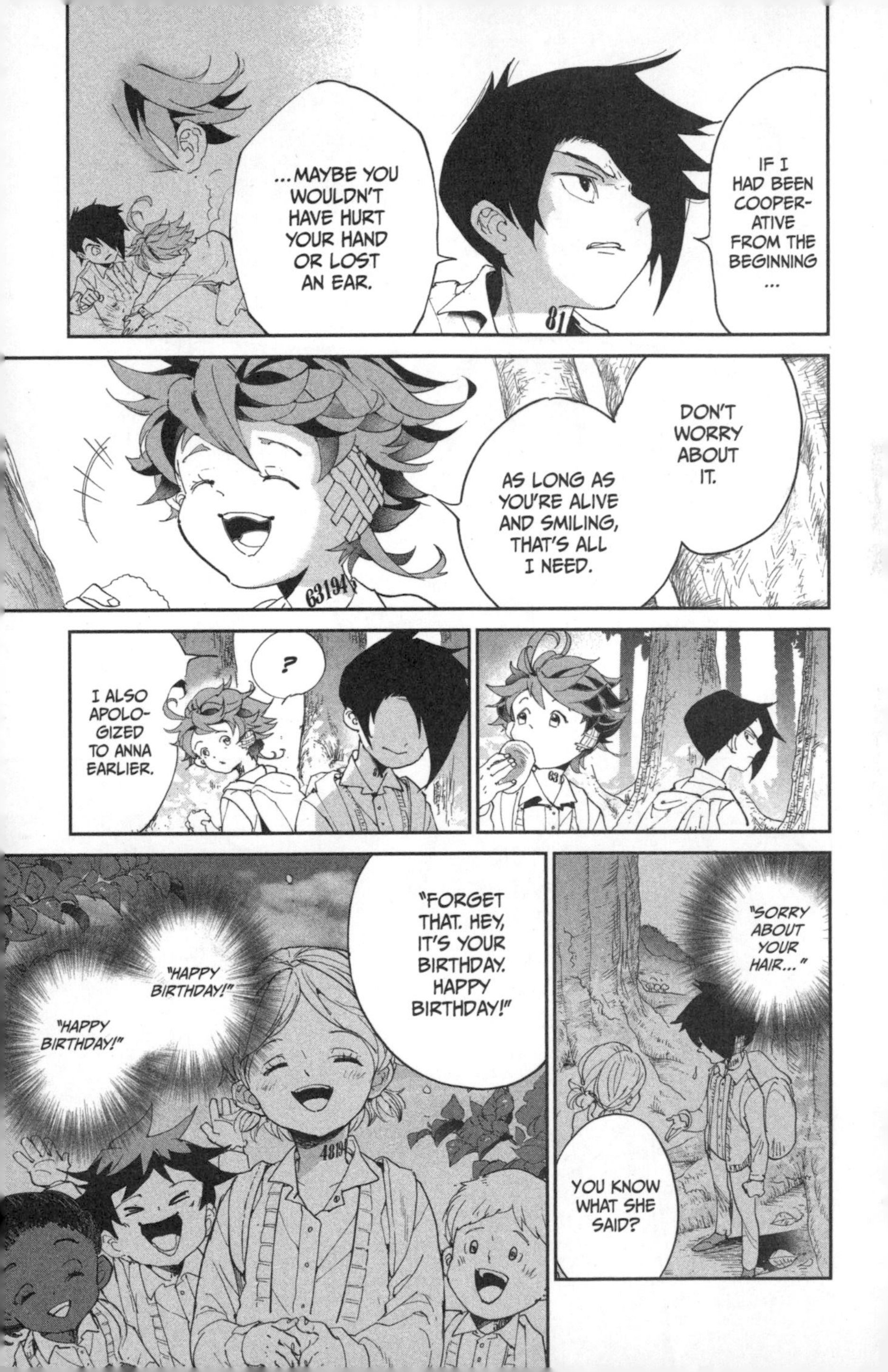
IF I HAD BEEN COOPERATIVE FROM THE BEGINNING...
...MAYBE YOU WOULDN'T HAVE HURT YOUR HAND OR LOST AN EAR.
DON'T WORRY ABOUT IT.
AS LONG AS YOU'RE ALIVE AND SMILING, THAT'S ALL I NEED.
?
I ALSO APOLOGIZED TO ANNA EARLIER.
"SORRY ABOUT YOUR HAIR..."
YOU KNOW WHAT SHE SAID?
"FORGET THAT. HEY, IT'S YOUR BIRTHDAY. HAPPY BIRTHDAY!"
"HAPPY BIRTHDAY!"
"HAPPY BIRTHDAY!"

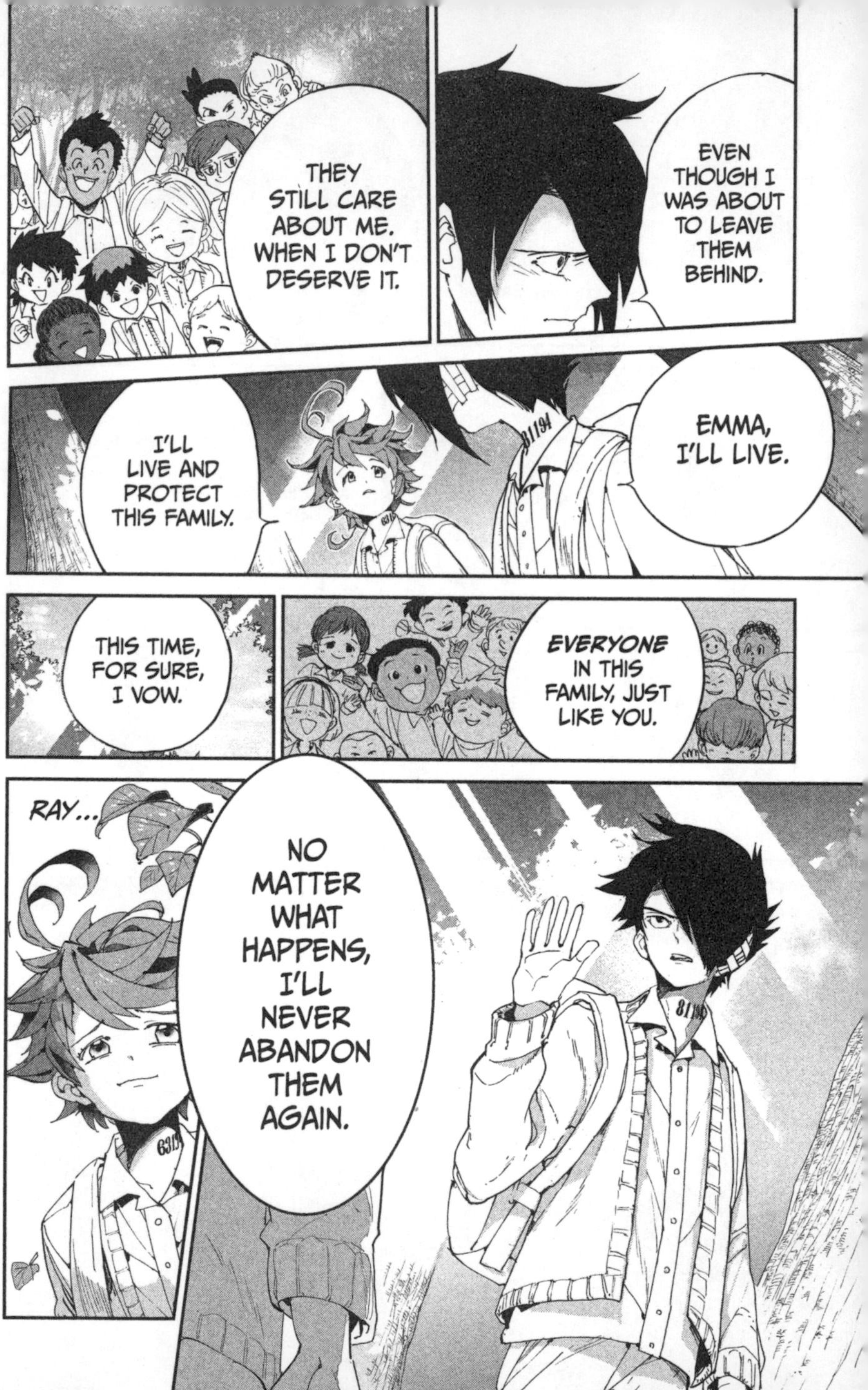
EVEN THOUGH I WAS ABOUT TO LEAVE THEM BEHIND.
THEY STILL CARE ABOUT ME. WHEN I DON'T DESERVE IT.
EMMA, I'LL LIVE.
I'LL LIVE AND PROTECT THIS FAMILY.
EVERYONE IN THIS FAMILY, JUST LIKE YOU.
THIS TIME, FOR SURE, I VOW.
NO MATTER WHAT HAPPENS, I'LL NEVER ABANDON THEM AGAIN.
RAY...

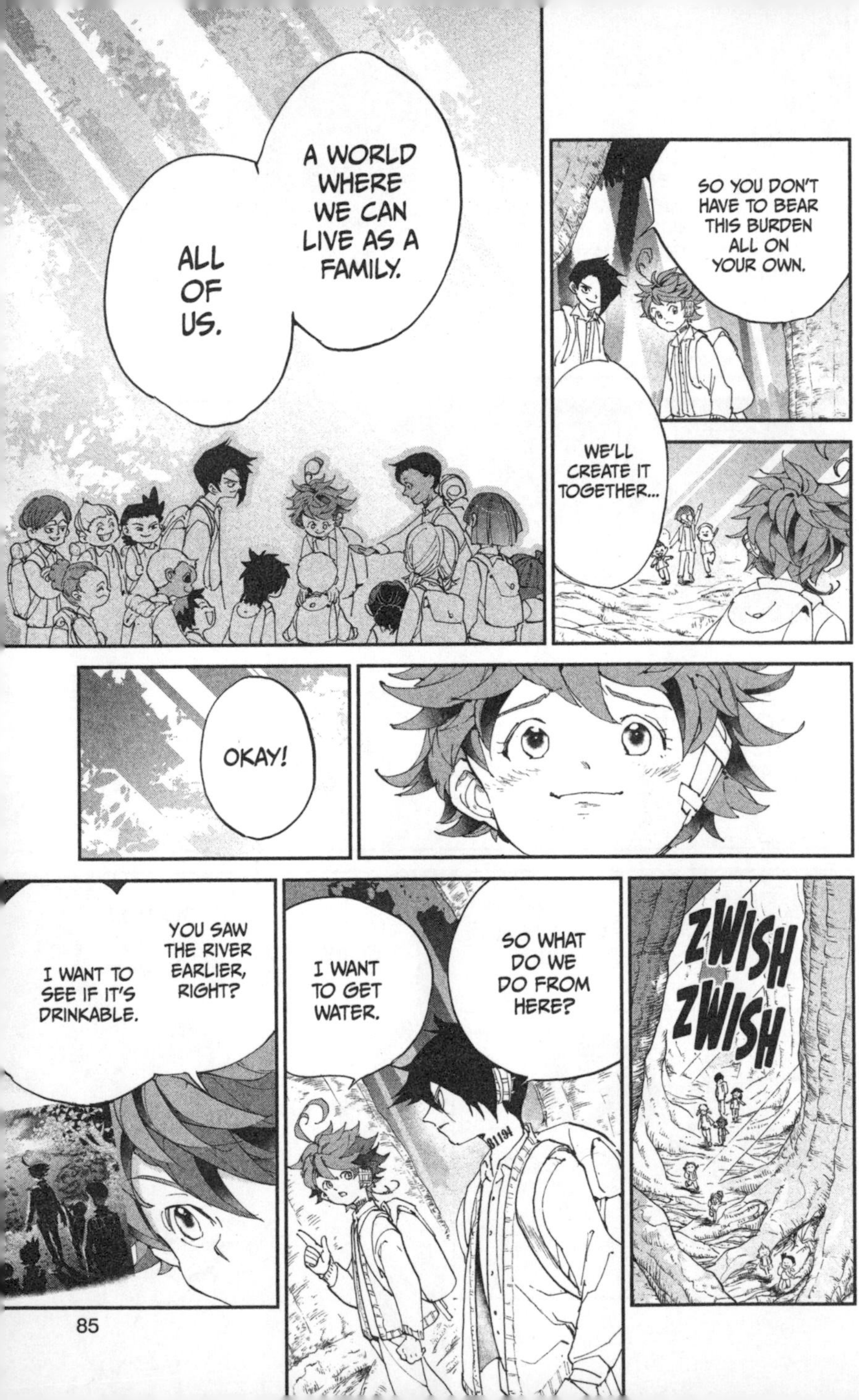
SO YOU DON'T HAVE TO BEAR THIS BURDEN ALL ON YOUR OWN.
WE'LL CREATE IT TOGETHER...
A WORLD WHERE WE CAN LIVE AS A FAMILY.
ALL OF US.
OKAY!
ZWISH
ZWISH
SO WHAT DO WE DO FROM HERE?
I WANT TO GET WATER.
YOU SAW THE RIVER EARLIER, RIGHT?
I WANT TO SEE IF IT'S DRINKABLE.

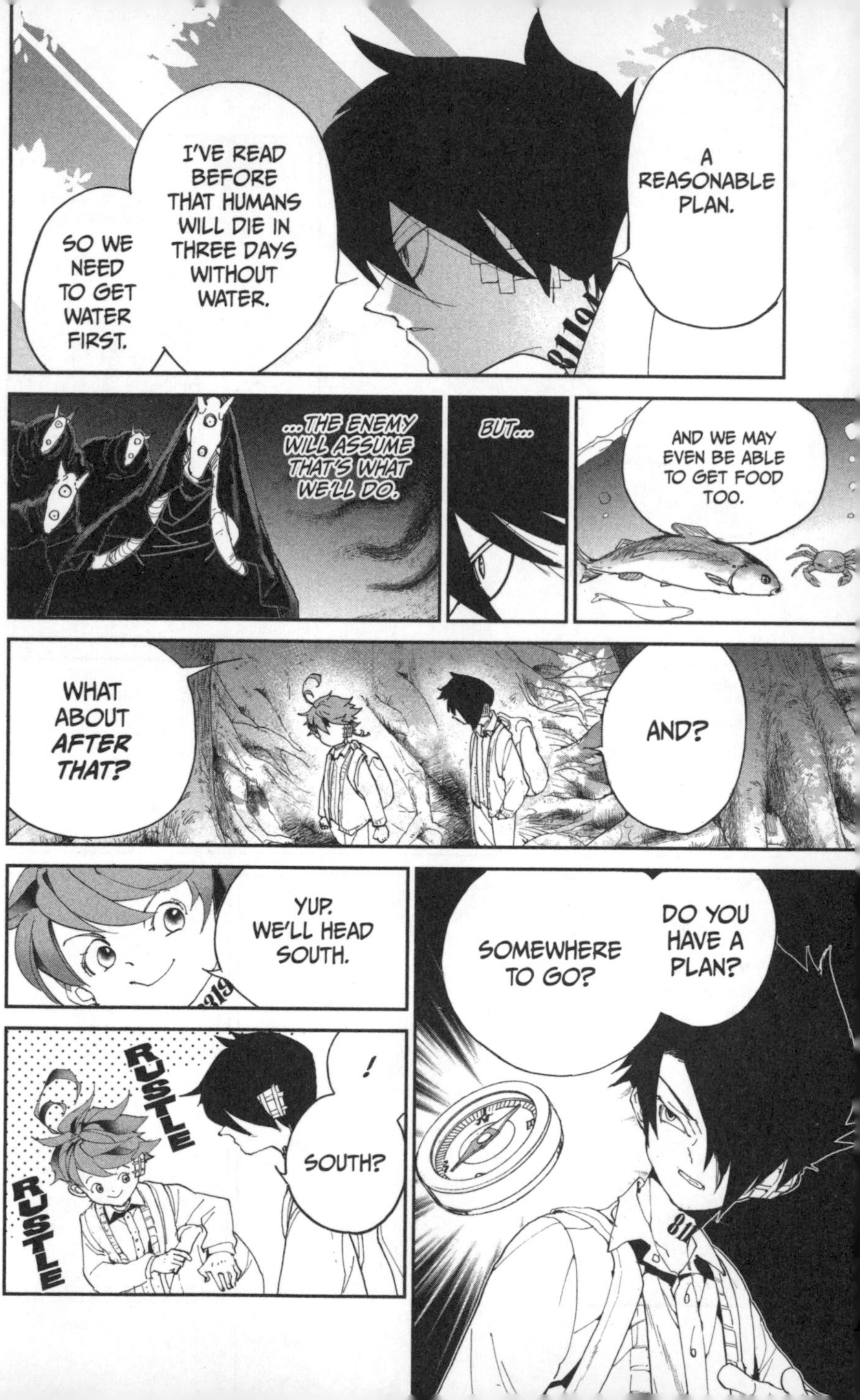
A REASONABLE PLAN.
I'VE READ BEFORE THAT HUMANS WILL DIE IN THREE DAYS WITHOUT WATER.
SO WE NEED TO GET WATER FIRST.
AND WE MAY EVEN BE ABLE TO GET FOOD TOO.
BUT...
...THE ENEMY WILL ASSUME THAT'S WHAT WE'LL DO.
AND?
WHAT ABOUT *AFTER* THAT?
DO YOU HAVE A PLAN?
SOMEWHERE TO GO?
YUP. WE'LL HEAD SOUTH.
RUSTLE
RUSTLE
!
SOUTH?

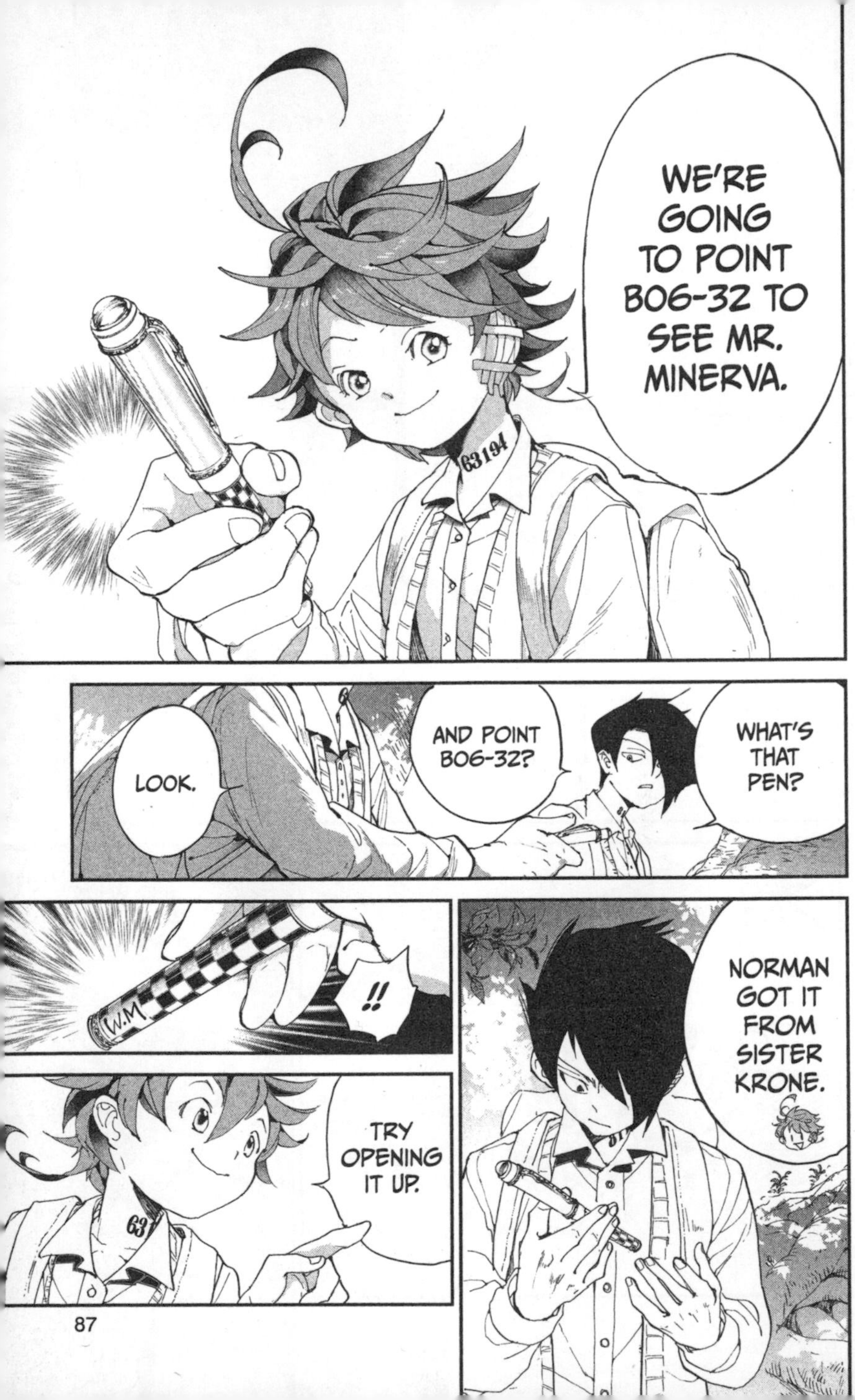

WE'RE GOING TO POINT B06-32 TO SEE MR. MINERVA.
WHAT'S THAT PEN?
AND POINT B06-32?
LOOK.
NORMAN GOT IT FROM SISTER KRONE.
!!
W.M
TRY OPENING IT UP.

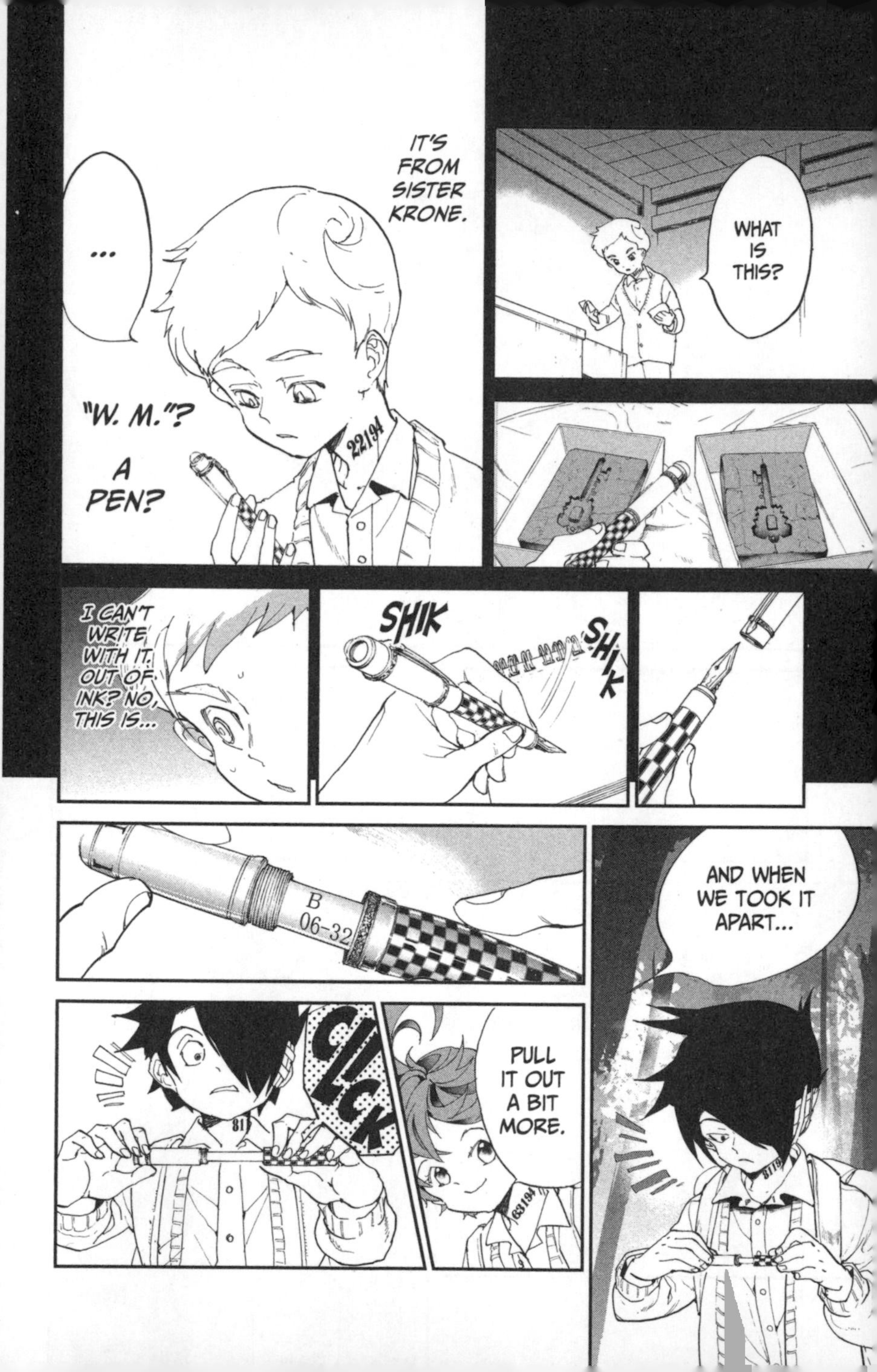
WHAT IS THIS?
IT'S FROM SISTER KRONE.
...
"W. M."?
A PEN?
SHIK
SHIK
I CAN'T WRITE WITH IT. OUT OF INK? NO, THIS IS...
AND WHEN WE TOOK IT APART...
B
06-32
PULL IT OUT A BIT MORE.
CLICK

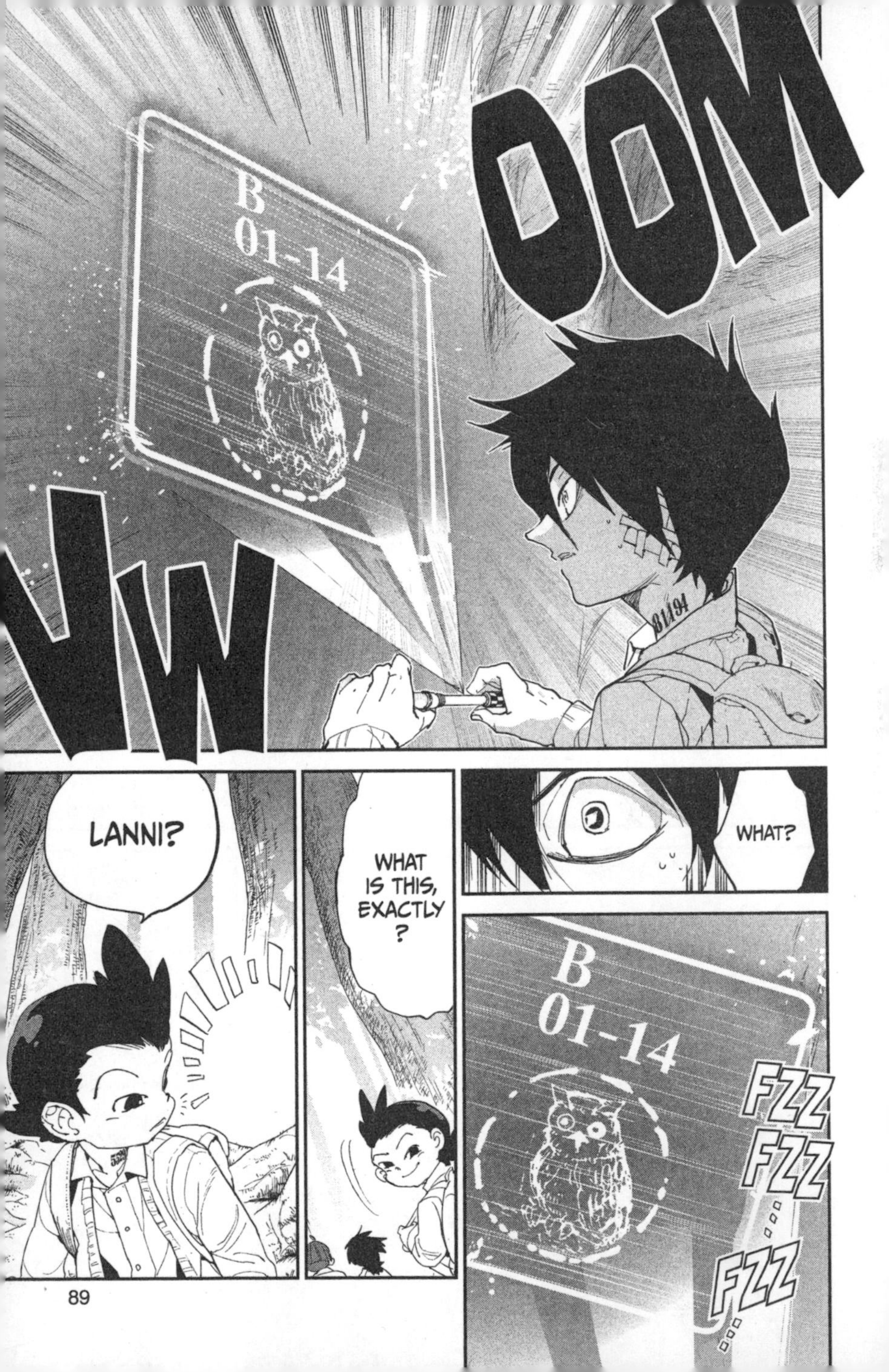
B
01-14
OOM
WHAT?
B
01-14
FZZ
FZZ
FZZ
WHAT IS THIS, EXACTLY?
LANNI?

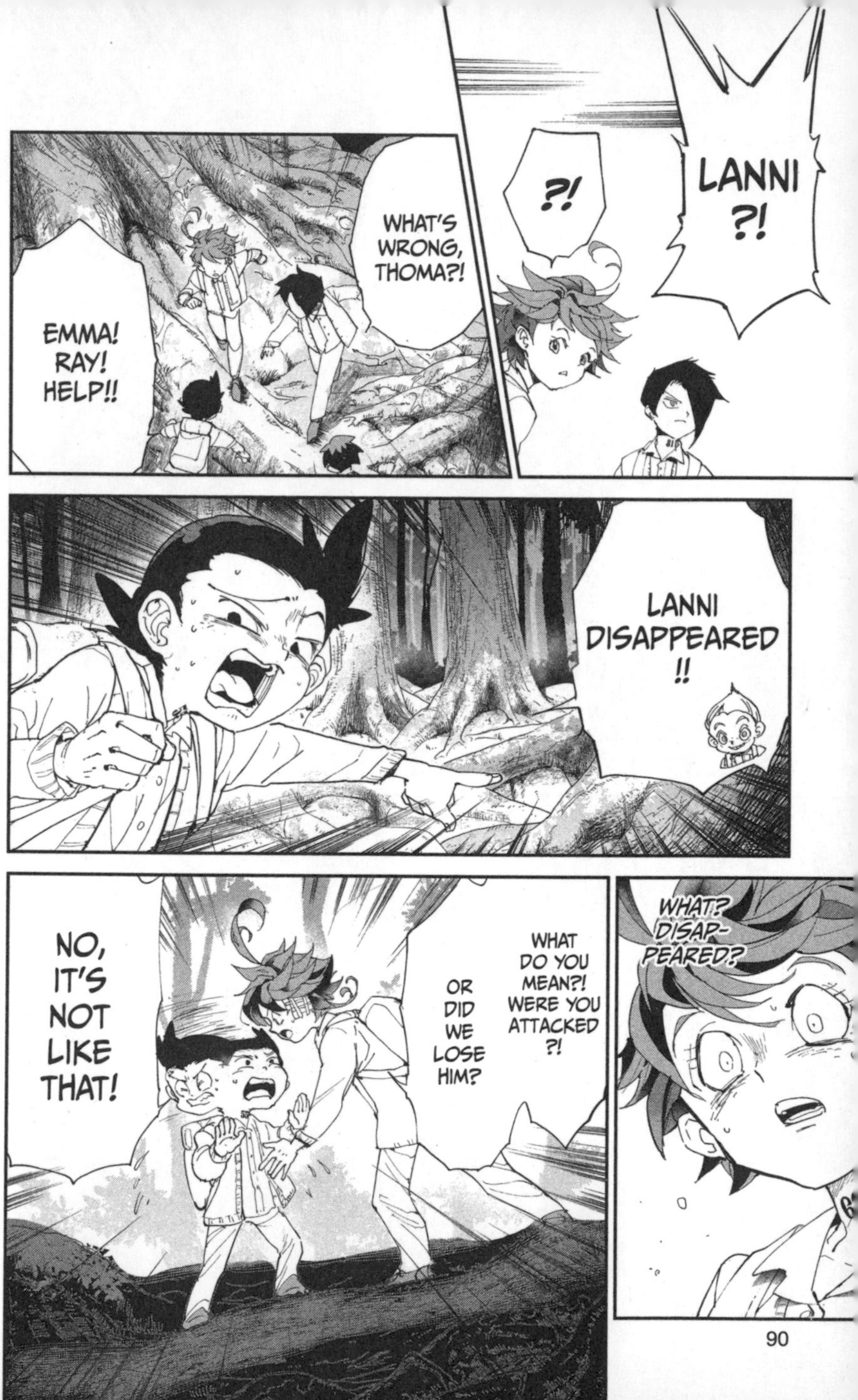
LANNI ?!
?!
WHAT'S WRONG, THOMA?!
EMMA! RAY! HELP!!
LANNI DISAPPEARED !!
WHAT? DISAP-PEARED?
WHAT DO YOU MEAN?! WERE YOU ATTACKED ?!
OR DID WE LOSE HIM?
NO, IT'S NOT LIKE THAT!

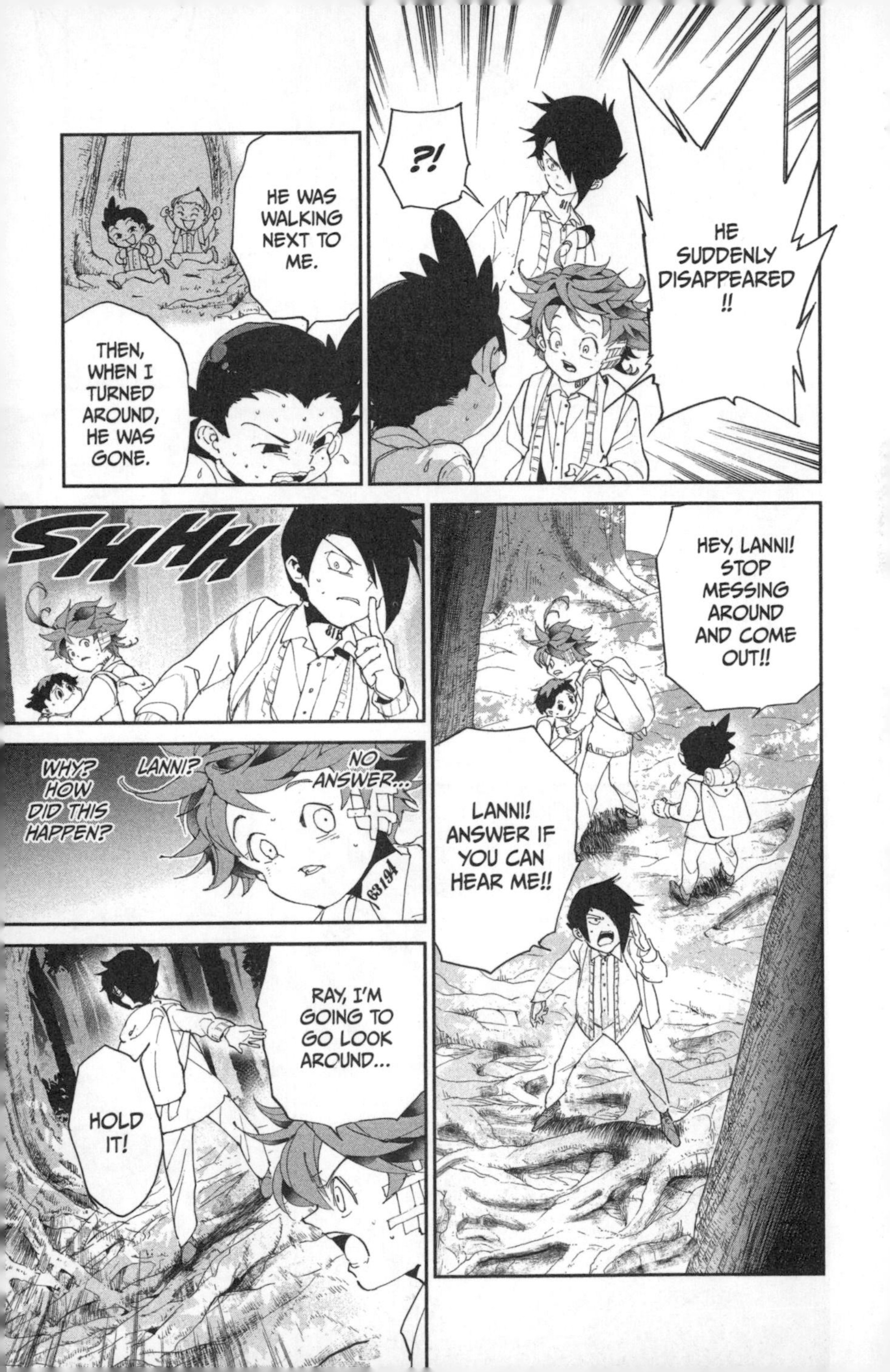
HE SUDDENLY DISAPPEARED!!
?!
HE WAS WALKING NEXT TO ME.
THEN, WHEN I TURNED AROUND, HE WAS GONE.
HEY, LANNI! STOP MESSING AROUND AND COME OUT!!
LANNI! ANSWER IF YOU CAN HEAR ME!!
SHHH
NO ANSWER...
LANNI?
WHY? HOW DID THIS HAPPEN?
RAY, I'M GOING TO GO LOOK AROUND...
HOLD IT!

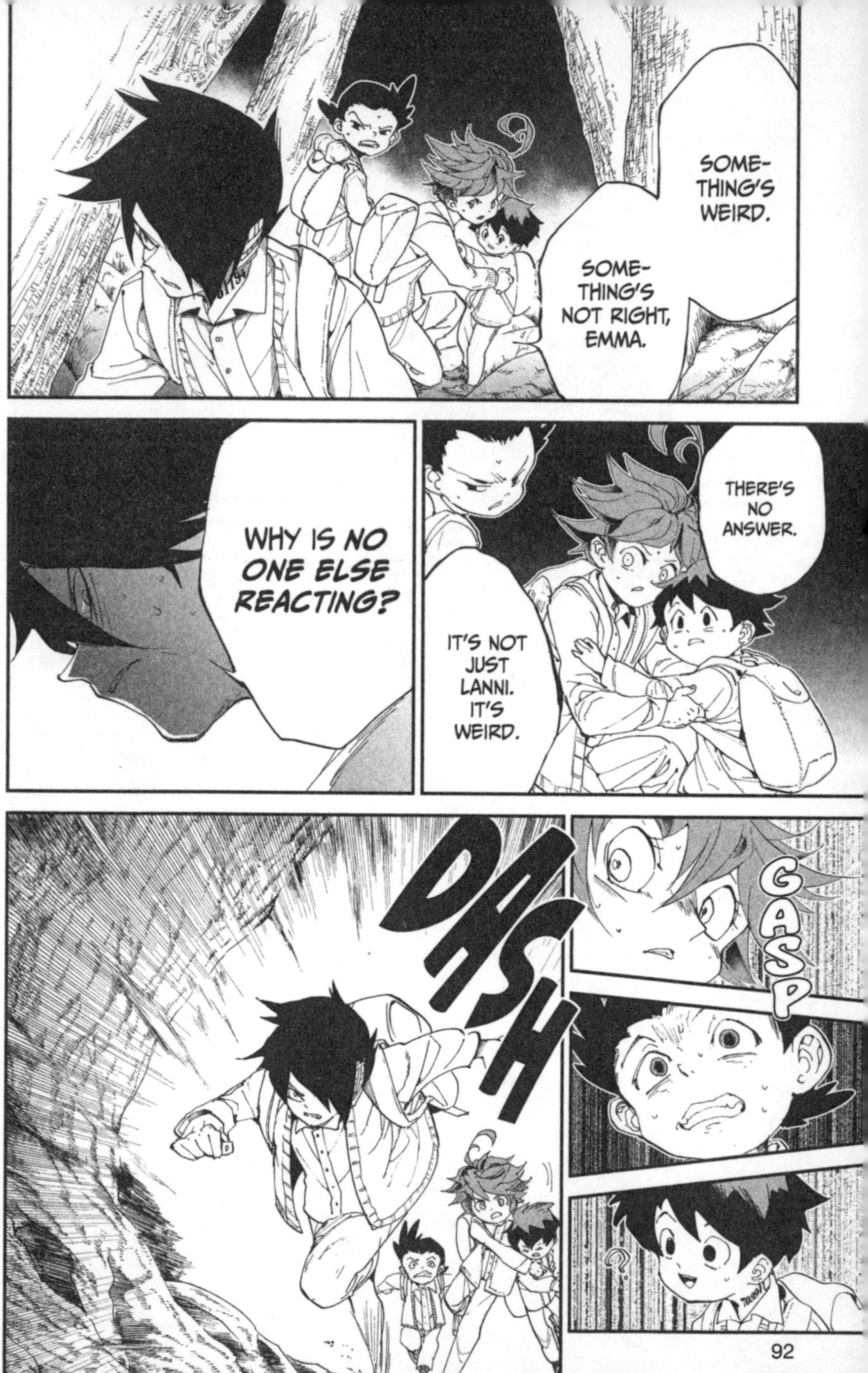
SOME-THING'S WEIRD.
SOME-THING'S NOT RIGHT, EMMA.
THERE'S NO ANSWER.
IT'S NOT JUST LANNI. IT'S WEIRD.
WHY IS NO ONE ELSE REACTING?
GASP
DASH

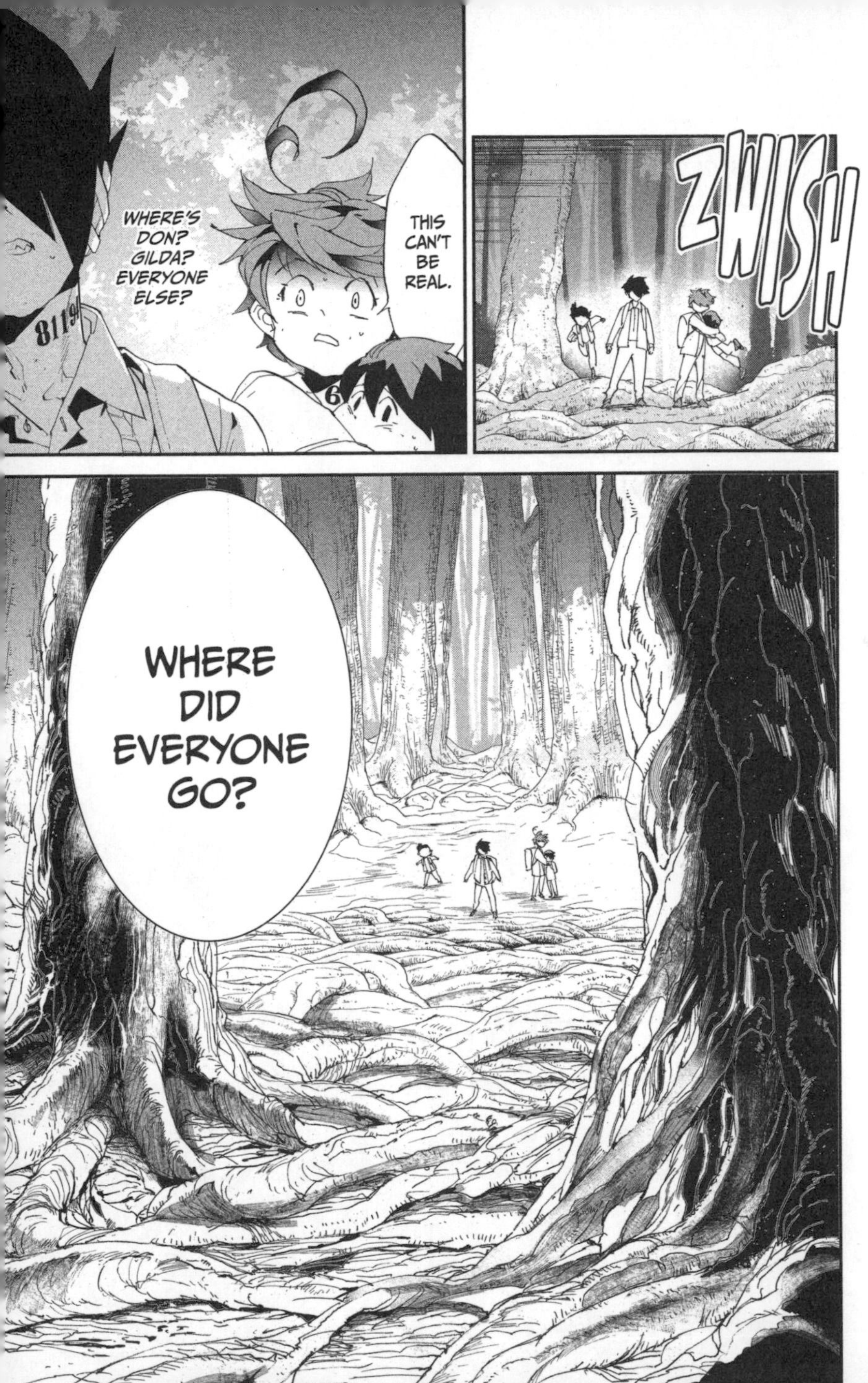
ZWISH
THIS CAN'T BE REAL.
WHERE'S DON? GILDA? EVERYONE ELSE?
WHERE DID EVERYONE GO?

SIDE STORY 2-1

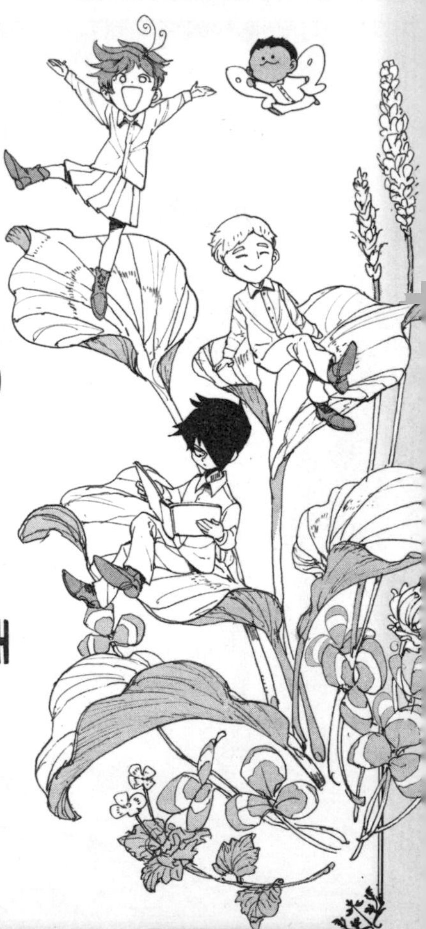

PERFECT DAY FOR LAUNDRY

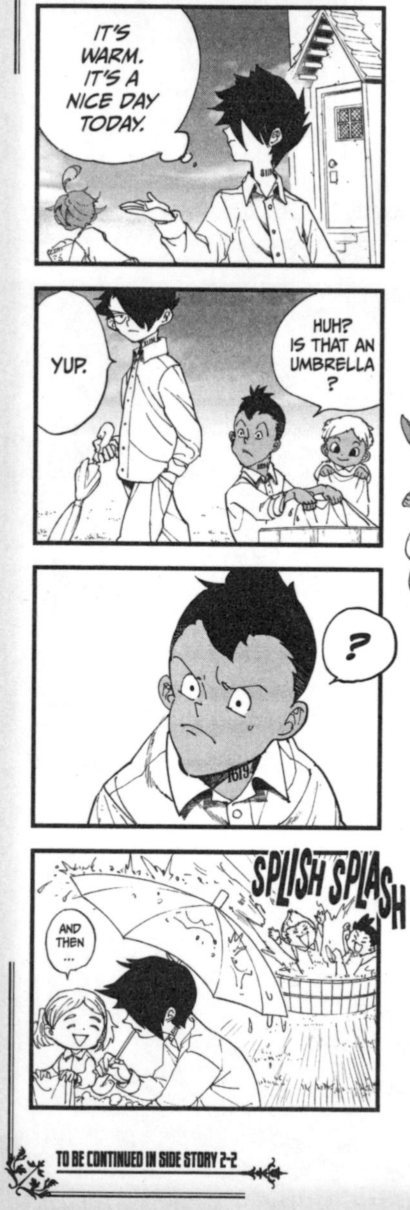
IT'S WARM. IT'S A NICE DAY TODAY.
HUH? IS THAT AN UMBRELLA ?
YUP.
?
SPLISH SPLASH
AND THEN ...

TO BE CONTINUED IN SIDE STORY 2-2

CHAPTER 39: BEYOND EXPECTATIONS

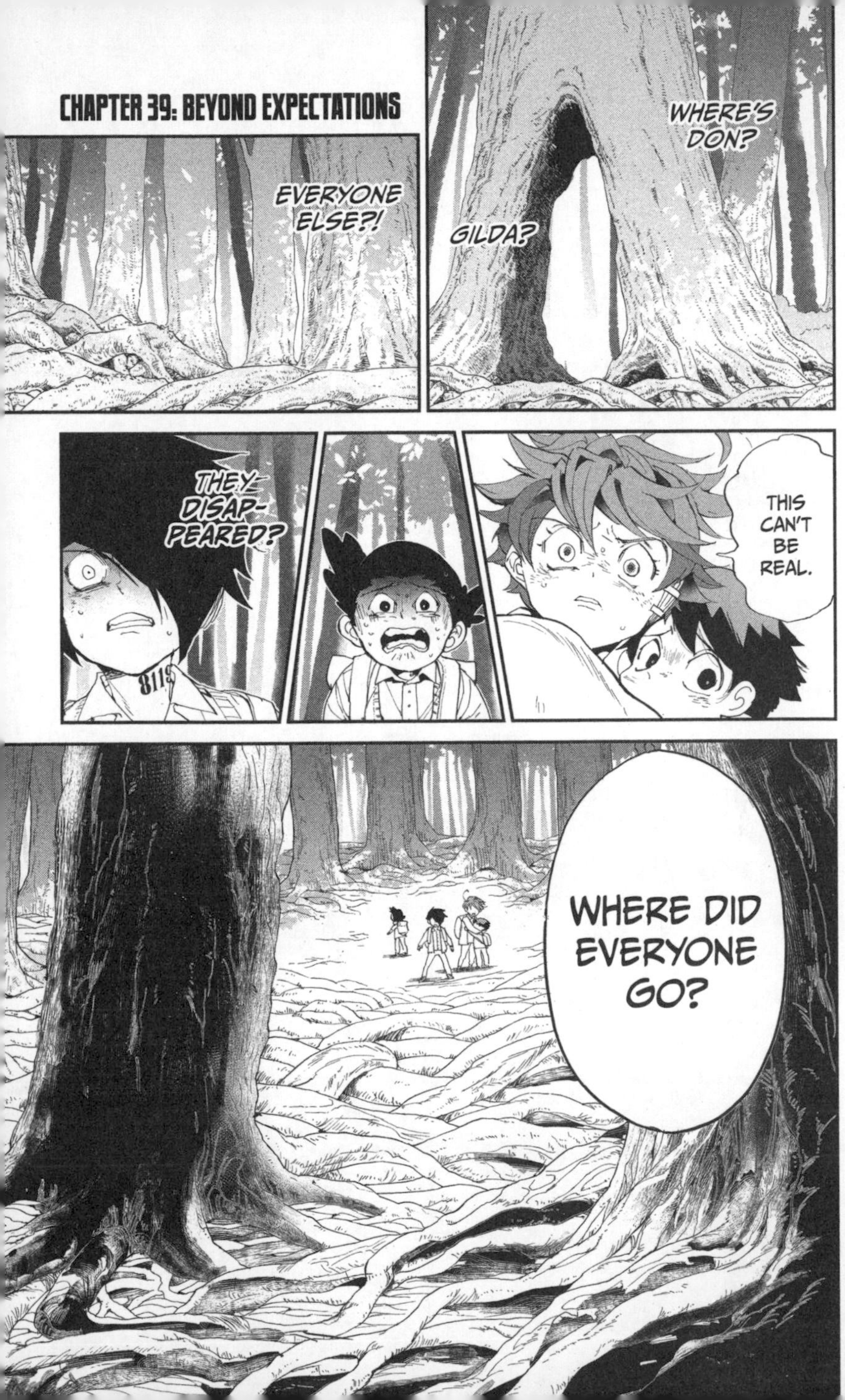
WHERE'S DON?
GILDA?
EVERYONE ELSE?!
THIS CAN'T BE REAL.
THEY DISAP-PEARED?
WHERE DID EVERYONE GO?

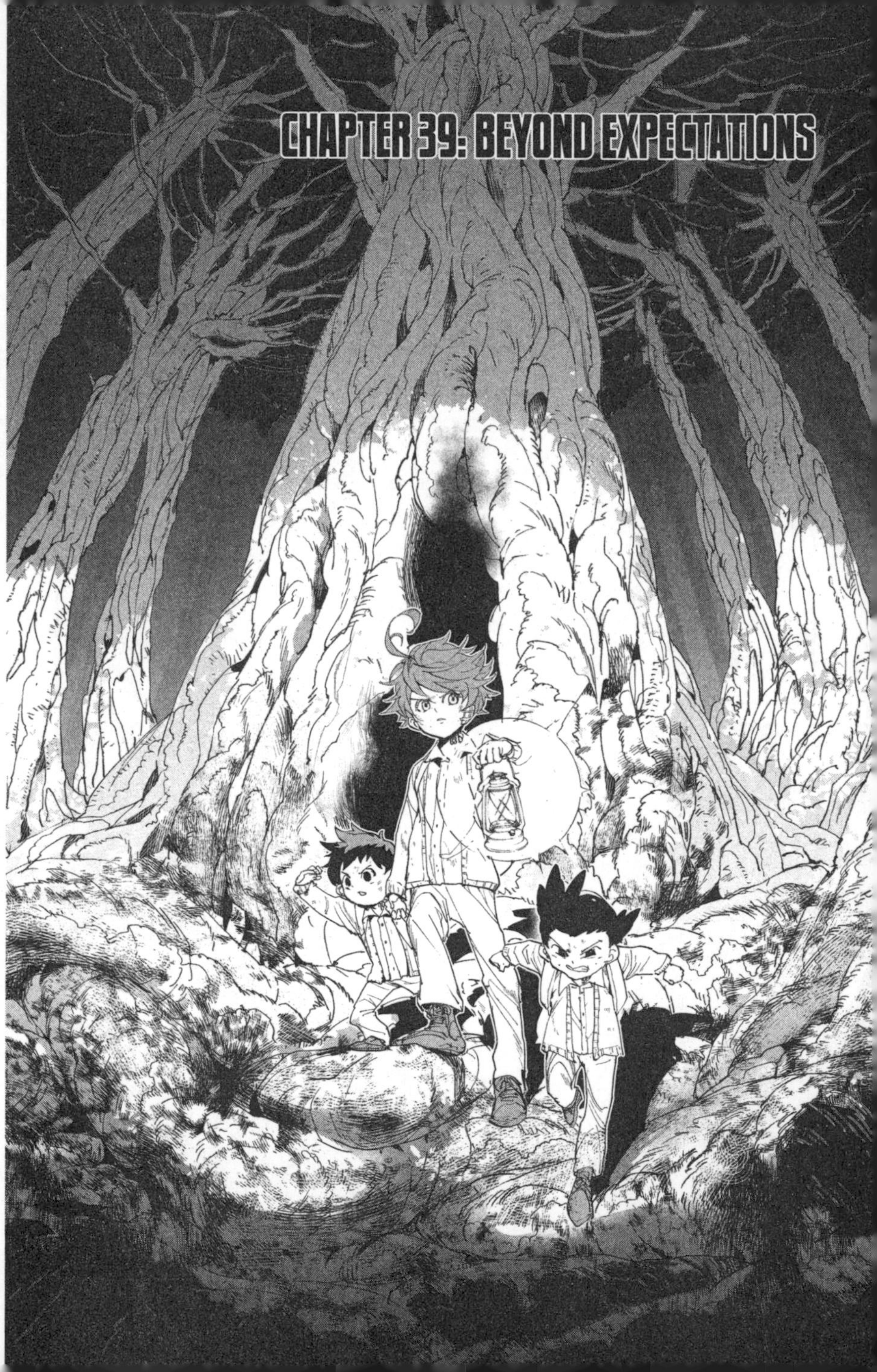
CHAPTER 39: BEYOND EXPECTATIONS

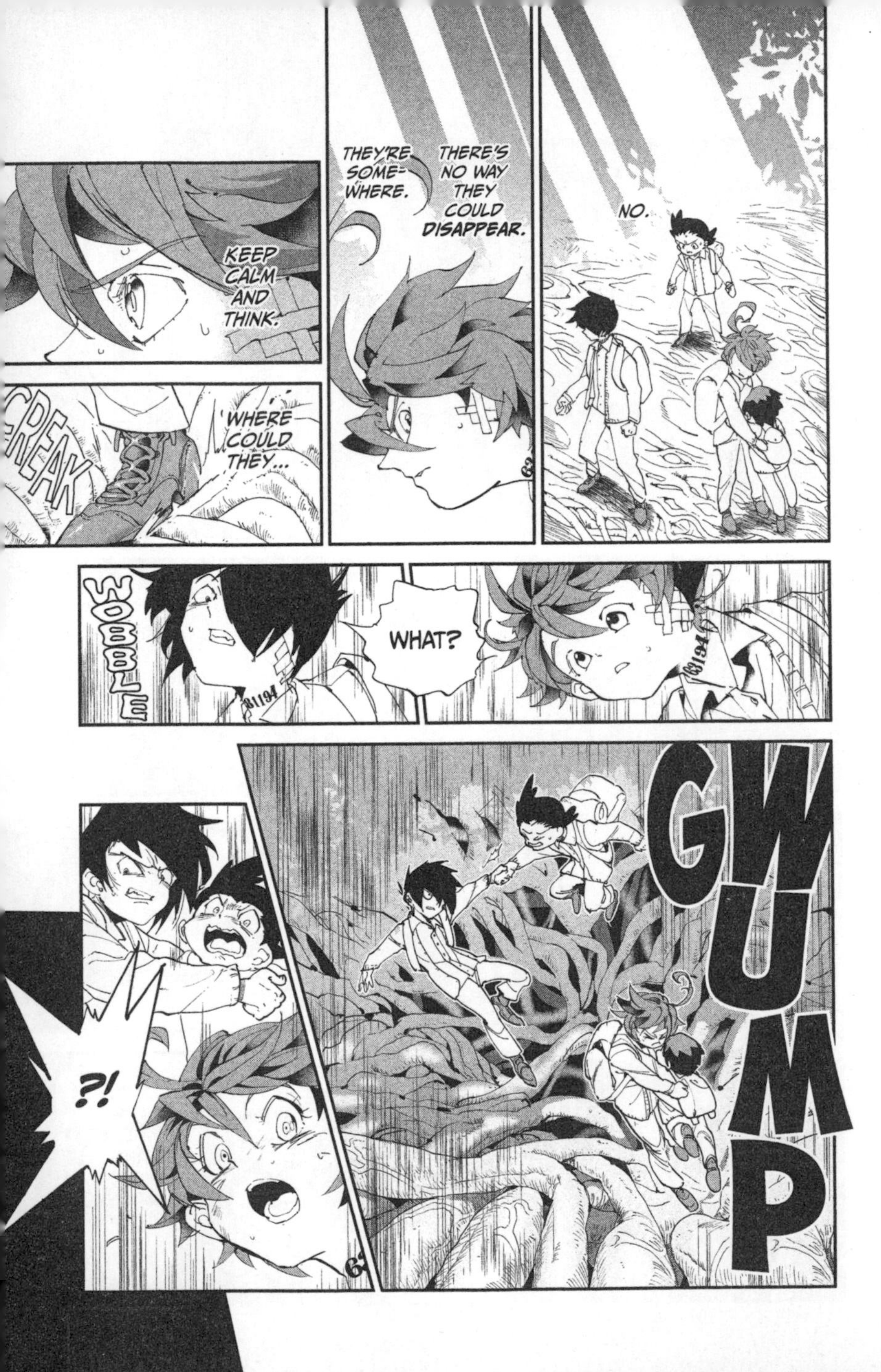
NO.
THERE'S NO WAY THEY COULD DISAPPEAR.
THEY'RE SOME-WHERE.
KEEP CALM AND THINK.
WHERE COULD THEY...
CREAK
WHAT?
WOBBLE
GWUMP
?!

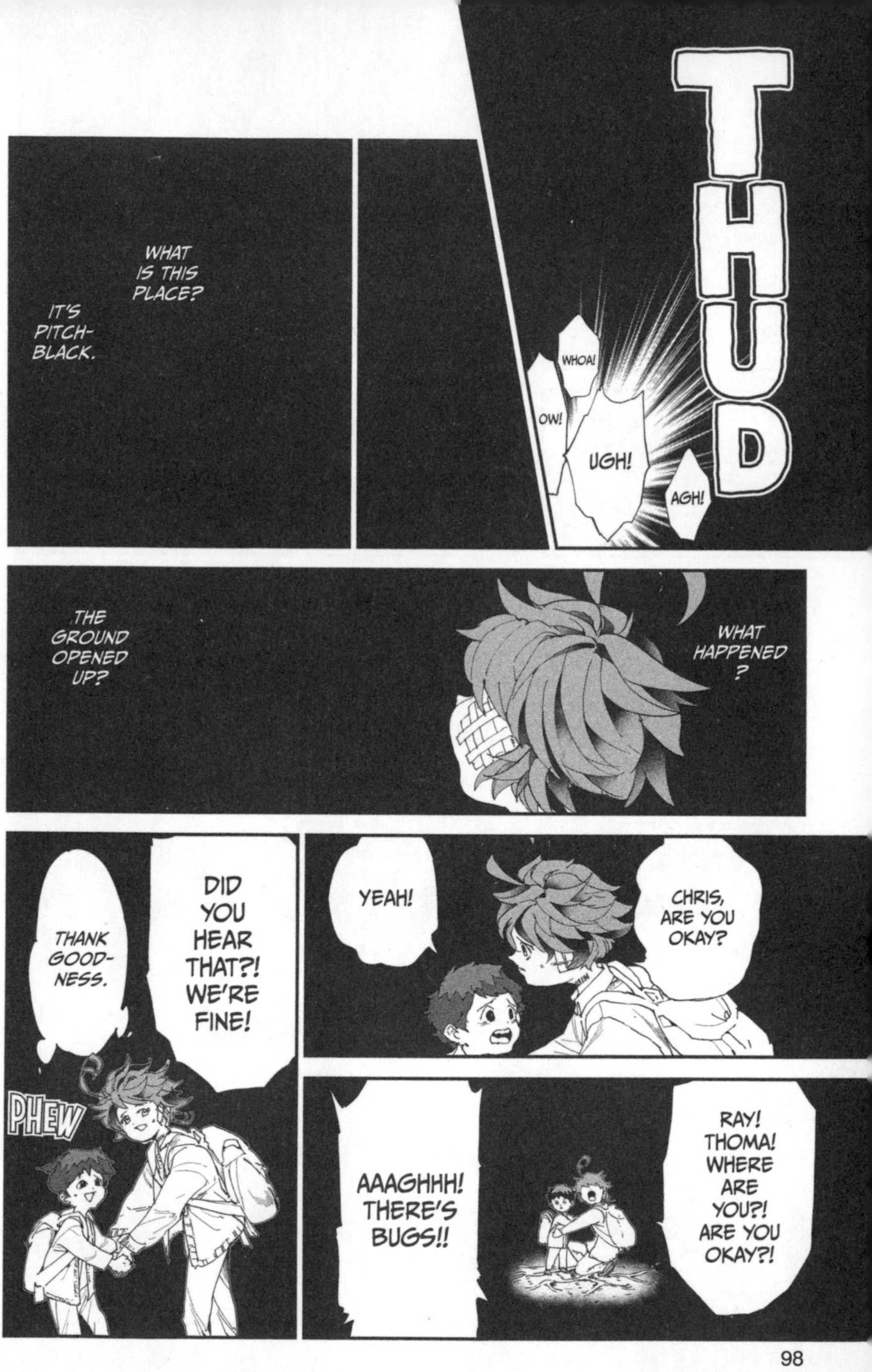
THUD
WHOA!
AGH!
UGH!
OW!
WHAT IS THIS PLACE?
IT'S PITCH-BLACK.
WHAT HAPPENED?
THE GROUND OPENED UP?
CHRIS, ARE YOU OKAY?
YEAH!
RAY! THOMA! WHERE ARE YOU?! ARE YOU OKAY?!
AAAGHHH! THERE'S BUGS!!
DID YOU HEAR THAT?! WE'RE FINE!
THANK GOODNESS.
PHEW

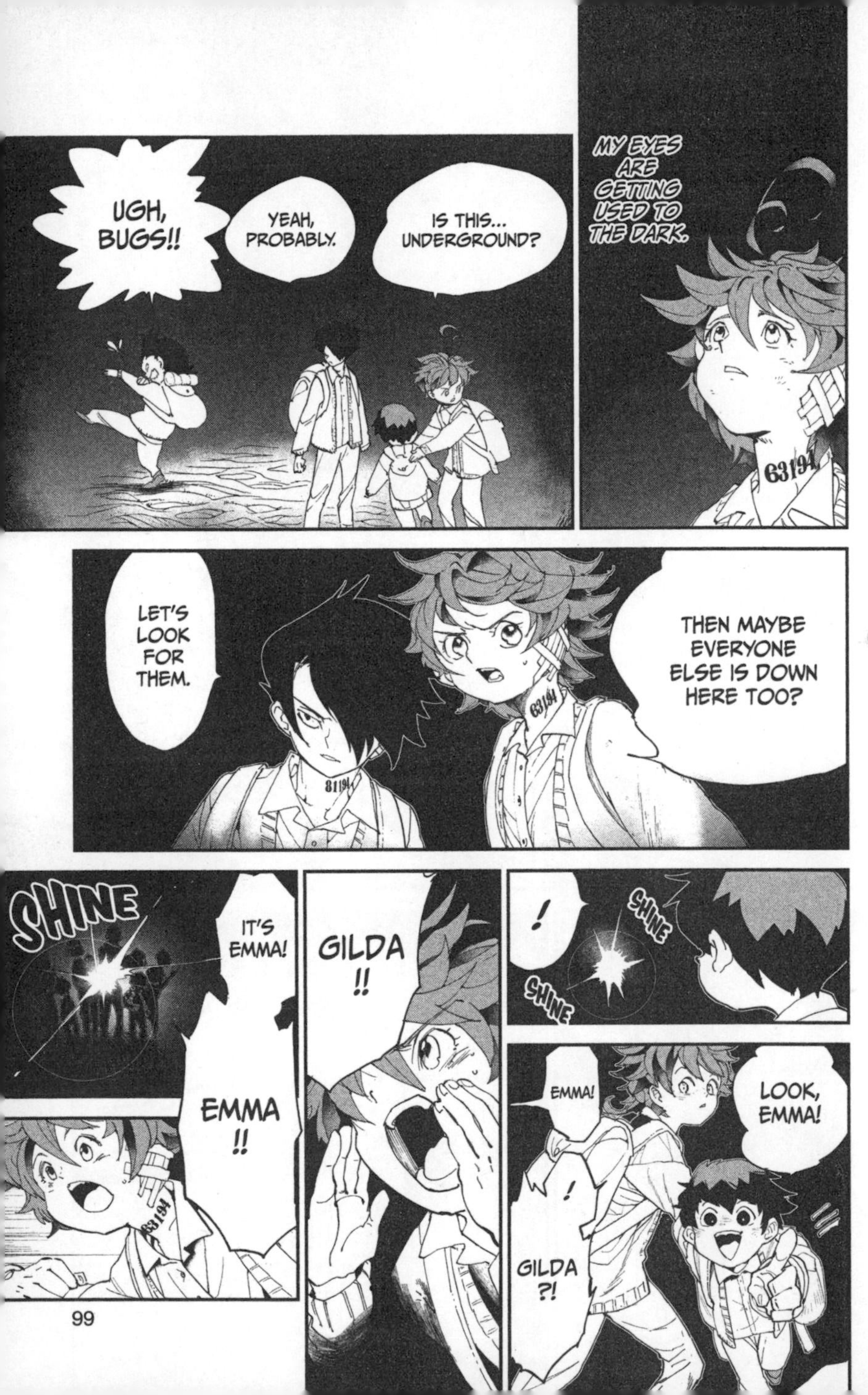
MY EYES ARE GETTING USED TO THE DARK.
IS THIS... UNDERGROUND?
YEAH, PROBABLY.
UGH, BUGS!!
THEN MAYBE EVERYONE ELSE IS DOWN HERE TOO?
LET'S LOOK FOR THEM.
!
SHINE
SHINE
LOOK, EMMA!
EMMA!
!
GILDA ?!
GILDA !!
SHINE
IT'S EMMA!
EMMA !!

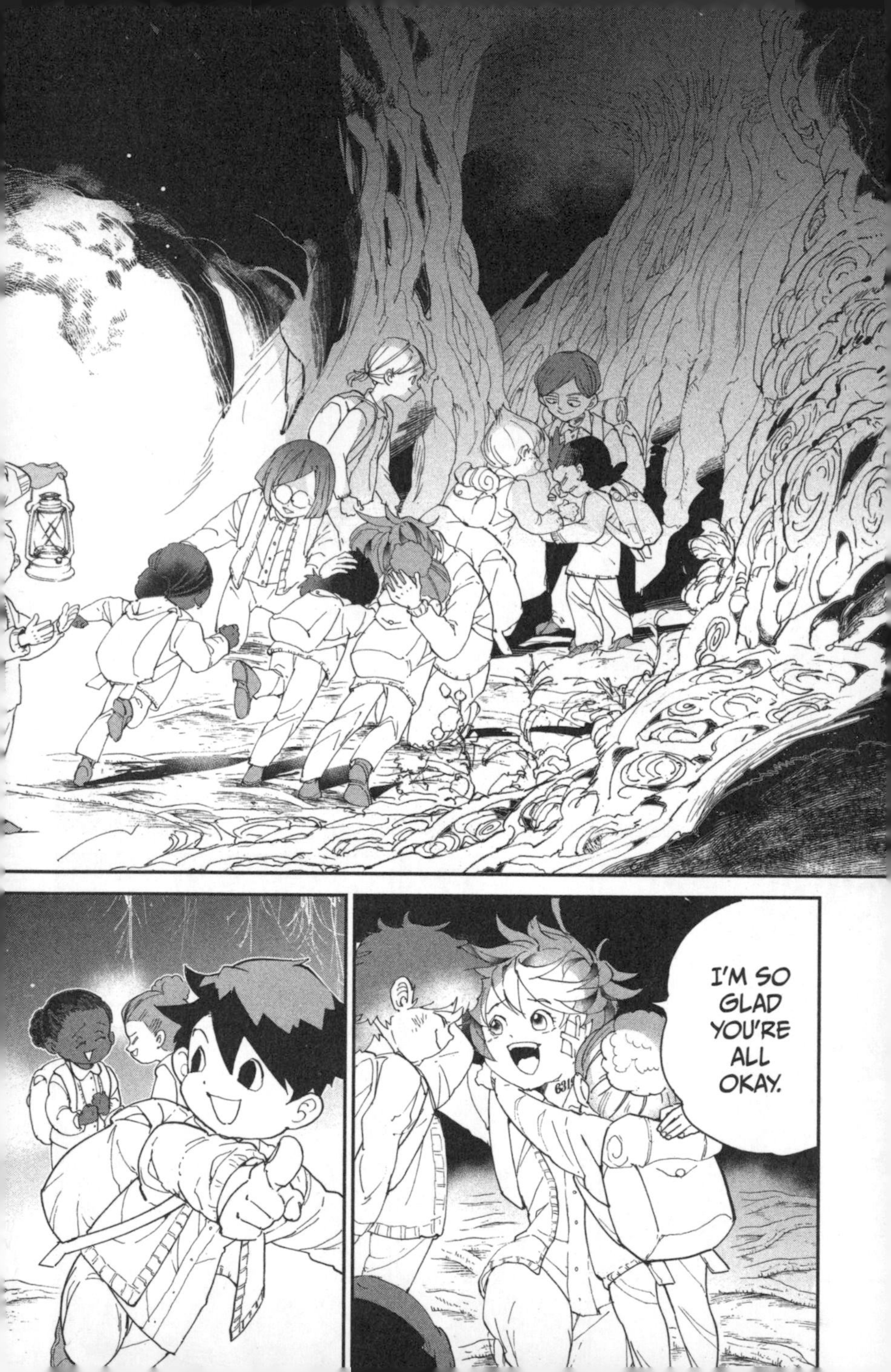
I'M SO GLAD YOU'RE ALL OKAY.

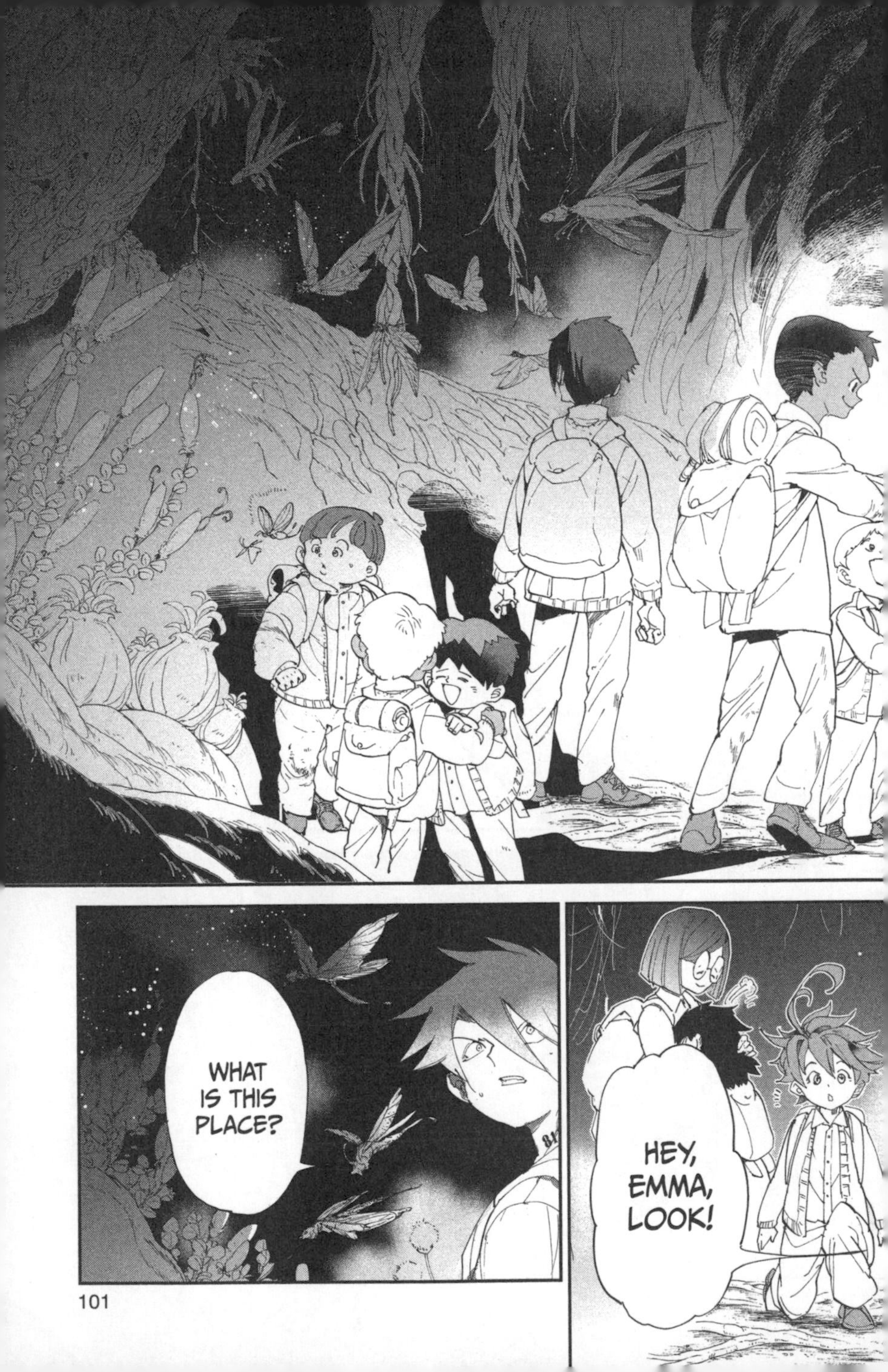
HEY, EMMA, LOOK!
WHAT IS THIS PLACE?

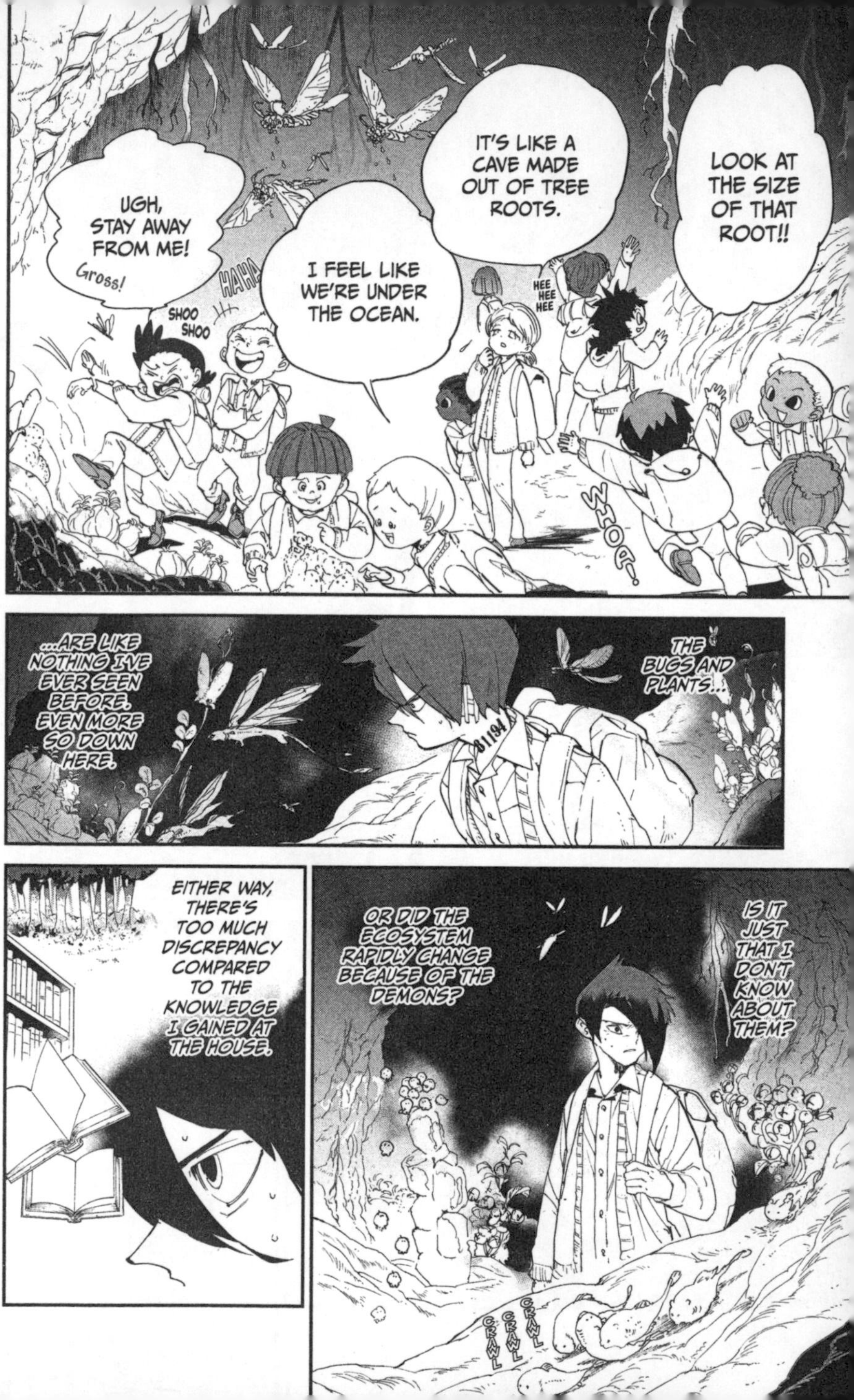
LOOK AT THE SIZE OF THAT ROOT!!
HEE HEE HEE
IT'S LIKE A CAVE MADE OUT OF TREE ROOTS.
I FEEL LIKE WE'RE UNDER THE OCEAN.
HAHA
UGH, STAY AWAY FROM ME!
Gross!
SHOO SHOO
WHOA!
THE BUGS AND PLANTS...
...ARE LIKE NOTHING I'VE EVER SEEN BEFORE. EVEN MORE SO DOWN HERE.
IS IT JUST THAT I DON'T KNOW ABOUT THEM?
OR DID THE ECOSYSTEM RAPIDLY CHANGE BECAUSE OF THE DEMONS?
CRAWL
CRAWL
CRAWL
EITHER WAY, THERE'S TOO MUCH DISCREPANCY COMPARED TO THE KNOWLEDGE I GAINED AT THE HOUSE.

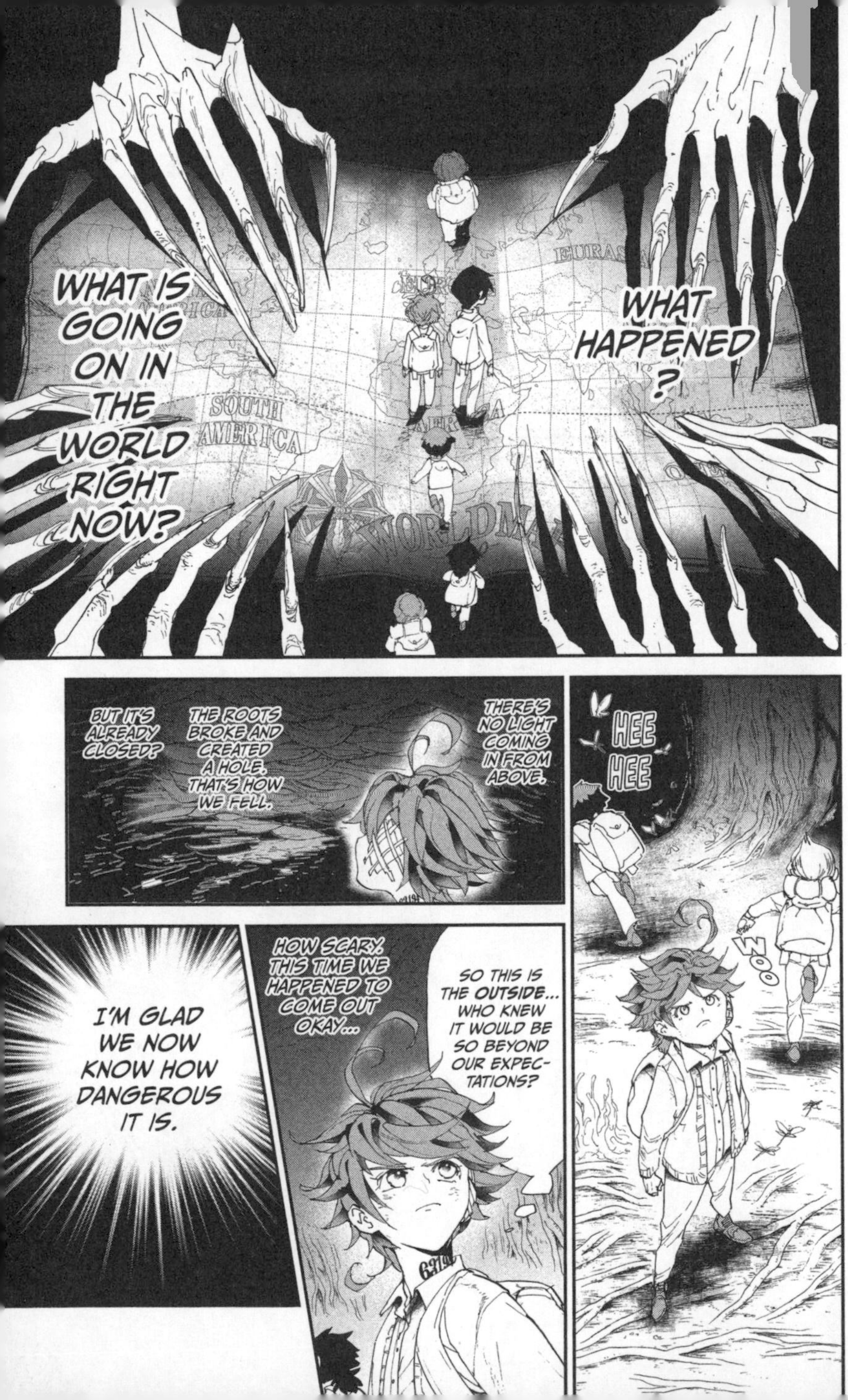
WHAT HAPPENED?
WHAT IS GOING ON IN THE WORLD RIGHT NOW?
SOUTH AMERICA
HEE HEE
WOO
THERE'S NO LIGHT COMING IN FROM ABOVE.
THE ROOTS BROKE AND CREATED A HOLE. THAT'S HOW WE FELL.
BUT IT'S ALREADY CLOSED?
SO THIS IS THE OUTSIDE... WHO KNEW IT WOULD BE SO BEYOND OUR EXPECTATIONS?
HOW SCARY. THIS TIME WE HAPPENED TO COME OUT OKAY...
I'M GLAD WE NOW KNOW HOW DANGEROUS IT IS.

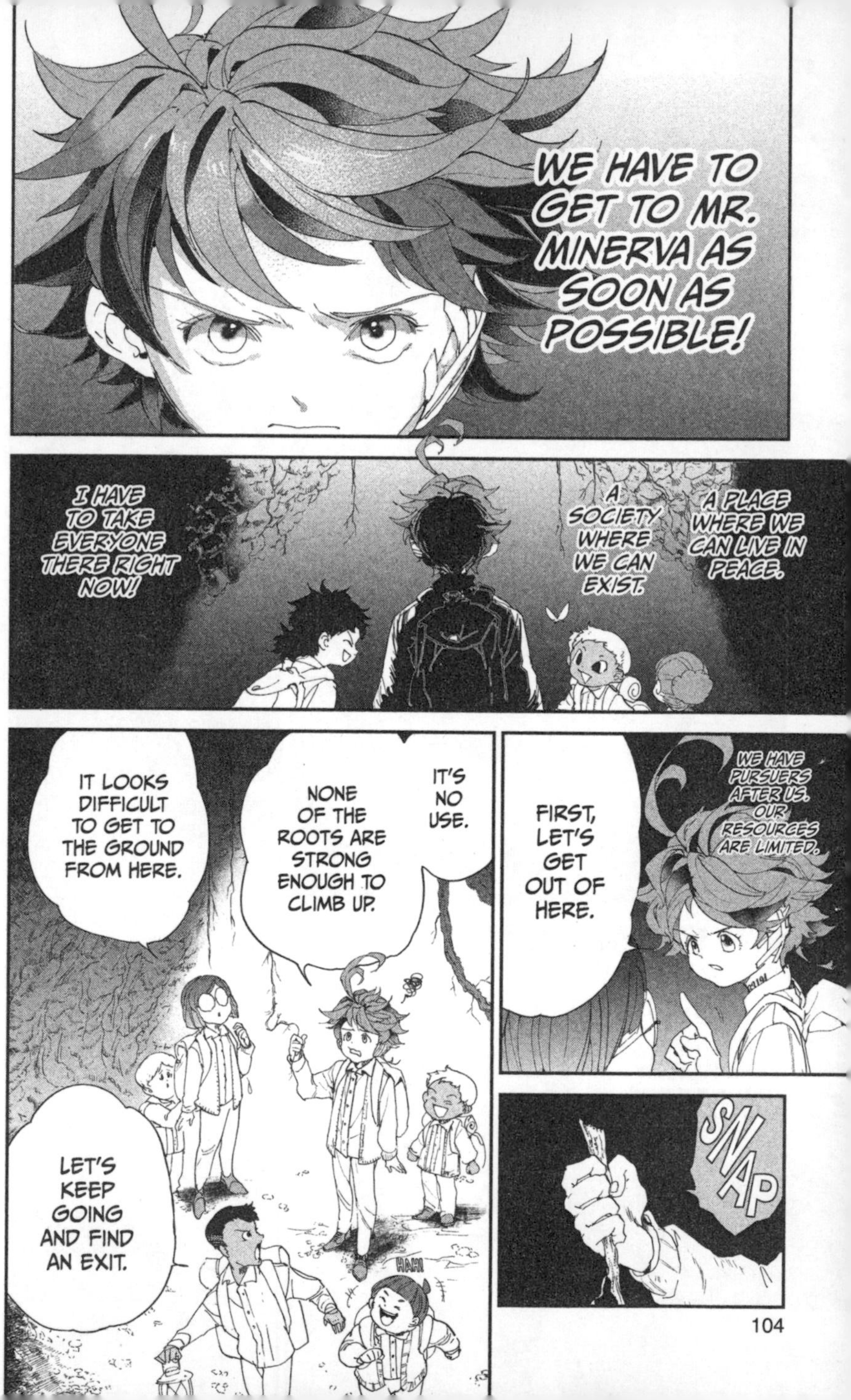
WE HAVE TO GET TO MR. MINERVA AS SOON AS POSSIBLE!
A PLACE WHERE WE CAN LIVE IN PEACE.
A SOCIETY WHERE WE CAN EXIST.
I HAVE TO TAKE EVERYONE THERE RIGHT NOW!
WE HAVE PURSUERS AFTER US. OUR RESOURCES ARE LIMITED.
FIRST, LET'S GET OUT OF HERE.
SNAP
IT'S NO USE.
NONE OF THE ROOTS ARE STRONG ENOUGH TO CLIMB UP.
IT LOOKS DIFFICULT TO GET TO THE GROUND FROM HERE.
HAH!
LET'S KEEP GOING AND FIND AN EXIT.

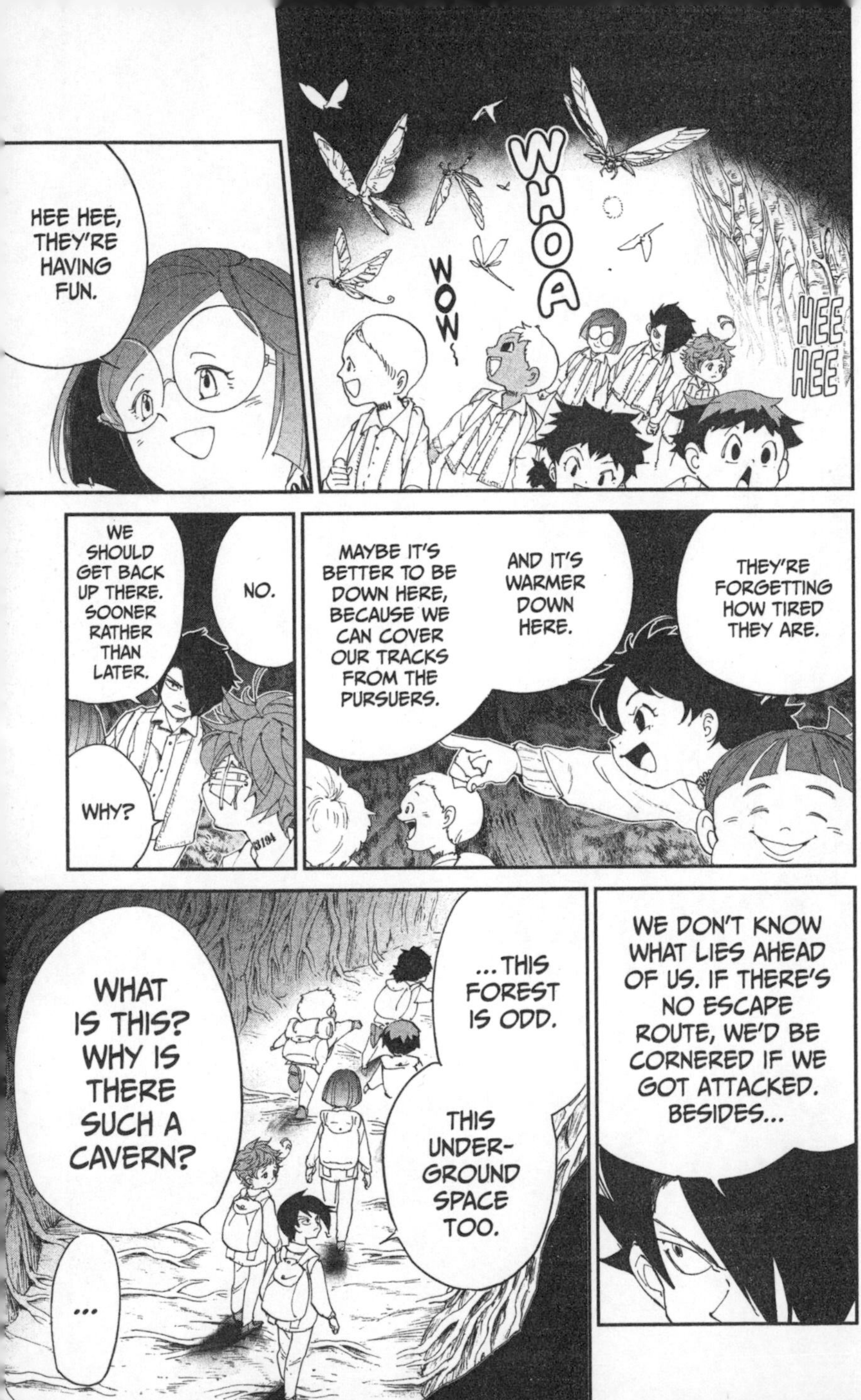
WHOA
WOW~
HEE HEE
HEE HEE, THEY'RE HAVING FUN.
THEY'RE FORGETTING HOW TIRED THEY ARE.
AND IT'S WARMER DOWN HERE.
MAYBE IT'S BETTER TO BE DOWN HERE, BECAUSE WE CAN COVER OUR TRACKS FROM THE PURSUERS.
NO.
WE SHOULD GET BACK UP THERE. SOONER RATHER THAN LATER.
WHY?
WE DON'T KNOW WHAT LIES AHEAD OF US. IF THERE'S NO ESCAPE ROUTE, WE'D BE CORNERED IF WE GOT ATTACKED. BESIDES...
...THIS FOREST IS ODD.
THIS UNDERGROUND SPACE TOO.
WHAT IS THIS? WHY IS THERE SUCH A CAVERN?
...

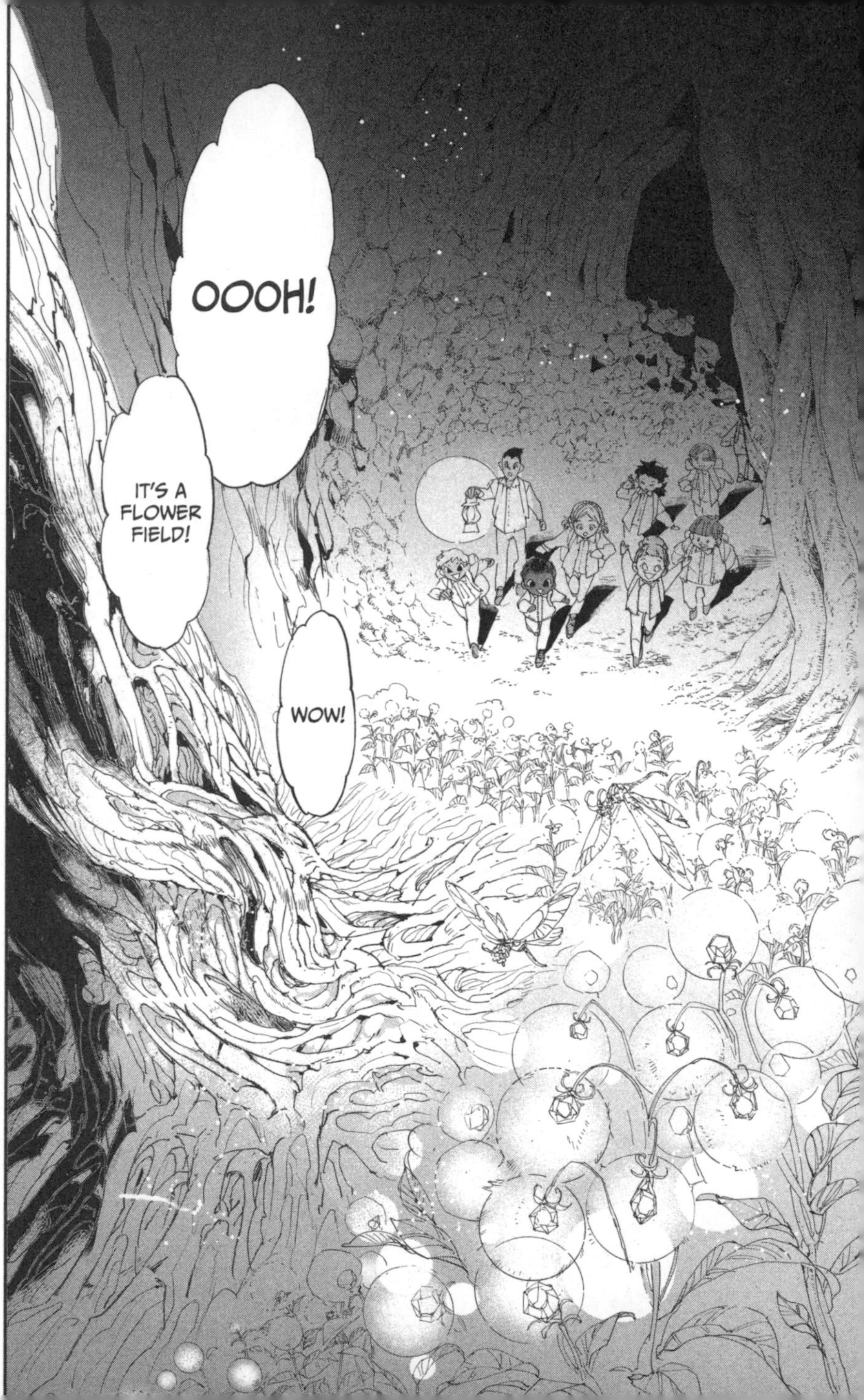
OOOH!
IT'S A FLOWER FIELD!
WOW!

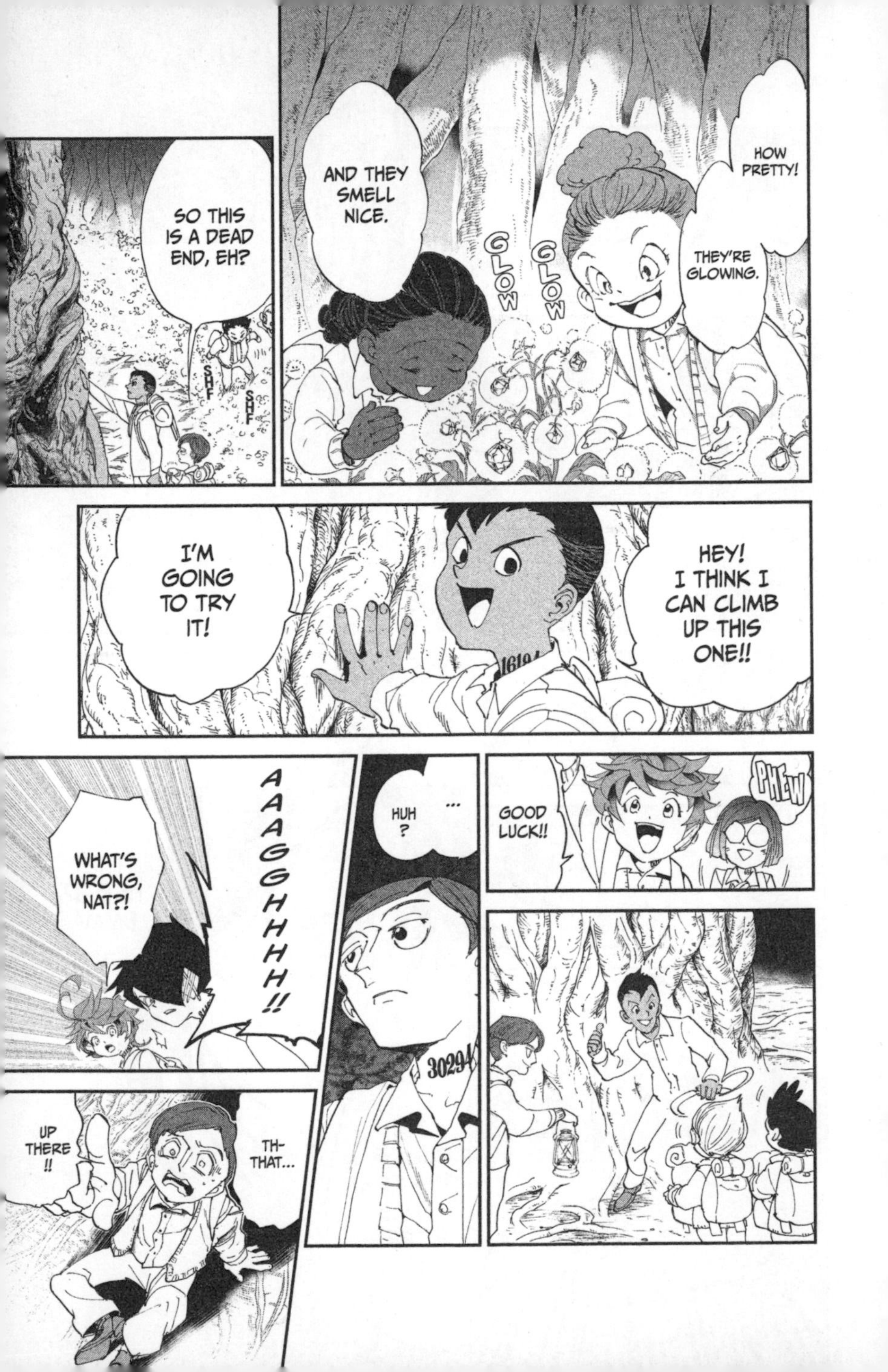
HOW PRETTY!
THEY'RE GLOWING.
GLOW
GLOW
AND THEY SMELL NICE.
SO THIS IS A DEAD END, EH?
SHF
SHF
HEY! I THINK I CAN CLIMB UP THIS ONE!!
I'M GOING TO TRY IT!
PHEW
GOOD LUCK!!
...
HUH?
30294
AAAAGGHHHHH!!
WHAT'S WRONG, NAT?!
TH-THAT...
UP THERE!!

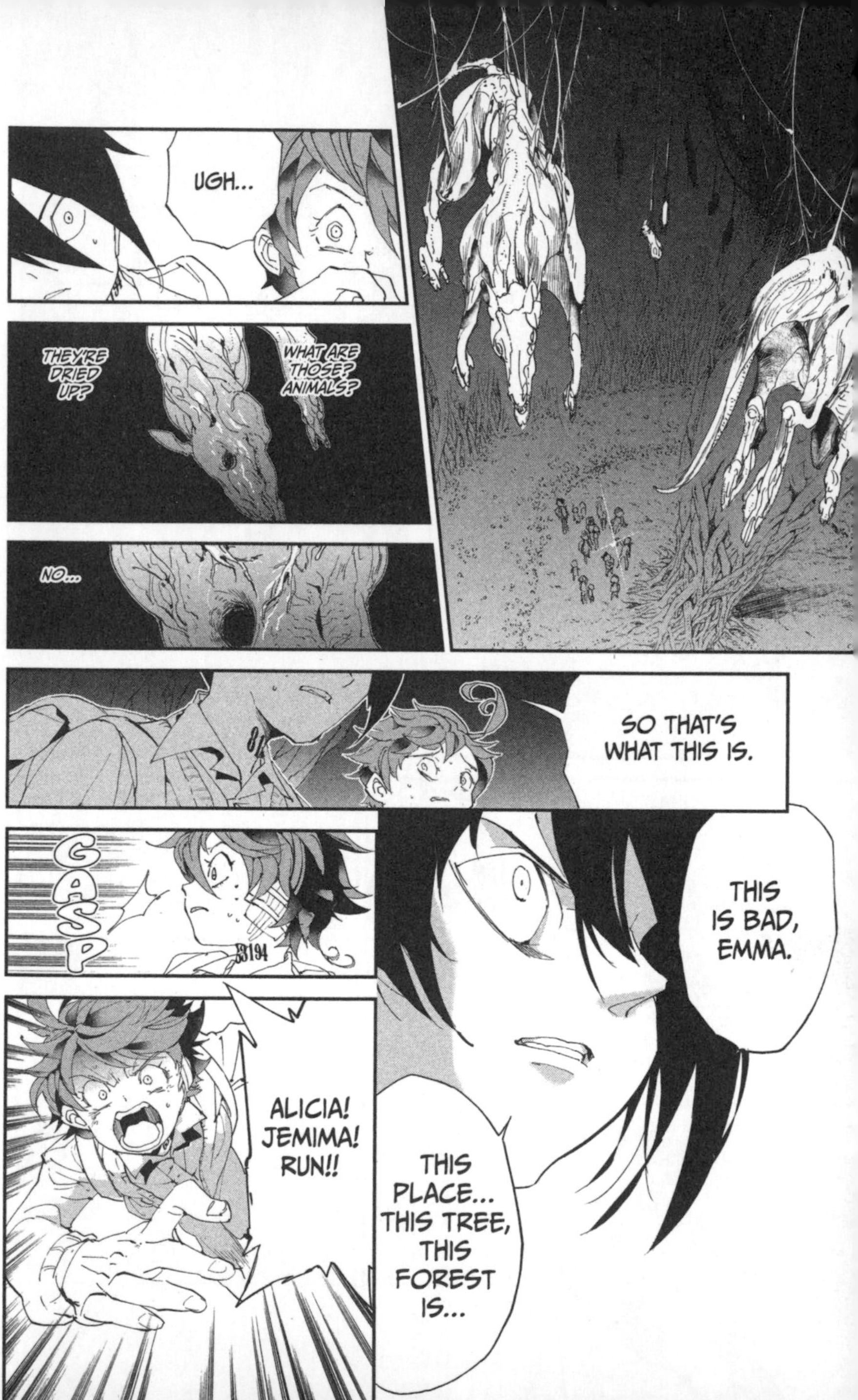
UGH...
WHAT ARE THOSE? ANIMALS?
THEY'RE DRIED UP?
NO...
SO THAT'S WHAT THIS IS.
THIS IS BAD, EMMA.
THIS PLACE... THIS TREE, THIS FOREST IS...
GASP
ALICIA! JEMIMA! RUN!!

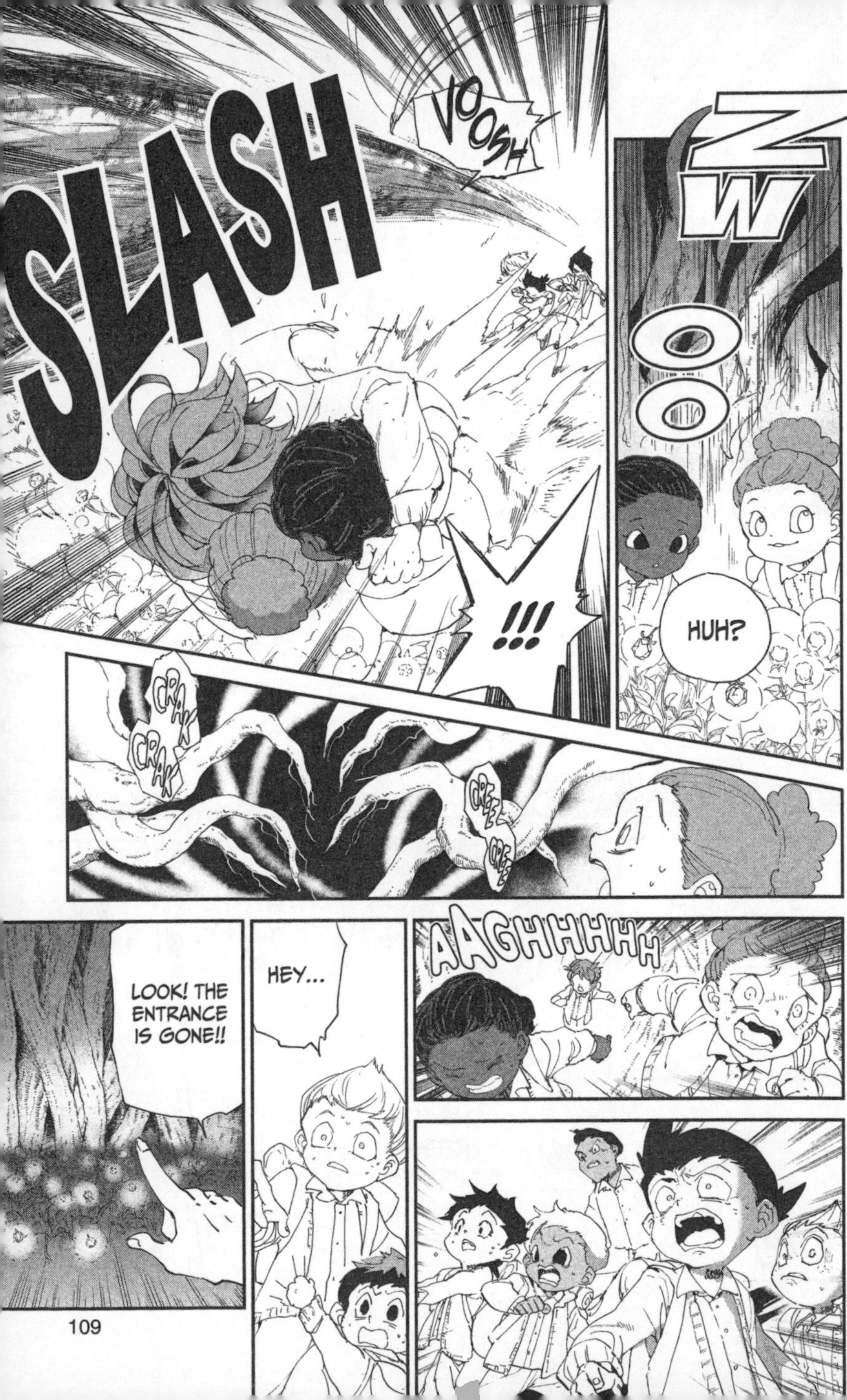
ZWOOO
HUH?
SLASH
VOOSH
!!!
CRAK CRAK
CREE CREE
AAGHHHHHH
HEY...
LOOK! THE ENTRANCE IS GONE!!

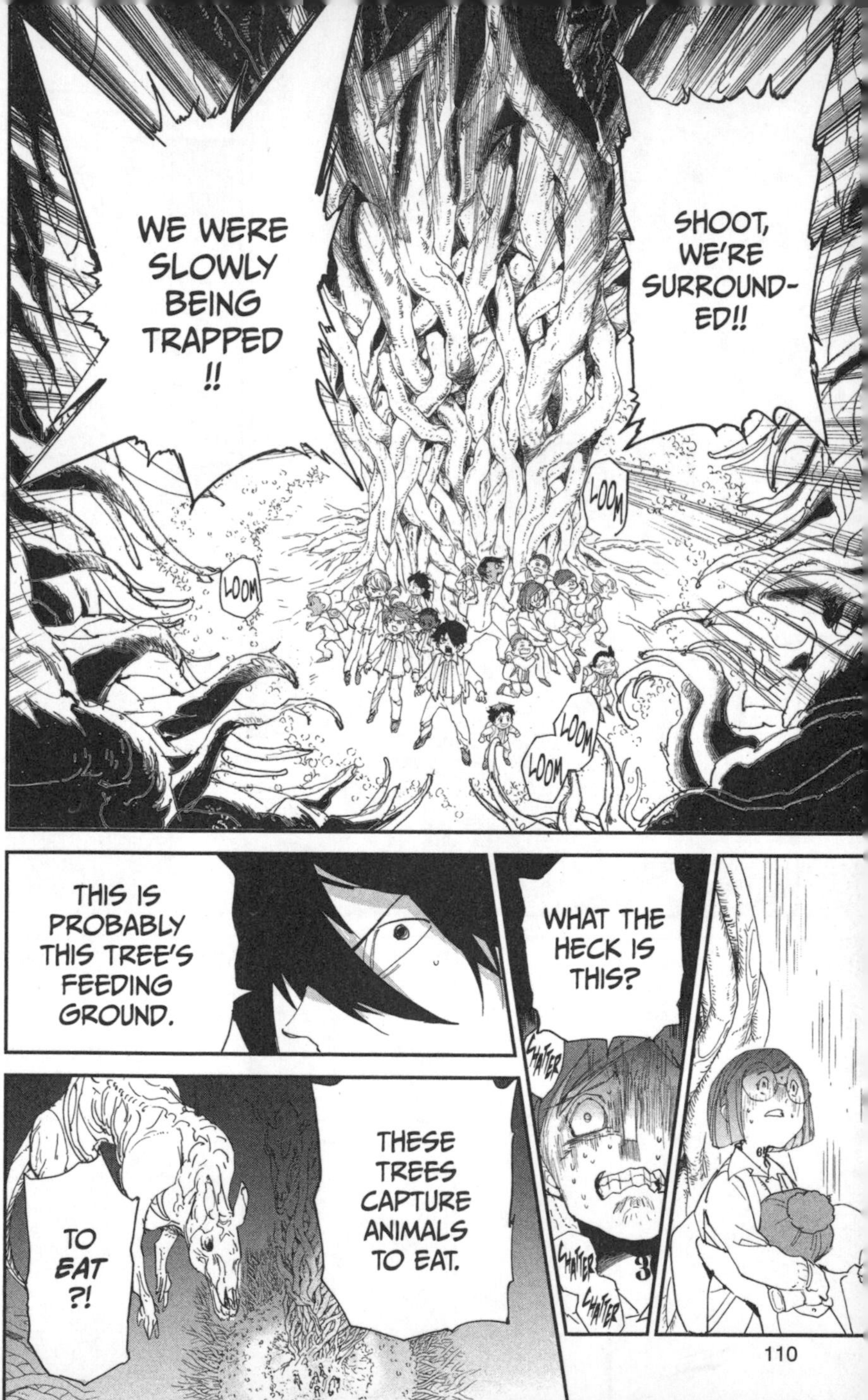
SHOOT, WE'RE SURROUND-ED!!
WE WERE SLOWLY BEING TRAPPED!!
LOOM
LOOM
LOOM
LOOM
WHAT THE HECK IS THIS?
CHATTER
CHATTER
CHATTER
THIS IS PROBABLY THIS TREE'S FEEDING GROUND.
THESE TREES CAPTURE ANIMALS TO EAT.
TO EAT?!

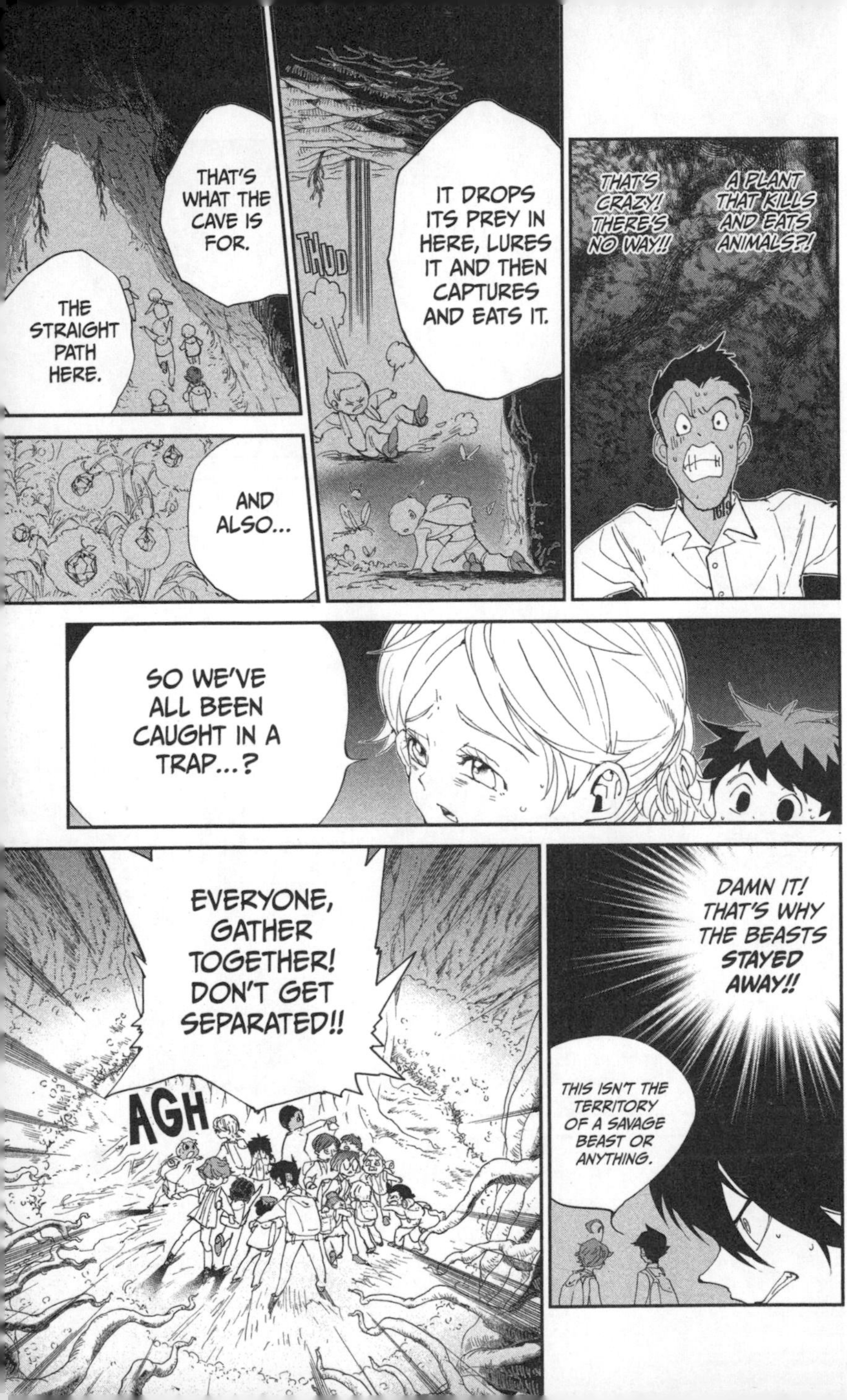
A PLANT THAT KILLS AND EATS ANIMALS?!
THAT'S CRAZY! THERE'S NO WAY!!
IT DROPS ITS PREY IN HERE, LURES IT AND THEN CAPTURES AND EATS IT.
THUD
THAT'S WHAT THE CAVE IS FOR.
THE STRAIGHT PATH HERE.
AND ALSO...
SO WE'VE ALL BEEN CAUGHT IN A TRAP...?
DAMN IT! THAT'S WHY THE BEASTS STAYED AWAY!!
THIS ISN'T THE TERRITORY OF A SAVAGE BEAST OR ANYTHING.
EVERYONE, GATHER TOGETHER! DON'T GET SEPARATED!!
AGH

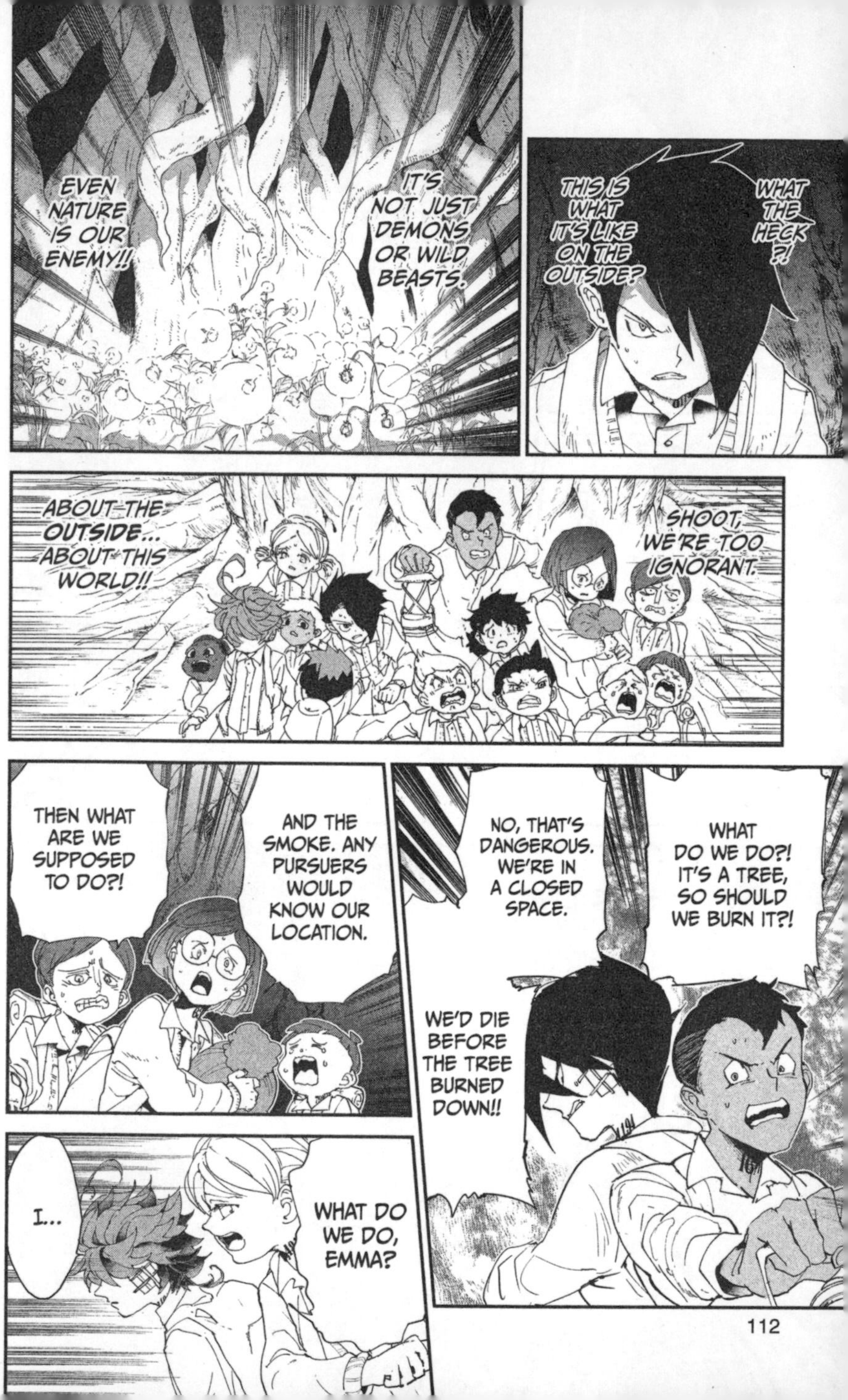
WHAT THE HECK?!
THIS IS WHAT IT'S LIKE ON THE OUTSIDE?
IT'S NOT JUST DEMONS OR WILD BEASTS.
EVEN NATURE IS OUR ENEMY!!
SHOOT, WE'RE TOO IGNORANT.
ABOUT THE OUTSIDE... ABOUT THIS WORLD!!
WHAT DO WE DO?! IT'S A TREE, SO SHOULD WE BURN IT?!
NO, THAT'S DANGEROUS. WE'RE IN A CLOSED SPACE.
WE'D DIE BEFORE THE TREE BURNED DOWN!!
AND THE SMOKE. ANY PURSUERS WOULD KNOW OUR LOCATION.
THEN WHAT ARE WE SUPPOSED TO DO?!
WHAT DO WE DO, EMMA?
I...

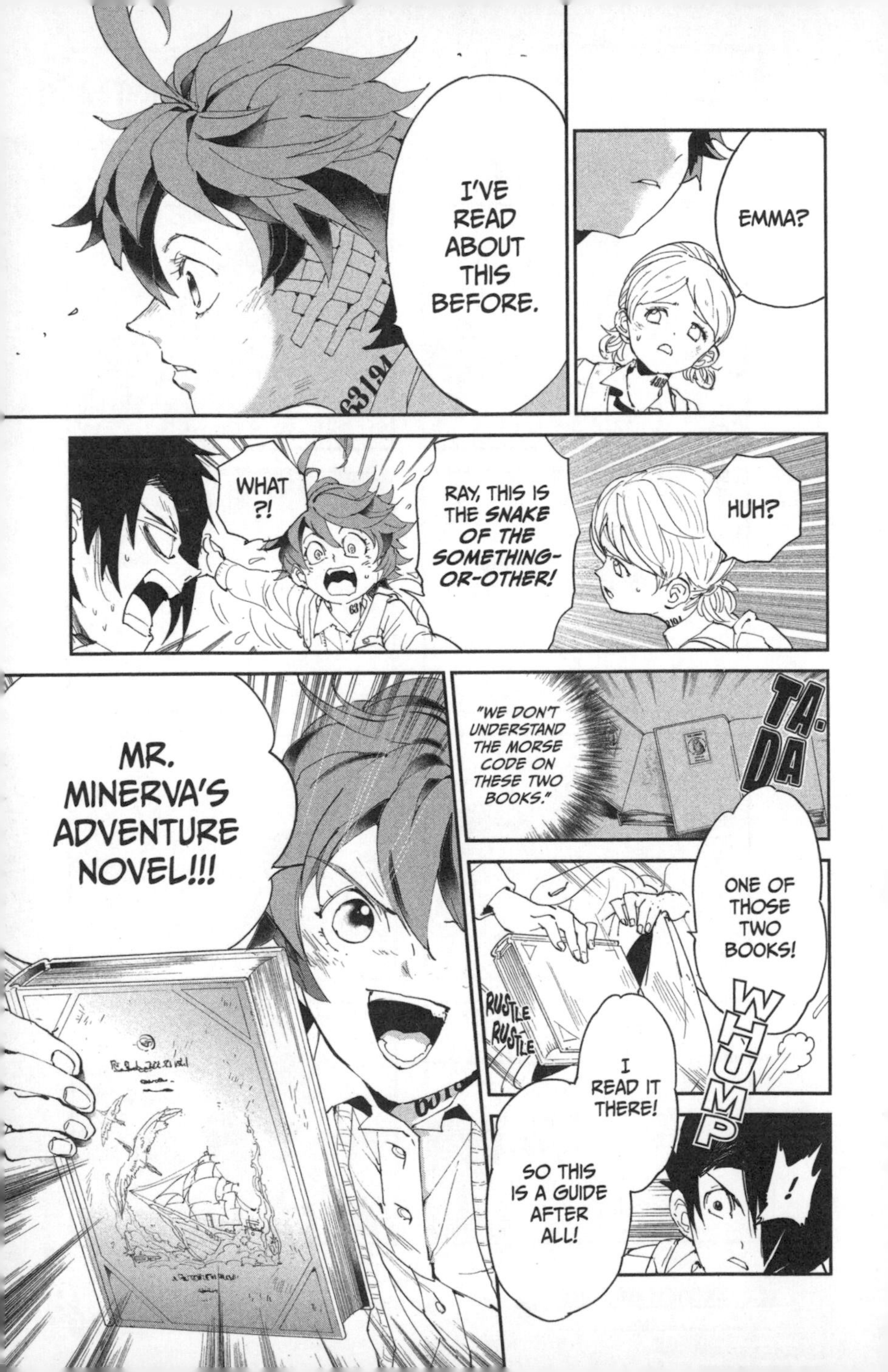
EMMA?
I'VE READ ABOUT THIS BEFORE.
HUH?
RAY, THIS IS THE *SNAKE OF THE SOMETHING-OR-OTHER!*
WHAT ?!
TA-DA
"WE DON'T UNDERSTAND THE MORSE CODE ON THESE TWO BOOKS."
ONE OF THOSE TWO BOOKS!
WHUMP
RUSTLE RUSTLE
!
MR. MINERVA'S ADVENTURE NOVEL!!!
I READ IT THERE!
SO THIS IS A GUIDE AFTER ALL!

SIDE STORY 2-2

ME TOO

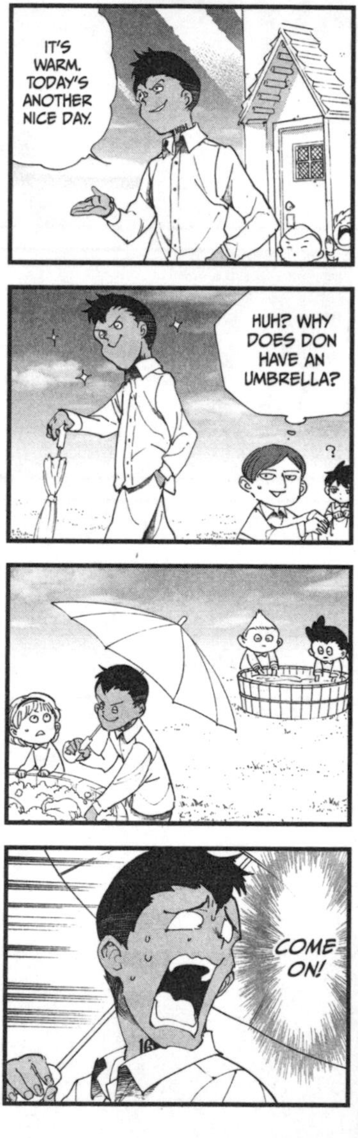
IT'S WARM. TODAY'S ANOTHER NICE DAY.
HUH? WHY DOES DON HAVE AN UMBRELLA?
?
COME ON!

THE UMBRELLA AND I

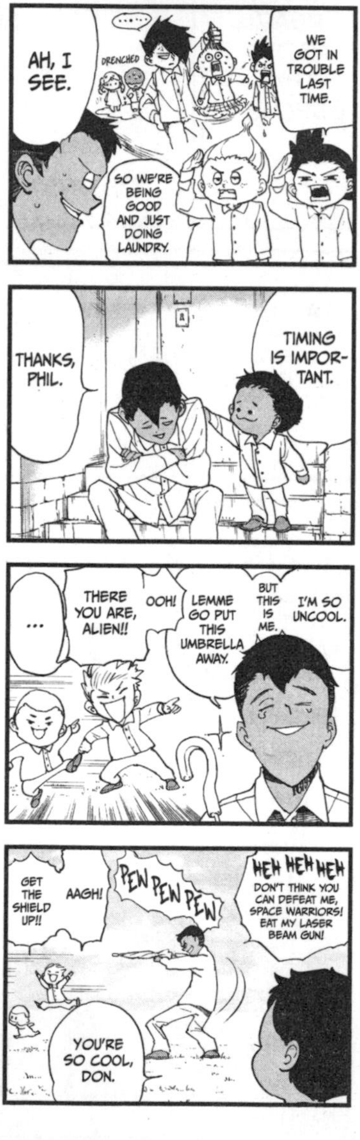
WE GOT IN TROUBLE LAST TIME.
......
DRENCHED
AH, I SEE.
SO WE'RE BEING GOOD AND JUST DOING LAUNDRY.
TIMING IS IMPORTANT.
THANKS, PHIL.
I'M SO UNCOOL.
BUT THIS IS ME.
LEMME GO PUT THIS UMBRELLA AWAY.
OOH!
THERE YOU ARE, ALIEN!!
...
HEH HEH HEH
DON'T THINK YOU CAN DEFEAT ME, SPACE WARRIORS! EAT MY LASER BEAM GUN!
PEW PEW PEW
AAGH!
GET THE SHIELD UP!!
YOU'RE SO COOL, DON.

TO BE CONTINUED IN SIDE STORY 2-3

CHAPTER 40: THE SNAKES OF ALVAPINERA

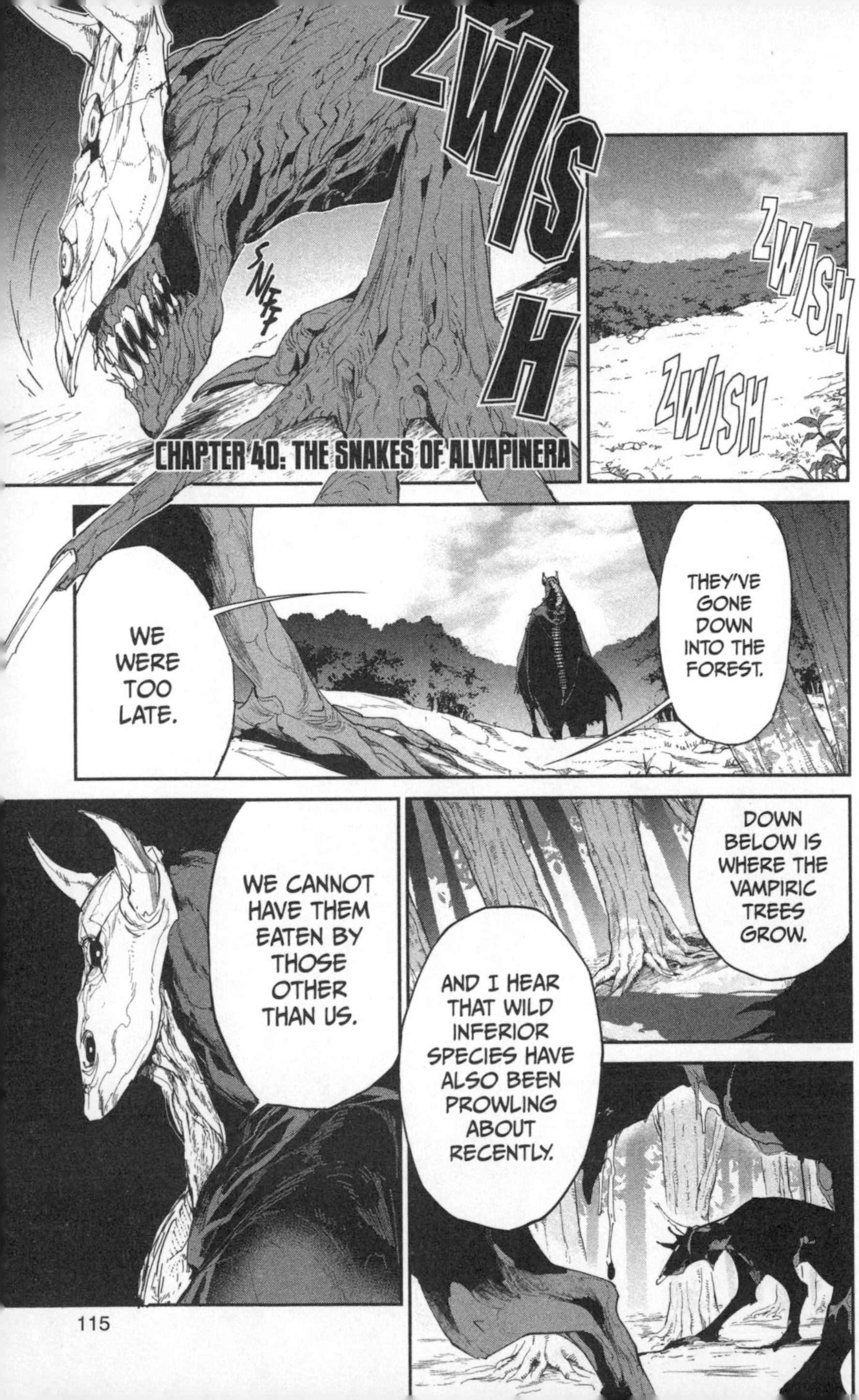
ZWISH
ZWISH
ZWISH
SNIFF
THEY'VE GONE DOWN INTO THE FOREST.
WE WERE TOO LATE.
DOWN BELOW IS WHERE THE VAMPIRIC TREES GROW.
AND I HEAR THAT WILD INFERIOR SPECIES HAVE ALSO BEEN PROWLING ABOUT RECENTLY.
WE CANNOT HAVE THEM EATEN BY THOSE OTHER THAN US.

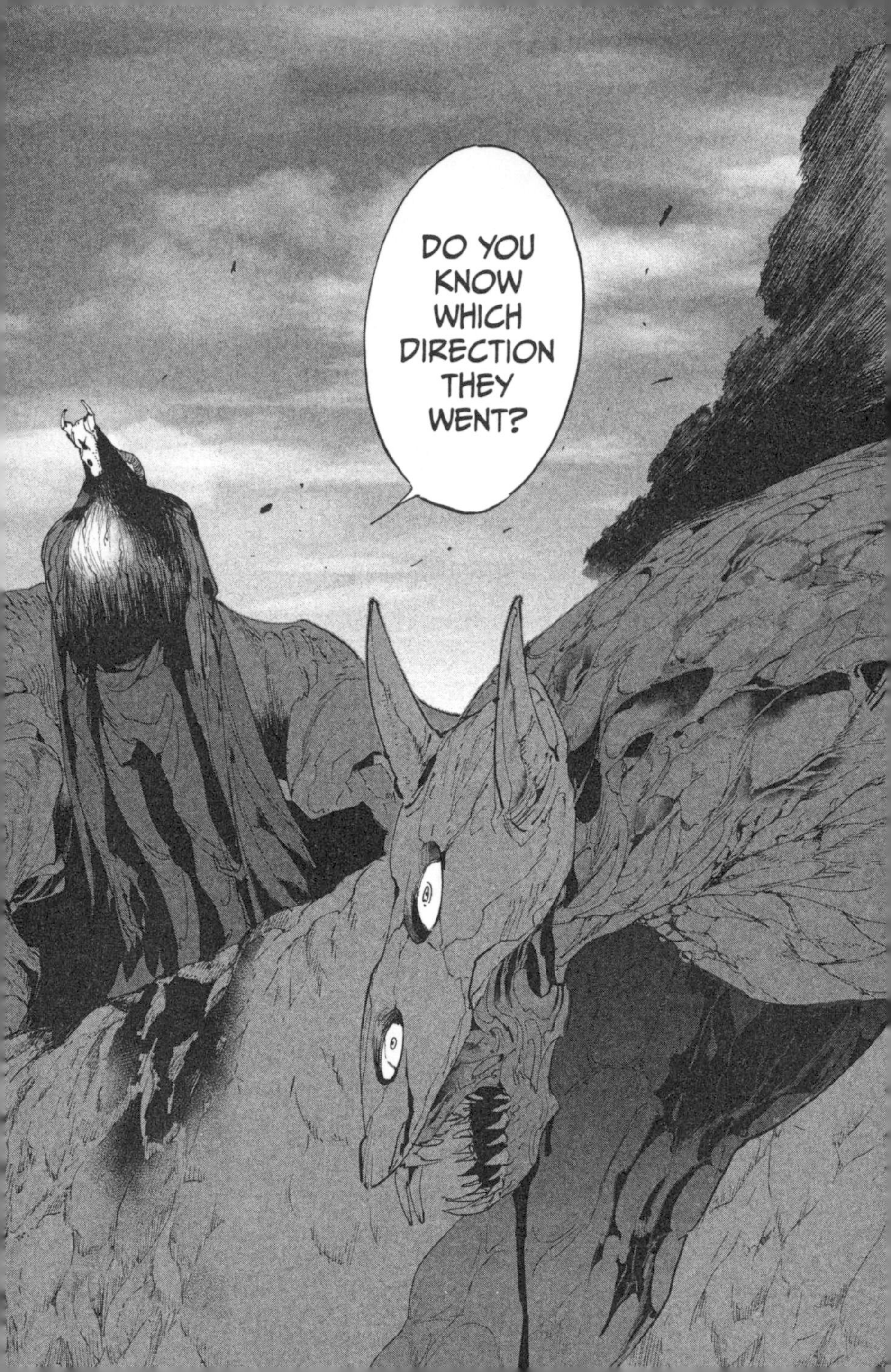
DO YOU KNOW WHICH DIRECTION THEY WENT?

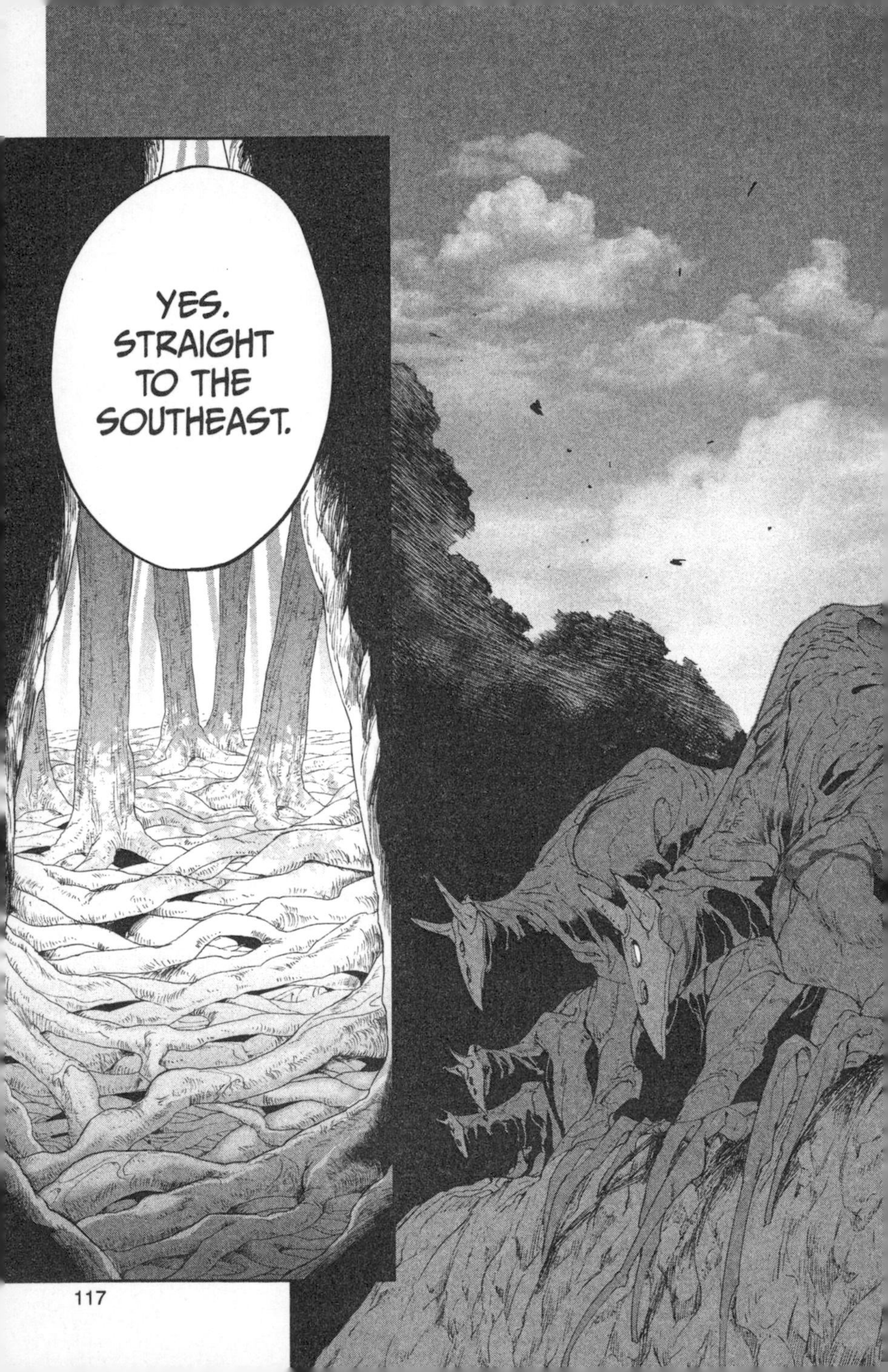
YES. STRAIGHT TO THE SOUTHEAST.

CHAPTER 40: THE SNAKES OF ALVAPINERA

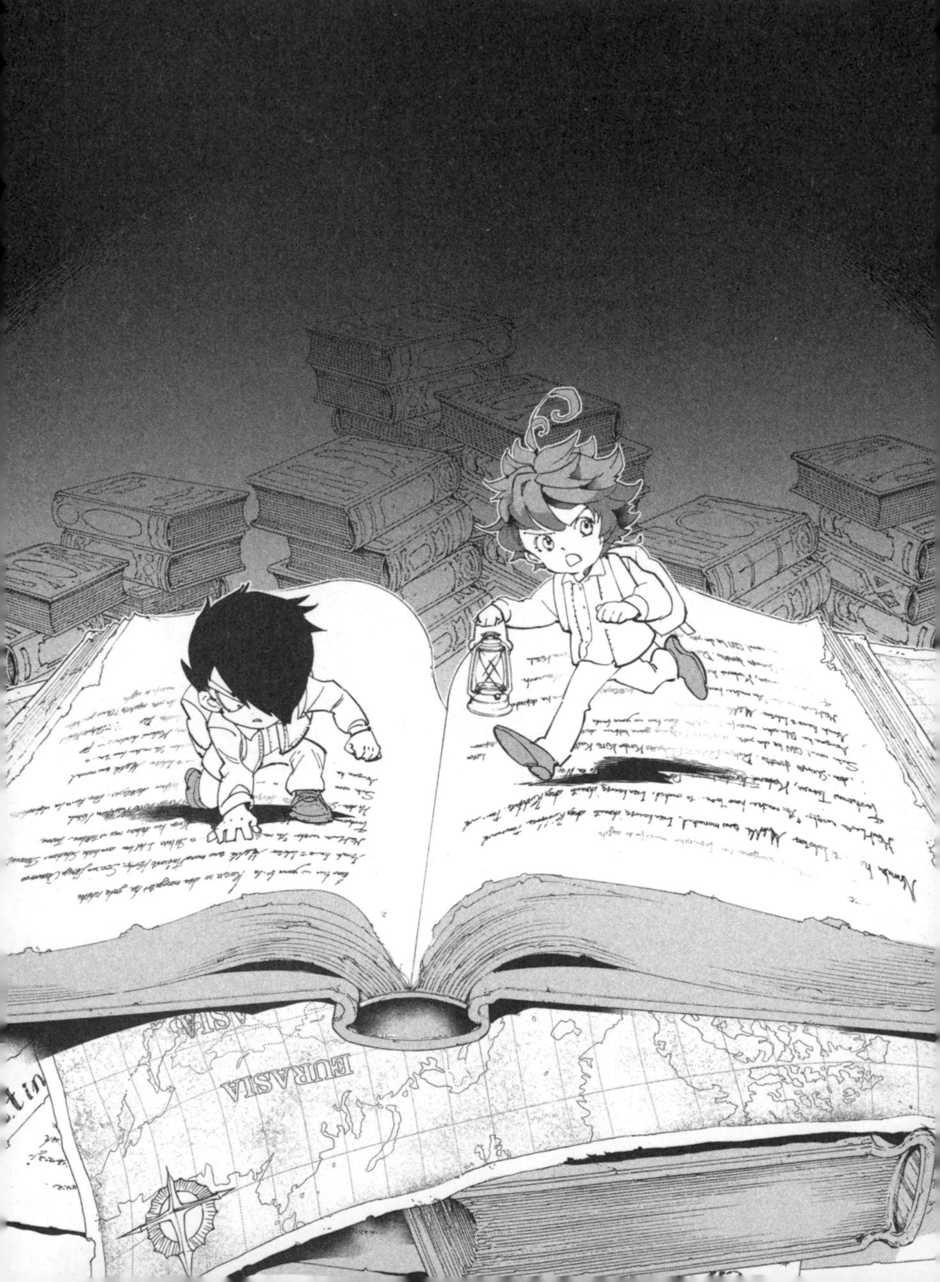
EURASIA

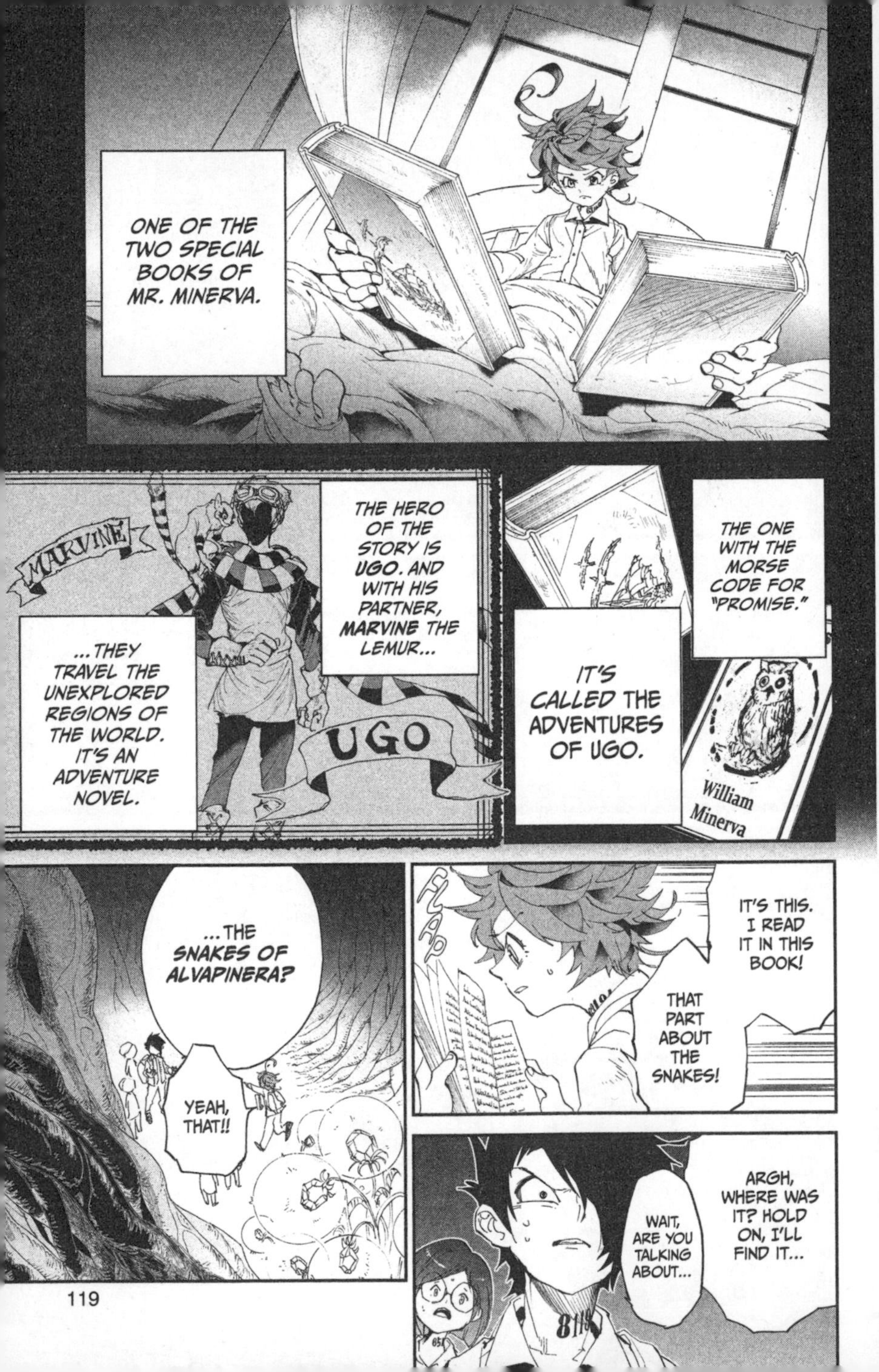
ONE OF THE TWO SPECIAL BOOKS OF MR. MINERVA.
THE ONE WITH THE MORSE CODE FOR "PROMISE."
IT'S CALLED THE ADVENTURES OF UGO.
William Minerva
THE HERO OF THE STORY IS UGO. AND WITH HIS PARTNER, MARVINE THE LEMUR...
MARVINE
UGO
...THEY TRAVEL THE UNEXPLORED REGIONS OF THE WORLD. IT'S AN ADVENTURE NOVEL.
FLAP
IT'S THIS. I READ IT IN THIS BOOK!
THAT PART ABOUT THE SNAKES!
ARGH, WHERE WAS IT? HOLD ON, I'LL FIND IT...
WAIT, ARE YOU TALKING ABOUT...
...THE SNAKES OF ALVAPINERA?
YEAH, THAT!!

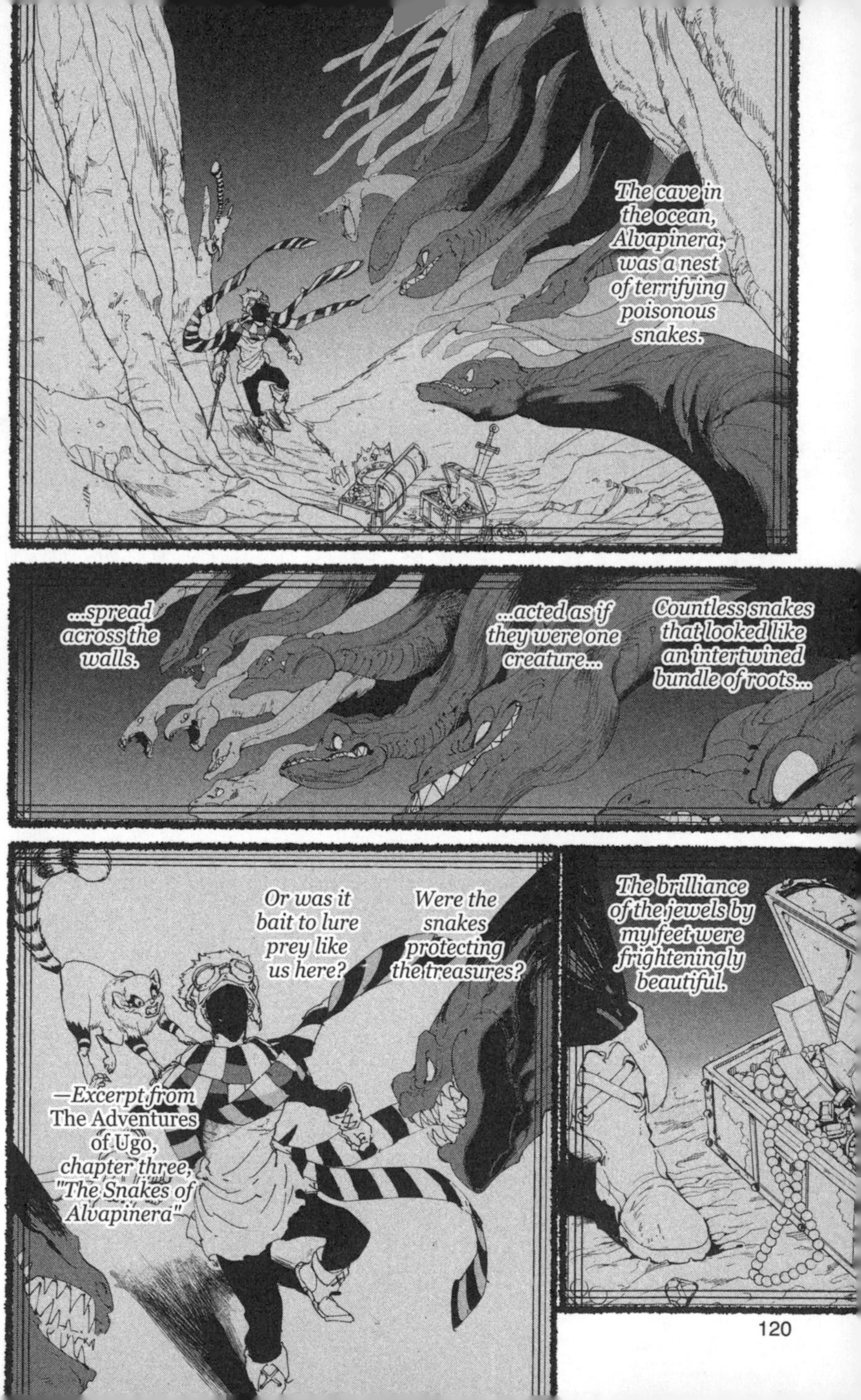
The cave in the ocean, Alvapinera, was a nest of terrifying poisonous snakes.
Countless snakes that looked like an intertwined bundle of roots...
...acted as if they were one creature...
...spread across the walls.
The brilliance of the jewels by my feet were frighteningly beautiful.
Were the snakes protecting the treasures?
Or was it bait to lure prey like us here?
—Excerpt from The Adventures of Ugo, chapter three, "The Snakes of Alvapinera"

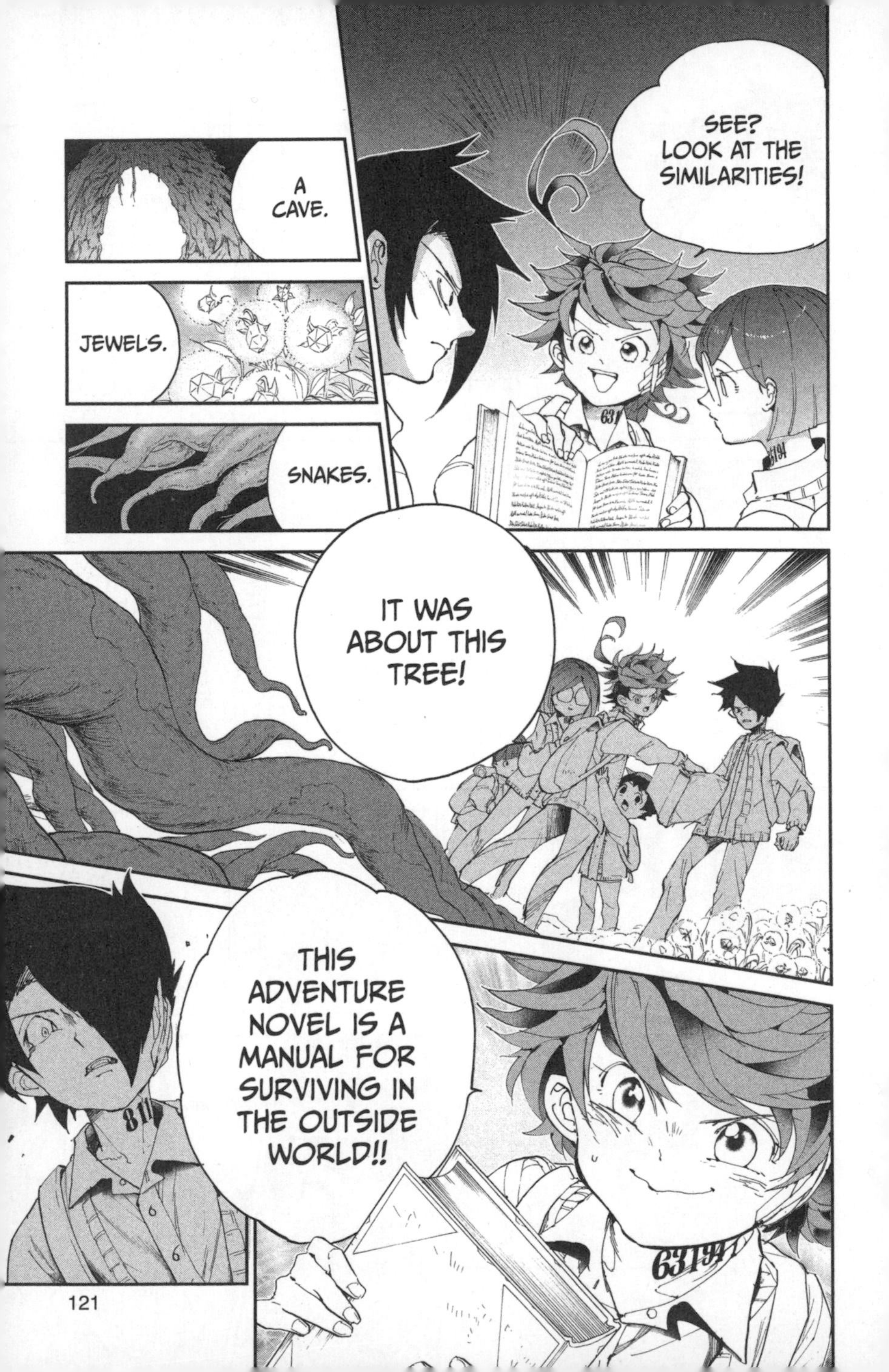
SEE? LOOK AT THE SIMILARITIES!
A CAVE.
JEWELS.
SNAKES.
IT WAS ABOUT THIS TREE!
THIS ADVENTURE NOVEL IS A MANUAL FOR SURVIVING IN THE OUTSIDE WORLD!!

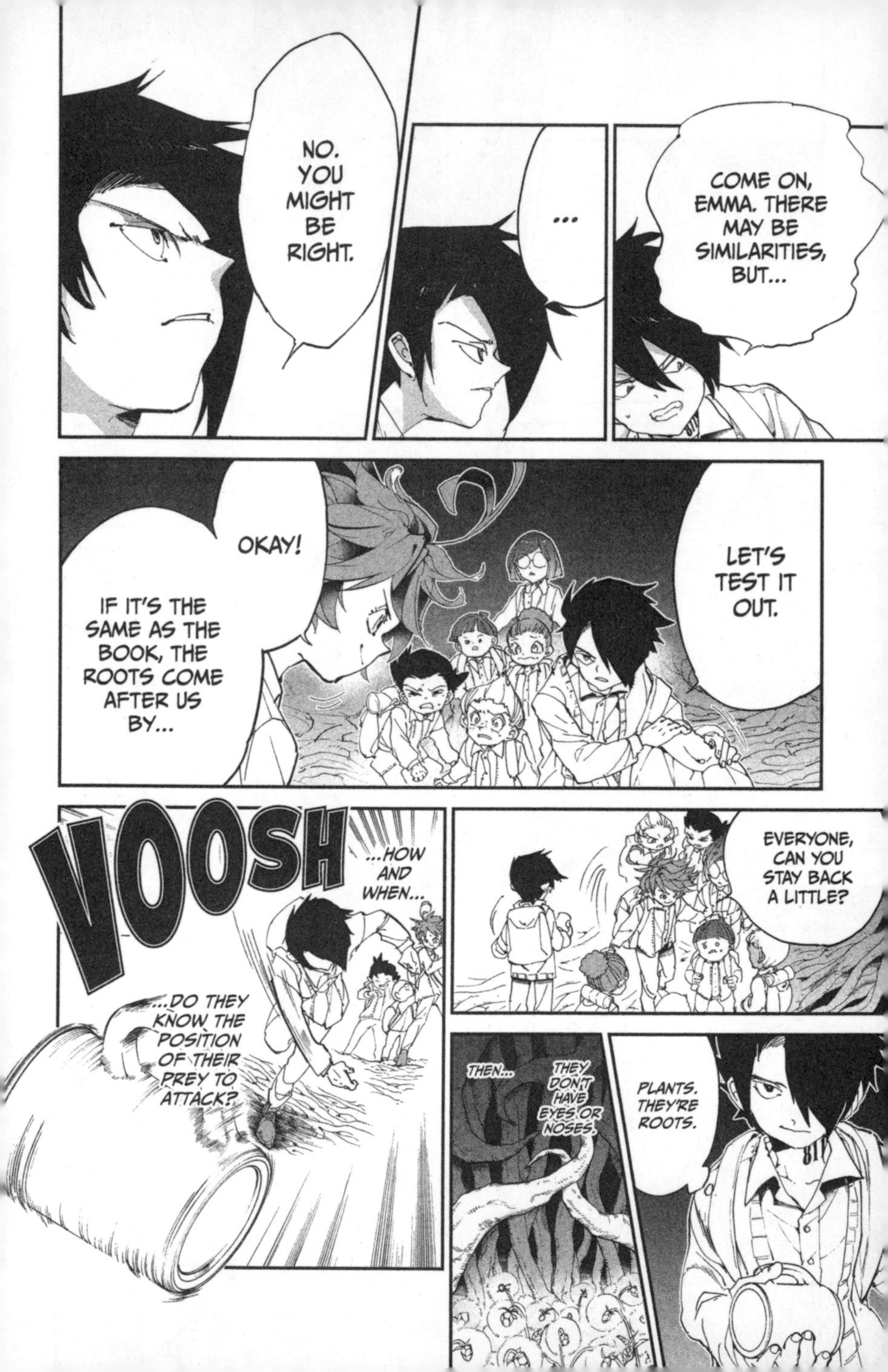
COME ON, EMMA. THERE MAY BE SIMILARITIES, BUT...
...
NO. YOU MIGHT BE RIGHT.
LET'S TEST IT OUT.
OKAY!
IF IT'S THE SAME AS THE BOOK, THE ROOTS COME AFTER US BY...
EVERYONE, CAN YOU STAY BACK A LITTLE?
PLANTS. THEY'RE ROOTS.
THEY DON'T HAVE EYES OR NOSES.
THEN...
VOOSH
...HOW AND WHEN...
...DO THEY KNOW THE POSITION OF THEIR PREY TO ATTACK?

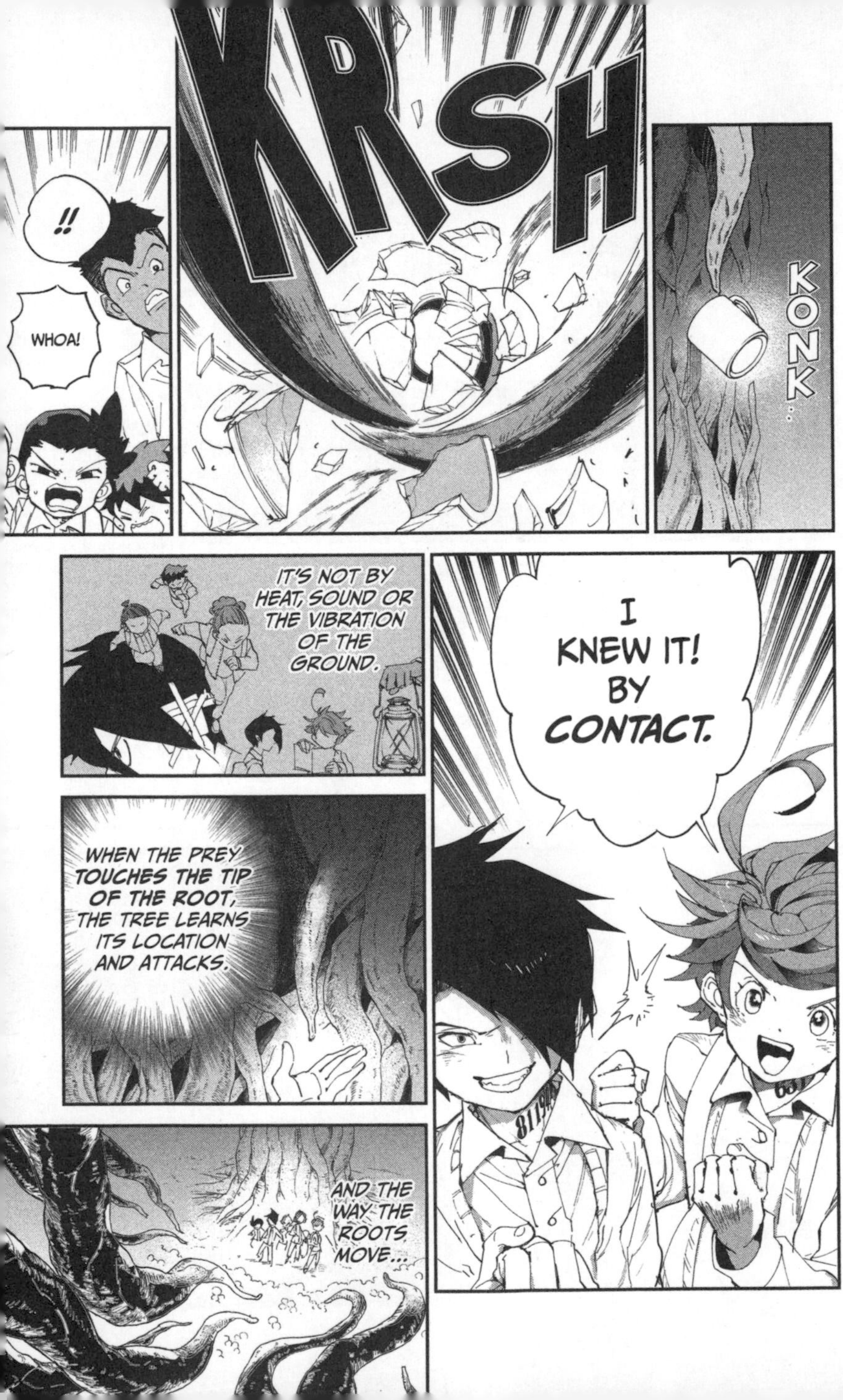
KONK...
KRSH
!!
WHOA!
I KNEW IT! BY CONTACT.
IT'S NOT BY HEAT, SOUND OR THE VIBRATION OF THE GROUND.
WHEN THE PREY TOUCHES THE TIP OF THE ROOT, THE TREE LEARNS ITS LOCATION AND ATTACKS.
AND THE WAY THE ROOTS MOVE...

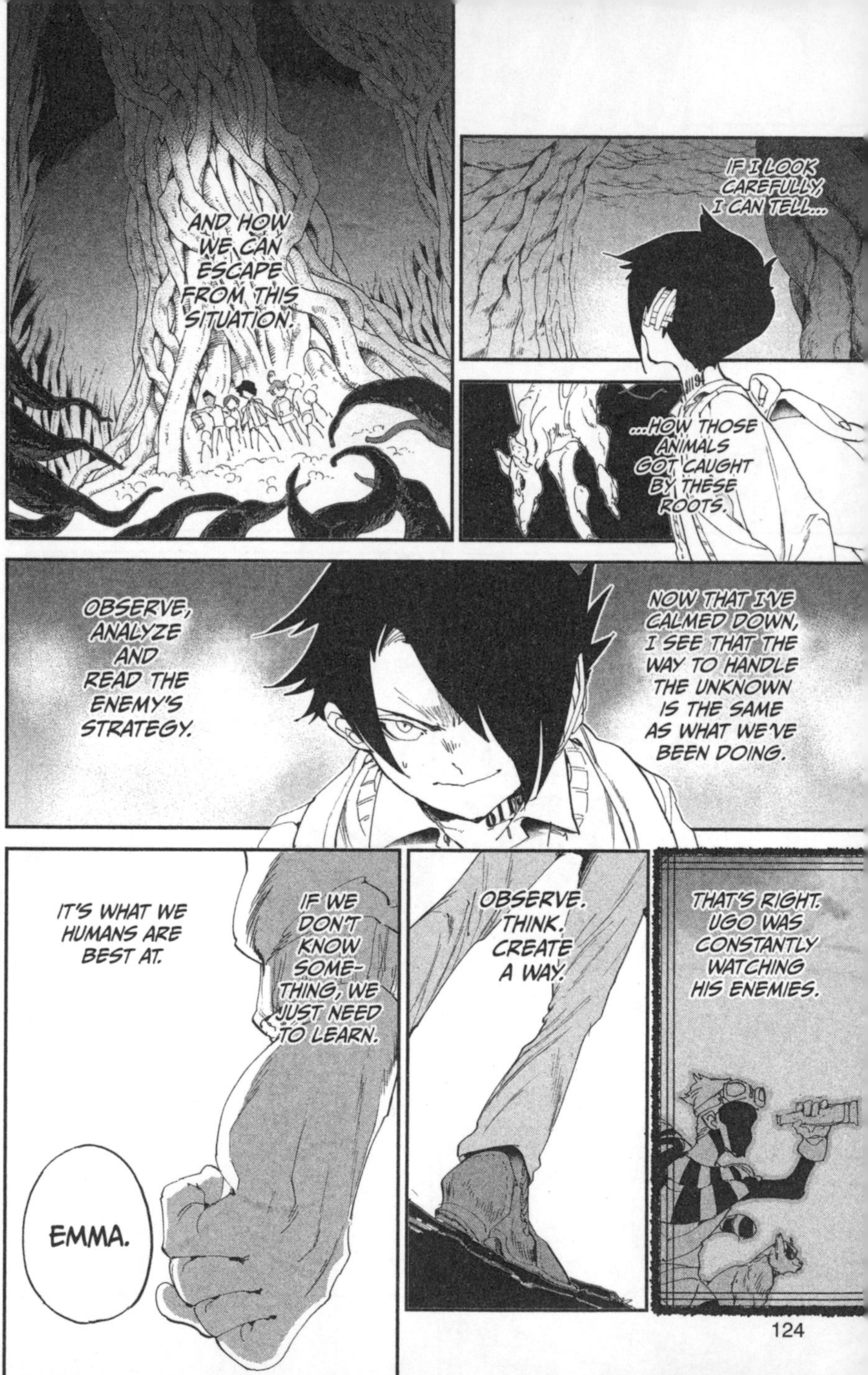

IF I LOOK CAREFULLY, I CAN TELL...
...HOW THOSE ANIMALS GOT CAUGHT BY THESE ROOTS.
AND HOW WE CAN ESCAPE FROM THIS SITUATION.
NOW THAT I'VE CALMED DOWN, I SEE THAT THE WAY TO HANDLE THE UNKNOWN IS THE SAME AS WHAT WE'VE BEEN DOING.
OBSERVE, ANALYZE AND READ THE ENEMY'S STRATEGY.
THAT'S RIGHT. UGO WAS CONSTANTLY WATCHING HIS ENEMIES.
OBSERVE. THINK. CREATE A WAY.
IF WE DON'T KNOW SOME-THING, WE JUST NEED TO LEARN.
IT'S WHAT WE HUMANS ARE BEST AT.
EMMA.

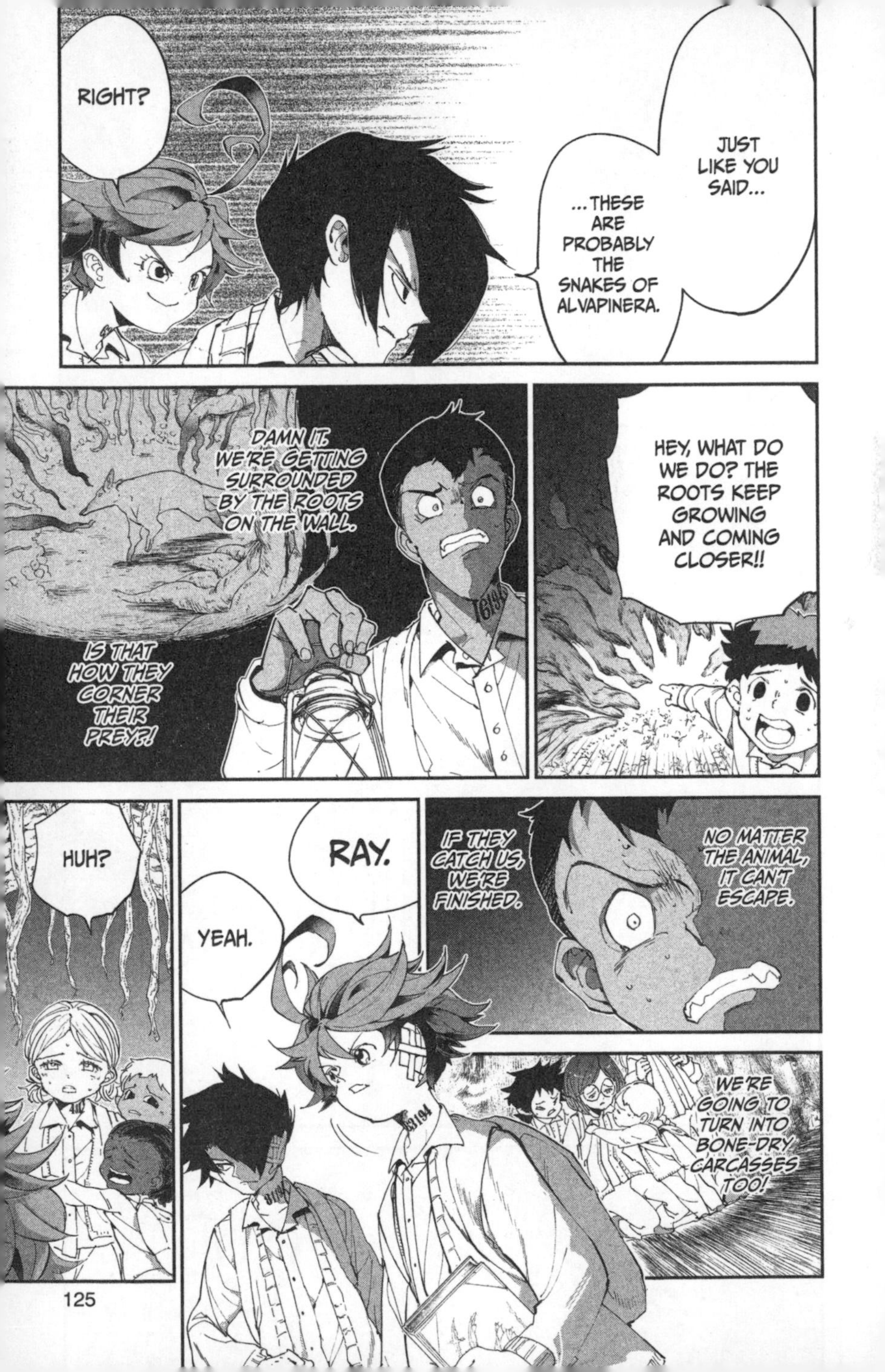
JUST LIKE YOU SAID...
...THESE ARE PROBABLY THE SNAKES OF ALVAPINERA.
RIGHT?
HEY, WHAT DO WE DO? THE ROOTS KEEP GROWING AND COMING CLOSER!!
DAMN IT. WE'RE GETTING SURROUNDED BY THE ROOTS ON THE WALL.
IS THAT HOW THEY CORNER THEIR PREY?!
NO MATTER THE ANIMAL, IT CAN'T ESCAPE.
IF THEY CATCH US, WE'RE FINISHED.
WE'RE GOING TO TURN INTO BONE-DRY CARCASSES TOO!
RAY.
YEAH.
HUH?

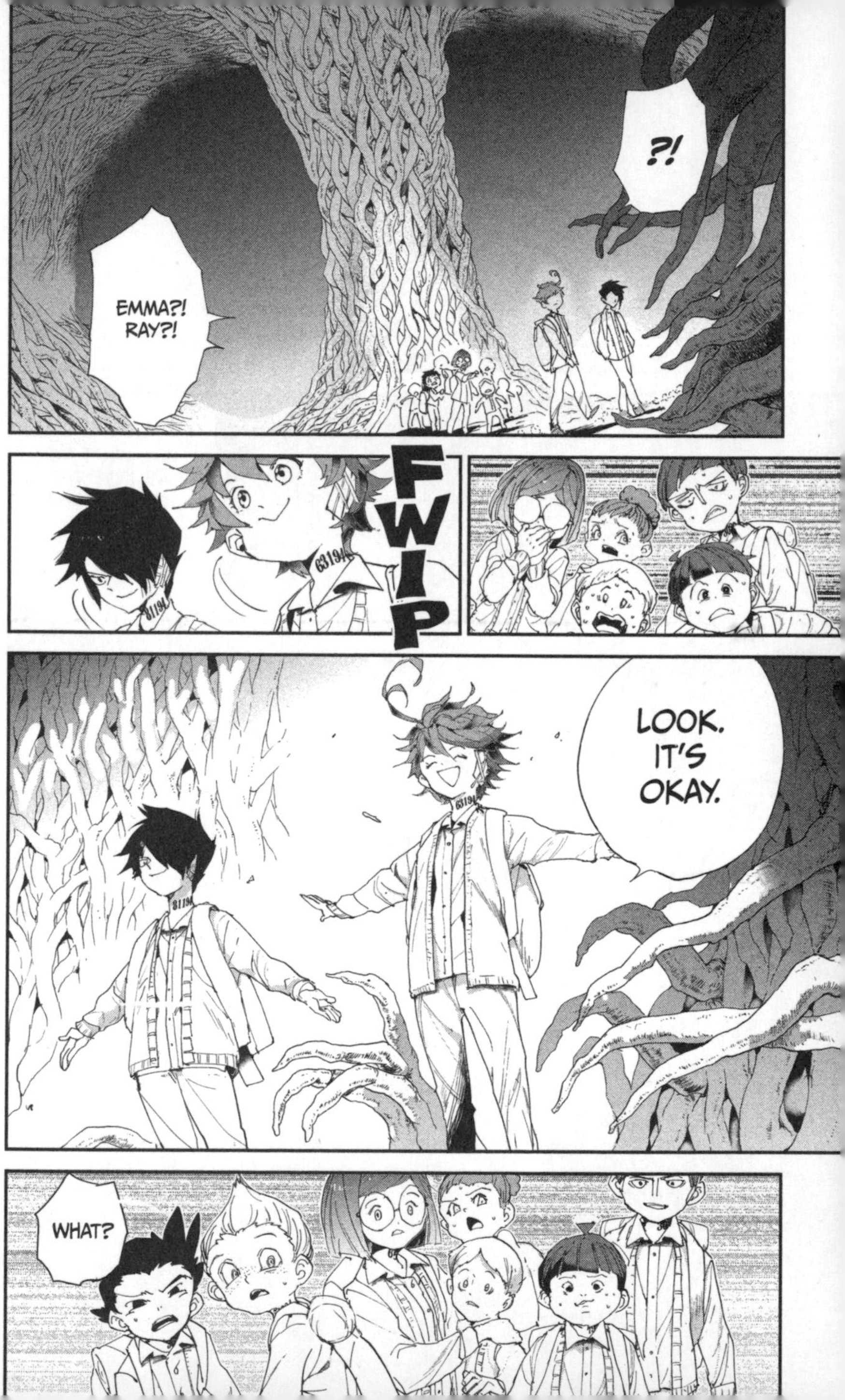
?!
EMMA?! RAY?!
FWIP
LOOK. IT'S OKAY.
WHAT?

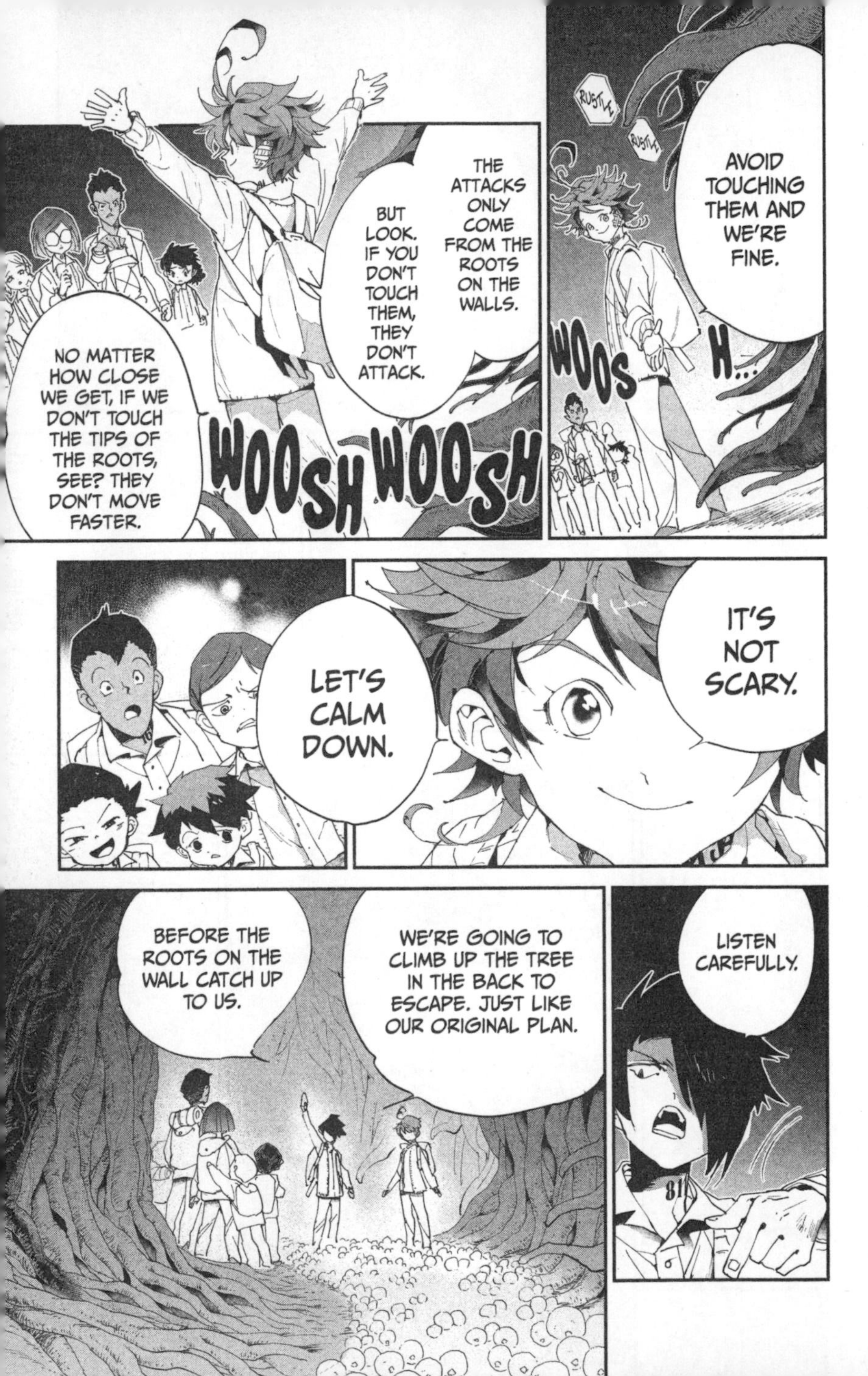
RUSTLE
RUSTLE
AVOID TOUCHING THEM AND WE'RE FINE.
WOOSH...
THE ATTACKS ONLY COME FROM THE ROOTS ON THE WALLS.
BUT LOOK. IF YOU DON'T TOUCH THEM, THEY DON'T ATTACK.
NO MATTER HOW CLOSE WE GET, IF WE DON'T TOUCH THE TIPS OF THE ROOTS, SEE? THEY DON'T MOVE FASTER.
WOOSH WOOSH
IT'S NOT SCARY.
LET'S CALM DOWN.
LISTEN CAREFULLY.
WE'RE GOING TO CLIMB UP THE TREE IN THE BACK TO ESCAPE. JUST LIKE OUR ORIGINAL PLAN.
BEFORE THE ROOTS ON THE WALL CATCH UP TO US.

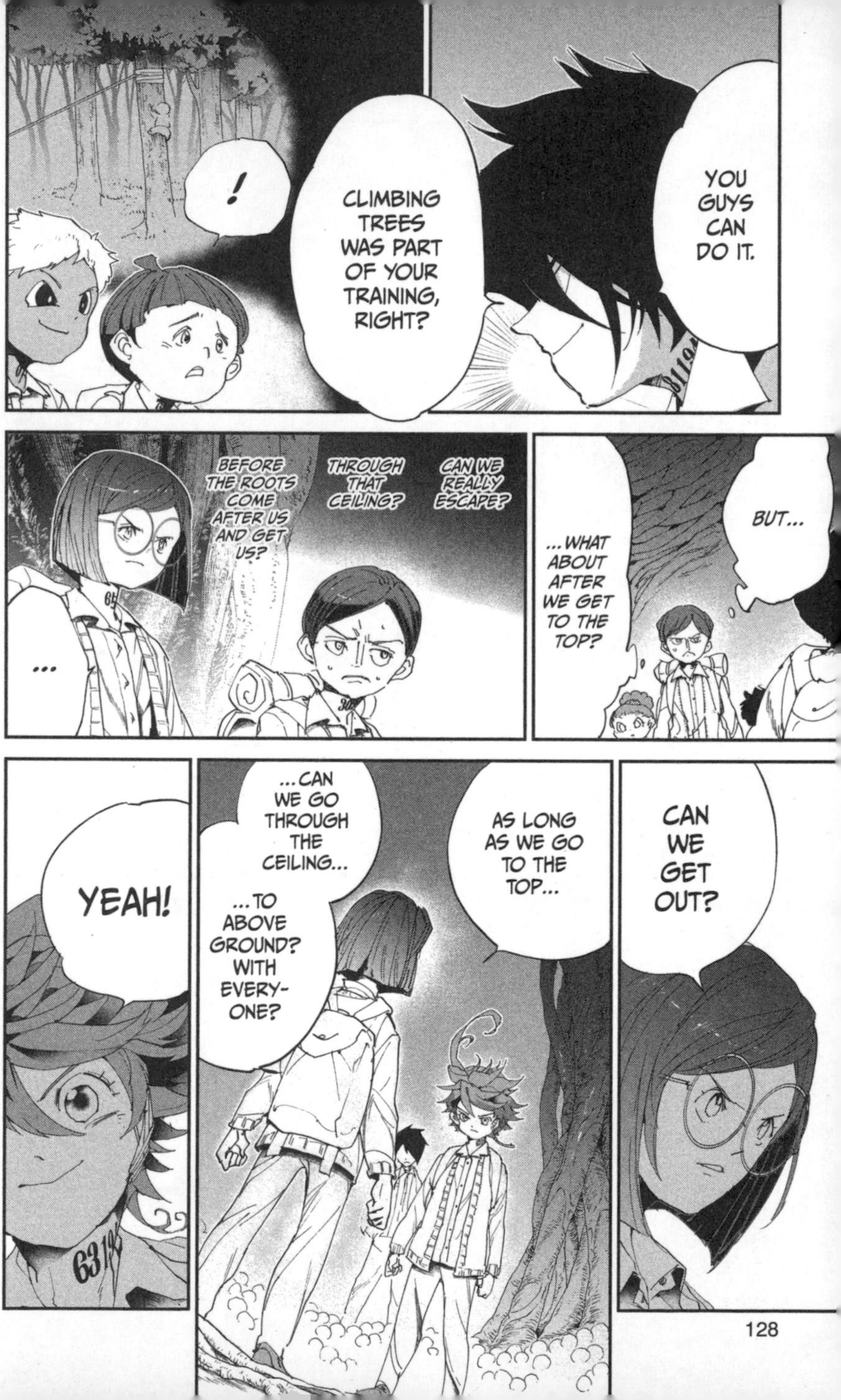
YOU GUYS CAN DO IT.
CLIMBING TREES WAS PART OF YOUR TRAINING, RIGHT?
!
BUT...
...WHAT ABOUT AFTER WE GET TO THE TOP?
CAN WE REALLY ESCAPE?
THROUGH THAT CEILING?
BEFORE THE ROOTS COME AFTER US AND GET US?
...
CAN WE GET OUT?
AS LONG AS WE GO TO THE TOP...
...CAN WE GO THROUGH THE CEILING...
...TO ABOVE GROUND? WITH EVERY-ONE?
YEAH!

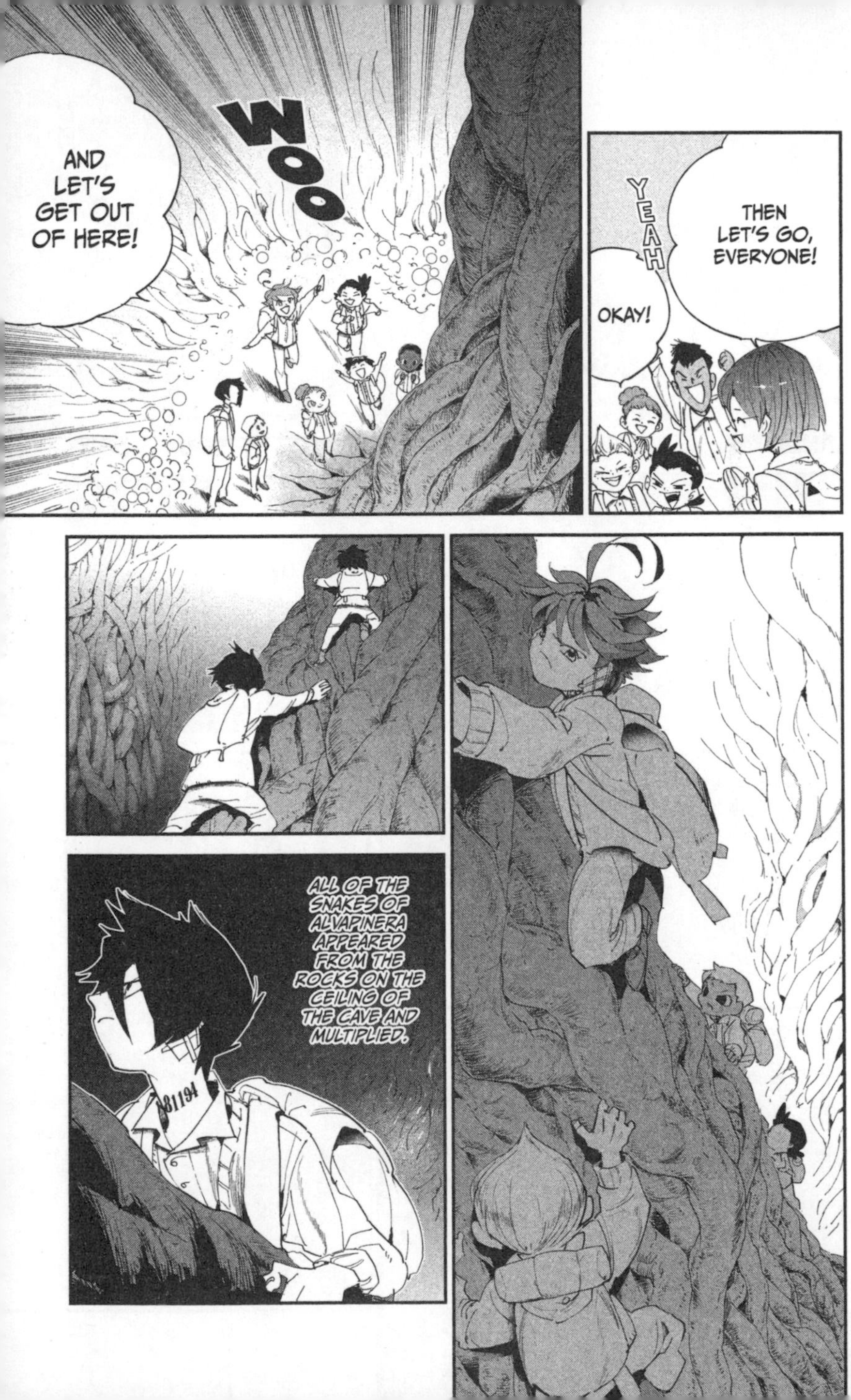
THEN LET'S GO, EVERYONE!
YEAH
OKAY!
WOO
AND LET'S GET OUT OF HERE!
ALL OF THE SNAKES OF ALVAPINERA APPEARED FROM THE ROCKS ON THE CEILING OF THE CAVE AND MULTIPLIED.

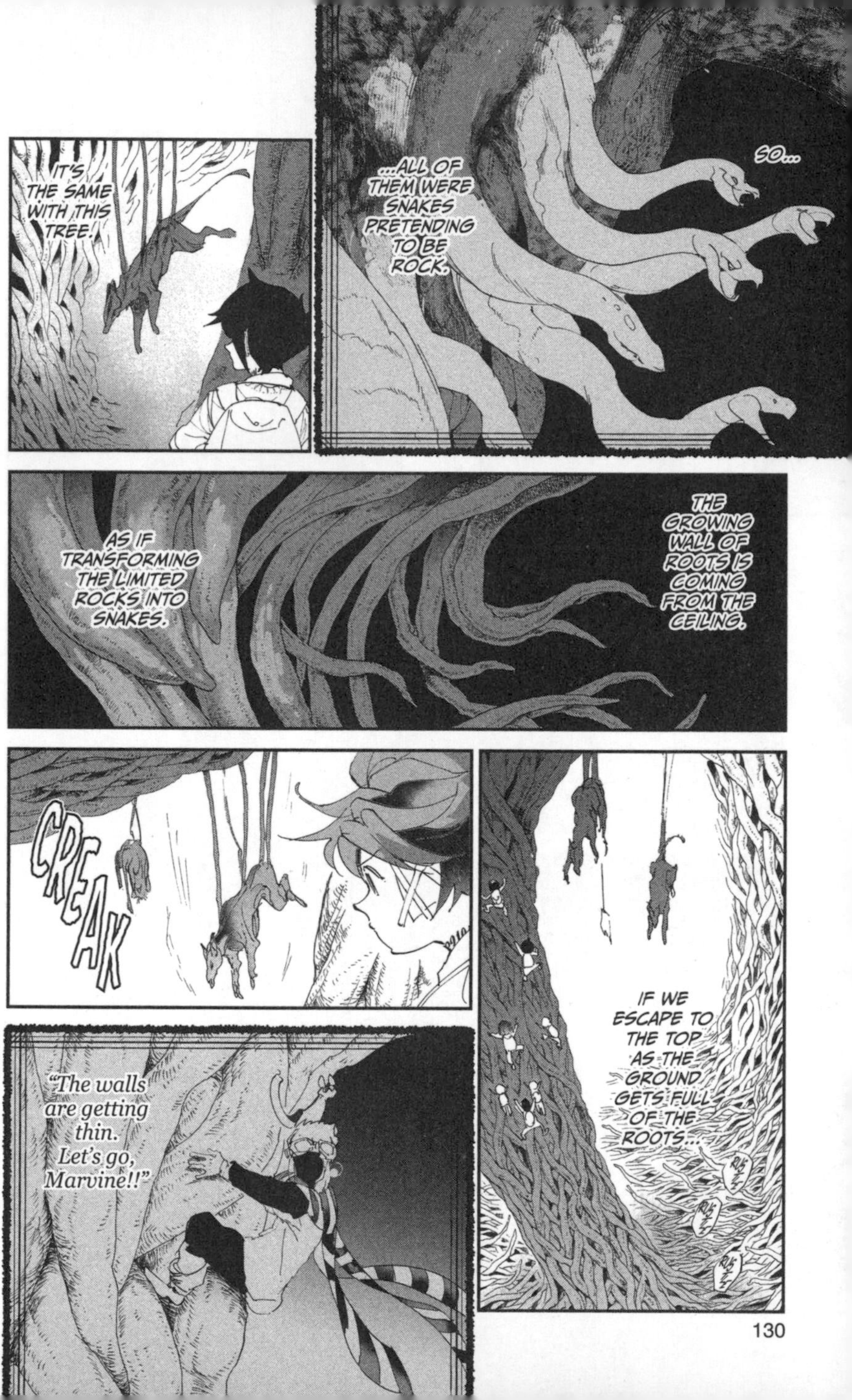
SO...
...ALL OF THEM WERE SNAKES PRETENDING TO BE ROCK.
IT'S THE SAME WITH THIS TREE.
THE GROWING WALL OF ROOTS IS COMING FROM THE CEILING.
AS IF TRANSFORMING THE LIMITED ROCKS INTO SNAKES.
IF WE ESCAPE TO THE TOP AS THE GROUND GETS FULL OF THE ROOTS...
CREAK
"The walls are getting thin. Let's go, Marvine!!"

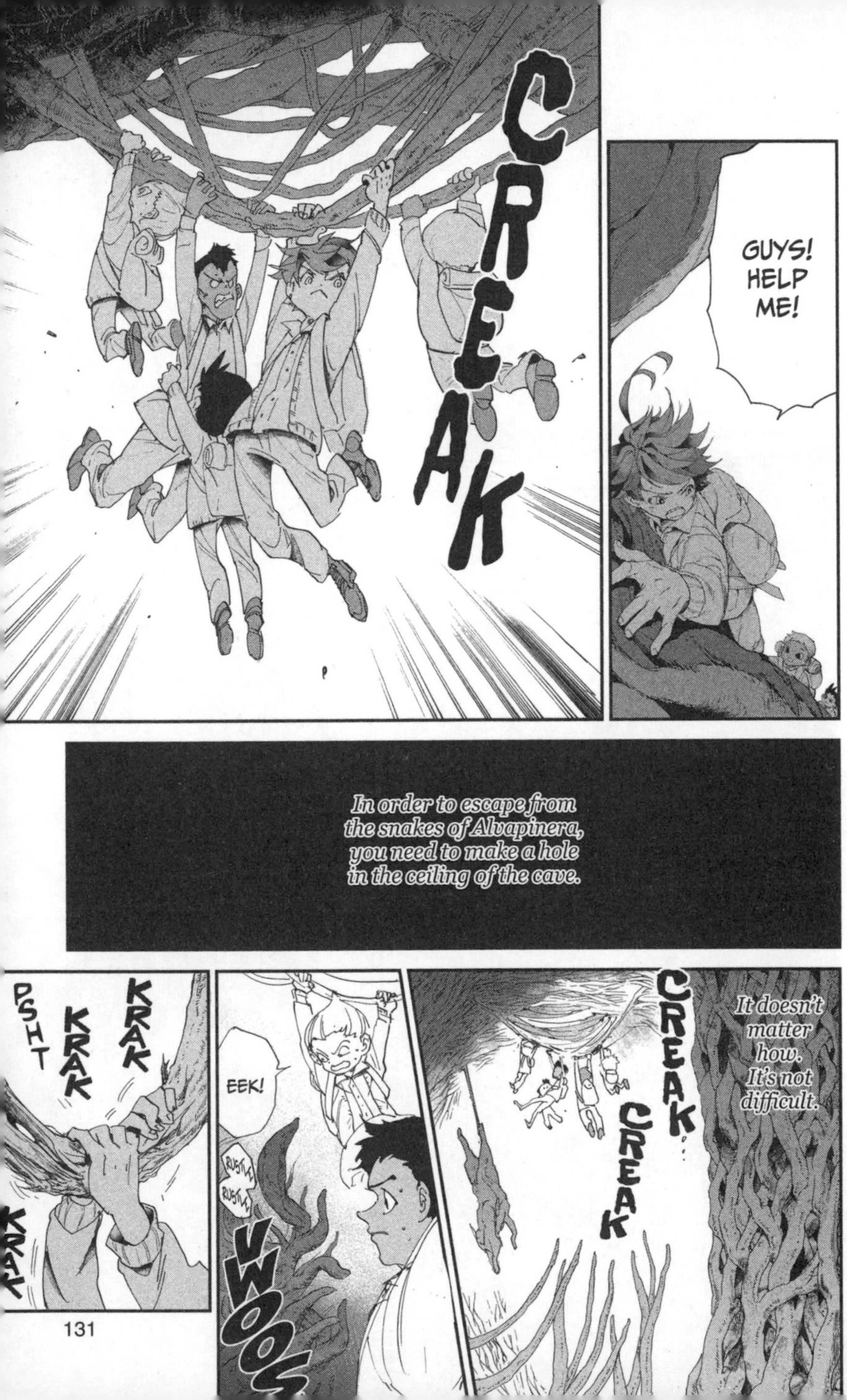
GUYS! HELP ME!
CREAK
In order to escape from the snakes of Alvapinera, you need to make a hole in the ceiling of the cave.
CREAK
CREAK
It doesn't matter how. It's not difficult.
EEK!
RUSTLE
RUSTLE
VWOOS
KRAK
KRAK
PSHT
KRAK

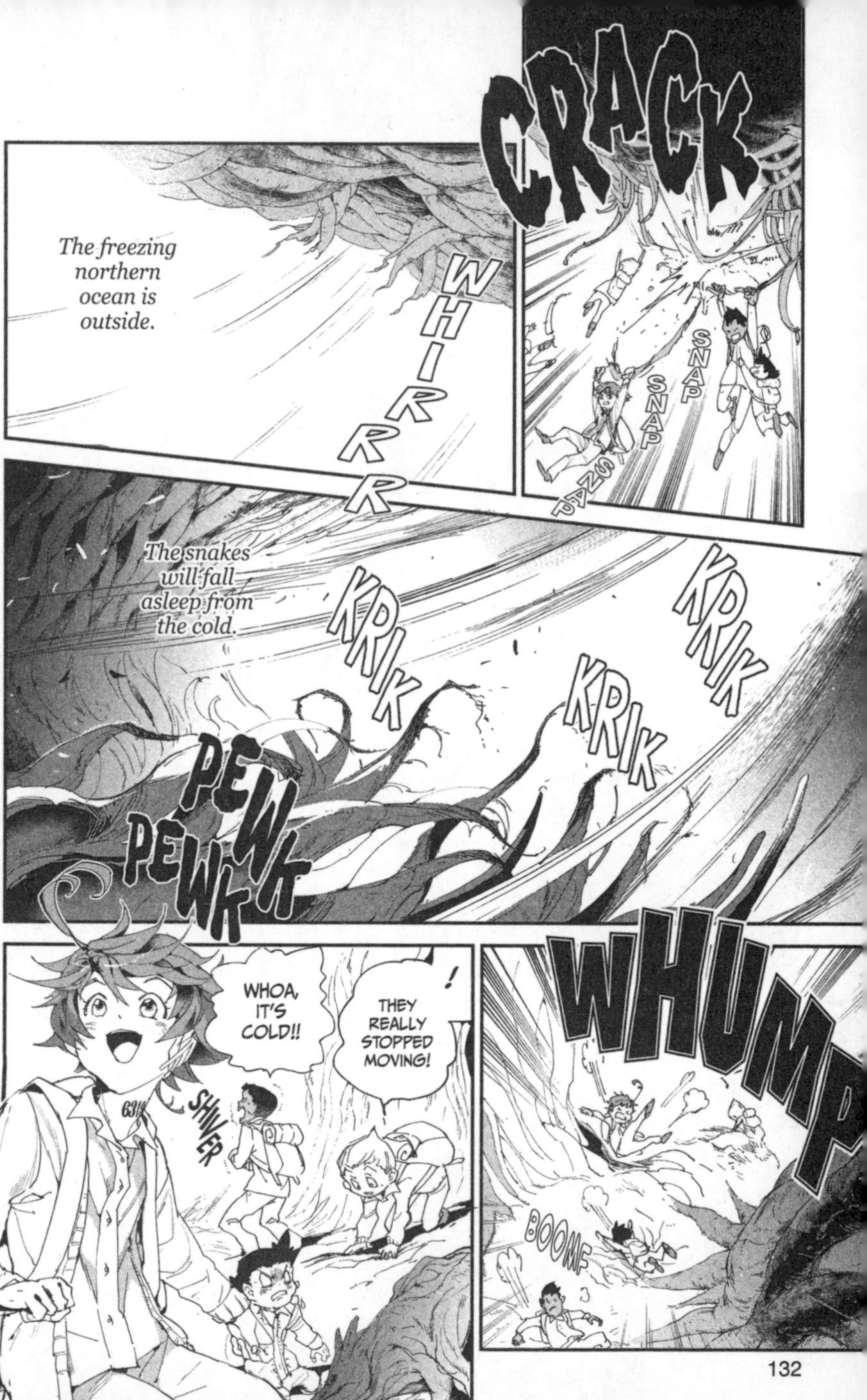
CRACK
SNAP
SNAP
SNAP
SNAP
The freezing northern ocean is outside.
WHIRRR
The snakes will fall asleep from the cold.
KRIK
KRIK
KRIK
PEWK
PEWK
WHUMP
BOOMF
!
THEY REALLY STOPPED MOVING!
WHOA, IT'S COLD!!
SHIVER

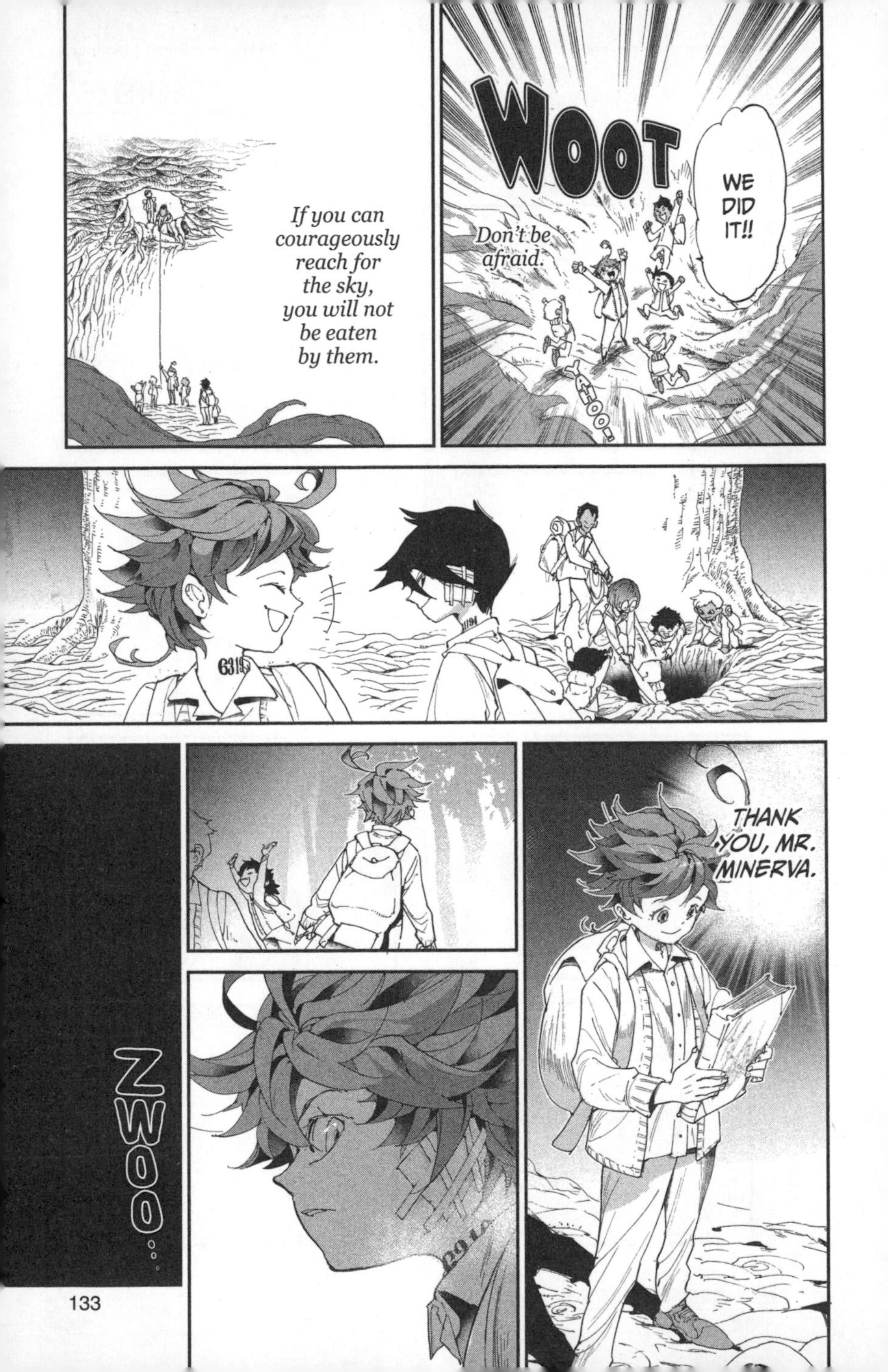
WOOT
WE DID IT!!
Don't be afraid.
YAHOO!
If you can courageously reach for the sky, you will not be eaten by them.
THANK YOU, MR. MINERVA.
ZWOO...

SIDE STORY 2-3

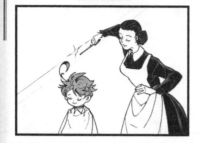

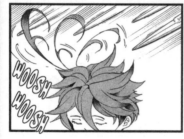

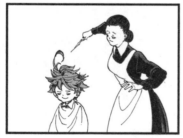

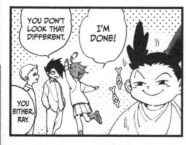

NEMESIS

WHEN OUR HAIR GETS LONG, MOM CUTS IT.
FWSH

NEMESES

WOOSH
WOOSH
YAY
YAY
I'M DONE!
YOU DON'T LOOK THAT DIFFERENT.
YOU EITHER, RAY.

TO BE CONTINUED IN SIDE STORY 2-4

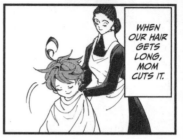

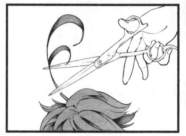

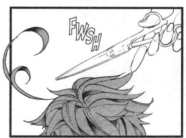

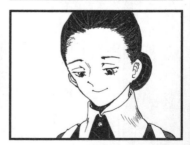

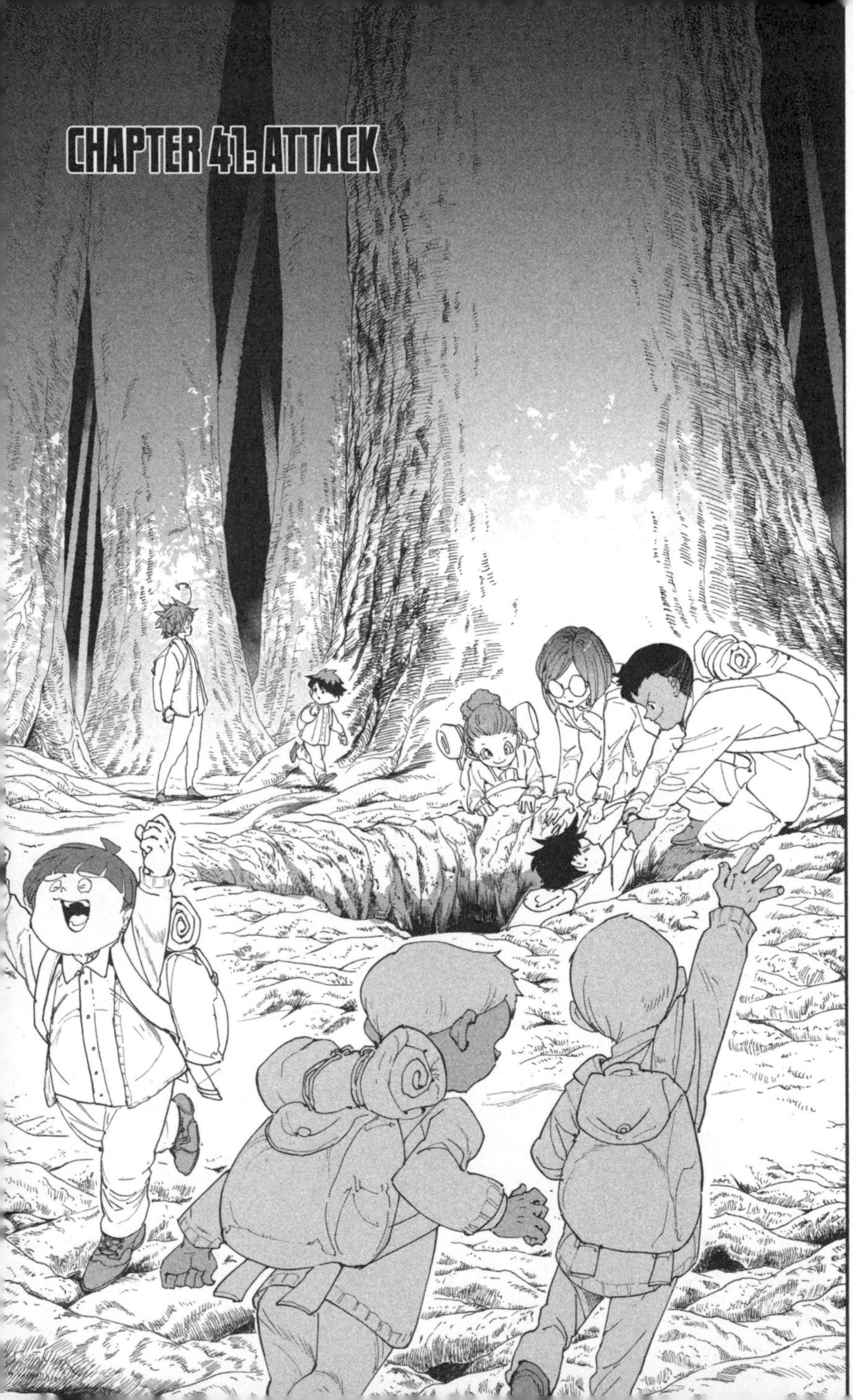
CHAPTER 41: ATTACK

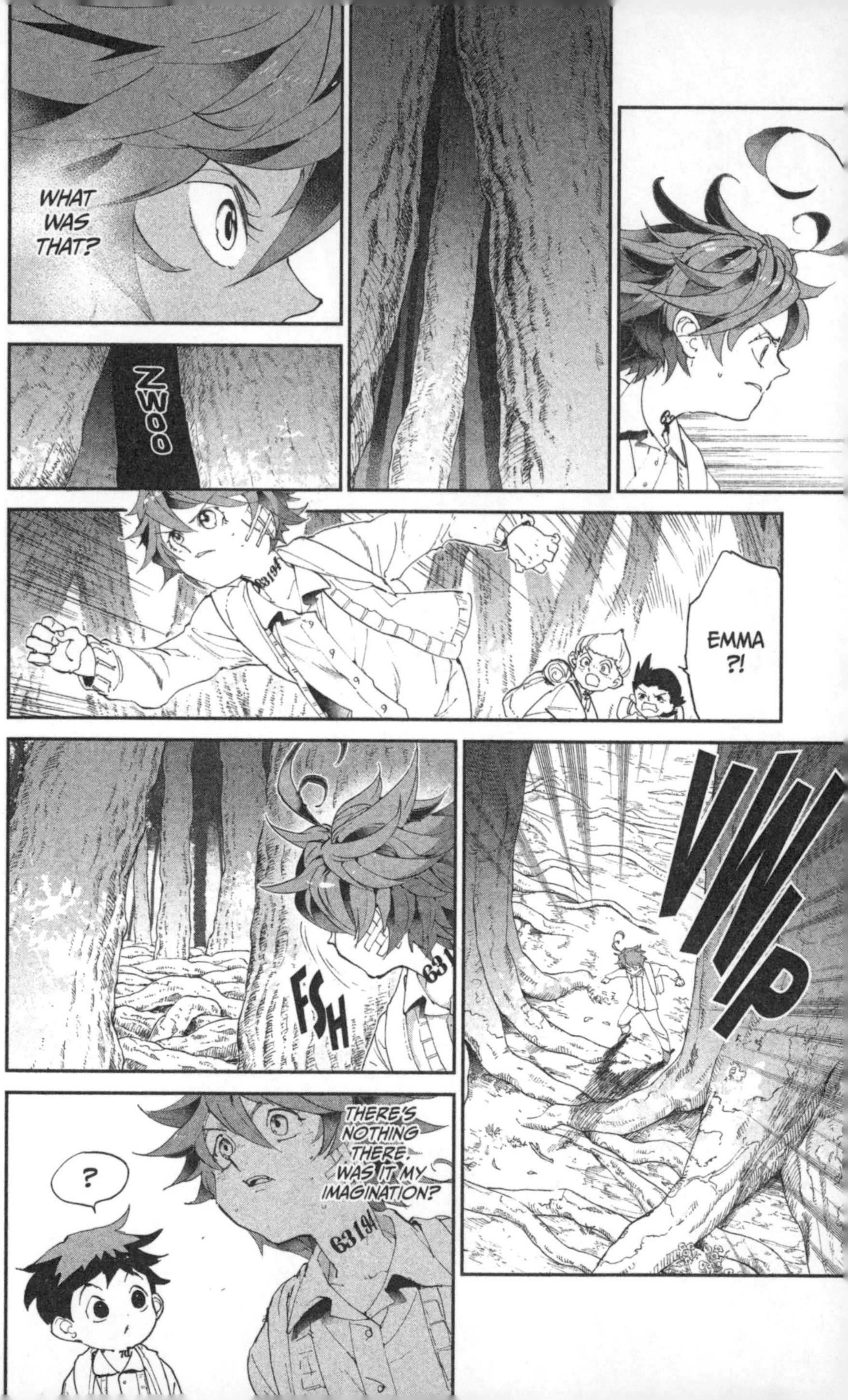
WHAT WAS THAT?
ZWOO
EMMA?!
WHIP
FSH
THERE'S NOTHING THERE. WAS IT MY IMAGINATION?
?

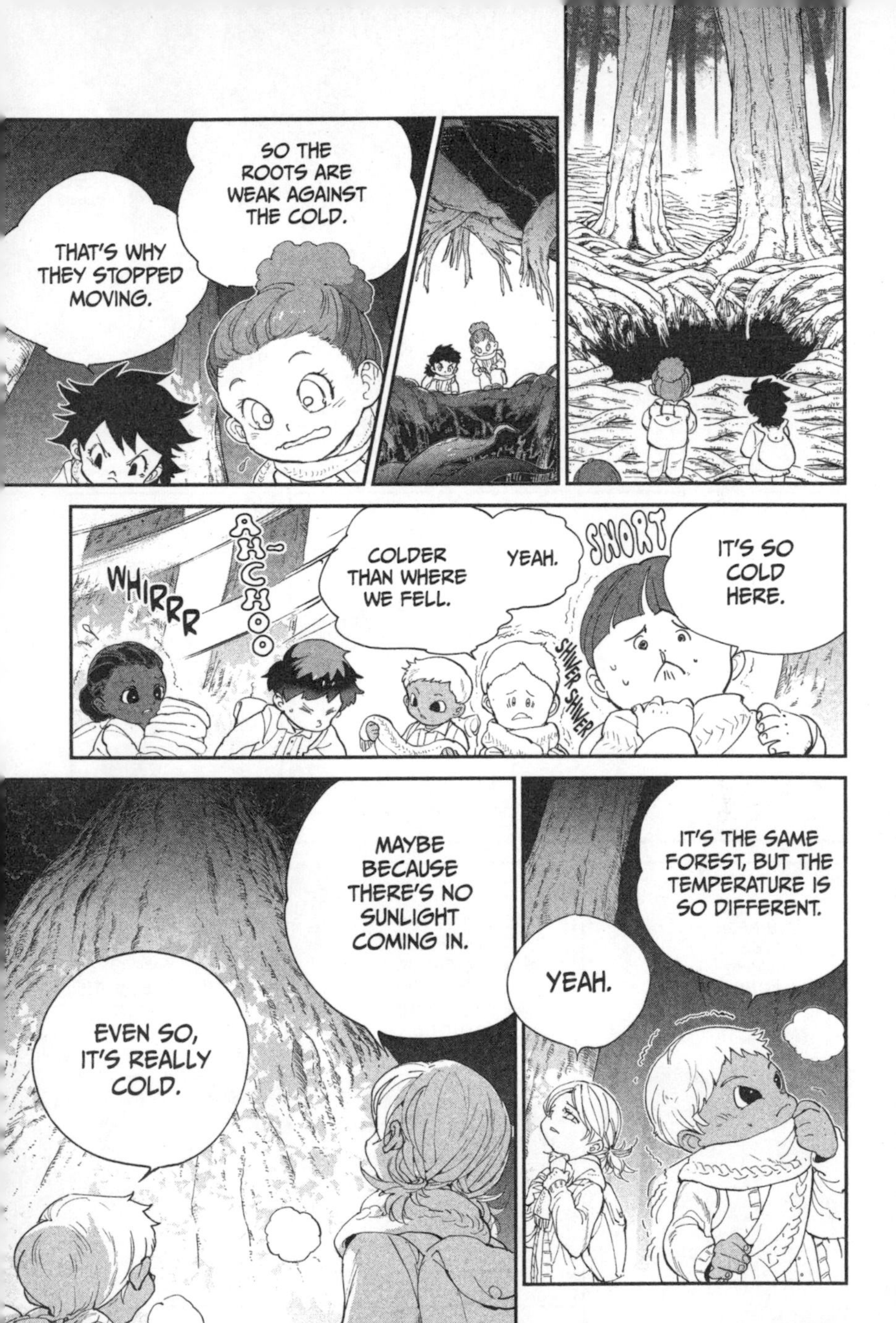
SO THE ROOTS ARE WEAK AGAINST THE COLD.
THAT'S WHY THEY STOPPED MOVING.
IT'S SO COLD HERE.
SNORT
SHIVER SHIVER
YEAH.
COLDER THAN WHERE WE FELL.
AH-CHOO
WHIRRR
IT'S THE SAME FOREST, BUT THE TEMPERATURE IS SO DIFFERENT.
YEAH.
MAYBE BECAUSE THERE'S NO SUNLIGHT COMING IN.
EVEN SO, IT'S REALLY COLD.

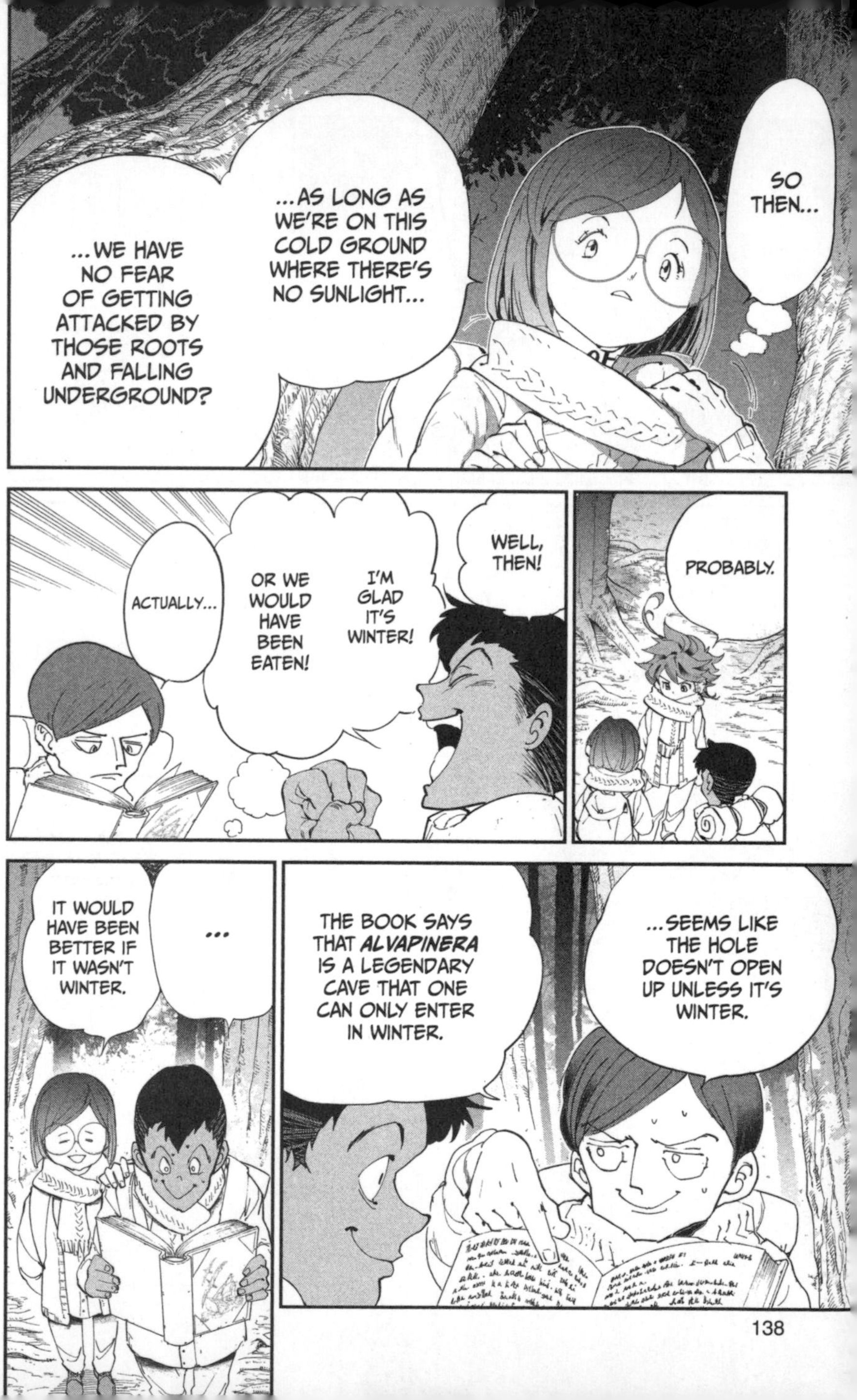
SO THEN...
...AS LONG AS WE'RE ON THIS COLD GROUND WHERE THERE'S NO SUNLIGHT...
...WE HAVE NO FEAR OF GETTING ATTACKED BY THOSE ROOTS AND FALLING UNDERGROUND?
PROBABLY.
WELL, THEN!
I'M GLAD IT'S WINTER!
OR WE WOULD HAVE BEEN EATEN!
ACTUALLY...
...SEEMS LIKE THE HOLE DOESN'T OPEN UP UNLESS IT'S WINTER.
THE BOOK SAYS THAT *ALVAPINERA* IS A LEGENDARY CAVE THAT ONE CAN ONLY ENTER IN WINTER.
...
IT WOULD HAVE BEEN BETTER IF IT WASN'T WINTER.

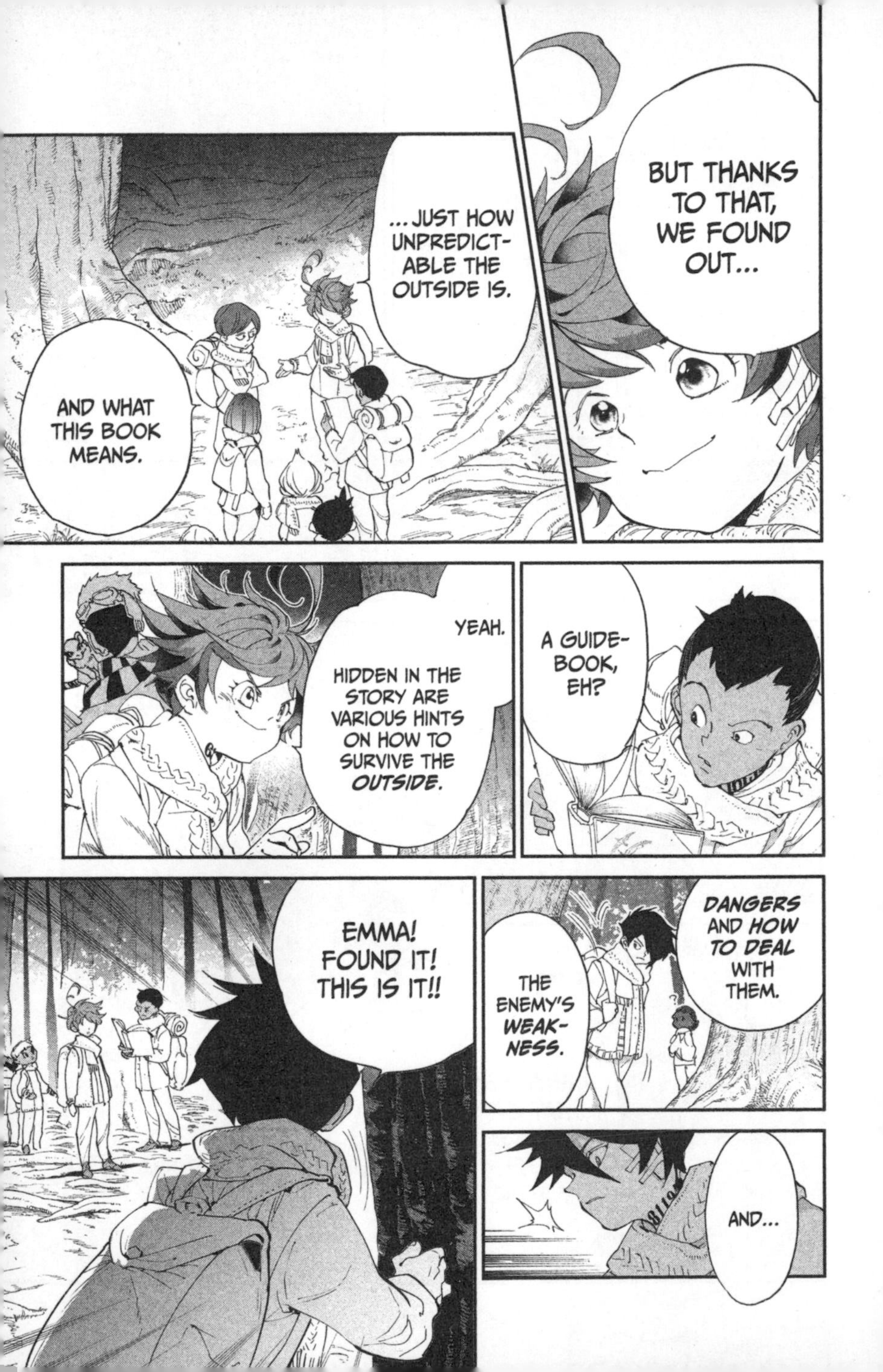
BUT THANKS TO THAT, WE FOUND OUT...
...JUST HOW UNPREDICT-ABLE THE OUTSIDE IS.
AND WHAT THIS BOOK MEANS.
A GUIDE-BOOK, EH?
YEAH.
HIDDEN IN THE STORY ARE VARIOUS HINTS ON HOW TO SURVIVE THE *OUTSIDE*.
DANGERS AND *HOW TO DEAL* WITH THEM.
THE ENEMY'S *WEAK-NESS*.
AND...
EMMA! FOUND IT! THIS IS IT!!

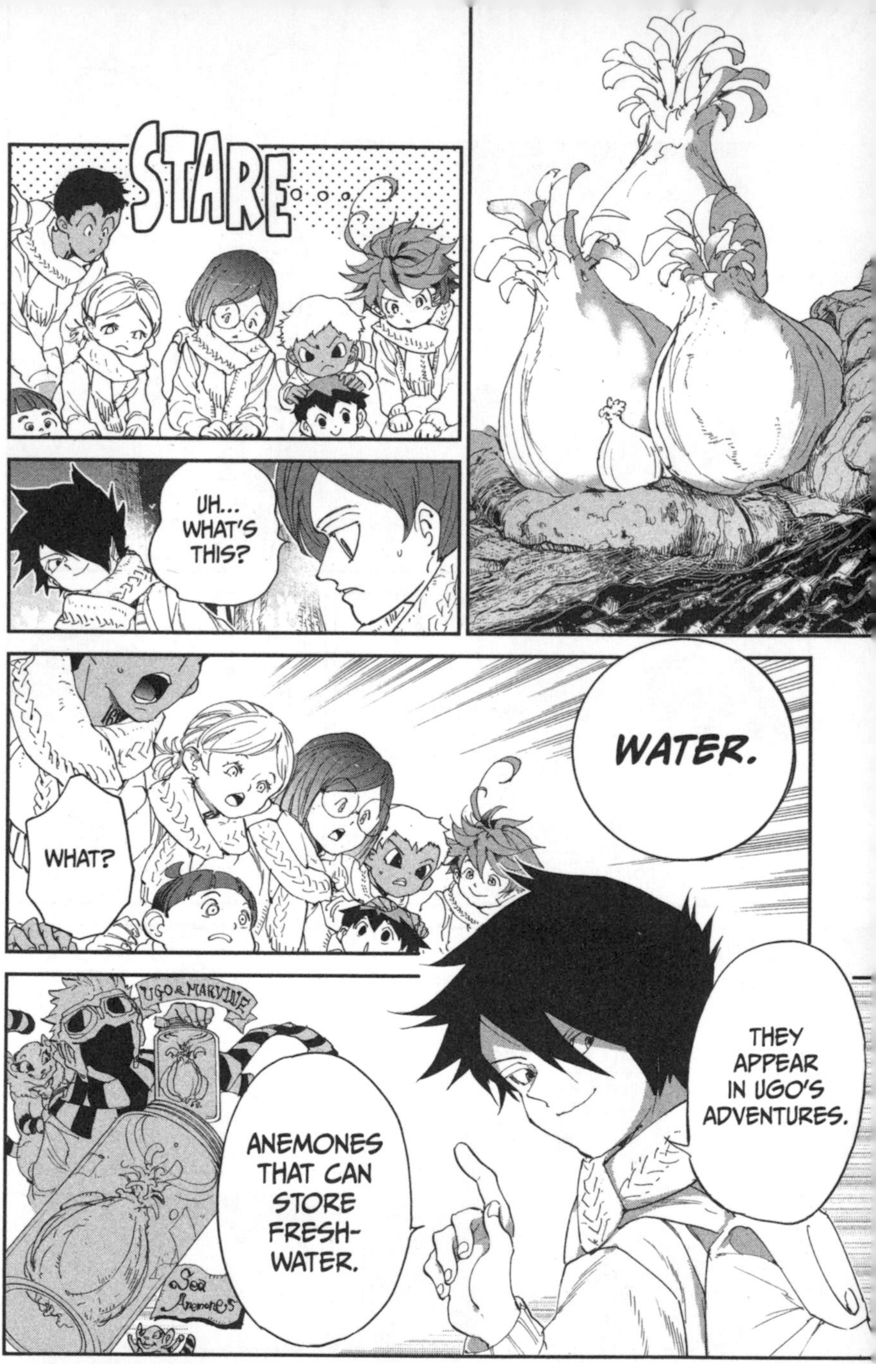
STARE...
UH... WHAT'S THIS?
WATER.
WHAT?
THEY APPEAR IN UGO'S ADVENTURES.
ANEMONES THAT CAN STORE FRESH-WATER.
UGO & MARVINE
Sea Anemones

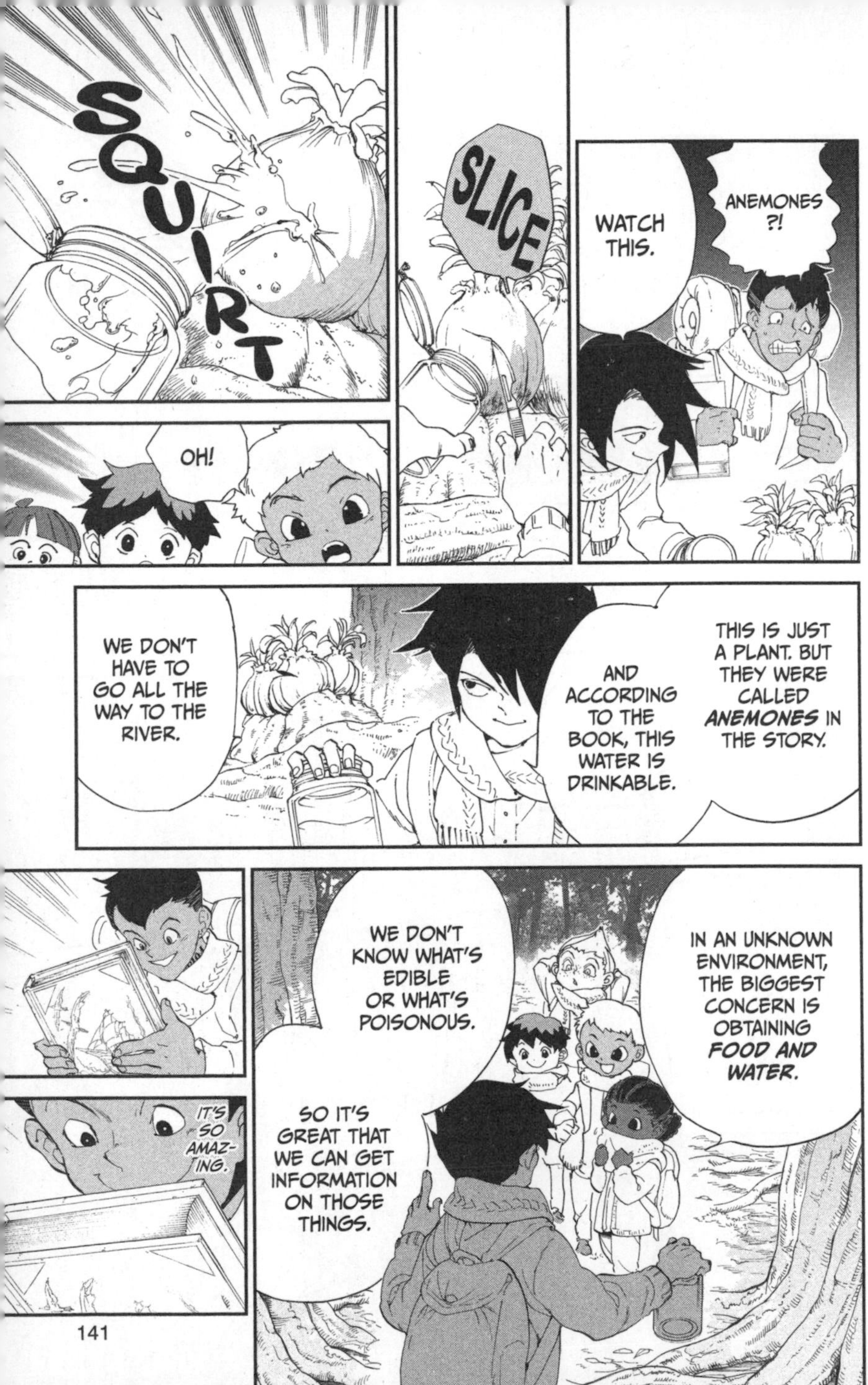
ANEMONES ?!
WATCH THIS.
SLICE
SQUIRT
OH!
THIS IS JUST A PLANT. BUT THEY WERE CALLED *ANEMONES* IN THE STORY.
AND ACCORDING TO THE BOOK, THIS WATER IS DRINKABLE.
WE DON'T HAVE TO GO ALL THE WAY TO THE RIVER.
IN AN UNKNOWN ENVIRONMENT, THE BIGGEST CONCERN IS OBTAINING *FOOD AND WATER.*
WE DON'T KNOW WHAT'S EDIBLE OR WHAT'S POISONOUS.
SO IT'S GREAT THAT WE CAN GET INFORMATION ON THOSE THINGS.
IT'S SO AMAZ-ING.

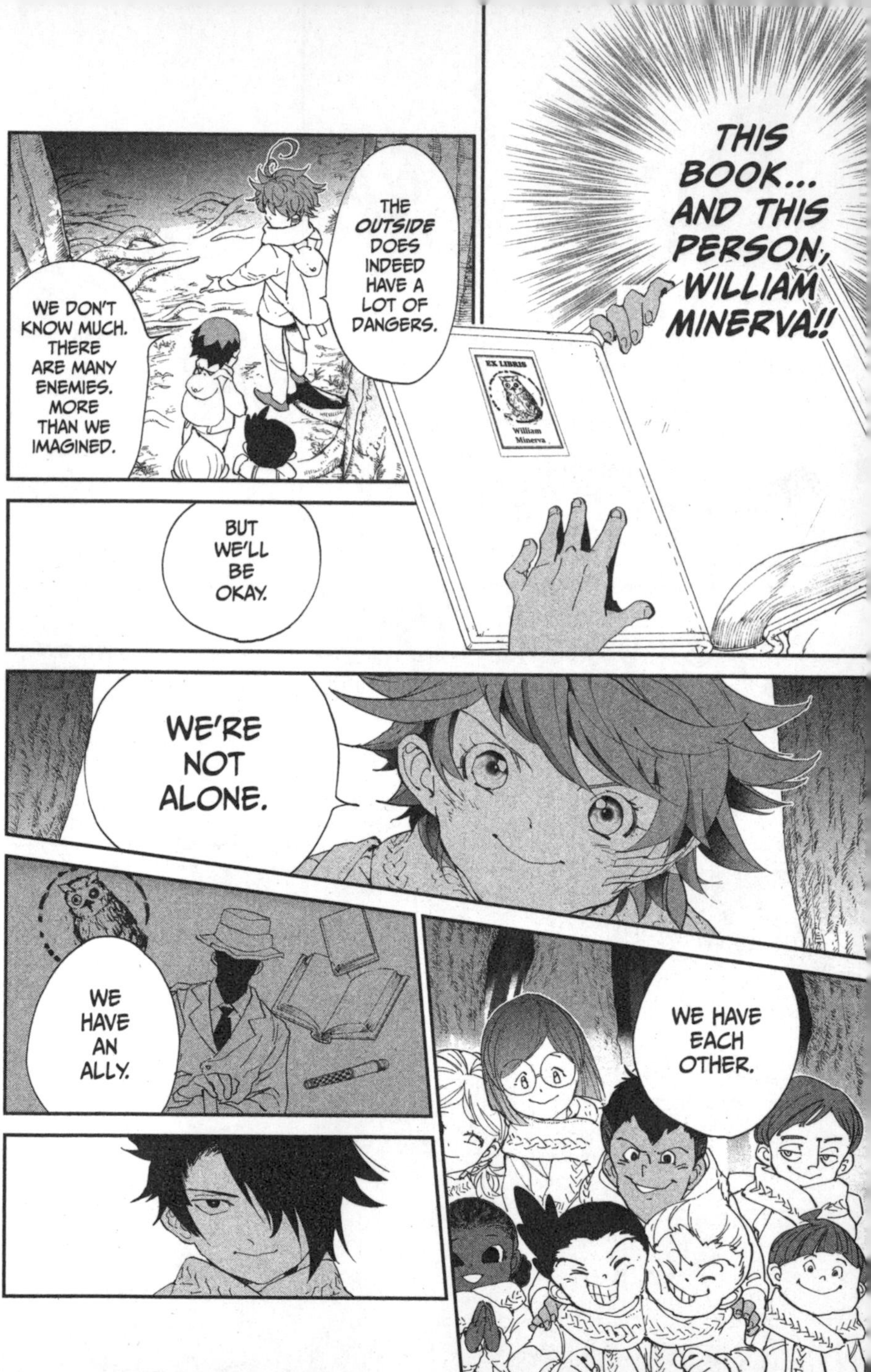
THIS BOOK... AND THIS PERSON, WILLIAM MINERVA!!
EX LIBRIS
William Minerva
THE *OUTSIDE* DOES INDEED HAVE A LOT OF DANGERS.
WE DON'T KNOW MUCH. THERE ARE MANY ENEMIES. MORE THAN WE IMAGINED.
BUT WE'LL BE OKAY.
WE'RE NOT ALONE.
WE HAVE EACH OTHER.
WE HAVE AN ALLY.

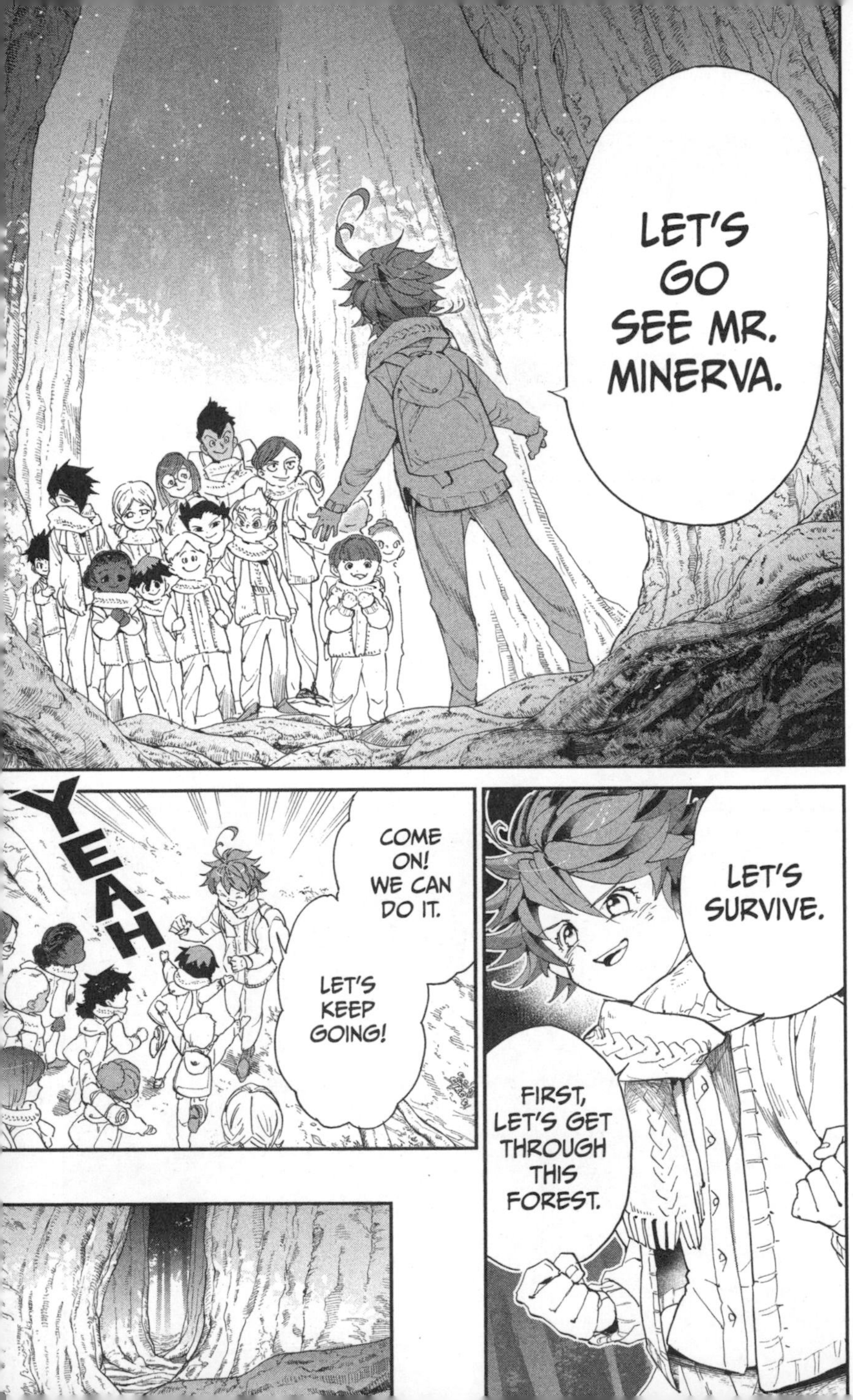
LET'S GO SEE MR. MINERVA.
LET'S SURVIVE.
FIRST, LET'S GET THROUGH THIS FOREST.
YEAH
COME ON! WE CAN DO IT.
LET'S KEEP GOING!

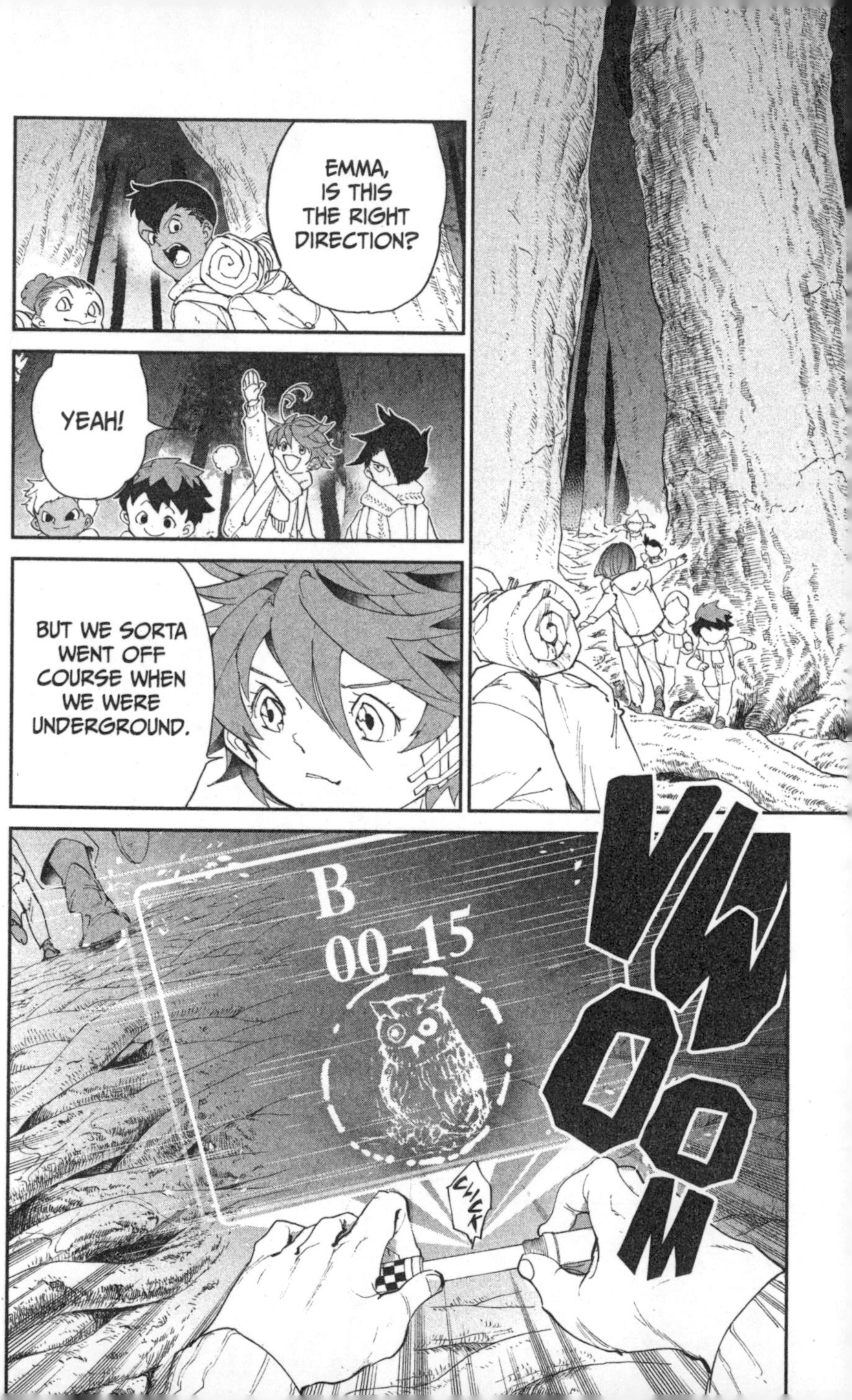
EMMA, IS THIS THE RIGHT DIRECTION?
YEAH!
BUT WE SORTA WENT OFF COURSE WHEN WE WERE UNDERGROUND.
VWOOOM
B
00-15
CLICK

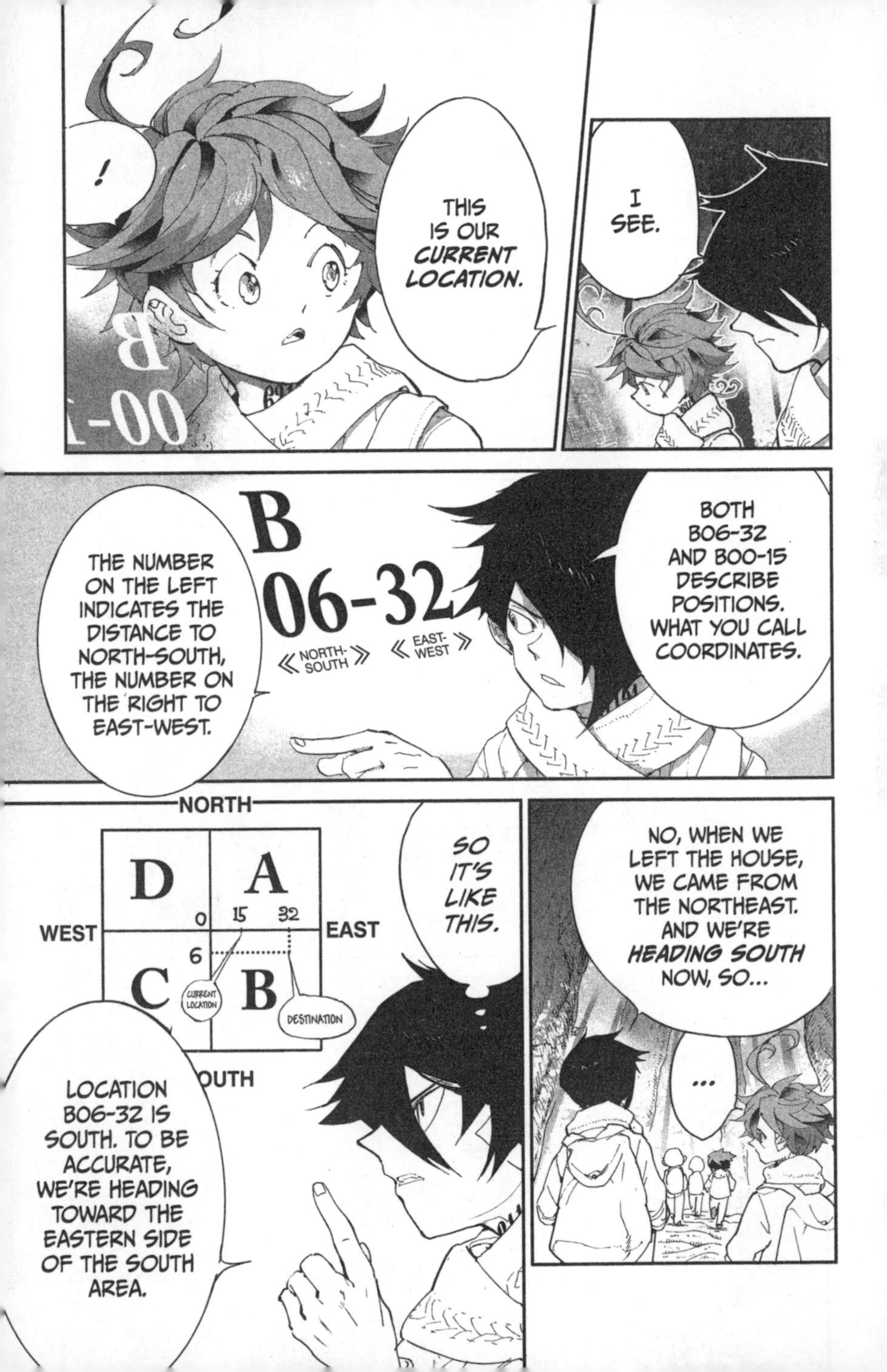
I SEE.
THIS IS OUR *CURRENT LOCATION.*
BOTH B06-32 AND B00-15 DESCRIBE POSITIONS. WHAT YOU CALL COORDINATES.
B 06-32
《NORTH-SOUTH》 《EAST-WEST》
THE NUMBER ON THE LEFT INDICATES THE DISTANCE TO NORTH-SOUTH, THE NUMBER ON THE RIGHT TO EAST-WEST.
NO, WHEN WE LEFT THE HOUSE, WE CAME FROM THE NORTHEAST. AND WE'RE *HEADING SOUTH* NOW, SO...
...
SO IT'S LIKE THIS.
NORTH
WEST
EAST
D
A
C
B
0
15
32
6
CURRENT LOCATION
DESTINATION
LOCATION B06-32 IS SOUTH. TO BE ACCURATE, WE'RE HEADING TOWARD THE EASTERN SIDE OF THE SOUTH AREA.

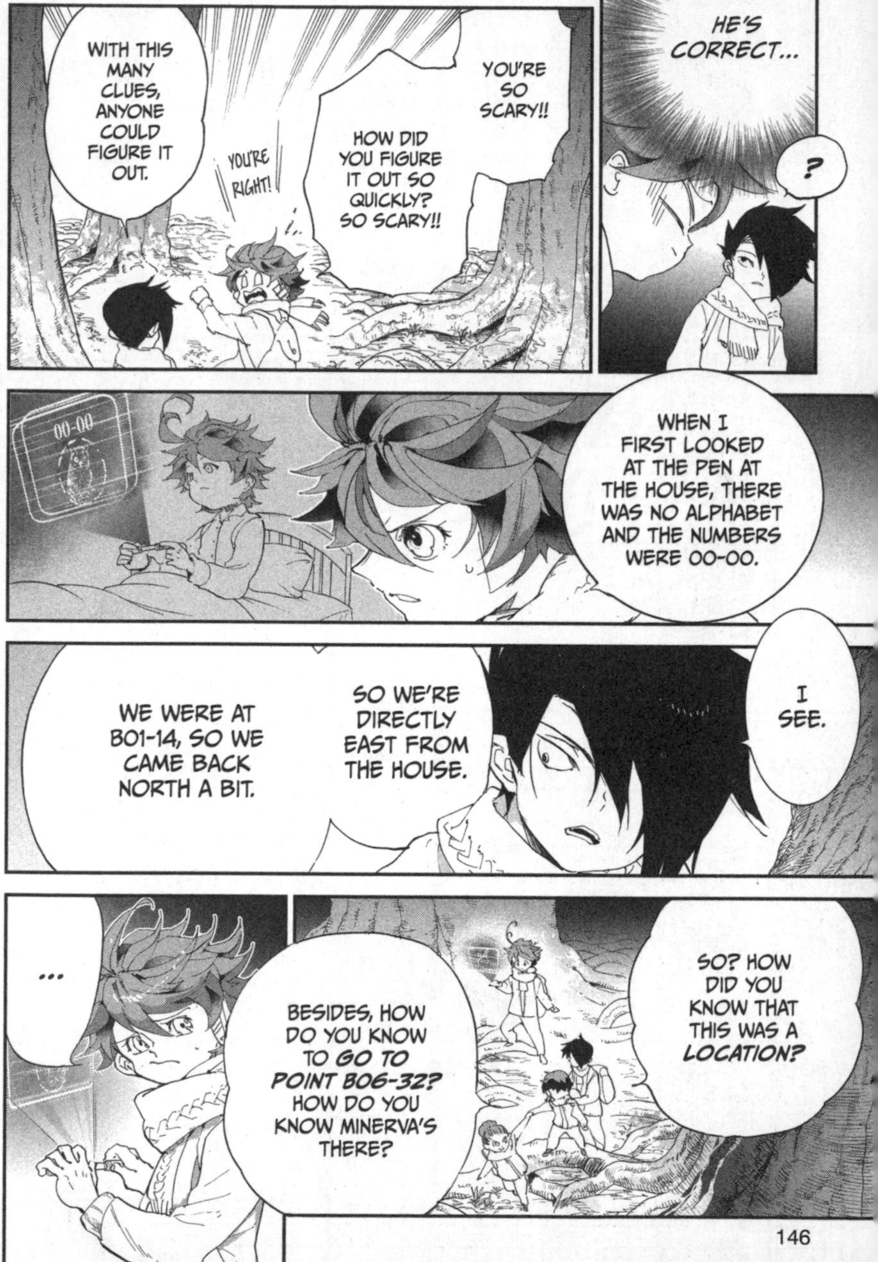
HE'S CORRECT...
?
YOU'RE SO SCARY!!
HOW DID YOU FIGURE IT OUT SO QUICKLY? SO SCARY!!
YOU'RE RIGHT!
WITH THIS MANY CLUES, ANYONE COULD FIGURE IT OUT.
00-00
WHEN I FIRST LOOKED AT THE PEN AT THE HOUSE, THERE WAS NO ALPHABET AND THE NUMBERS WERE 00-00.
I SEE.
SO WE'RE DIRECTLY EAST FROM THE HOUSE.
WE WERE AT B01-14, SO WE CAME BACK NORTH A BIT.
SO? HOW DID YOU KNOW THAT THIS WAS A *LOCATION?*
BESIDES, HOW DO YOU KNOW TO *GO TO POINT B06-32?* HOW DO YOU KNOW MINERVA'S THERE?
...

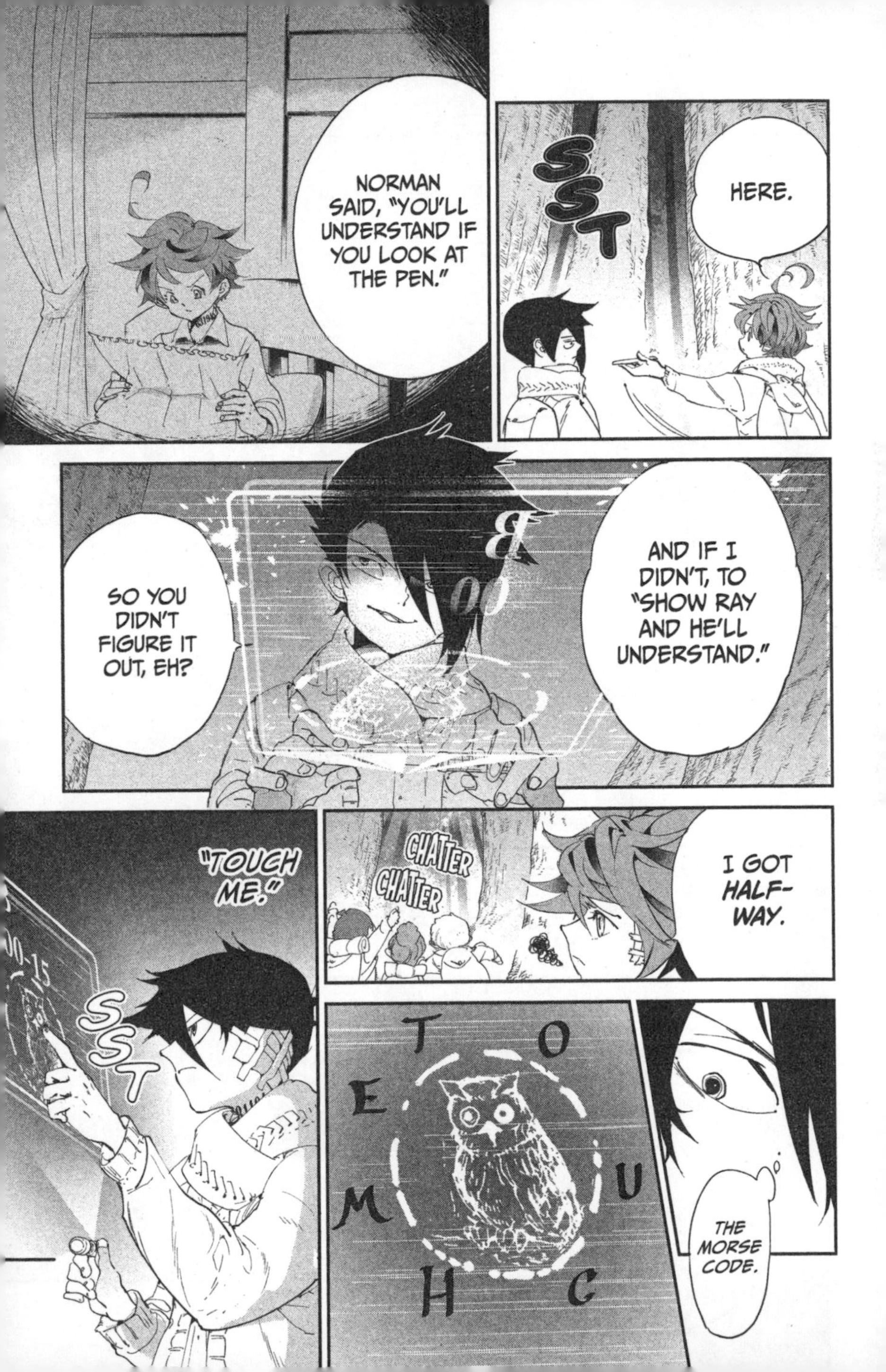
SST
HERE.
NORMAN SAID, "YOU'LL UNDERSTAND IF YOU LOOK AT THE PEN."
AND IF I DIDN'T, TO "SHOW RAY AND HE'LL UNDERSTAND."
SO YOU DIDN'T FIGURE IT OUT, EH?
CHATTER
CHATTER
I GOT HALF-WAY.
THE MORSE CODE.
"TOUCH ME."
SST

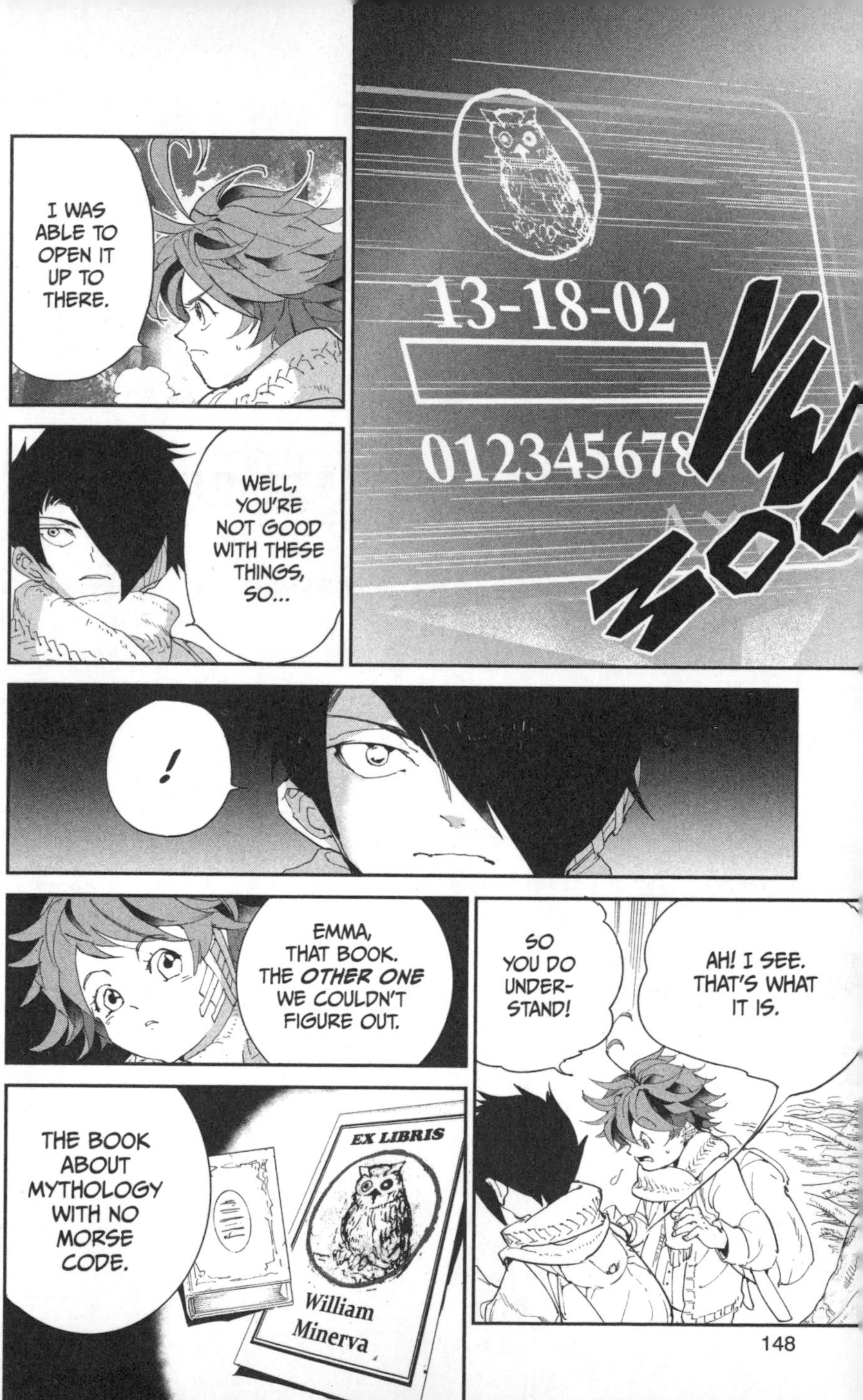
13-18-02
01234567
I WAS ABLE TO OPEN IT UP TO THERE.
WELL, YOU'RE NOT GOOD WITH THESE THINGS, SO...
!
AH! I SEE. THAT'S WHAT IT IS.
SO YOU DO UNDER-STAND!
EMMA, THAT BOOK. THE *OTHER ONE* WE COULDN'T FIGURE OUT.
THE BOOK ABOUT MYTHOLOGY WITH NO MORSE CODE.
EX LIBRIS
William Minerva

THAT BOOK IS THE CODEBOOK FOR THIS PEN.

YEAH.

A CODE-BOOK?

LOOK.

THERE'S THE SAME LABEL WITH NO MORSE CODE, RIGHT?

SO YOU USE THIS BOOK TO DECIPHER THE CODE.

13-18-02 IS THE CODE.

YOU CAN MOVE ON IF YOU ENTER THE ANSWER.

FOR EXAMPLE, WE LOOK IN THE BOOK FOR PAGE 13, LINE 18, THE SECOND WORD.

THE WORD IS "HUMAN."

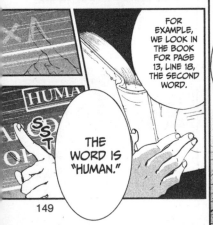

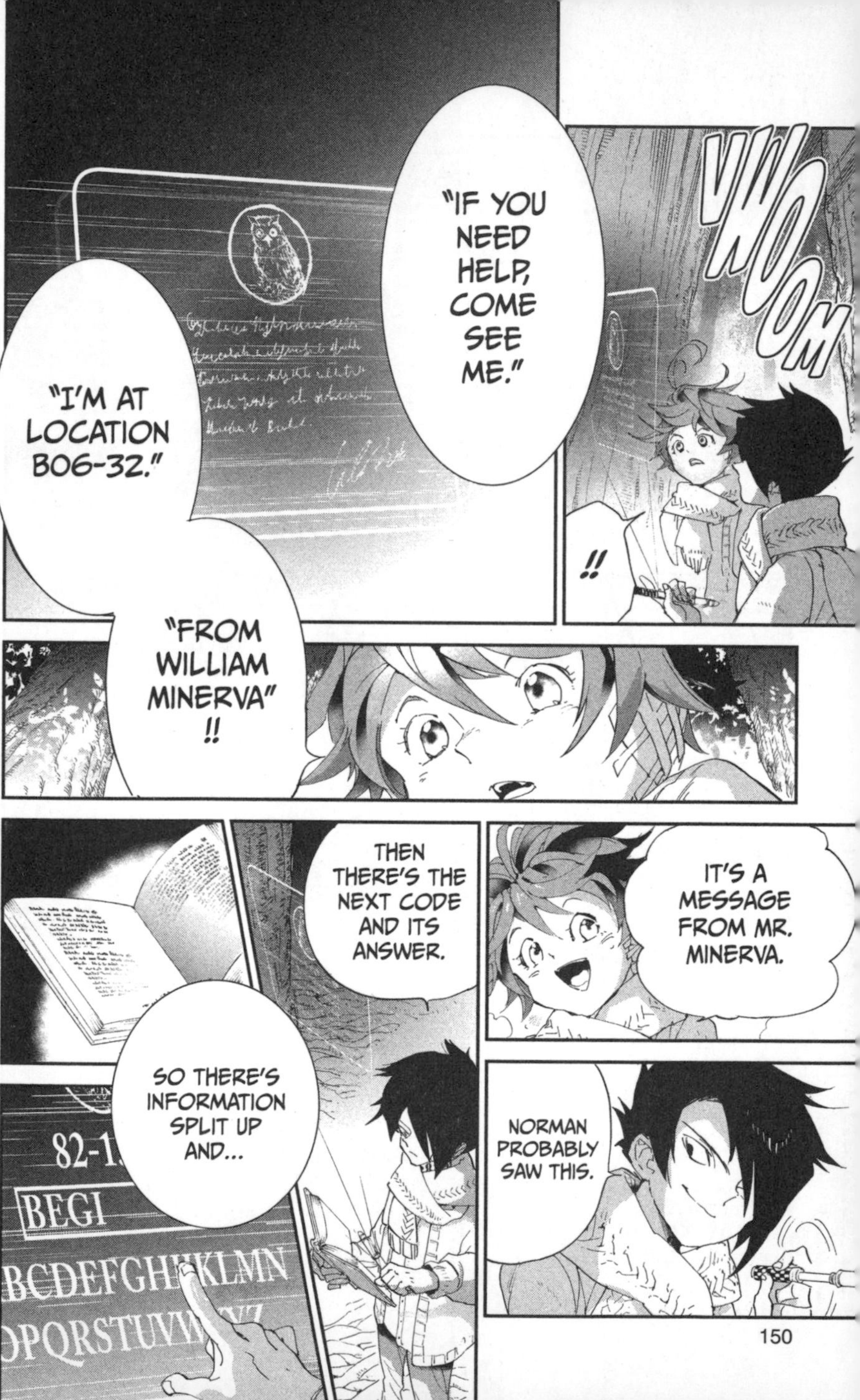
WHOOM
!!
"IF YOU NEED HELP, COME SEE ME."
"I'M AT LOCATION B06-32."
"FROM WILLIAM MINERVA" !!
IT'S A MESSAGE FROM MR. MINERVA.
THEN THERE'S THE NEXT CODE AND ITS ANSWER.
NORMAN PROBABLY SAW THIS.
SO THERE'S INFORMATION SPLIT UP AND...

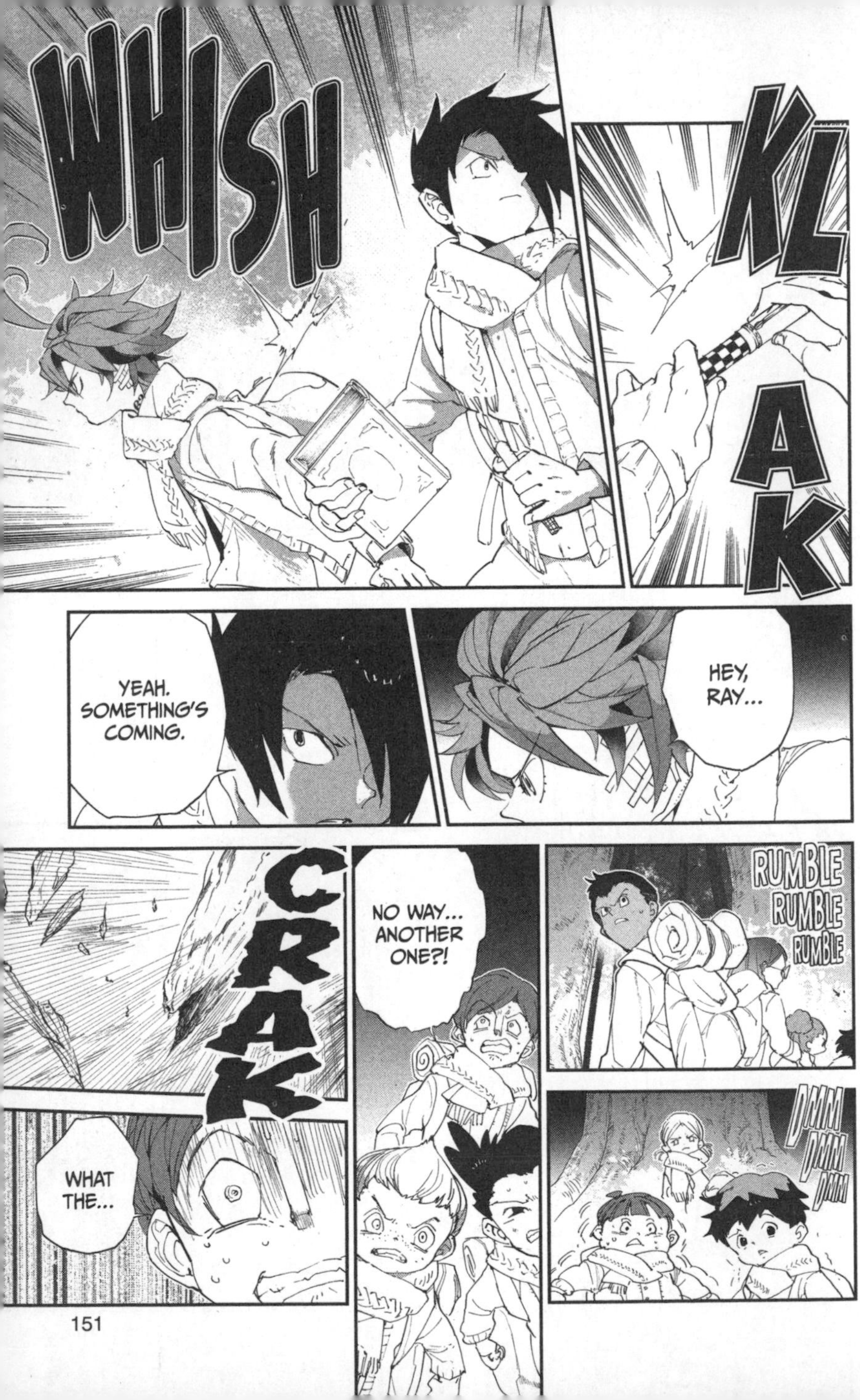
KLAK
WHISH
HEY, RAY...
YEAH. SOMETHING'S COMING.
RUMBLE RUMBLE RUMBLE
DMM DMM DMM
NO WAY... ANOTHER ONE?!
CRAK
WHAT THE...

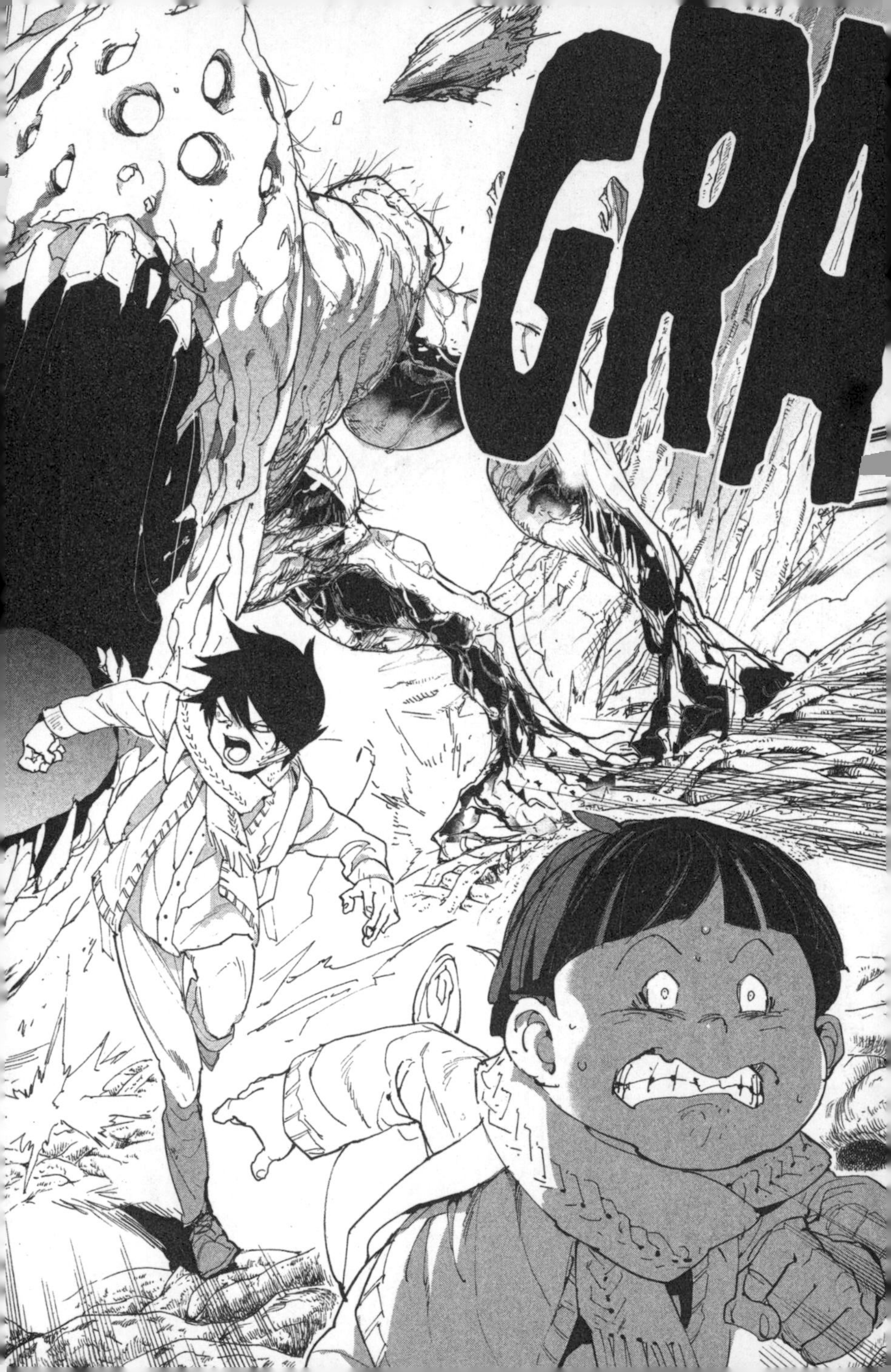
GRA

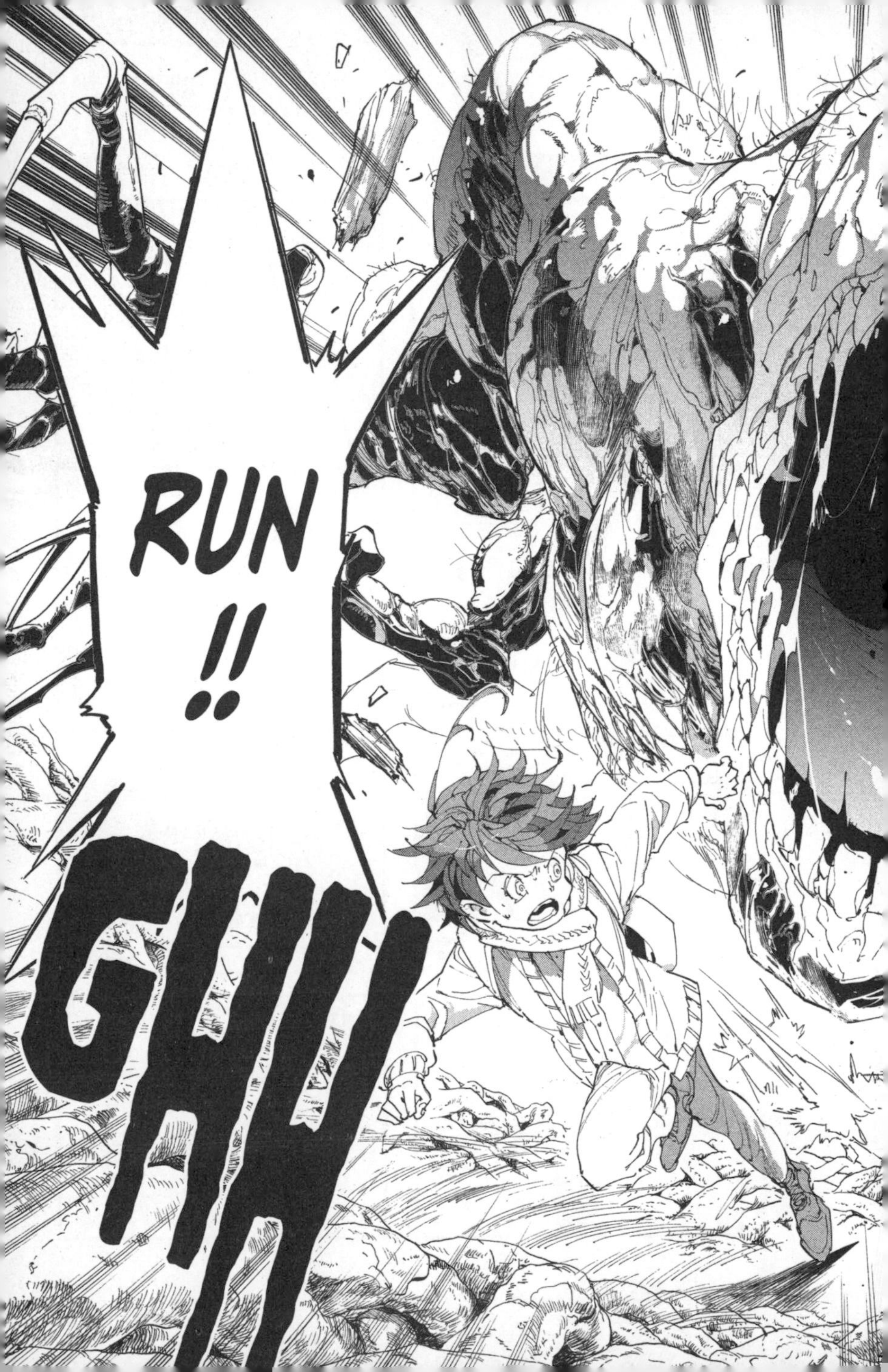
RUN!!
GHHH

SIDE STORY 2-4

GONE

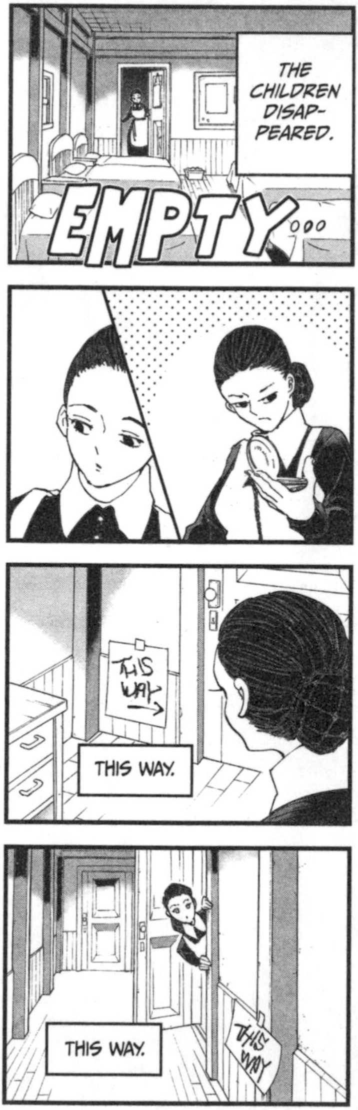
THE CHILDREN DISAP-PEARED.
EMPTY...
THIS WAY.
THIS WAY
THIS WAY.
THIS WAY

FIND US

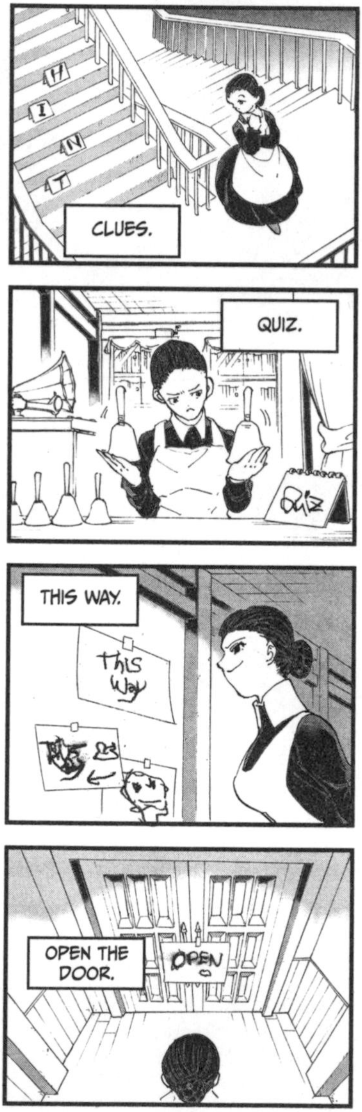
H
I
N
T
CLUES.
QUIZ.
QUIZ
THIS WAY.
This way
OPEN THE DOOR.
OPEN

TO BE CONTINUED IN SIDE STORY 2-5

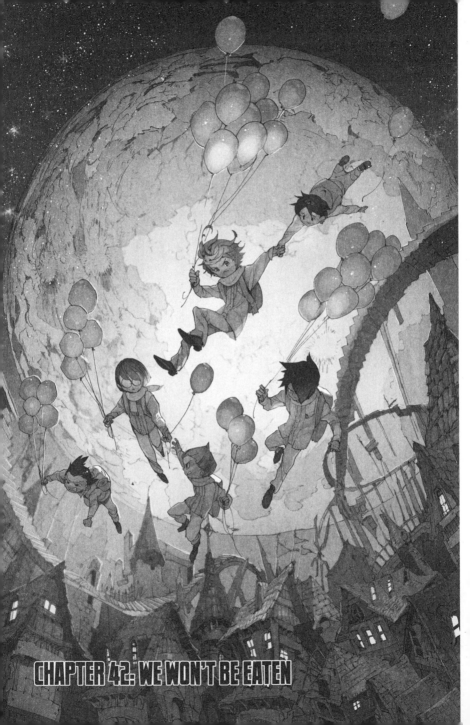

CHAPTER 42: WE WON'T BE EATEN

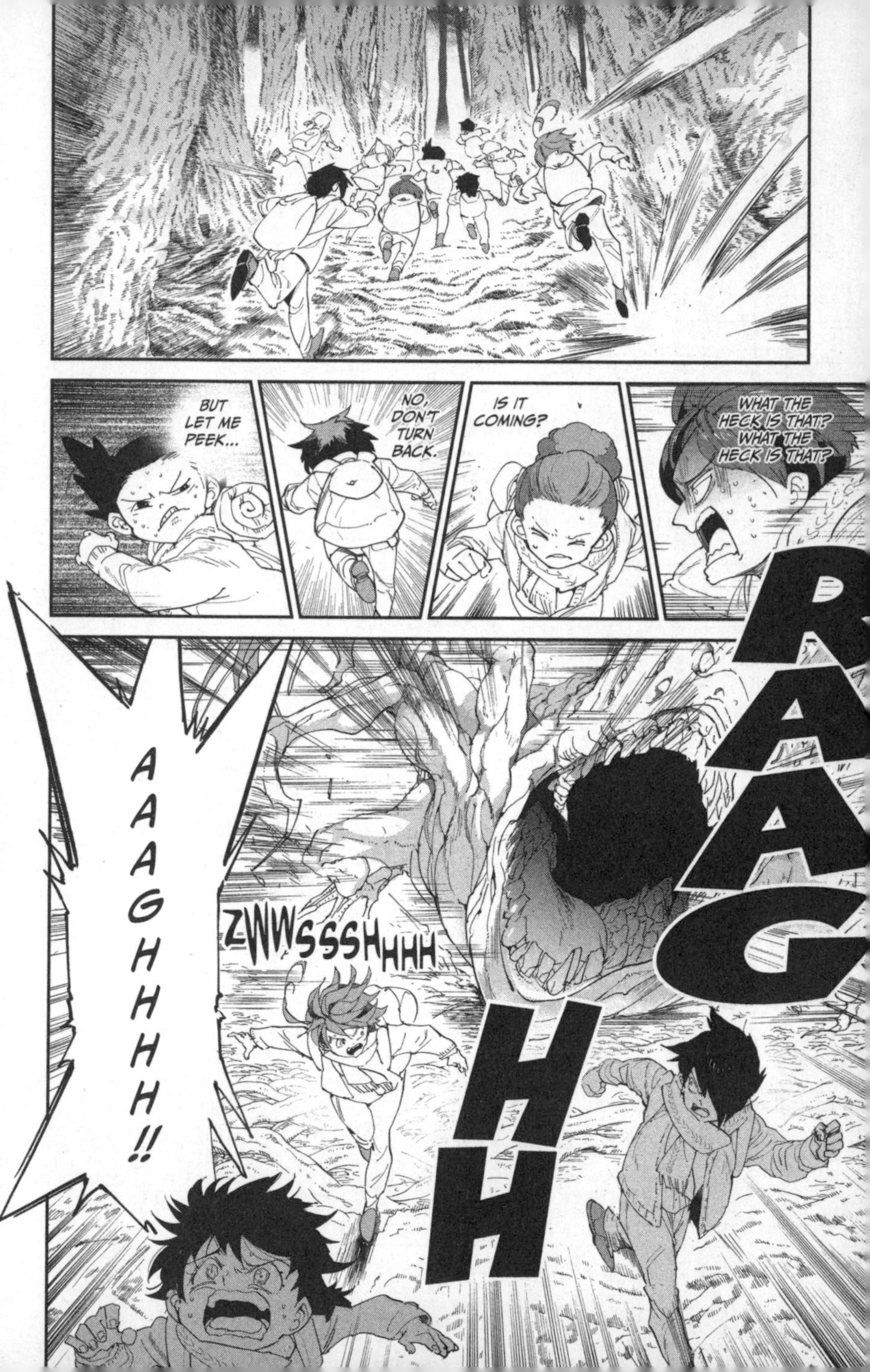
WHAT THE HECK IS THAT? WHAT THE HECK IS THAT?
IS IT COMING?
NO, DON'T TURN BACK.
BUT LET ME PEEK...
RAAAGHHH
ZWWSSSHHHH
AAAAGHHHHHH!!

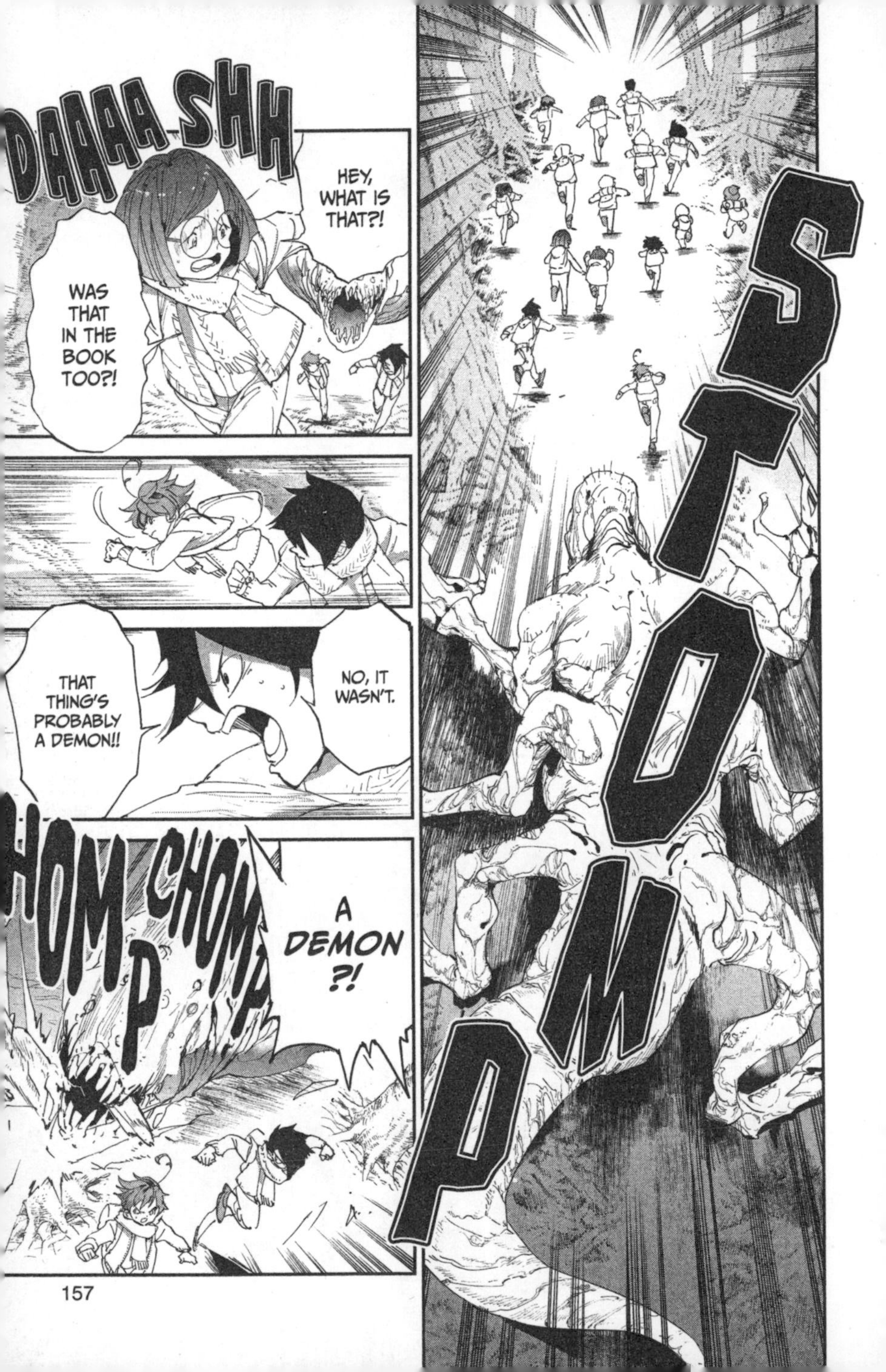
STOMP
DAAAA SHH
HEY, WHAT IS THAT?!
WAS THAT IN THE BOOK TOO?!
NO, IT WASN'T.
THAT THING'S PROBABLY A DEMON!!
CHOMP
HOM
A DEMON ?!

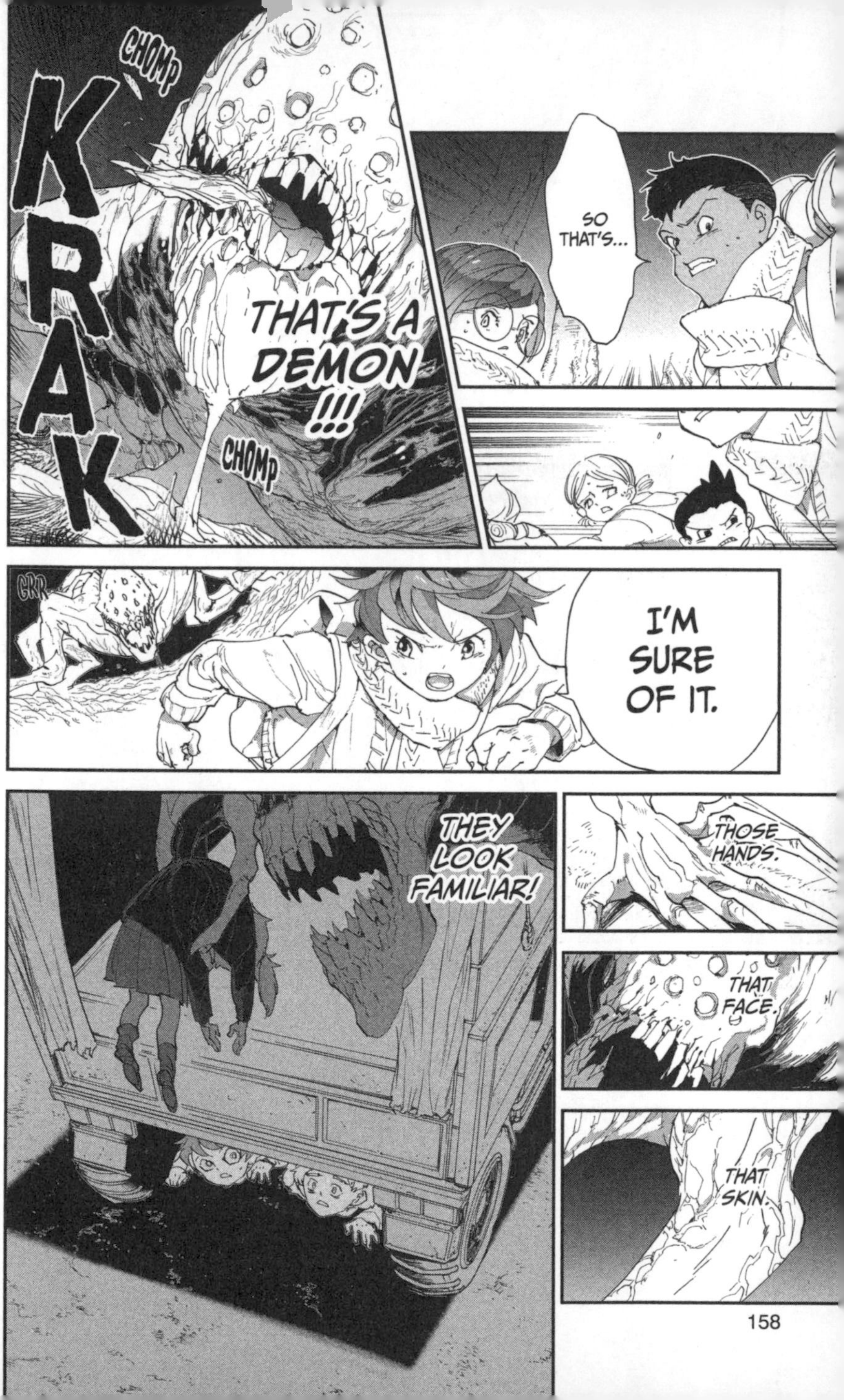
SO THAT'S...
CHOMP
KRAK
THAT'S A DEMON!!!
CHOMP
I'M SURE OF IT.
GRR
THOSE HANDS.
THAT FACE.
THAT SKIN.
THEY LOOK FAMILIAR!

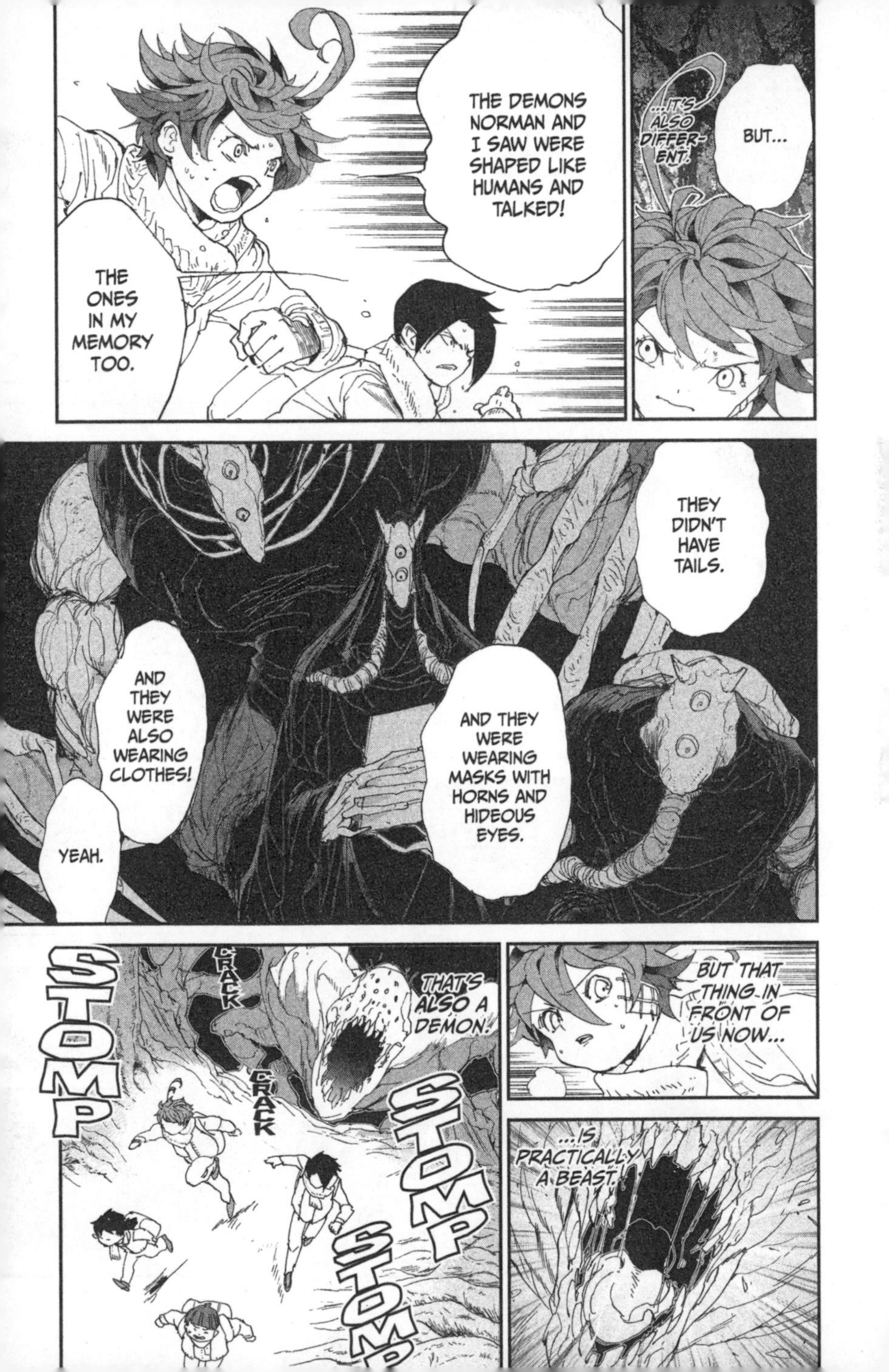
BUT...
...IT'S ALSO DIFFERENT.
THE DEMONS NORMAN AND I SAW WERE SHAPED LIKE HUMANS AND TALKED!
THE ONES IN MY MEMORY TOO.
THEY DIDN'T HAVE TAILS.
AND THEY WERE WEARING MASKS WITH HORNS AND HIDEOUS EYES.
AND THEY WERE ALSO WEARING CLOTHES!
YEAH.
BUT THAT THING IN FRONT OF US NOW...
...IS PRACTICALLY A BEAST.
THAT'S ALSO A DEMON.
CRACK
CRACK
STOMP
STOMP
STOMP

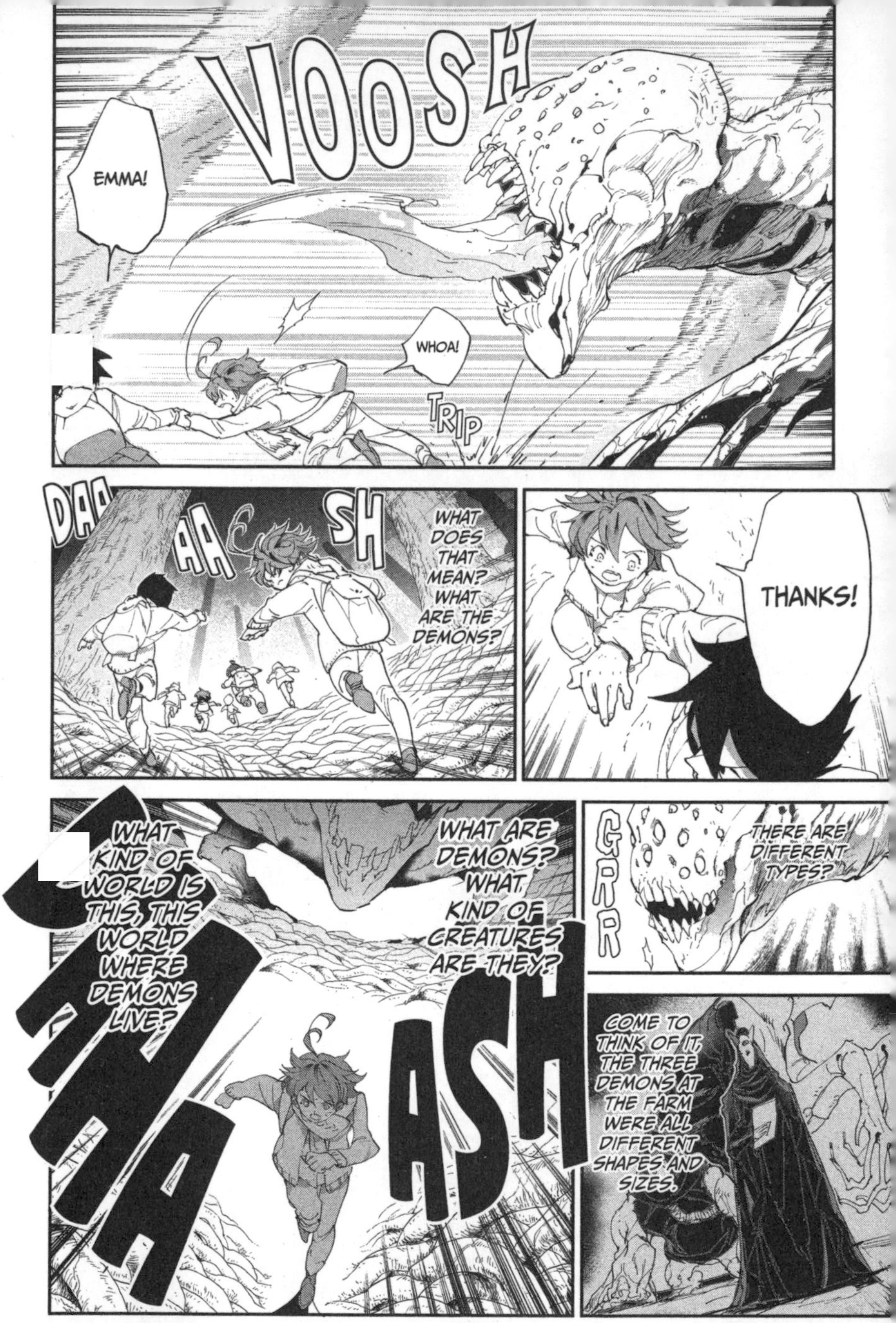

VOOSH
EMMA!
WHOA!
TRIP
THANKS!
DAAAASH
WHAT DOES THAT MEAN? WHAT ARE THE DEMONS?
GRR
THERE ARE DIFFERENT TYPES?
COME TO THINK OF IT, THE THREE DEMONS AT THE FARM WERE ALL DIFFERENT SHAPES AND SIZES.
WHAT ARE DEMONS? WHAT KIND OF CREATURES ARE THEY?
WHAT KIND OF WORLD IS THIS, THIS WORLD WHERE DEMONS LIVE?
DAAAASH

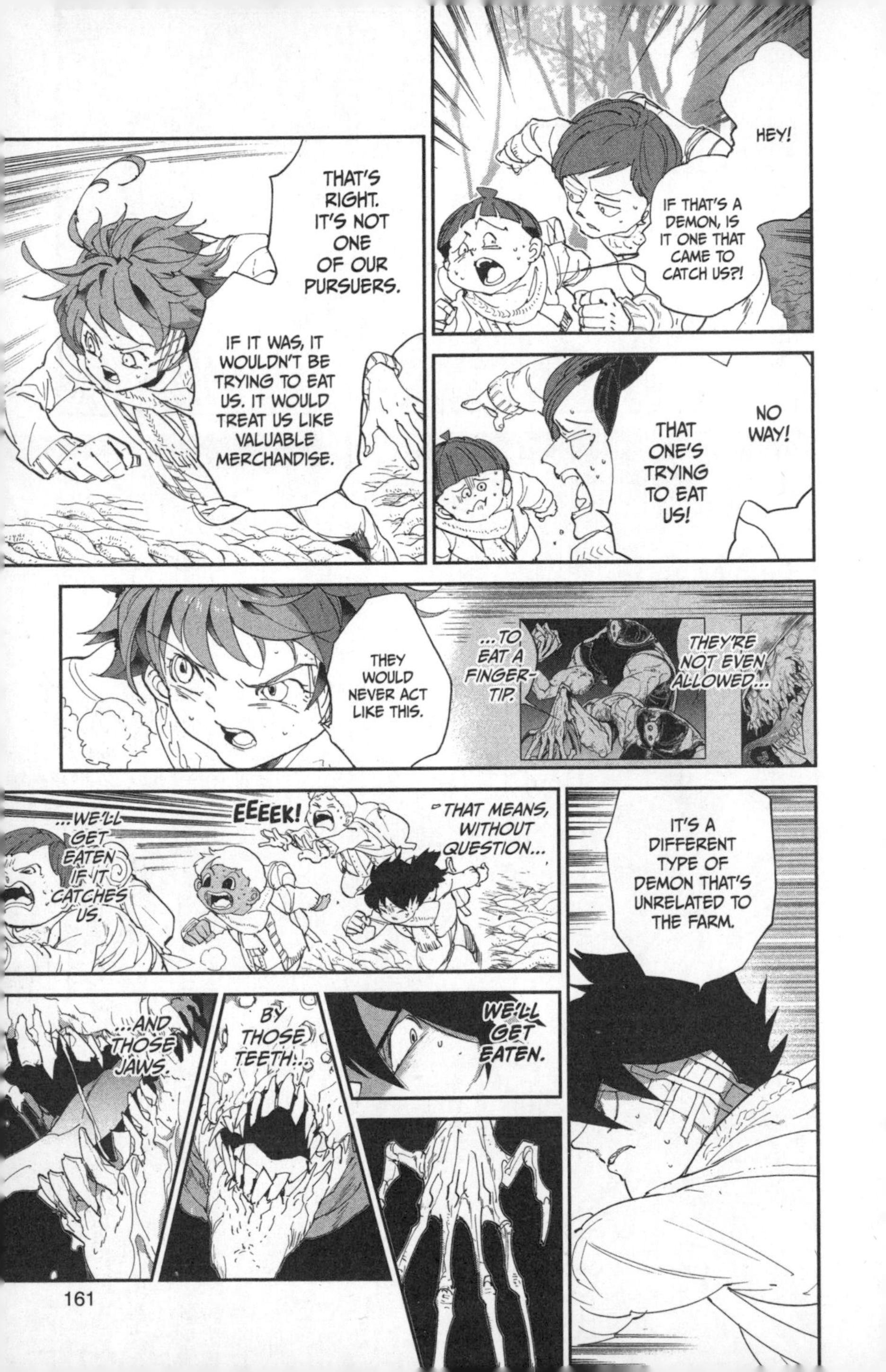
HEY!
IF THAT'S A DEMON, IS IT ONE THAT CAME TO CATCH US?!
NO WAY!
THAT ONE'S TRYING TO EAT US!
THAT'S RIGHT. IT'S NOT ONE OF OUR PURSUERS.
IF IT WAS, IT WOULDN'T BE TRYING TO EAT US. IT WOULD TREAT US LIKE VALUABLE MERCHANDISE.
THEY'RE NOT EVEN ALLOWED...
...TO EAT A FINGER-TIP.
THEY WOULD NEVER ACT LIKE THIS.
IT'S A DIFFERENT TYPE OF DEMON THAT'S UNRELATED TO THE FARM.
THAT MEANS, WITHOUT QUESTION...
EEEEK!
...WE'LL GET EATEN IF IT CATCHES US.
WE'LL GET EATEN.
BY THOSE TEETH...
...AND THOSE JAWS.

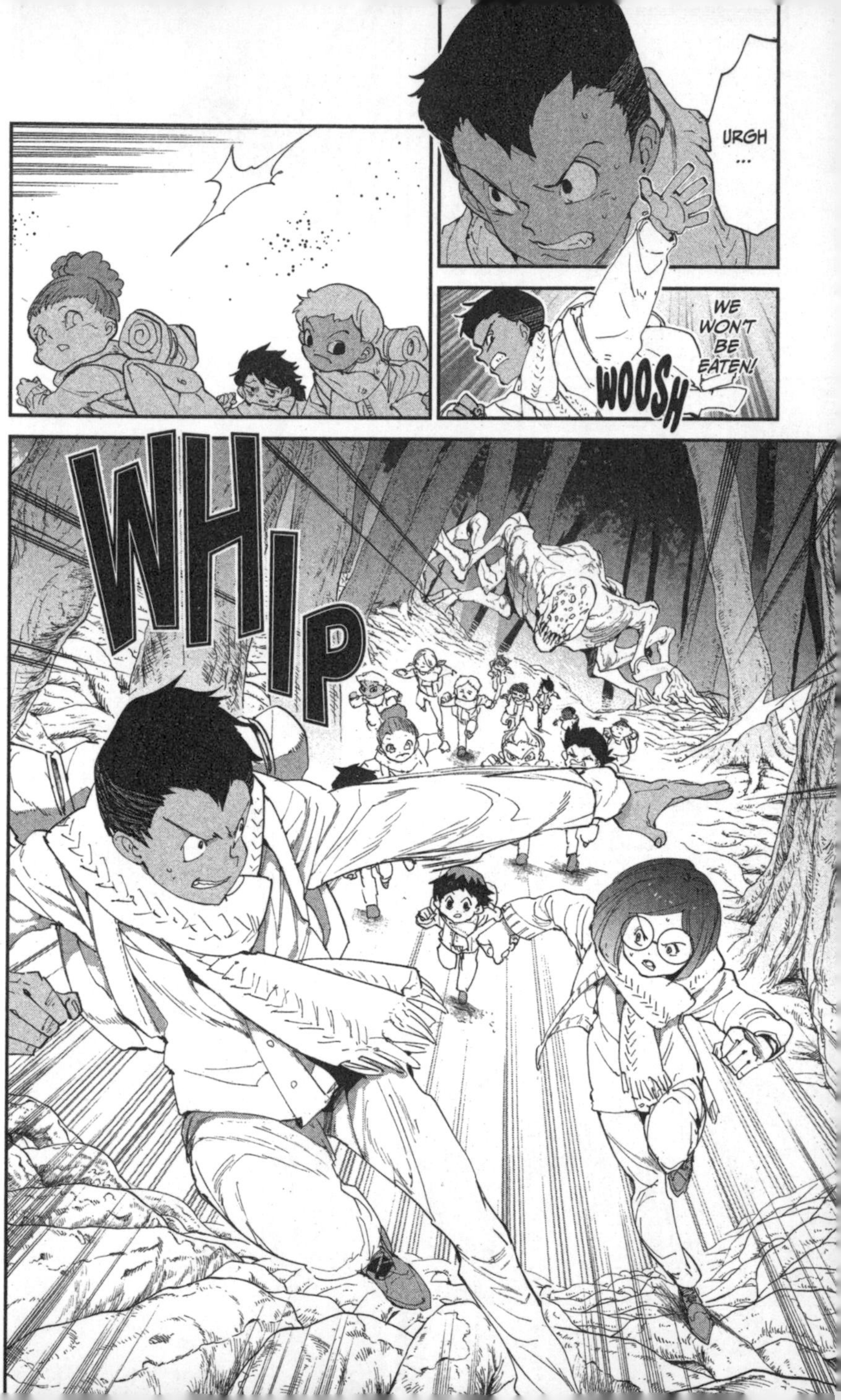
URGH ...
WE WON'T BE EATEN!
WOOSH
WHIP

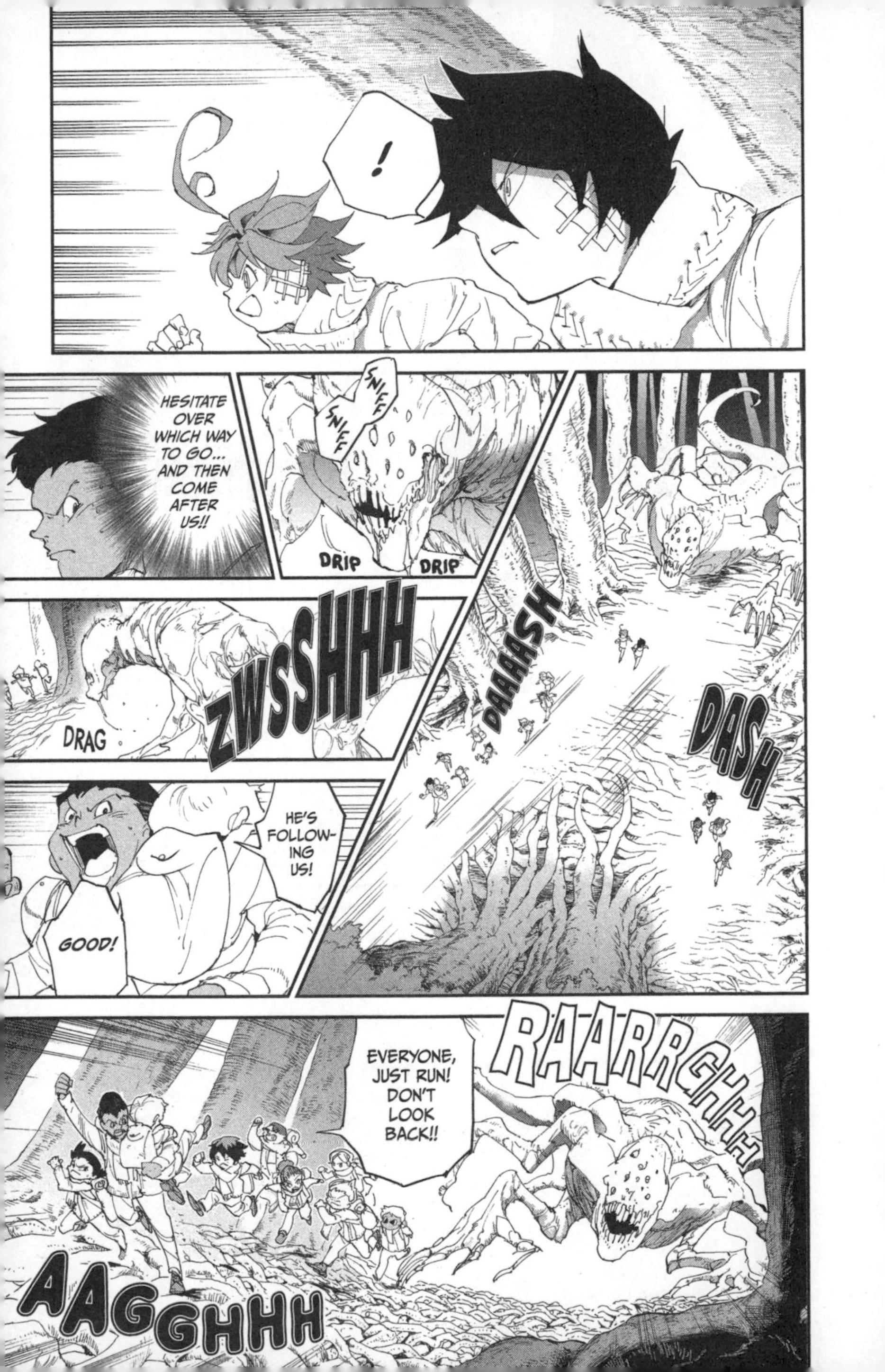
!
DAAAASH
DASH
SNIFF SNIFF
DRIP DRIP
HESITATE OVER WHICH WAY TO GO... AND THEN COME AFTER US!!
ZWSSHHH
DRAG
HE'S FOLLOWING US!
GOOD!
RAARRGHHH
EVERYONE, JUST RUN! DON'T LOOK BACK!!
AAGGHHH

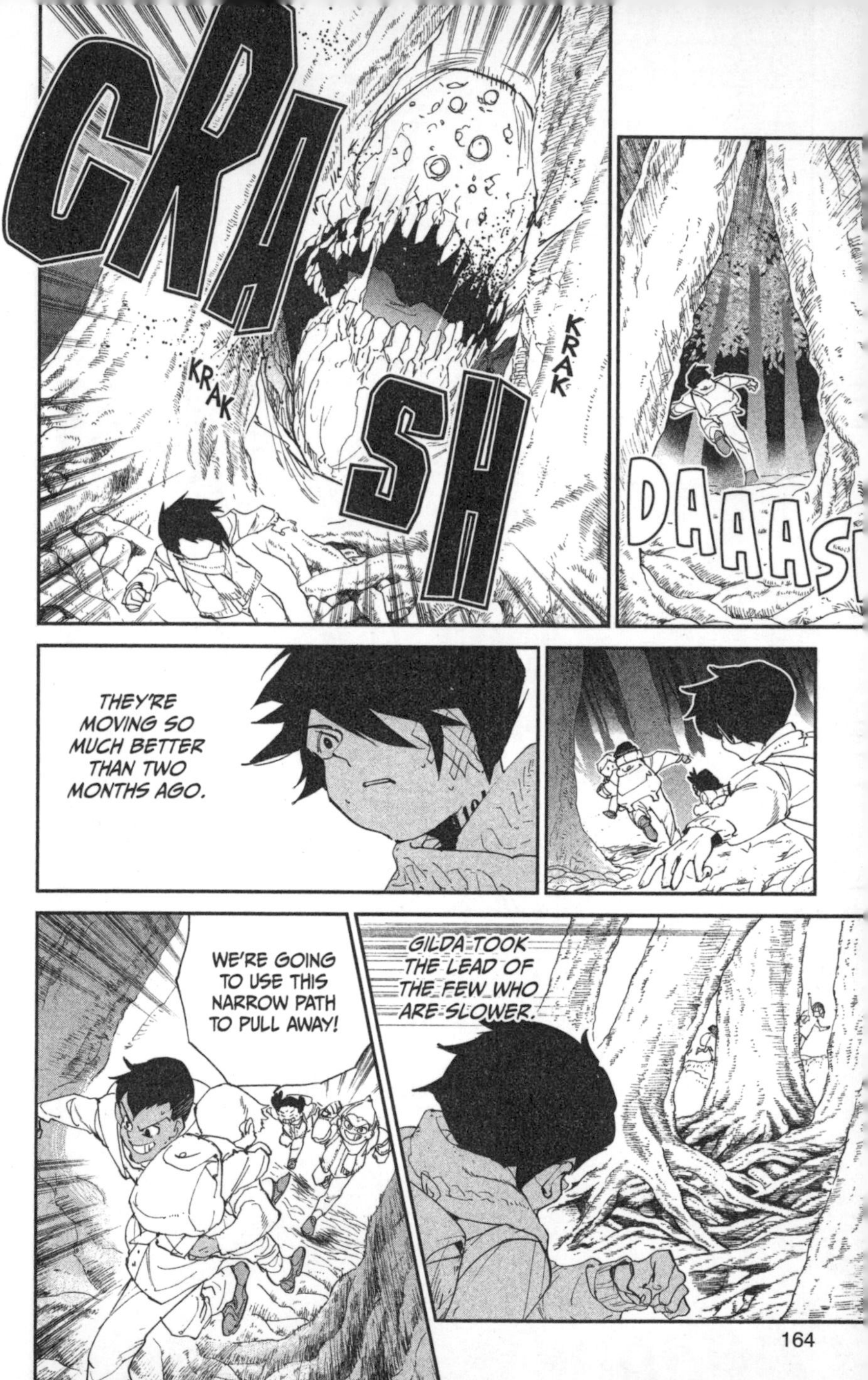
DAAAS
CRASH
KRAK
KRAK
THEY'RE MOVING SO MUCH BETTER THAN TWO MONTHS AGO.
GILDA TOOK THE LEAD OF THE FEW WHO ARE SLOWER.
WE'RE GOING TO USE THIS NARROW PATH TO PULL AWAY!

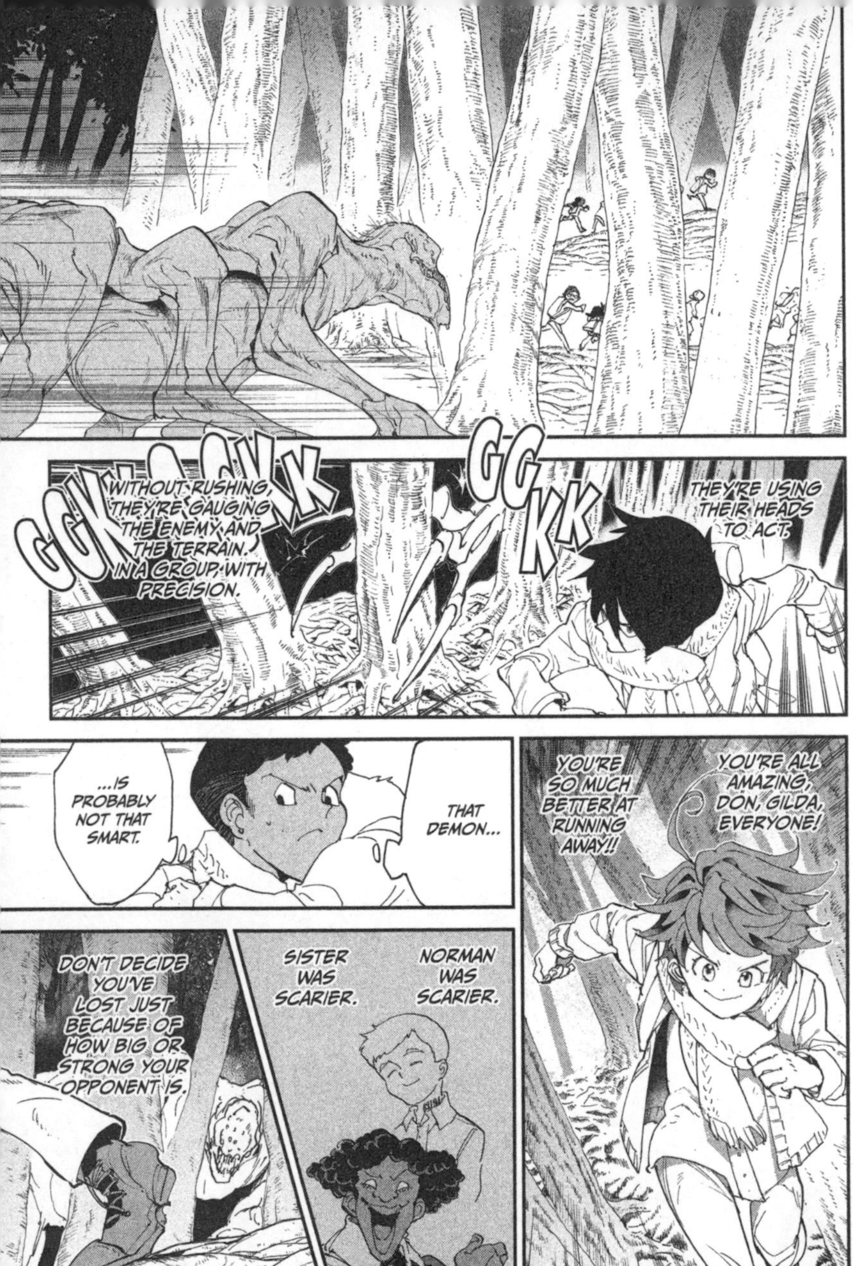
THEY'RE USING THEIR HEADS TO ACT.
GGKK
WITHOUT RUSHING, THEY'RE GAUGING THE ENEMY AND THE TERRAIN. IN A GROUP, WITH PRECISION.
YOU'RE ALL AMAZING, DON, GILDA, EVERYONE!
YOU'RE SO MUCH BETTER AT RUNNING AWAY!!
THAT DEMON...
...IS PROBABLY NOT THAT SMART.
NORMAN WAS SCARIER.
SISTER WAS SCARIER.
DON'T DECIDE YOU'VE LOST JUST BECAUSE OF HOW BIG OR STRONG YOUR OPPONENT IS.

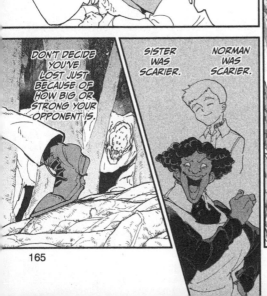

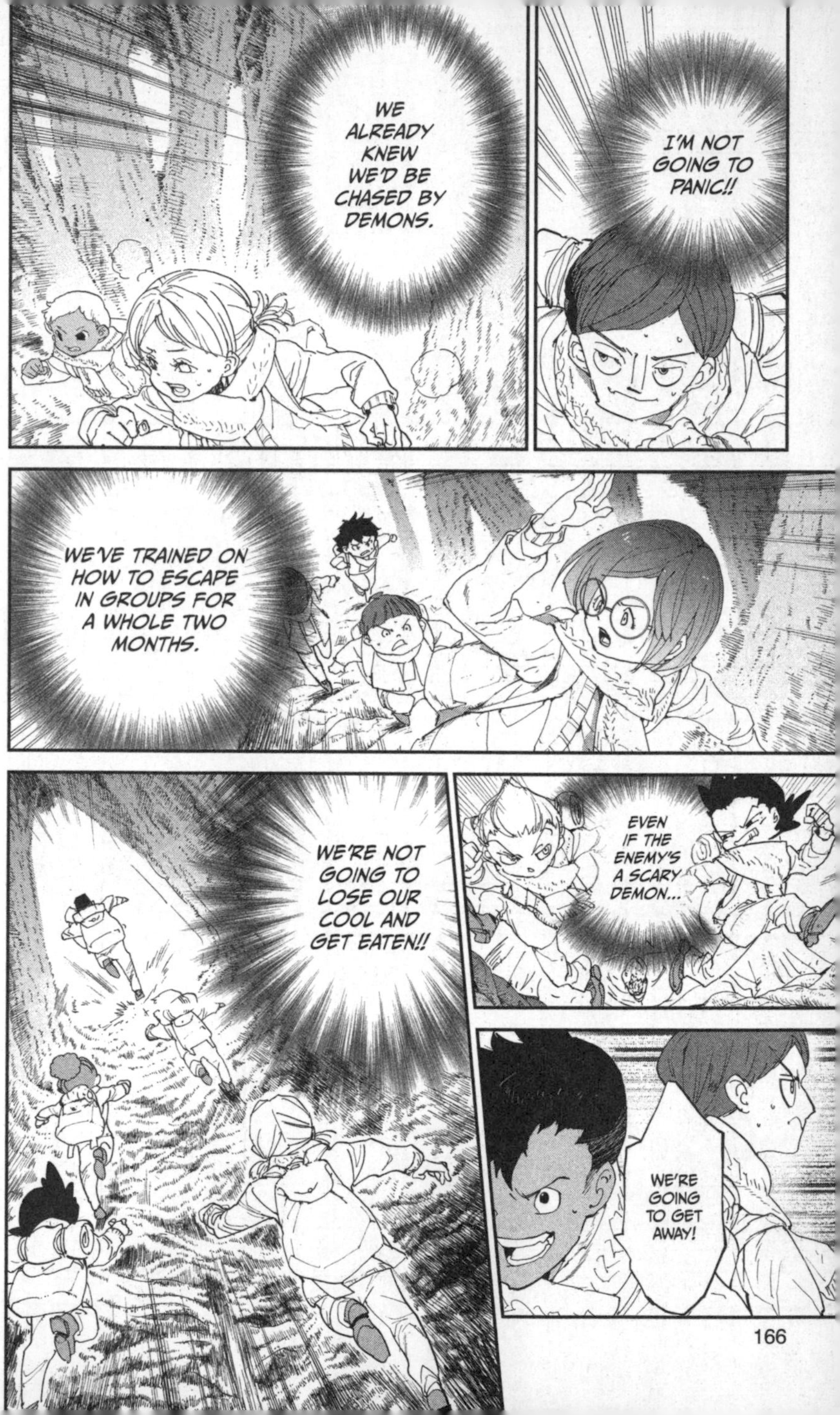
I'M NOT GOING TO PANIC!!
WE ALREADY KNEW WE'D BE CHASED BY DEMONS.
WE'VE TRAINED ON HOW TO ESCAPE IN GROUPS FOR A WHOLE TWO MONTHS.
EVEN IF THE ENEMY'S A SCARY DEMON...
WE'RE GOING TO GET AWAY!
WE'RE NOT GOING TO LOSE OUR COOL AND GET EATEN!!

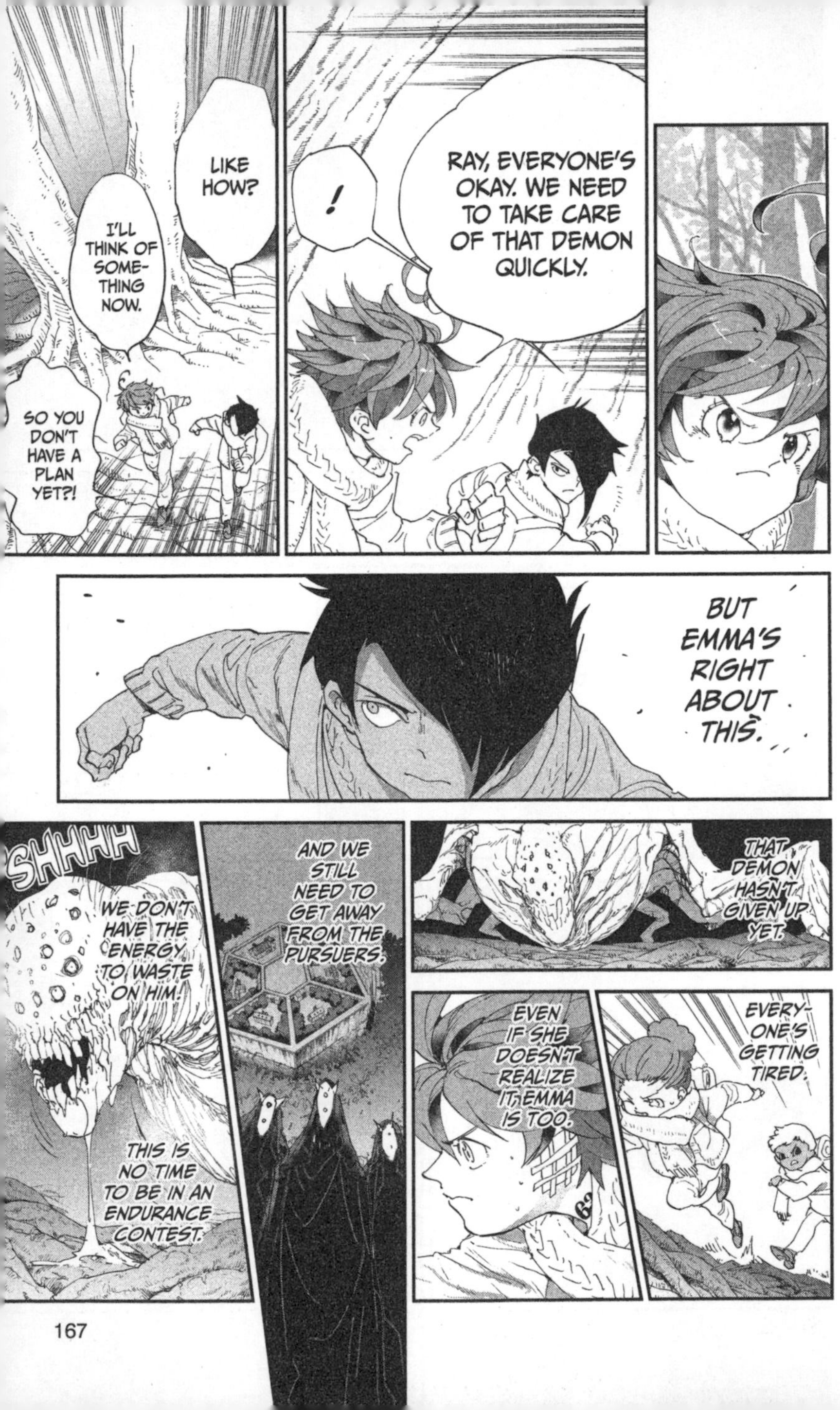
RAY, EVERYONE'S OKAY. WE NEED TO TAKE CARE OF THAT DEMON QUICKLY.
!
LIKE HOW?
I'LL THINK OF SOME-THING NOW.
SO YOU DON'T HAVE A PLAN YET?!
BUT EMMA'S RIGHT ABOUT THIS.
THAT DEMON HASN'T GIVEN UP YET.
EVERY-ONE'S GETTING TIRED.
EVEN IF SHE DOESN'T REALIZE IT, EMMA IS TOO.
AND WE STILL NEED TO GET AWAY FROM THE PURSUERS.
SHHHH
WE DON'T HAVE THE ENERGY TO WASTE ON HIM.
THIS IS NO TIME TO BE IN AN ENDURANCE CONTEST.

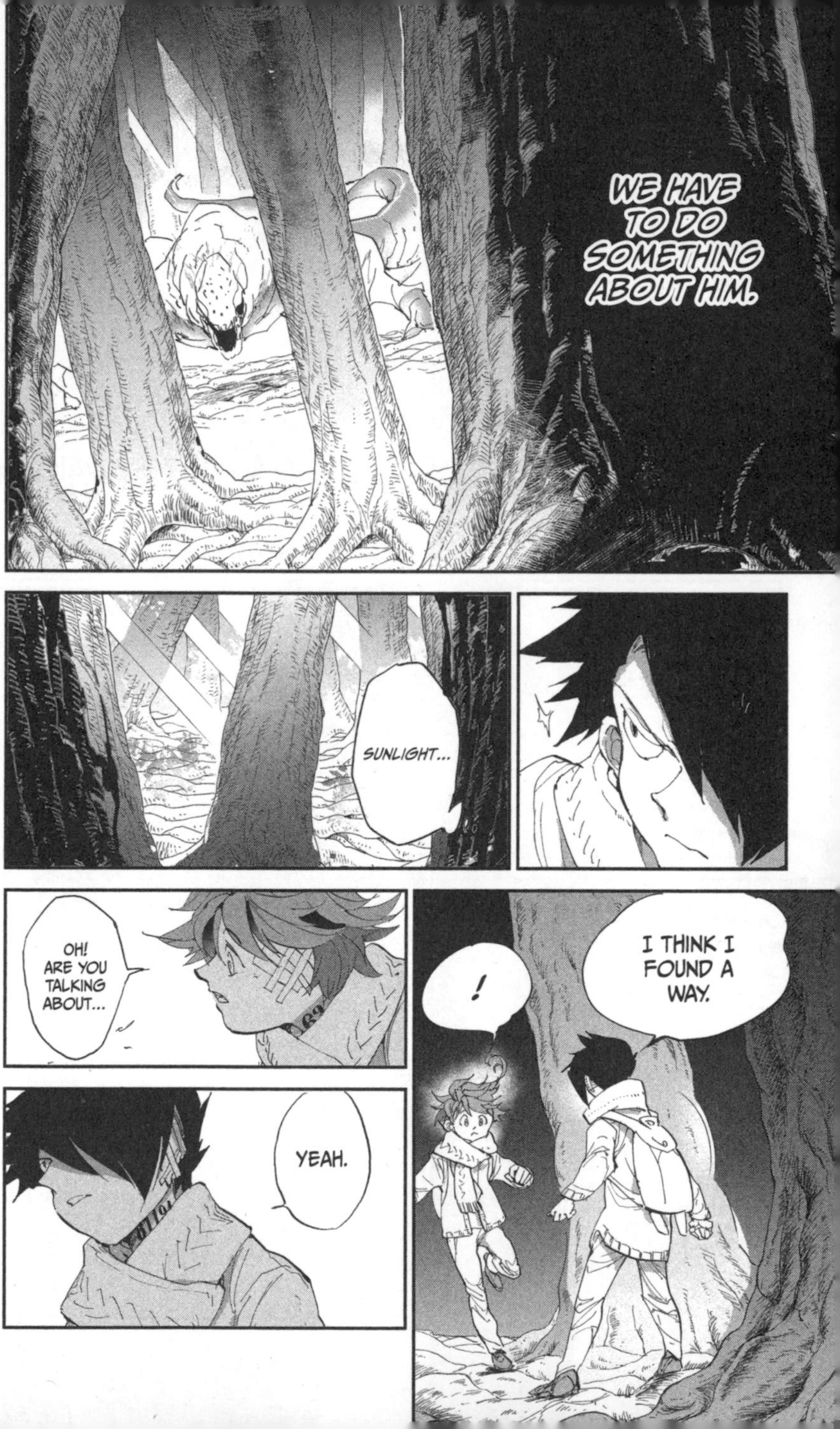
WE HAVE TO DO SOMETHING ABOUT HIM.
SUNLIGHT...
I THINK I FOUND A WAY.
!
OH! ARE YOU TALKING ABOUT...
YEAH.

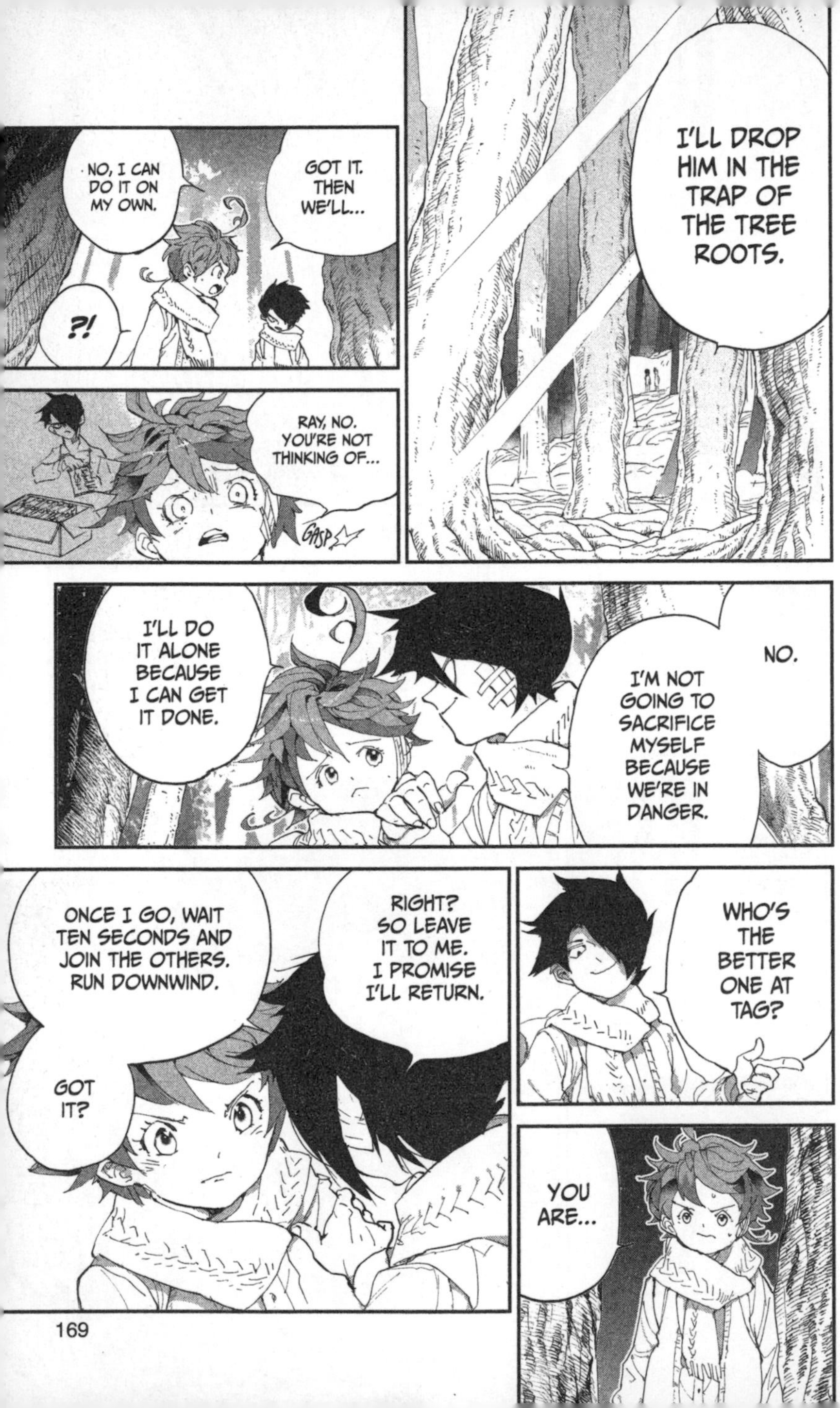
I'LL DROP HIM IN THE TRAP OF THE TREE ROOTS.
GOT IT. THEN WE'LL...
NO, I CAN DO IT ON MY OWN.
?!
RAY, NO. YOU'RE NOT THINKING OF...
GASP
NO.
I'M NOT GOING TO SACRIFICE MYSELF BECAUSE WE'RE IN DANGER.
I'LL DO IT ALONE BECAUSE I CAN GET IT DONE.
WHO'S THE BETTER ONE AT TAG?
YOU ARE...
RIGHT? SO LEAVE IT TO ME. I PROMISE I'LL RETURN.
ONCE I GO, WAIT TEN SECONDS AND JOIN THE OTHERS. RUN DOWNWIND.
GOT IT?

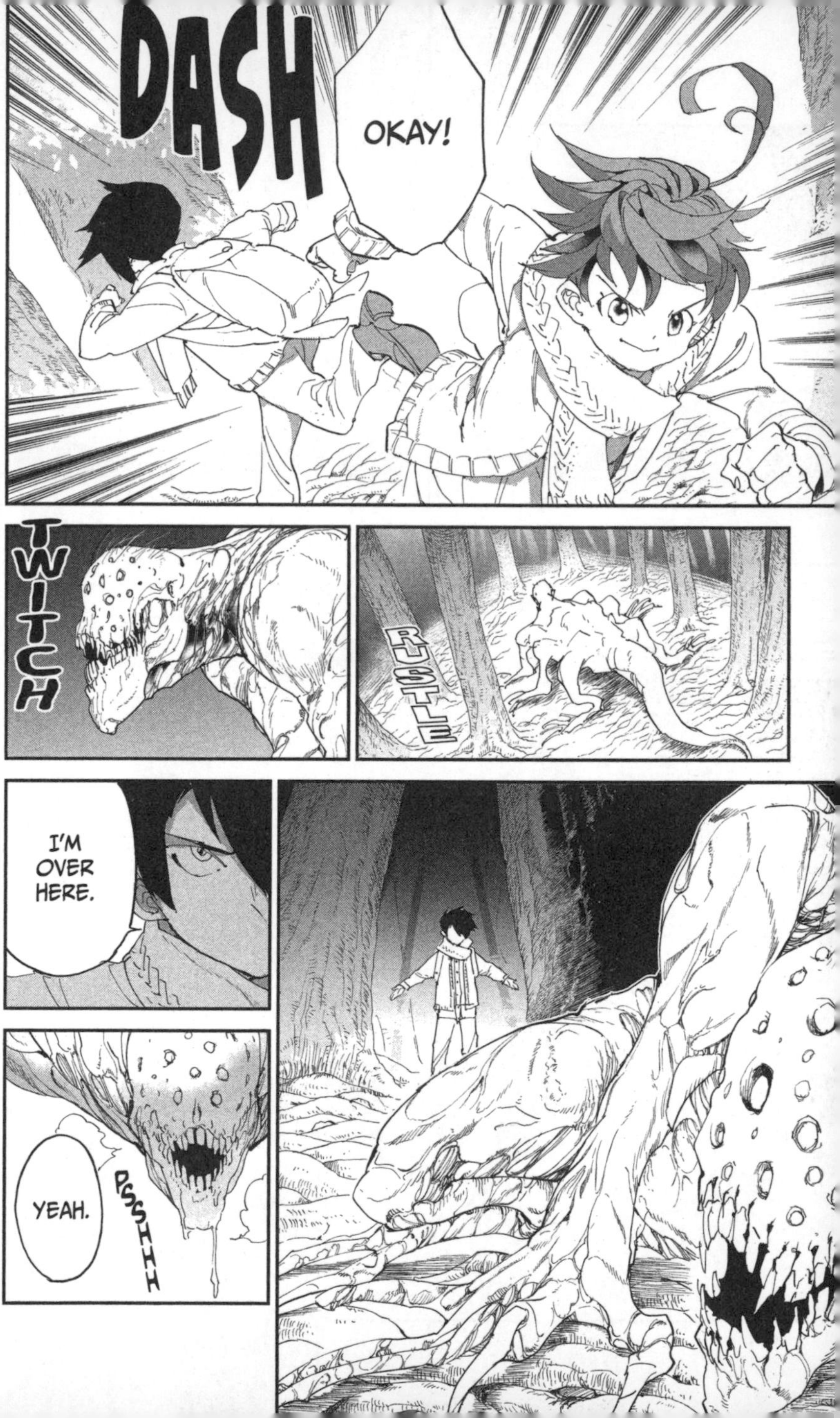
OKAY!
DASH
RUSTLE
TWITCH
I'M OVER HERE.
YEAH.
PSSHHH

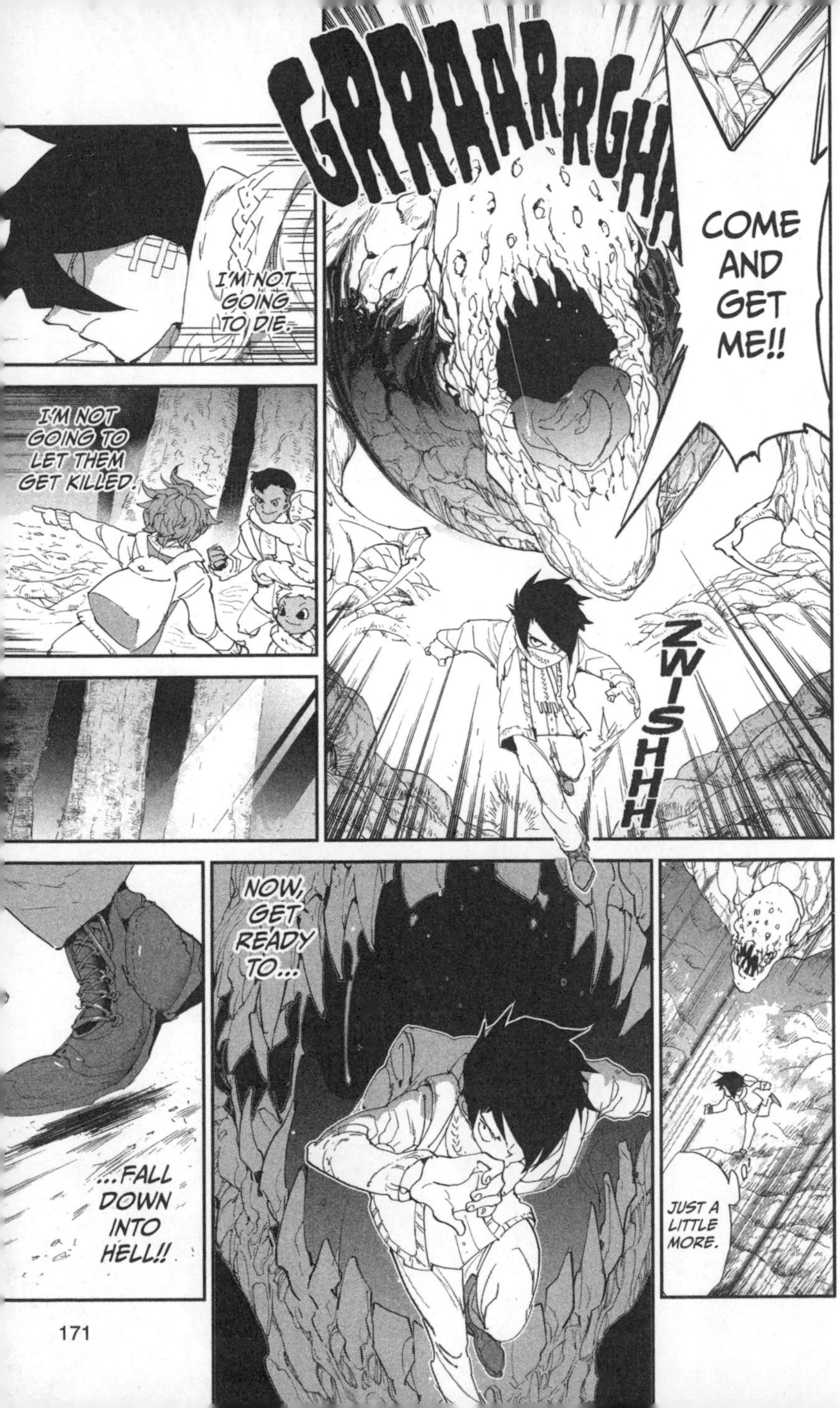
GRRAARRGHA
COME AND GET ME!!
ZWISHHH
I'M NOT GOING TO DIE.
I'M NOT GOING TO LET THEM GET KILLED.
JUST A LITTLE MORE.
NOW, GET READY TO...
...FALL DOWN INTO HELL!!

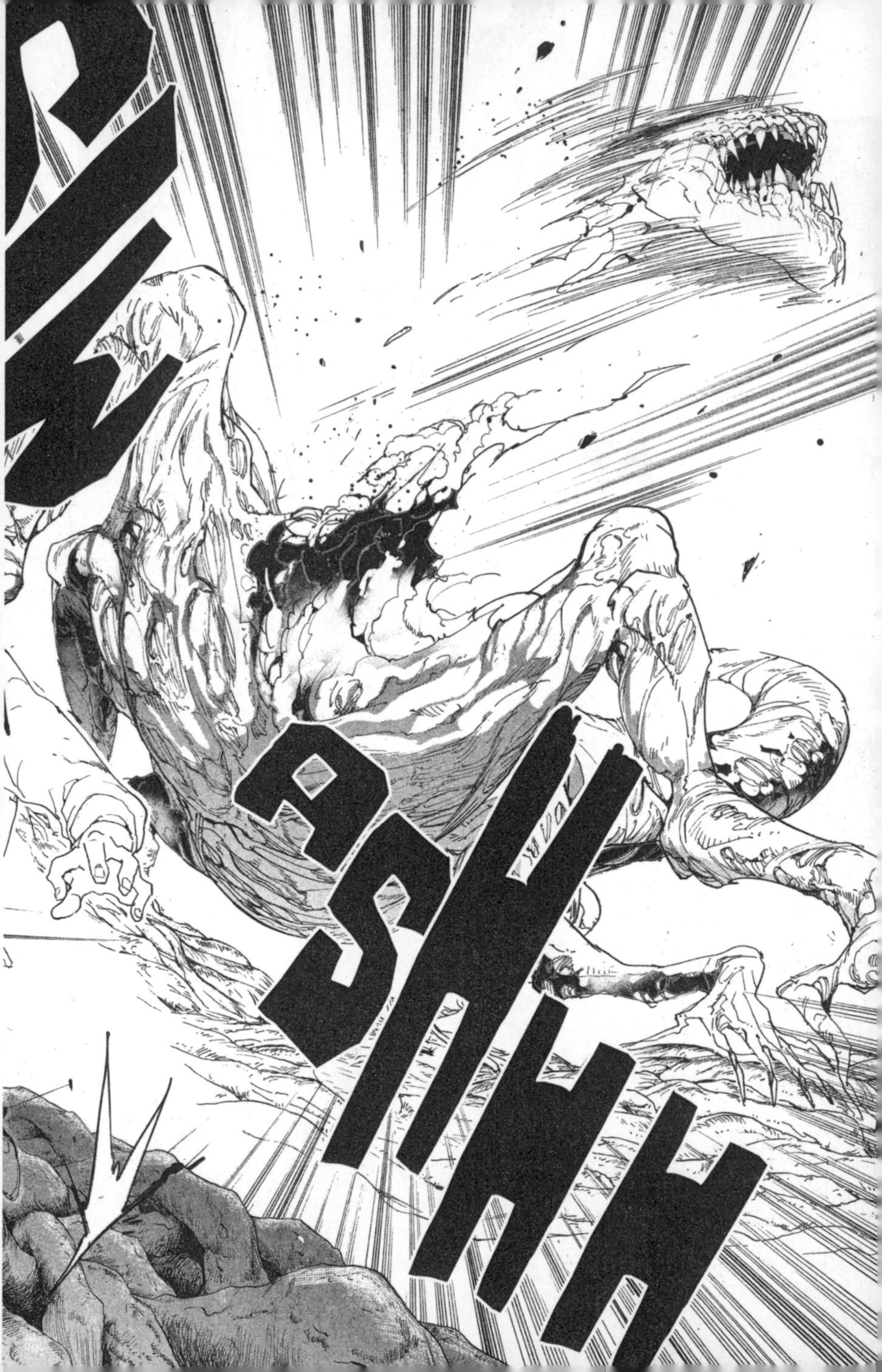
ASHHHH

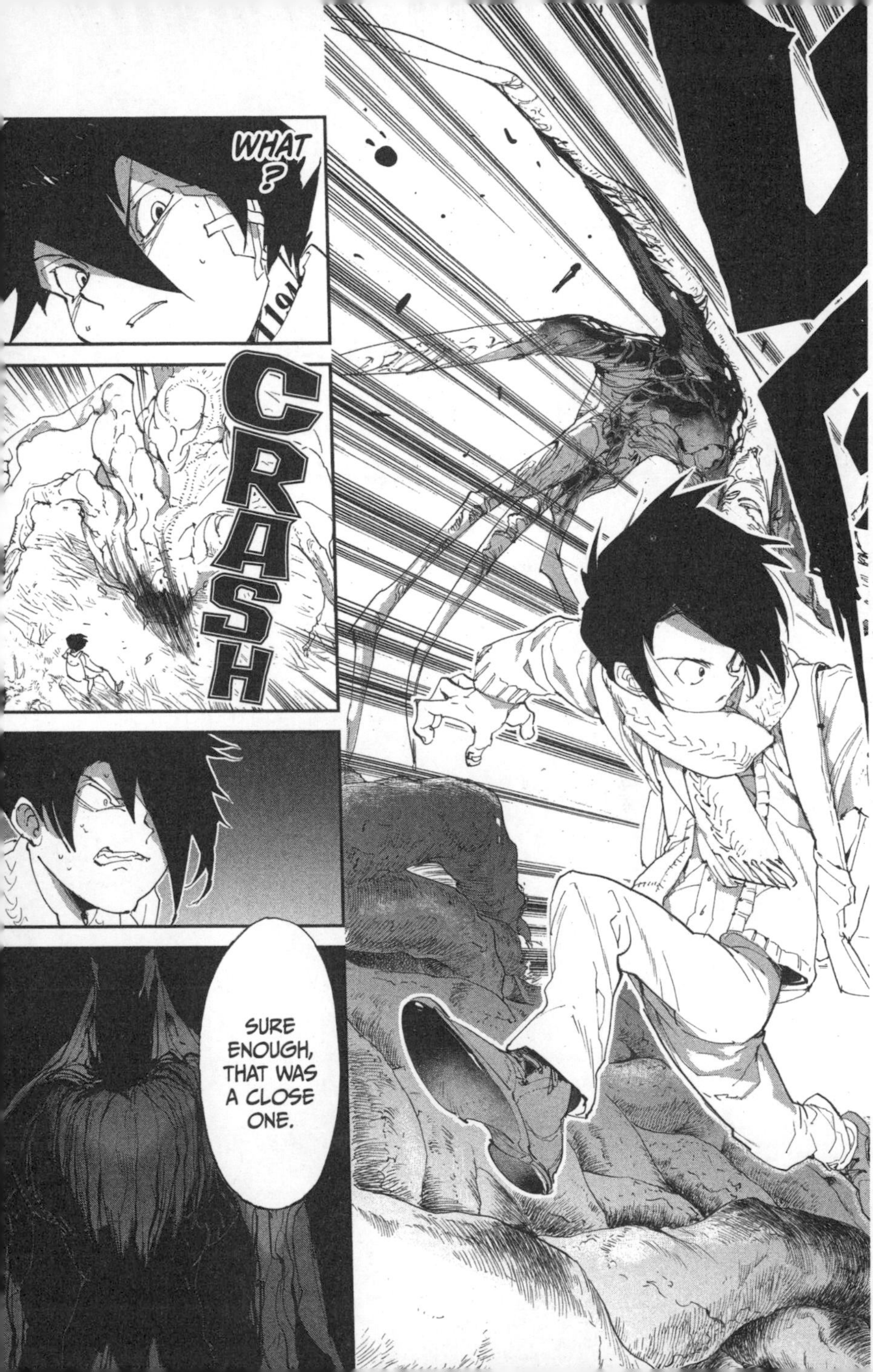
WHAT?
CRASH
SURE ENOUGH, THAT WAS A CLOSE ONE.

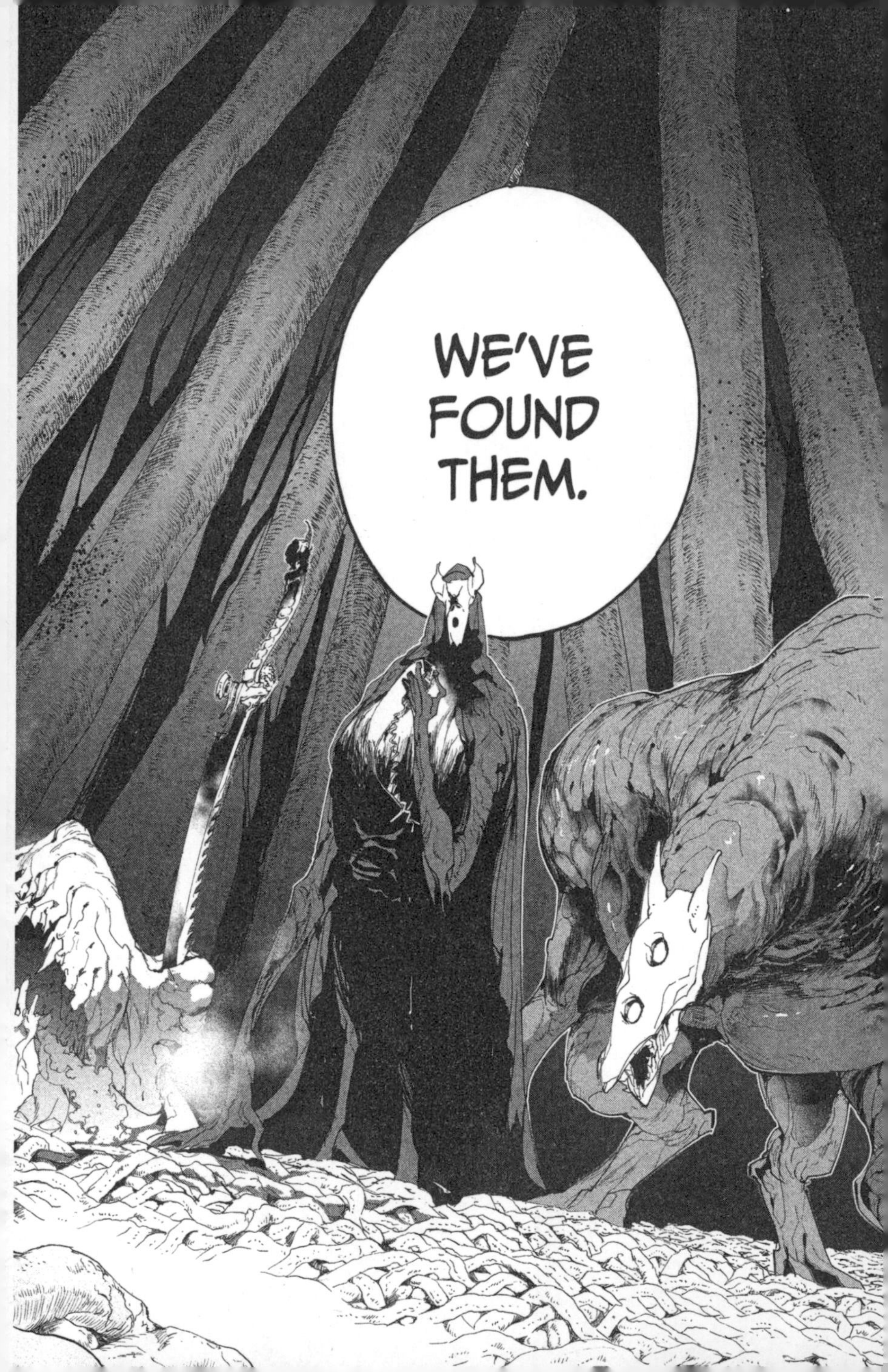
WE'VE FOUND THEM.

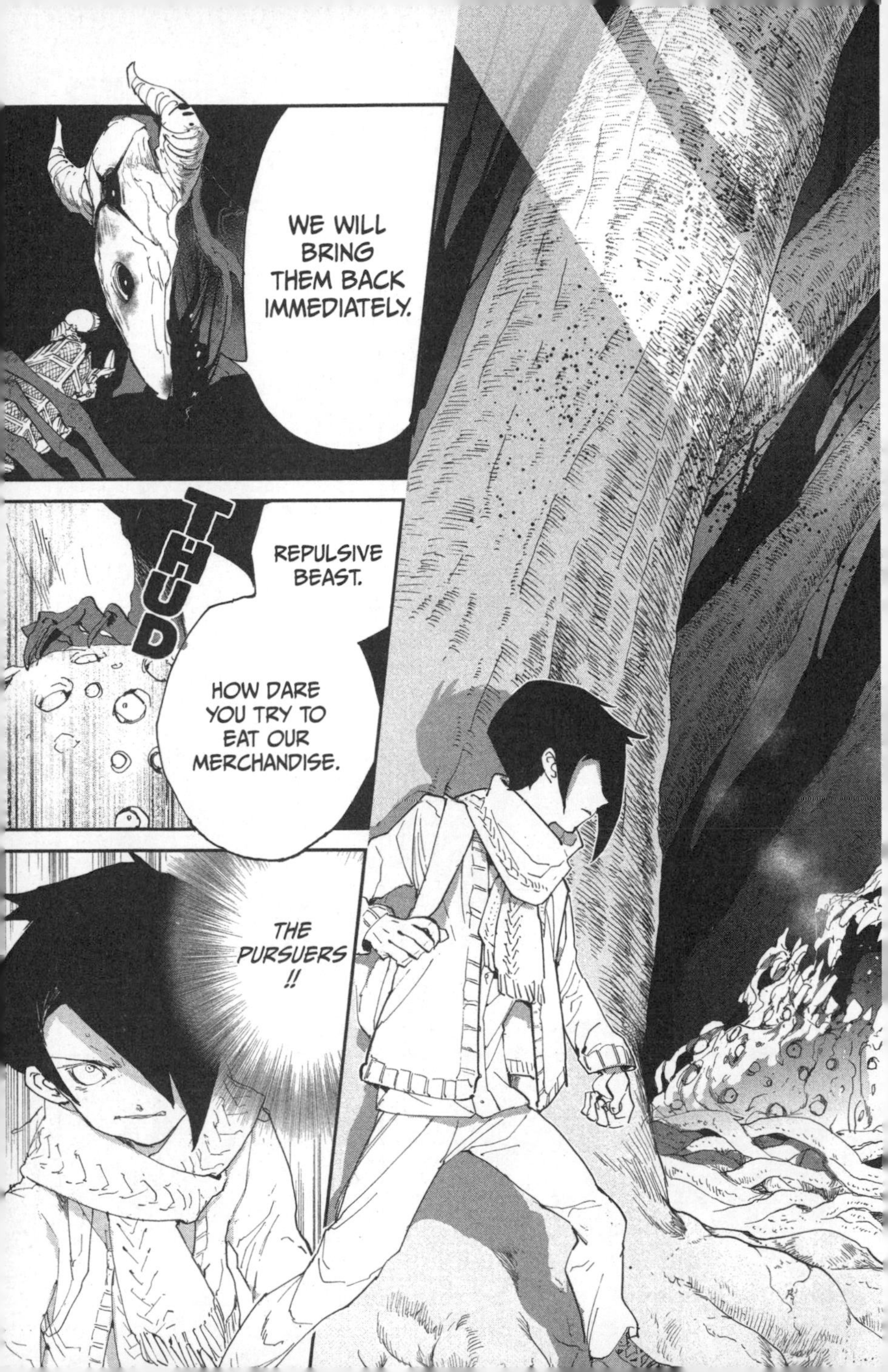
WE WILL BRING THEM BACK IMMEDIATELY.
REPULSIVE BEAST.
HOW DARE YOU TRY TO EAT OUR MERCHANDISE.
THUD
THE PURSUERS !!

SIDE STORY 2-5

I LOVE YOU

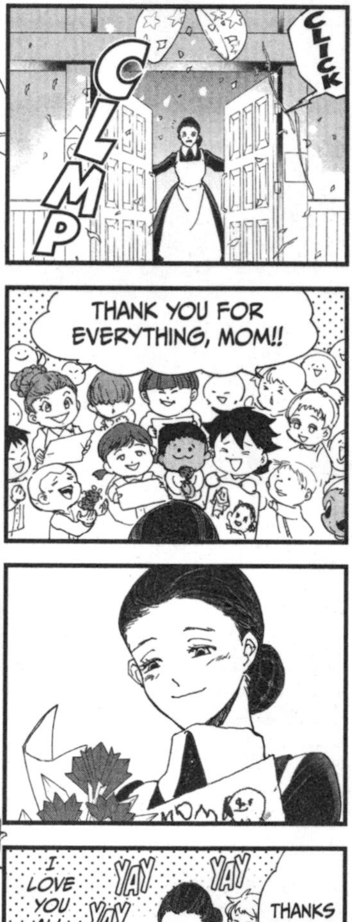
CLICK
CLMP
THANK YOU FOR EVERYTHING, MOM!!
MOM
THANKS TO YOU TOO.
YAY
YAY
YAY
I LOVE YOU ALL, MY CHIL-DREN.

SIDE STORY 2 – FIN –

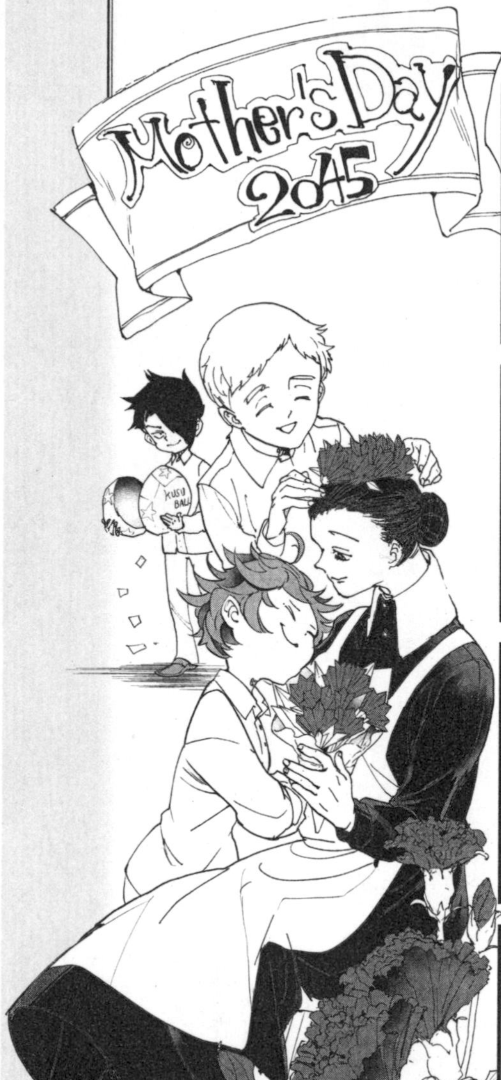
Mother's Day 2045
KUSU BALL

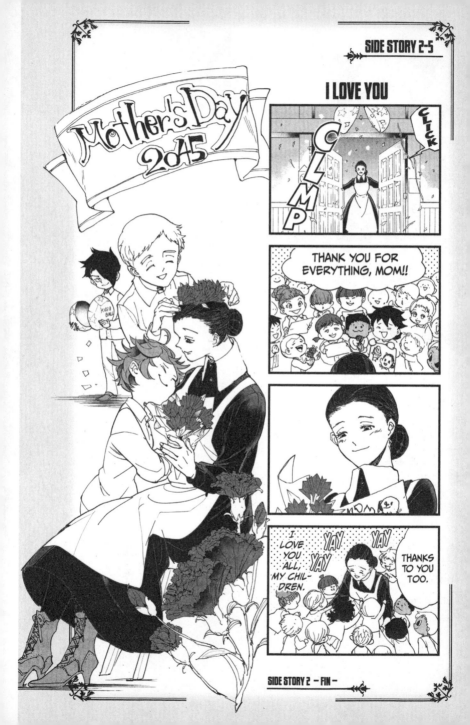

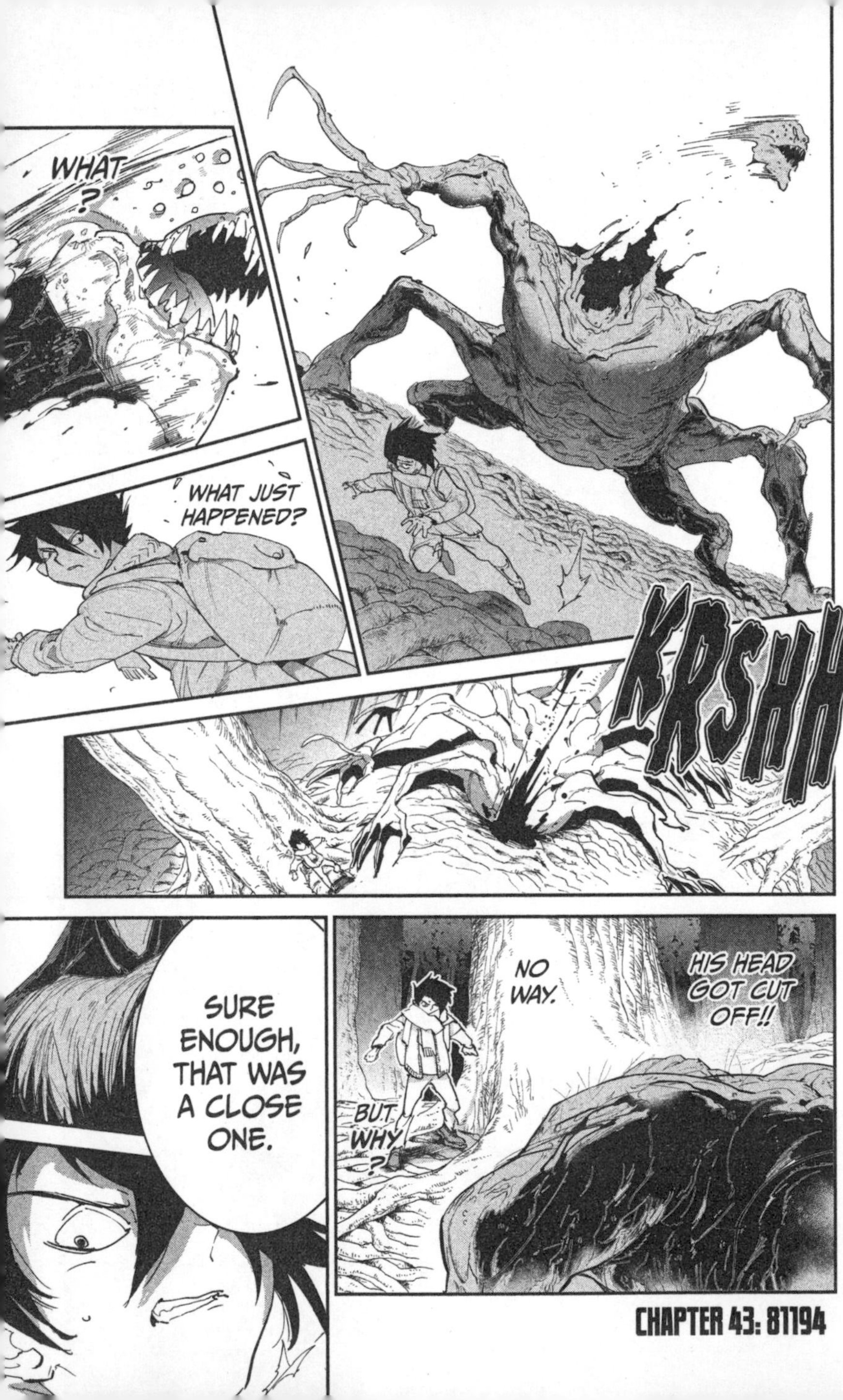
WHAT ?
WHAT JUST HAPPENED?
KRSHH
HIS HEAD GOT CUT OFF!!
NO WAY.
BUT WHY ?
SURE ENOUGH, THAT WAS A CLOSE ONE.

CHAPTER 43: 81194

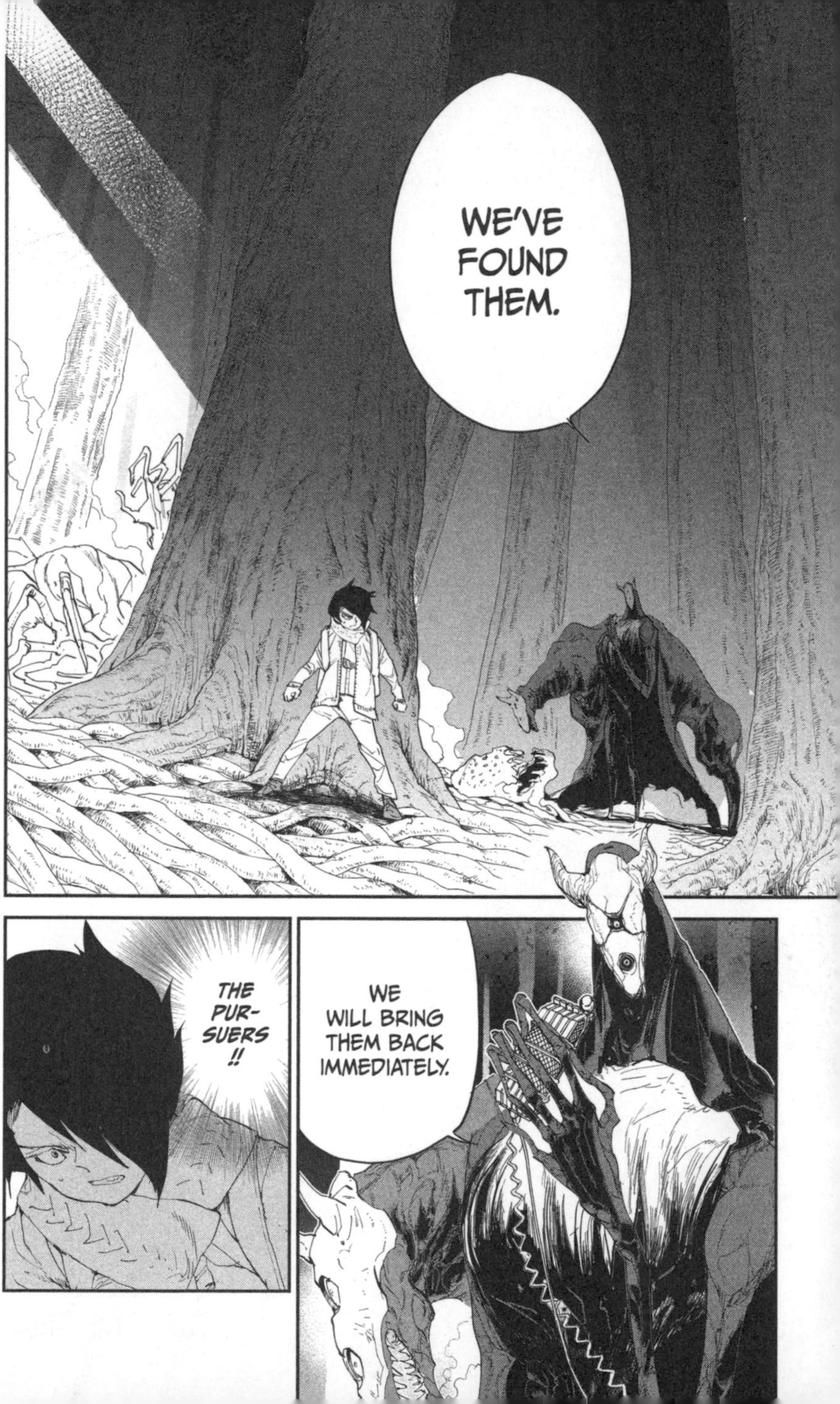
WE'VE FOUND THEM.
WE WILL BRING THEM BACK IMMEDIATELY.
THE PURSUERS!!

CHAPTER 43: 81194

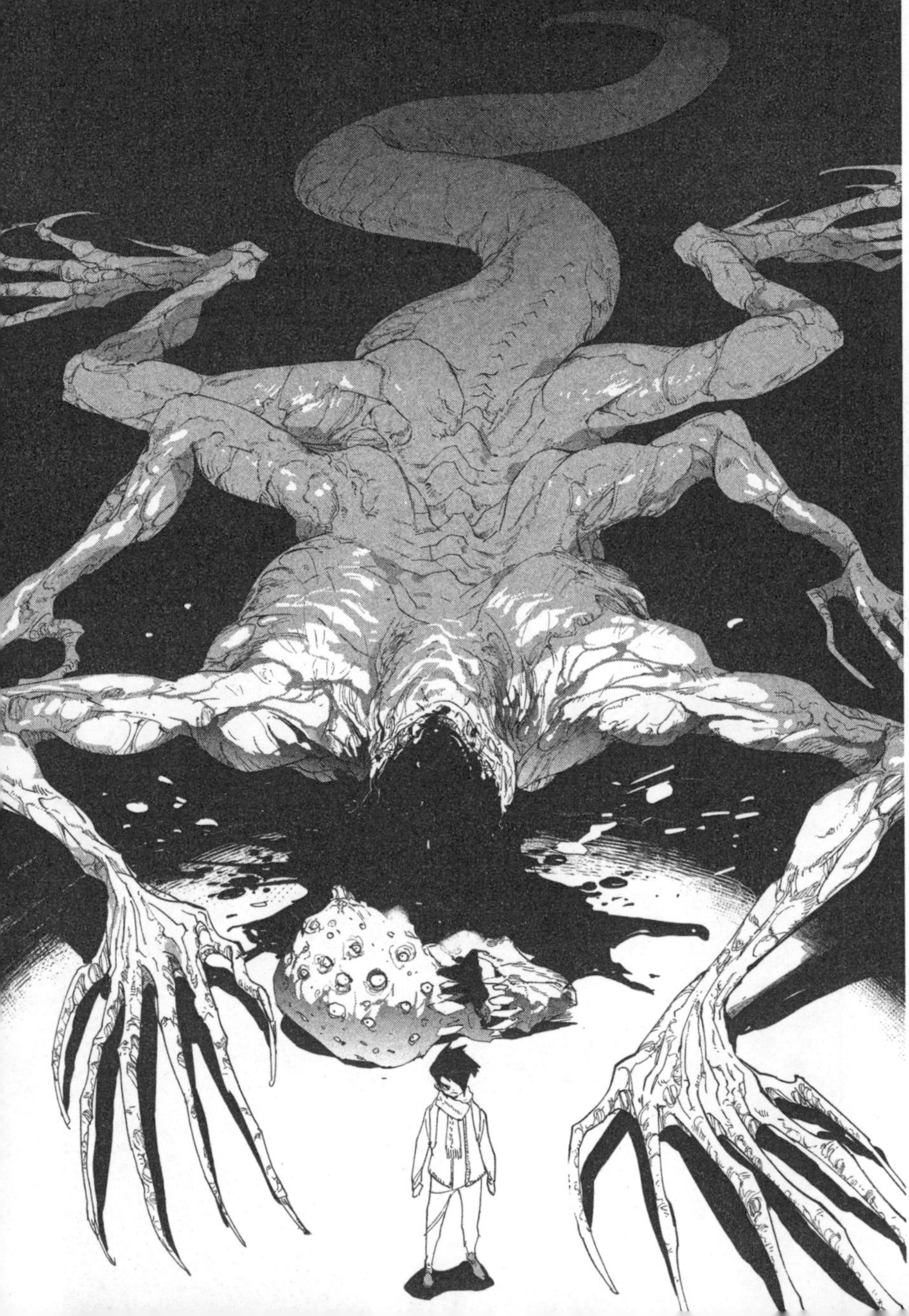

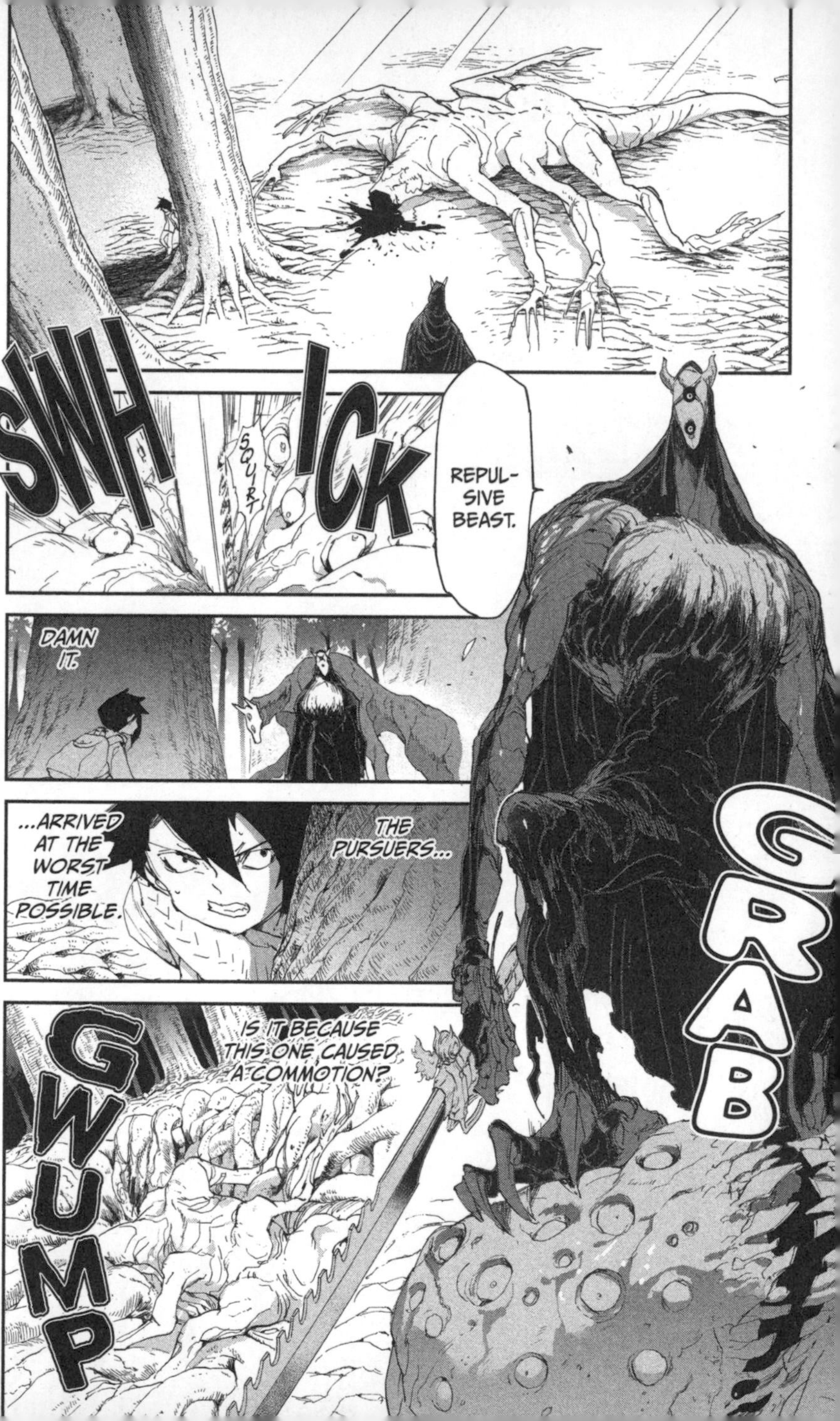
REPUL-
SIVE
BEAST.
GRAB
SWH
ICK
SQUIRT
DAMN IT.
THE PURSUERS...
...ARRIVED AT THE WORST TIME POSSIBLE.
IS IT BECAUSE THIS ONE CAUSED A COMMOTION?
GWUMP

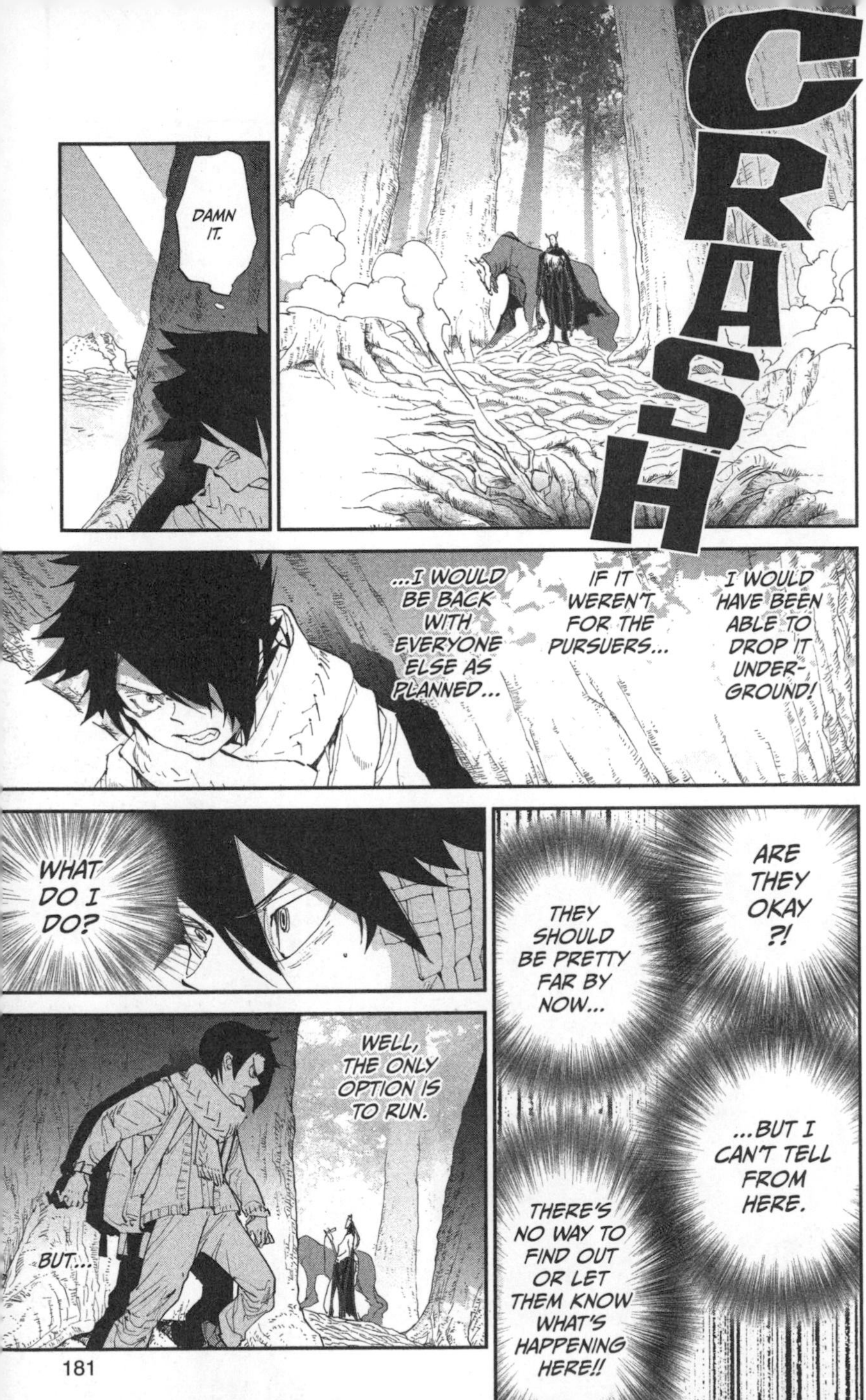
CRASH
DAMN IT.
I WOULD HAVE BEEN ABLE TO DROP IT UNDER-GROUND!
IF IT WEREN'T FOR THE PURSUERS...
...I WOULD BE BACK WITH EVERYONE ELSE AS PLANNED...
ARE THEY OKAY?!
THEY SHOULD BE PRETTY FAR BY NOW...
...BUT I CAN'T TELL FROM HERE.
THERE'S NO WAY TO FIND OUT OR LET THEM KNOW WHAT'S HAPPENING HERE!!
WHAT DO I DO?
WELL, THE ONLY OPTION IS TO RUN.
BUT...

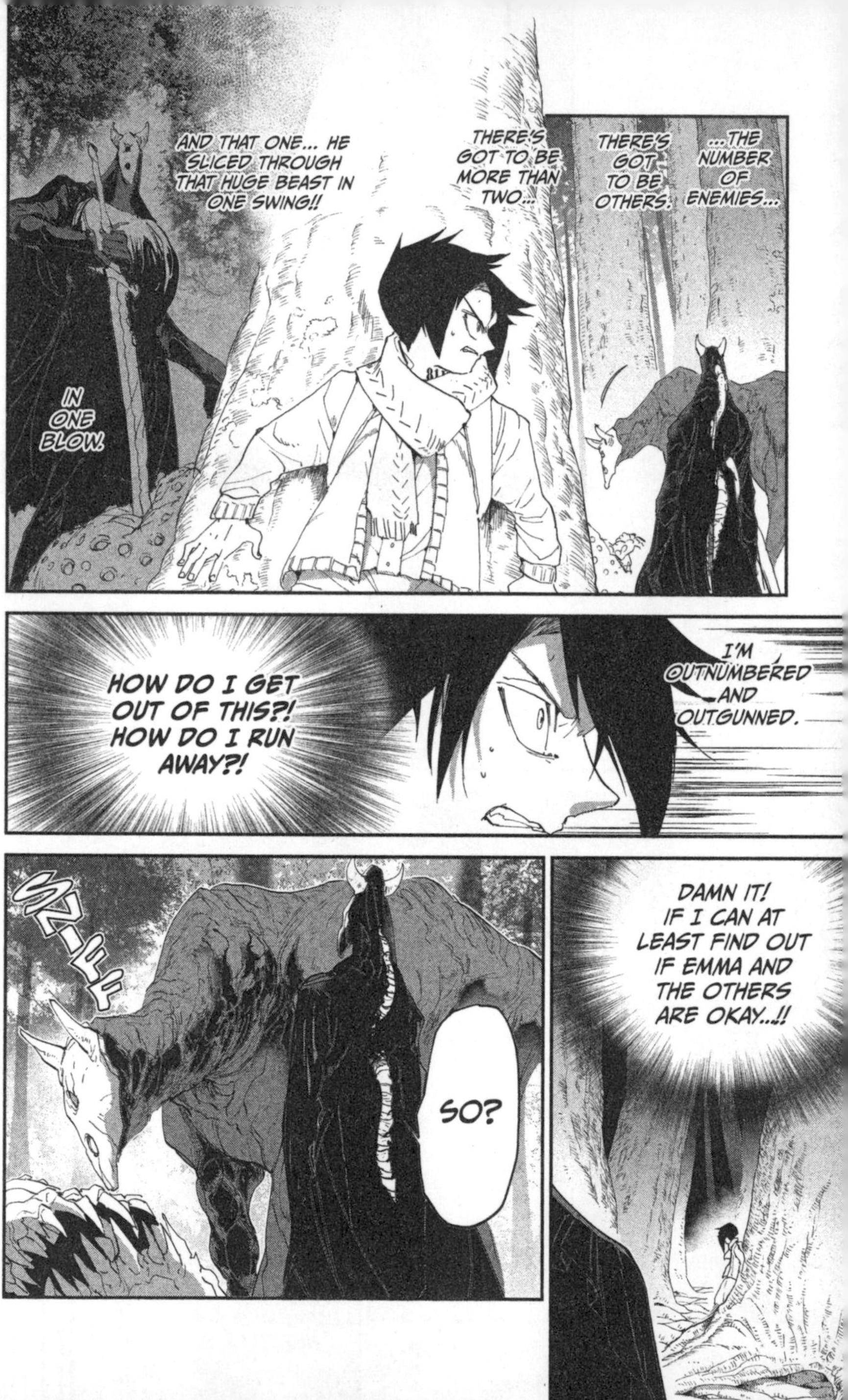
...THE NUMBER OF ENEMIES...
THERE'S GOT TO BE OTHERS.
THERE'S GOT TO BE MORE THAN TWO...
AND THAT ONE... HE SLICED THROUGH THAT HUGE BEAST IN ONE SWING!!
IN ONE BLOW.
I'M OUTNUMBERED AND OUTGUNNED.
HOW DO I GET OUT OF THIS?! HOW DO I RUN AWAY?!
DAMN IT! IF I CAN AT LEAST FIND OUT IF EMMA AND THE OTHERS ARE OKAY...!!
SNIFF
SO?

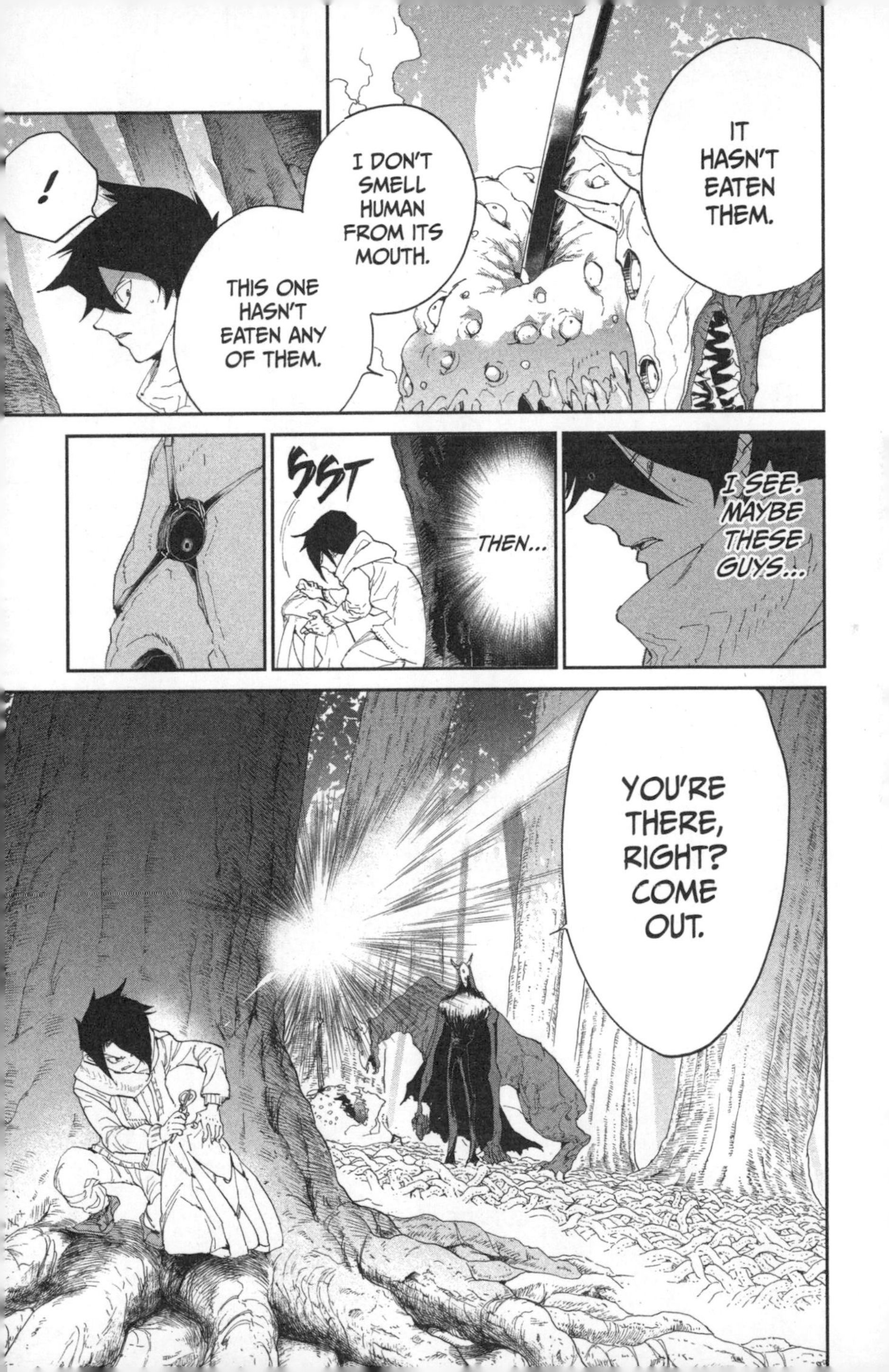
IT HASN'T EATEN THEM.
I DON'T SMELL HUMAN FROM ITS MOUTH.
THIS ONE HASN'T EATEN ANY OF THEM.
!
I SEE. MAYBE THESE GUYS...
SST
THEN...
YOU'RE THERE, RIGHT? COME OUT.

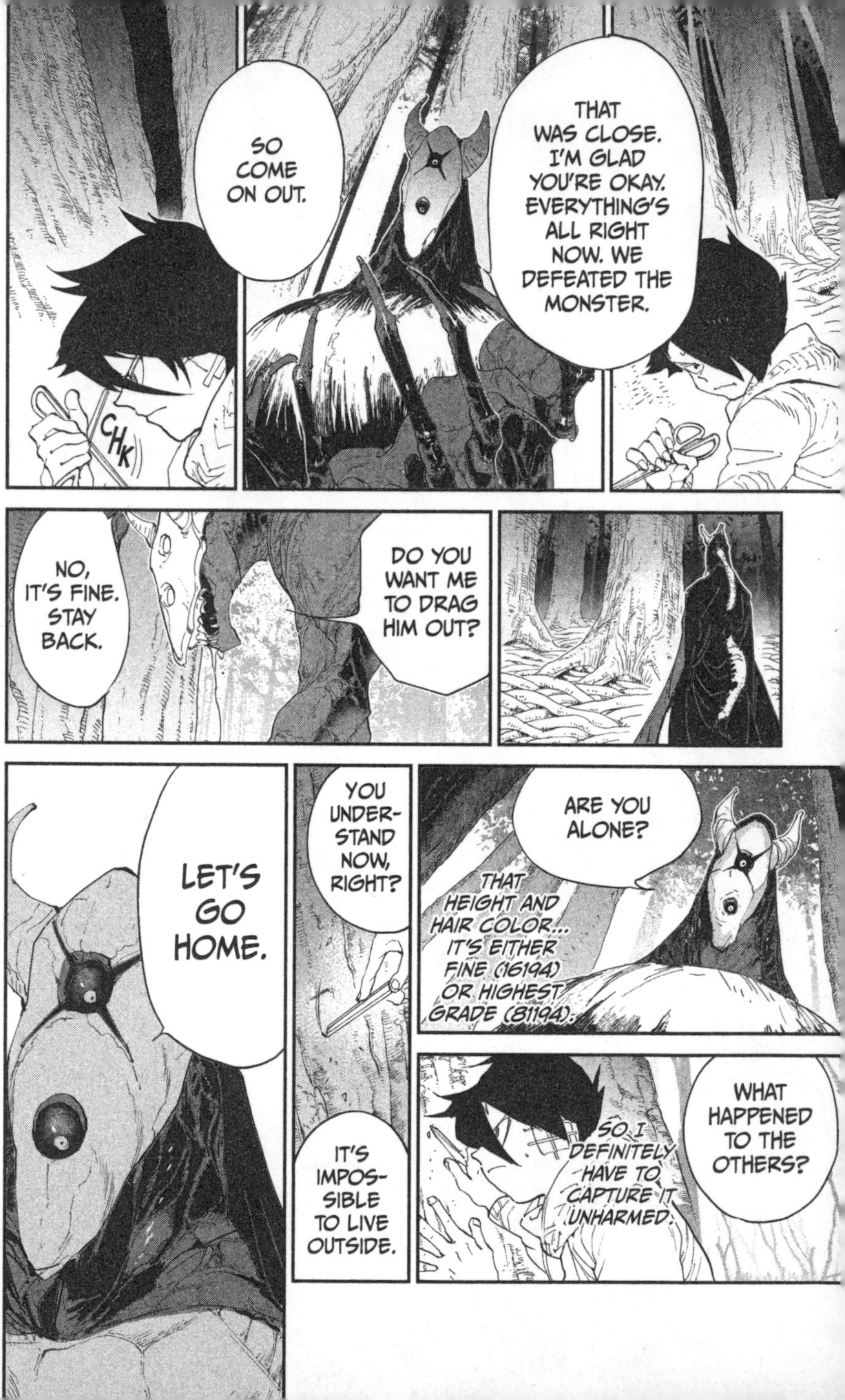
THAT WAS CLOSE. I'M GLAD YOU'RE OKAY. EVERYTHING'S ALL RIGHT NOW. WE DEFEATED THE MONSTER.
SO COME ON OUT.
CHK
DO YOU WANT ME TO DRAG HIM OUT?
NO, IT'S FINE. STAY BACK.
ARE YOU ALONE?
THAT HEIGHT AND HAIR COLOR... IT'S EITHER FINE (16194) OR HIGHEST GRADE (81194).
WHAT HAPPENED TO THE OTHERS?
SO I DEFINITELY HAVE TO CAPTURE IT UNHARMED.
YOU UNDER-STAND NOW, RIGHT?
IT'S IMPOS-SIBLE TO LIVE OUTSIDE.
LET'S GO HOME.

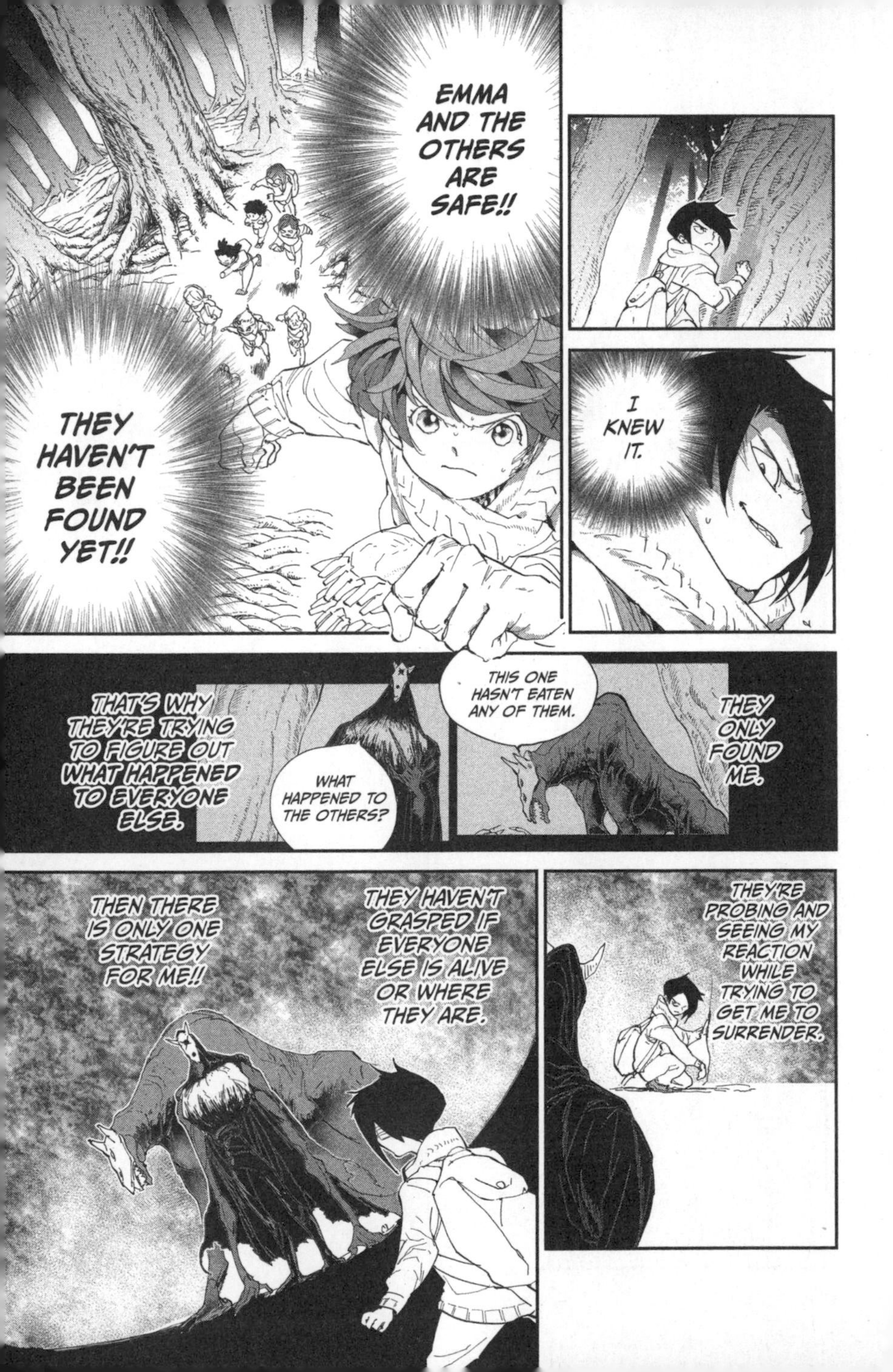
I KNEW IT.
EMMA AND THE OTHERS ARE SAFE!!
THEY HAVEN'T BEEN FOUND YET!!
THEY ONLY FOUND ME.
THIS ONE HASN'T EATEN ANY OF THEM.
WHAT HAPPENED TO THE OTHERS?
THAT'S WHY THEY'RE TRYING TO FIGURE OUT WHAT HAPPENED TO EVERYONE ELSE.
THEY'RE PROBING AND SEEING MY REACTION WHILE TRYING TO GET ME TO SURRENDER.
THEY HAVEN'T GRASPED IF EVERYONE ELSE IS ALIVE OR WHERE THEY ARE.
THEN THERE IS ONLY ONE STRATEGY FOR ME!!

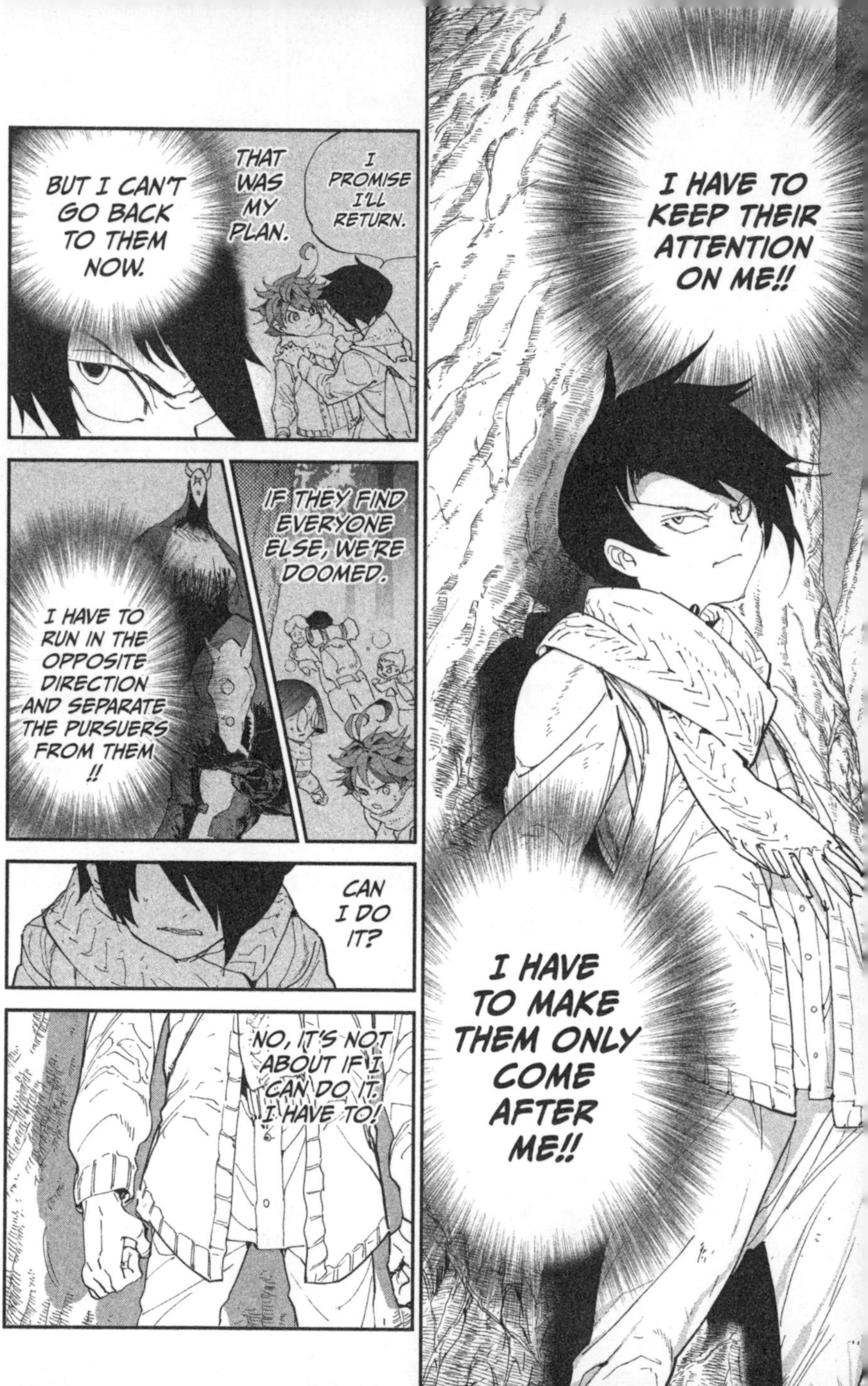
I HAVE TO KEEP THEIR ATTENTION ON ME!!
I HAVE TO MAKE THEM ONLY COME AFTER ME!!
I PROMISE I'LL RETURN.
THAT WAS MY PLAN.
BUT I CAN'T GO BACK TO THEM NOW.
IF THEY FIND EVERYONE ELSE, WE'RE DOOMED.
I HAVE TO RUN IN THE OPPOSITE DIRECTION AND SEPARATE THE PURSUERS FROM THEM !!
CAN I DO IT?
NO, IT'S NOT ABOUT IF I CAN DO IT. I HAVE TO!

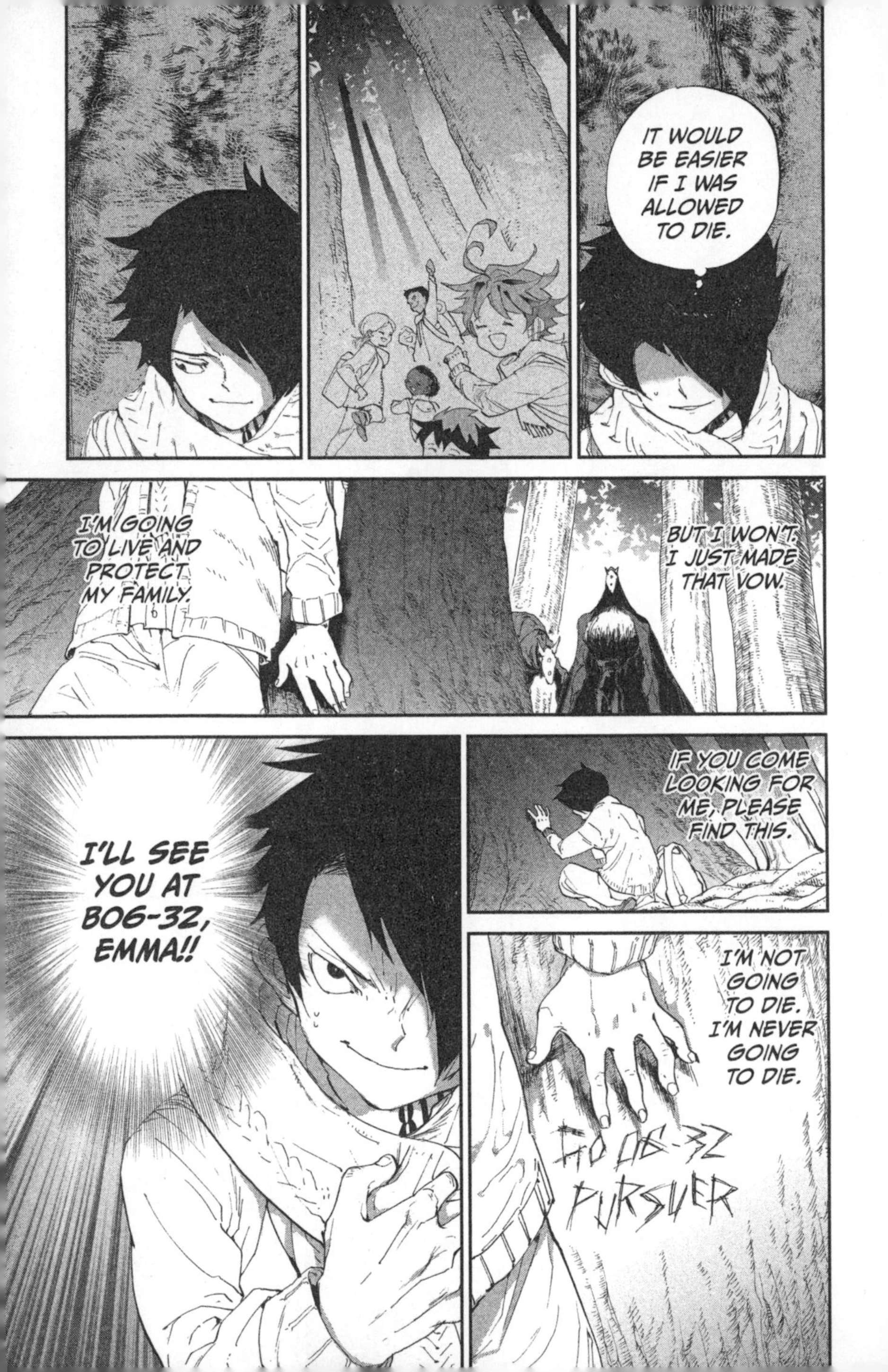
IT WOULD BE EASIER IF I WAS ALLOWED TO DIE.
BUT I WON'T. I JUST MADE THAT VOW.
I'M GOING TO LIVE AND PROTECT MY FAMILY.
IF YOU COME LOOKING FOR ME, PLEASE FIND THIS.
I'M NOT GOING TO DIE. I'M NEVER GOING TO DIE.
GO 06-32
PURSUER
I'LL SEE YOU AT B06-32, EMMA!!

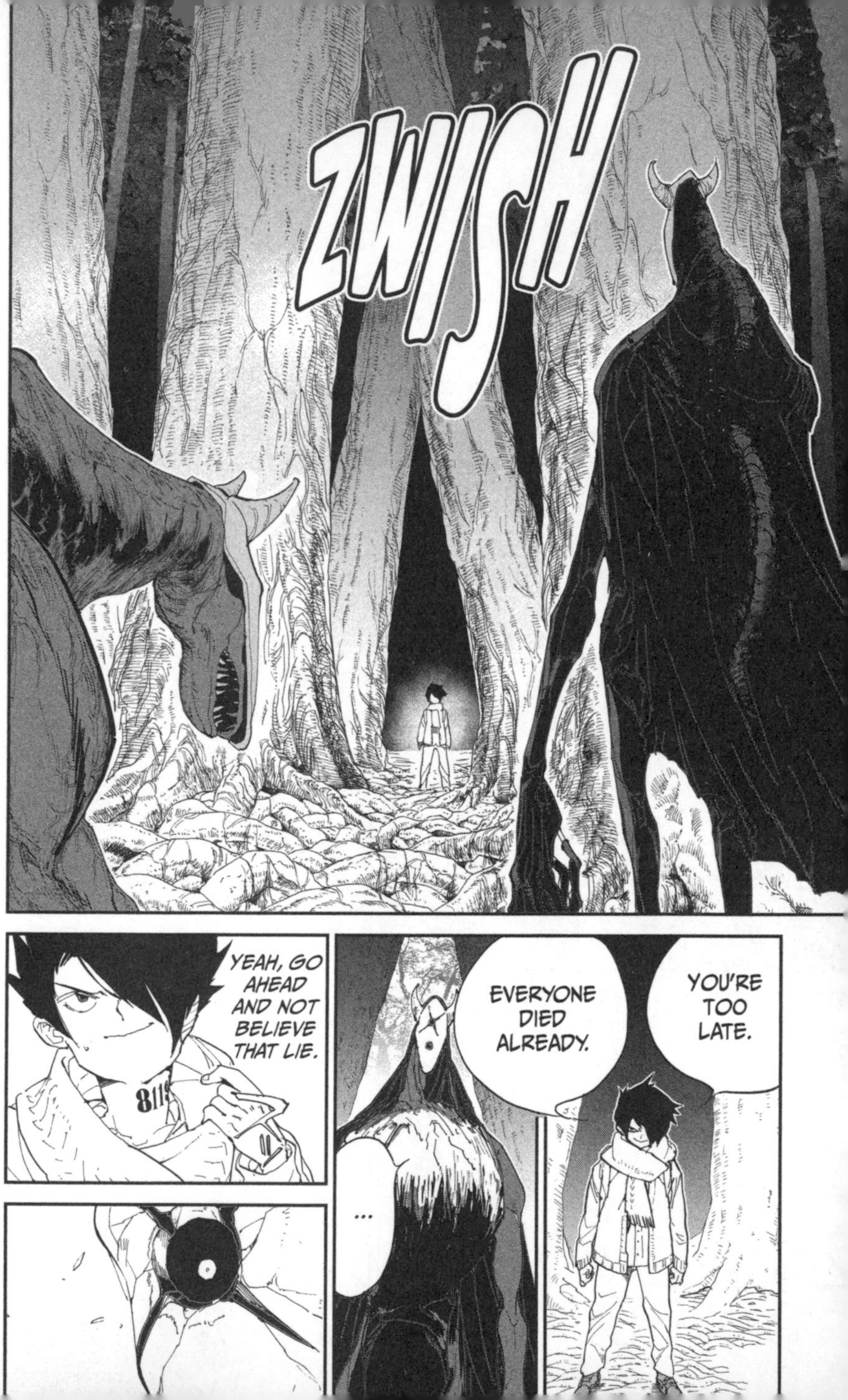
ZWISH
YOU'RE TOO LATE.
EVERYONE DIED ALREADY.
...
YEAH, GO AHEAD AND NOT BELIEVE THAT LIE.

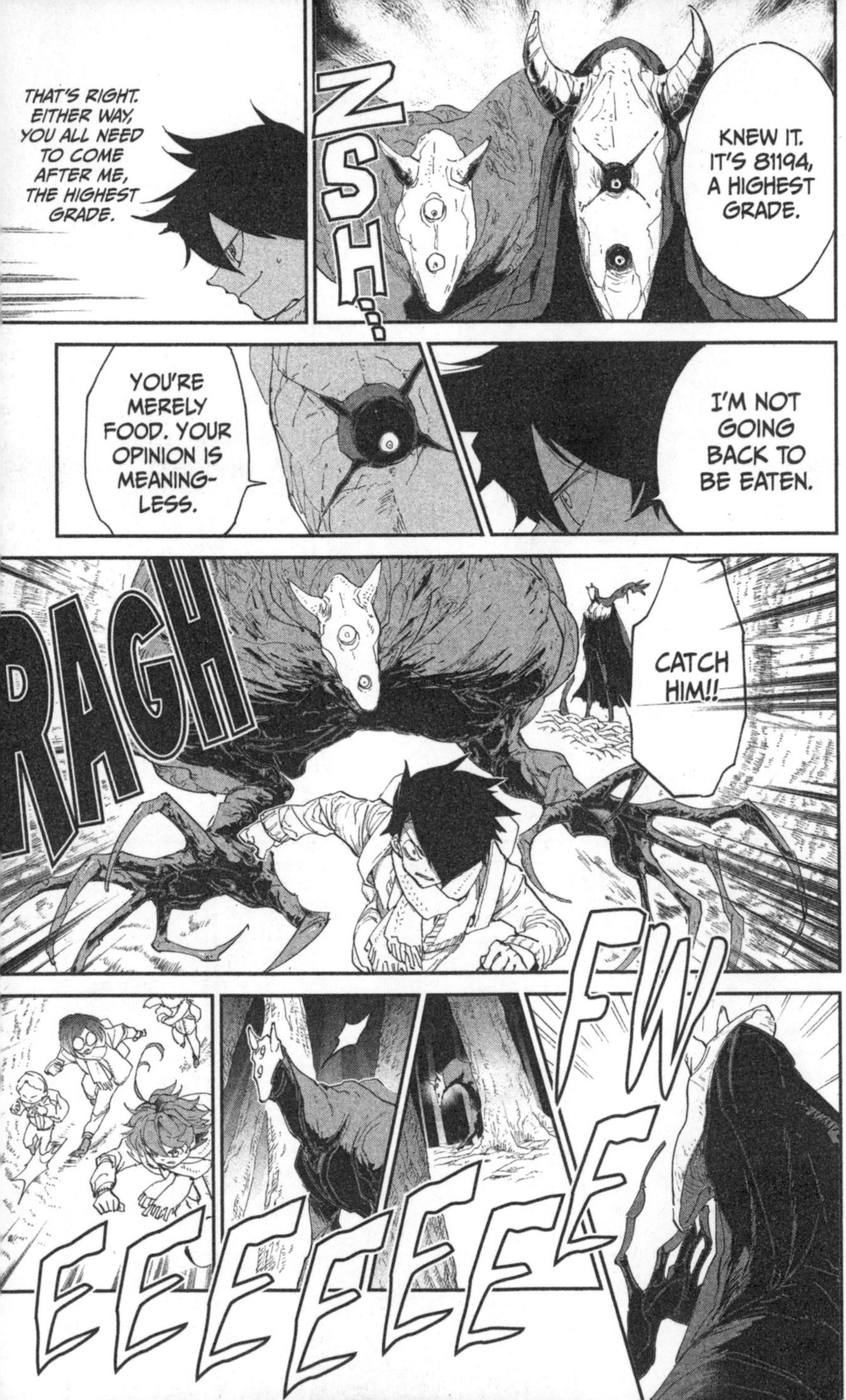
KNEW IT. IT'S 81194, A HIGHEST GRADE.
ZSH...
THAT'S RIGHT. EITHER WAY, YOU ALL NEED TO COME AFTER ME, THE HIGHEST GRADE.
I'M NOT GOING BACK TO BE EATEN.
YOU'RE MERELY FOOD. YOUR OPINION IS MEANING-LESS.
CATCH HIM!!
RAGH
FWEEEEEEEE

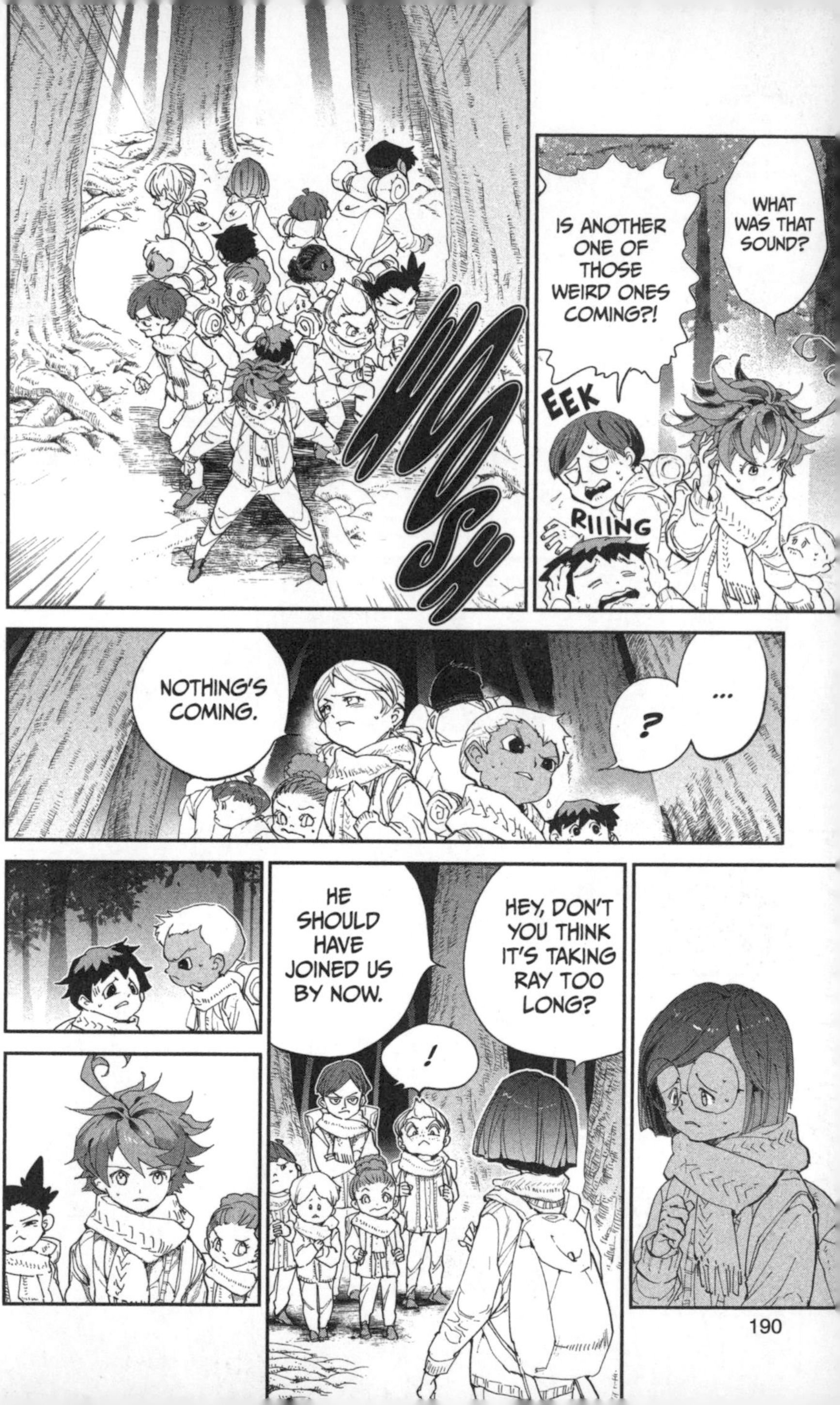
WHAT WAS THAT SOUND?
IS ANOTHER ONE OF THOSE WEIRD ONES COMING?!
EEK
RIIING
WHOOSH
...
?
NOTHING'S COMING.
HEY, DON'T YOU THINK IT'S TAKING RAY TOO LONG?
HE SHOULD HAVE JOINED US BY NOW.
!

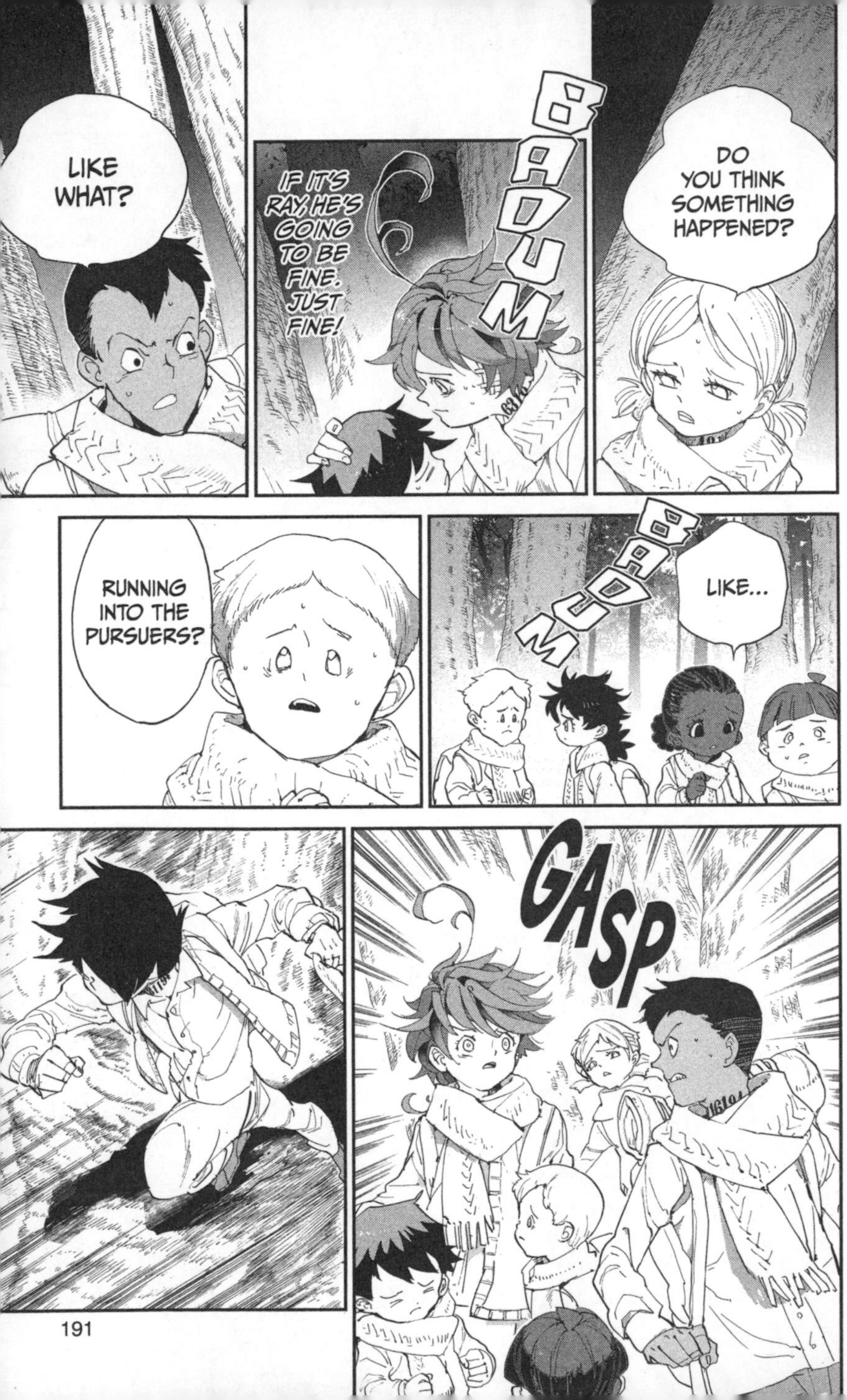
DO YOU THINK SOMETHING HAPPENED?
BADUM
IF IT'S RAY, HE'S GOING TO BE FINE. JUST FINE!
LIKE WHAT?
BADUM
LIKE...
RUNNING INTO THE PURSUERS?
GASP

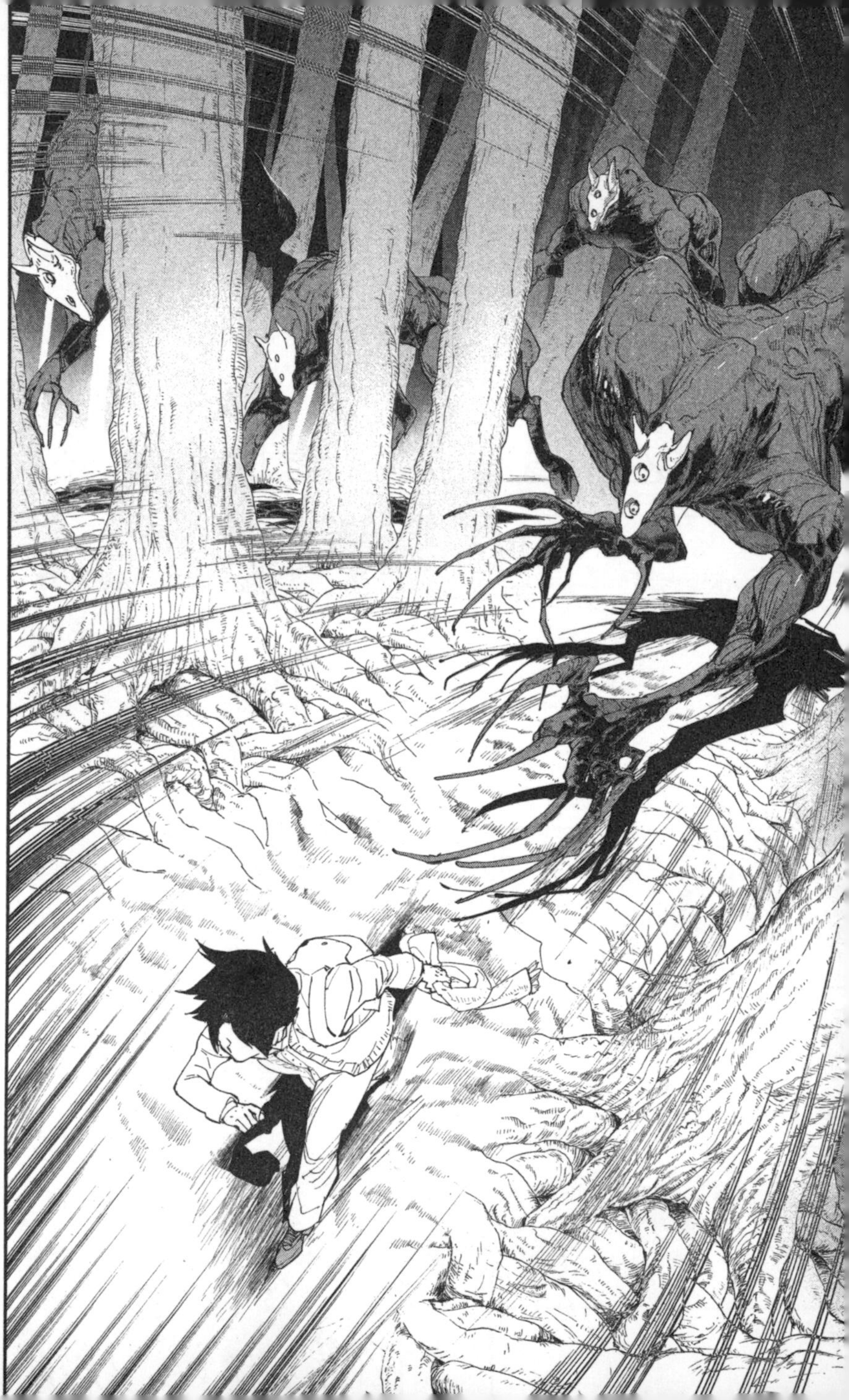

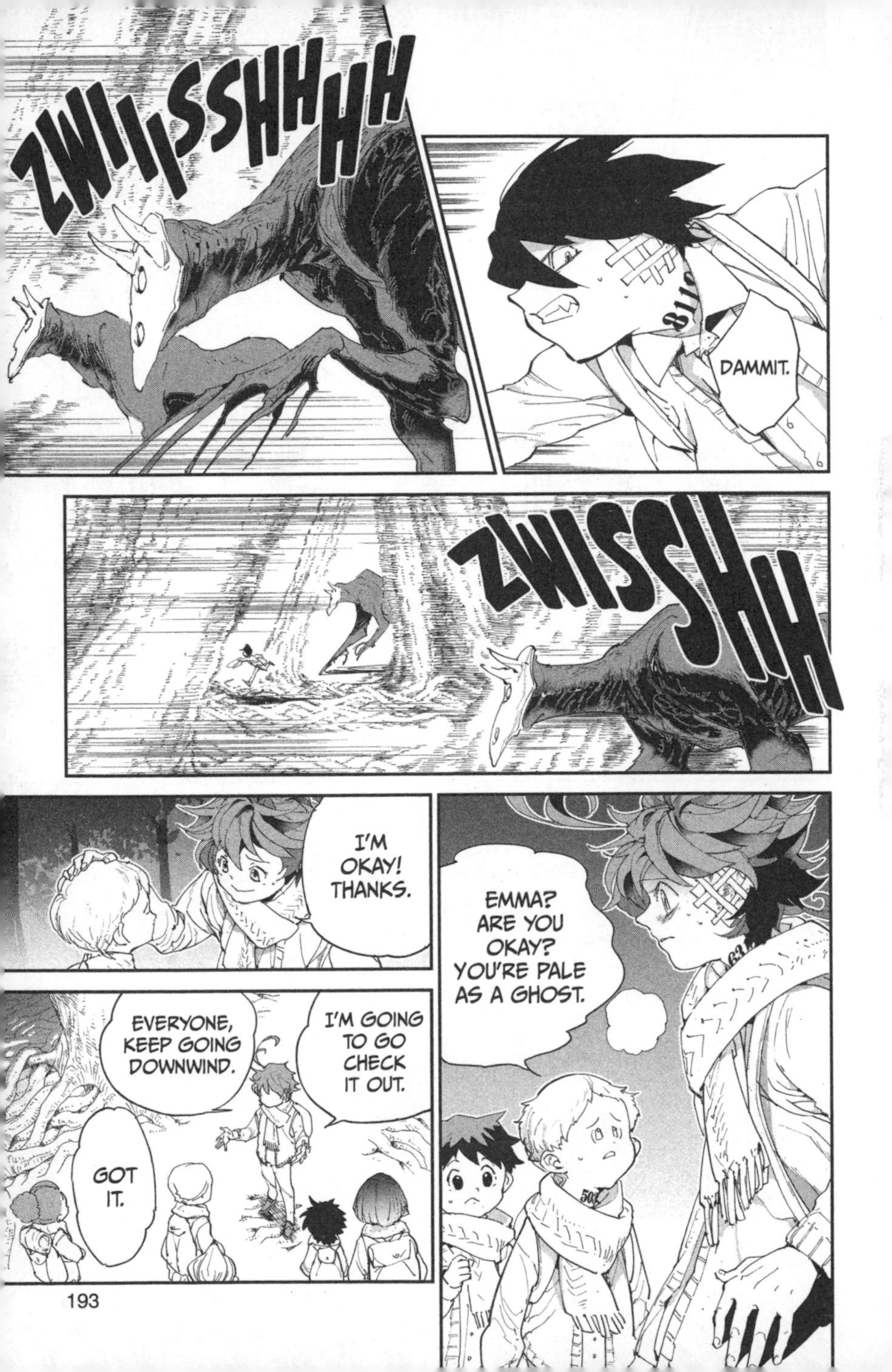
DAMMIT.
ZWIIISSHHHHH
ZWISSHHH
EMMA? ARE YOU OKAY? YOU'RE PALE AS A GHOST.
I'M OKAY! THANKS.
I'M GOING TO GO CHECK IT OUT.
EVERYONE, KEEP GOING DOWNWIND.
GOT IT.

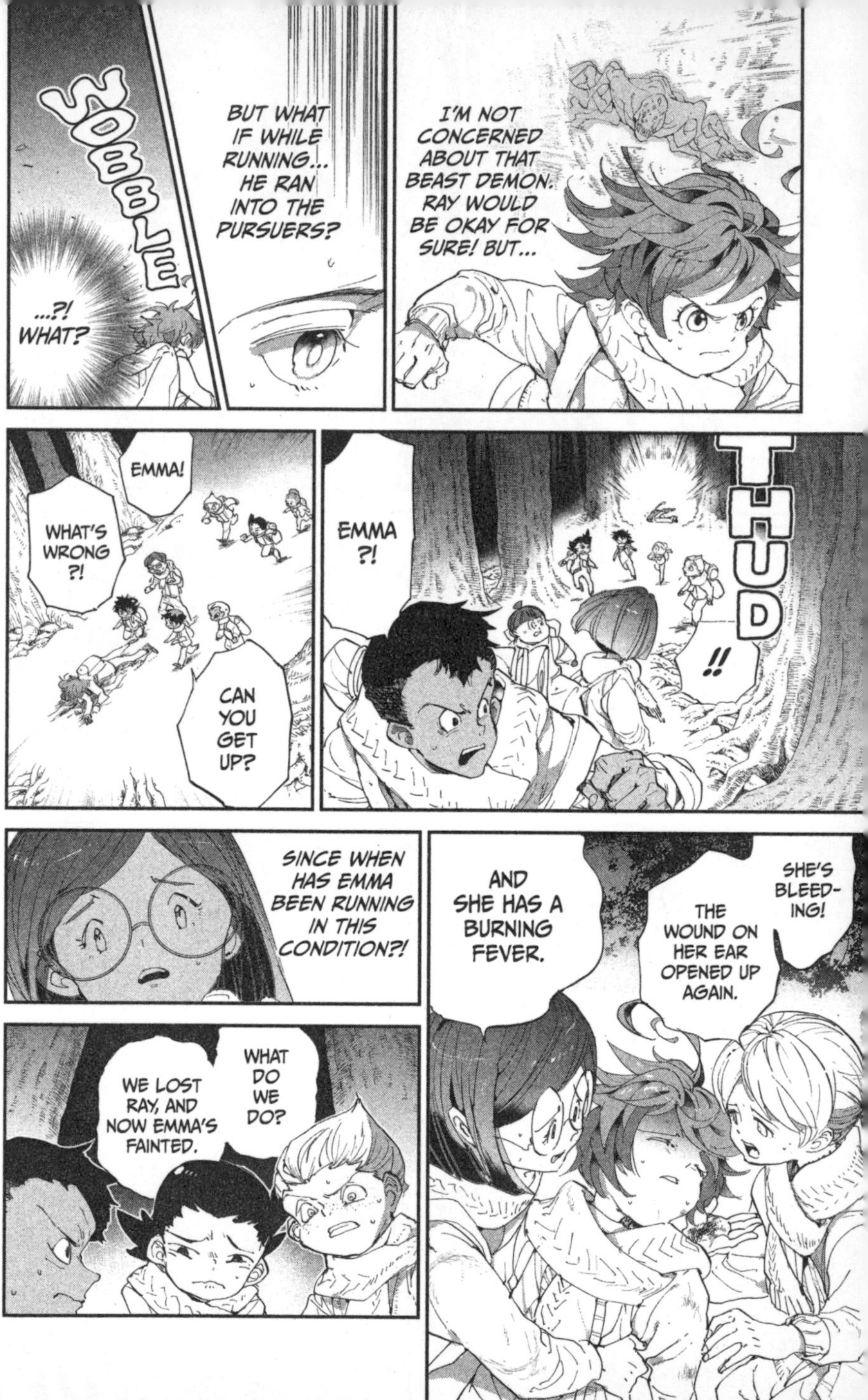
I'M NOT CONCERNED ABOUT THAT BEAST DEMON. RAY WOULD BE OKAY FOR SURE! BUT...
BUT WHAT IF WHILE RUNNING... HE RAN INTO THE PURSUERS?
WOBBLE
...?! WHAT?
THUD
!!
EMMA ?!
EMMA!
WHAT'S WRONG ?!
CAN YOU GET UP?
SHE'S BLEEDING!
THE WOUND ON HER EAR OPENED UP AGAIN.
AND SHE HAS A BURNING FEVER.
SINCE WHEN HAS EMMA BEEN RUNNING IN THIS CONDITION?!
WHAT DO WE DO?
WE LOST RAY, AND NOW EMMA'S FAINTED.

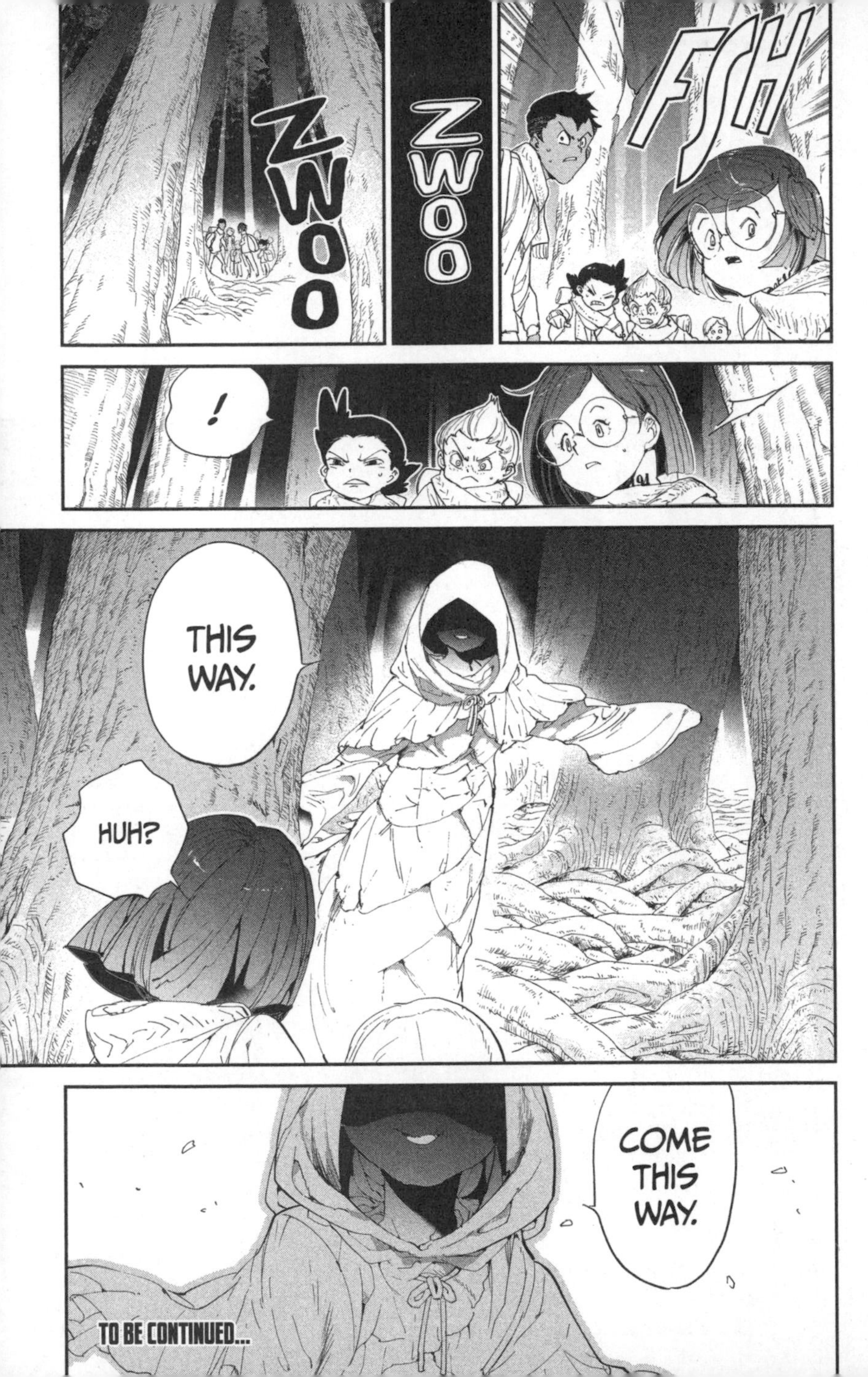
FSH
ZWOO
ZWOO
!
THIS WAY.
HUH?
COME THIS WAY.
TO BE CONTINUED...

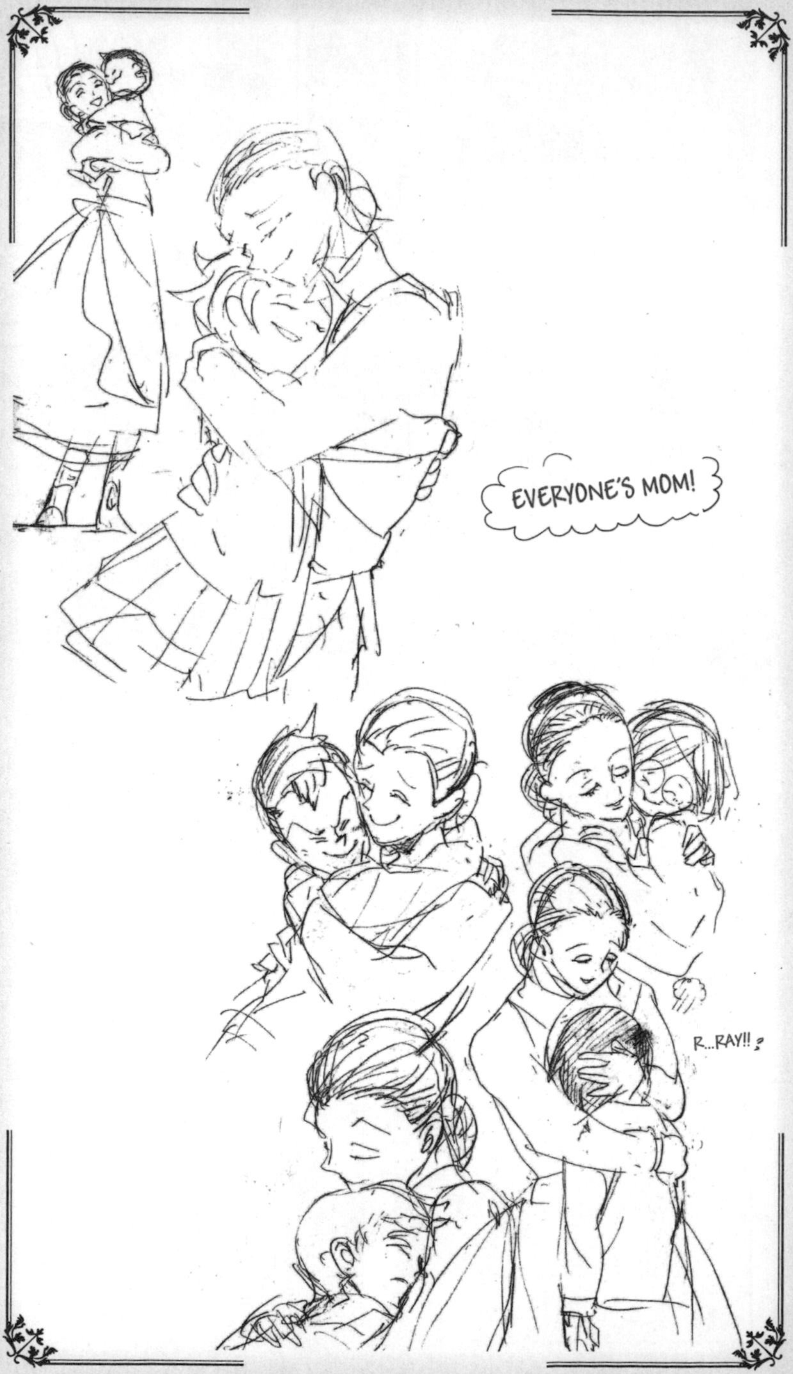
EVERYONE'S MOM!
R...RAY!!

ECSTATIC SISTER

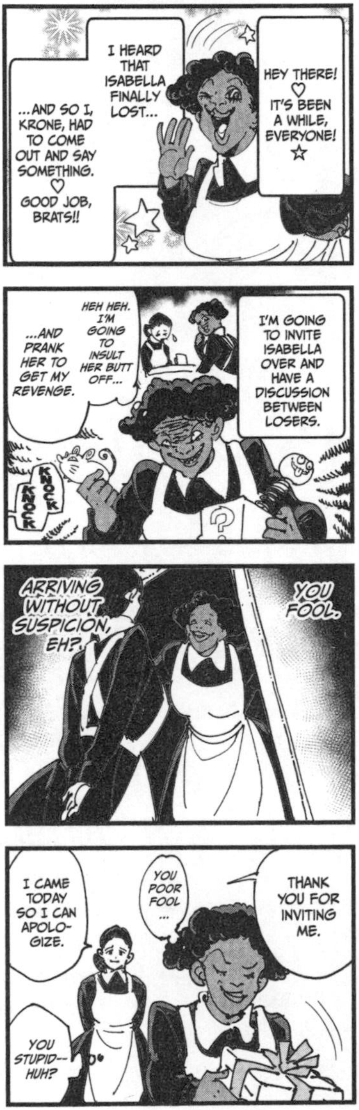
HEY THERE! ♡ IT'S BEEN A WHILE, EVERYONE! ☆
I HEARD THAT ISABELLA FINALLY LOST...
...AND SO I, KRONE, HAD TO COME OUT AND SAY SOMETHING. ♡ GOOD JOB, BRATS!!
I'M GOING TO INVITE ISABELLA OVER AND HAVE A DISCUSSION BETWEEN LOSERS.
HEH HEH. I'M GOING TO INSULT HER BUTT OFF...
...AND PRANK HER TO GET MY REVENGE.
KNOCK KNOCK
YOU FOOL.
ARRIVING WITHOUT SUSPICION, EH?
THANK YOU FOR INVITING ME.
YOU POOR FOOL...
I CAME TODAY SO I CAN APOLO-GIZE.
YOU STUPID-- HUH?

ISABELLA AND KRONE

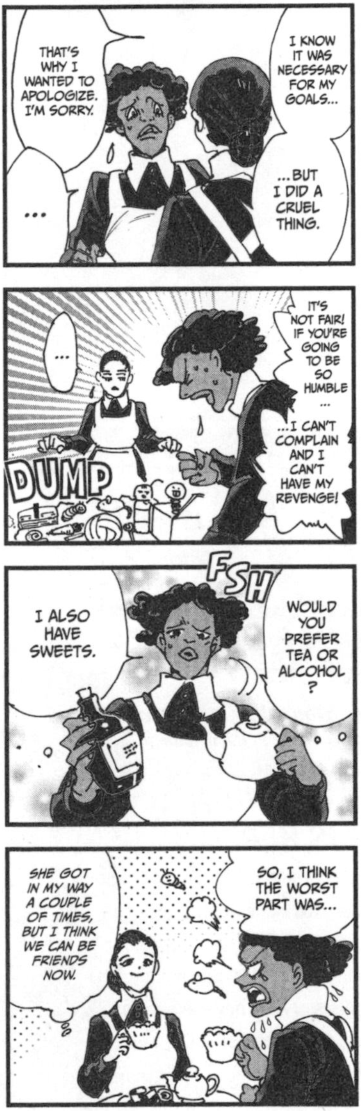
I KNOW IT WAS NECESSARY FOR MY GOALS...
...BUT I DID A CRUEL THING.
THAT'S WHY I WANTED TO APOLOGIZE. I'M SORRY.
...
IT'S NOT FAIR! IF YOU'RE GOING TO BE SO HUMBLE...
...I CAN'T COMPLAIN AND I CAN'T HAVE MY REVENGE!
...
DUMP
FSH
WOULD YOU PREFER TEA OR ALCOHOL?
I ALSO HAVE SWEETS.
SO, I THINK THE WORST PART WAS...
SHE GOT IN MY WAY A COUPLE OF TIMES, BUT I THINK WE CAN BE FRIENDS NOW.

SIDE STORY 3 –FIN–

YOU'RE READING THE **WRONG WAY!**

The Promised Neverland reads from right to left, starting in the upper-right corner. Japanese is read from right to left, meaning that action, sound effects and word-balloon order are completely reversed from English order.